Opinion Writing and Case Preparation

put your knowledge into practice

- Written specifically for students on the Bar Professional Training Course

- Expert author teams include barristers and BPTC tutors

- Clear, authoritative guides to legal practice and procedure

Advocacy

Company Law in Practice

Conference Skills

Criminal Litigation & Sentencing

Drafting

Employment Law in Practice

Evidence

Family Law in Practice

Opinion Writing & Case Preparation

Professional Ethics

Remedies

 Online Resource Centre

www.oxfordtextbooks.co.uk/orc/barmanuals

The Bar Manuals are also supported by an Online Resource Centre with further materials and updates to selected manuals.

The Bar Manuals are published by Oxford University Press in conjunction with The City Law School

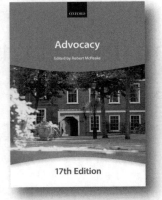

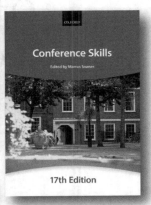

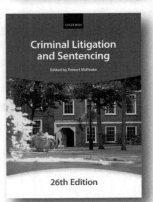

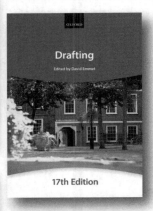

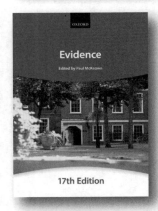

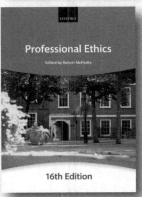

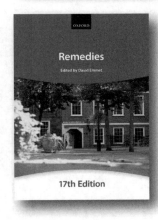

Opinion Writing and Case Preparation

The City Law School
CITY UNIVERSITY LONDON

Authors

Paul Banks, Head of Library Services, The City Law School

Susan Blake, Barrister, Associate Dean, The City Law School

Matthew Boyle, Barrister, Gray's Inn

Nigel Duncan, Professor of Legal Education, The City Law School

Nina Ellin, Barrister, former Lecturer, The City Law School

David Emmet, Barrister, former Reader, The City Law School

Guy Holborn, Librarian, Lincoln's Inn

Peter Hungerford-Welch, Barrister, Assistant Dean, The City Law School

Snigdha Nag, Barrister, Senior Lecturer, The City Law School

Marian Riley-Poku, Barrister, Lecturer, The City Law School

Richard Salter QC, Barrister, Inner Temple

Stuart Sime, Barrister, Professor of Law, The City Law School

Hester Swift, Foreign and International Law Librarian, Institute of Advanced Legal Studies

Margot Taylor, Solicitor, former Principal Lecturer, The City Law School

Editors

Nigel Duncan, Professor of Legal Education, The City Law School

Allison Wolfgarten, Barrister, Senior Lecturer, The City Law School

Series Editor

Julie Browne, Barrister, Senior Lecturer, The City Law School

OXFORD

UNIVERSITY PRESS

OXFORD
UNIVERSITY PRESS

Great Clarendon Street, Oxford, OX2 6DP,
United Kingdom

Oxford University Press is a department of the University of Oxford.
It furthers the University's objective of excellence in research, scholarship,
and education by publishing worldwide. Oxford is a registered trade mark of
Oxford University Press in the UK and in certain other countries

Published in the United States of America by Oxford University Press
198 Madison Avenue, New York, NY 10016, United States of America

British Library Cataloguing in Publication Data
Data available

ISBN 978–0–19–871443–9

Printed in Great Britain by
Ashford Colour Press Ltd, Gosport, Hampshire

Links to third party websites are provided by Oxford in good faith and
for information only. Oxford disclaims any responsibility for the materials
contained in any third party website referenced in this work.

FOREWORD

These manuals have been written by a combination of practitioners and members of staff of the City Law School (formerly the Inns of Court School of Law), and are designed primarily to support training on the Bar Professional Training Course (BPTC), wherever it is taught. They provide an extremely useful resource to assist in acquiring the skills and knowledge that practising barristers need. They are updated regularly and are supported by an Online Resource Centre, which can be used by readers to keep up-to-date throughout the academic year.

This series of manuals exemplifies the practical and professional approach that is central to the BPTC. I congratulate the authors on the excellent standard of the manuals and I am grateful to Oxford University Press for their ongoing and enthusiastic support.

Peter Hungerford-Welch
Barrister
Assistant Dean (Professional Programmes)
The City Law School
City University London
2014

PREFACE

This manual brings together in one volume the skill of case preparation with that of opinion writing, the major way in which barristers advise their lay and professional clients.

The first two sections explain and demonstrate, in the context of the work of a barrister, the underlying skills of legal research and fact management which will ensure that a case has been thoroughly prepared so that every relevant consideration has been taken into account before the client is given any advice, any document is drafted, or any case presented in court. Their purpose is to assist those who read them to develop effective techniques which, it is hoped, will ensure that the advice they give is sound and the arguments they put forward are convincing.

The development of professional legal skills training with its emphasis on the ability to perform lawyers' tasks has underlined the need to develop case preparation skills to a high standard. If a relevant law or fact is not identified, or if there is only a superficial assessment of the strength of evidence, the advice given is unlikely to be sound, and the arguments presented when attempting to settle or before a tribunal are unlikely to succeed.

The experience of those studying and teaching on the Bar Professional Training Course has identified the need to provide clear guidance on how to carry out legal research efficiently and to identify, analyse, and present relevant facts to ensure the best outcome for the client. The methods and techniques adopted in this manual are the outcome of our experience over many years and our discussions with the many practitioners and academics who have kindly contributed to the debate about how best to develop effective case preparation skills.

The advice given in this manual is not intended to be prescriptive. The aim is to provide practical advice and to demonstrate through the inclusion of worked examples how particular techniques can be applied to the preparation of a case. It is hoped that this will provide a framework which will assist each individual to develop his or her own intellectual skills in order to carry out the task of preparation competently and professionally.

Students will find that they will have opportunities to apply these techniques throughout the Bar Professional Training Course. In particular, the sections assisting you with legal research and fact management processes will be invaluable when you are working with sets of papers for the skills exercises and should be particularly useful in preparing for assessment and later when you enter practice.

The third part of this manual introduces you to opinion writing.

ACKNOWLEDGEMENTS

Grateful acknowledgement is made to the publishers of copyright material that appears in this book.

BBC Enterprises: extract from *Yes, Prime Minister*
City University: screenshot of Lawbore
Incorporated Council of Law Reporting: extracts from *Lewis v Lady Rook* [1992] 1 WLR 662
Jordan Publishing Ltd: screenshot of Jordans Family Law Online
Lexis Nexis: screenshot of Lexis Library
Sweet & Maxwell: screenshots of Lawtel and Westlaw UK

GUIDE TO USING THIS BOOK

The Bar Manuals series includes a range of tools and features to aid your learning. This guide will outline the approach to using this book, and help you to make the most out of each of the features within.

Practical approach

The authors have taken a practical approach to teaching opinion writing and case preparation. This will help you to enhance the skills that you will need, not only for exams but in practice when it is necessary to apply the law to real-life scenarios.

A step-by-step approach

This book features a step-by-step approach to giving advice on evidence in both a civil and a criminal case, which acts as a checklist for students and barristers to ensure that they have considered all relevant points.

Exercises

A number of self-assessment exercises are provided as a practical tool to help you to prepare for a case. A variety of exercises are included within the appendix (which can be found on the Online Resource Centre) to test your knowledge and understanding of opinion writing and case preparation and improve your writing skills.

Examples

Opinion Writing and Case Preparation features examples of barristers' opinions which will serve to give you some idea of differences in style and how opinions can be tailored for different circumstances.

Pedagogical features

Tables and diagrams offer visual representations of more complex subjects. This feature helps you to simplify more difficult subjects and provides a range of documentation within case notes.

Online Resource Centre updates

For further material and updates to selected manuals in this series please visit the Online Resource Centre at www.oxfordtextbooks.co.uk/orc/barmanuals/.

OUTLINE CONTENTS

Foreword   v
Preface   vi
Acknowledgements   vii
Guide to using this book   viii

PART I	**Legal Research**	**1**
1	Preparation: a forensic skill	3
2	Introduction to practical legal research	5
3	Legal research methods and techniques	9
4	Legal resources for the practitioner	25
5	Using electronic resources for research	64
6	Researching words and phrases	80
7	Reading and interpreting a case	90
8	Practical legal research: a summary	117
9	Legal sources for the practitioner: a bibliography	126

PART II	**Fact Management**	**139**
10	Overview of a civil case	141
11	Anatomy of a criminal case	171
12	The fact management process	187
13	Presentation for the practitioner: the CAP approach in action	223
14	Dealing with figures	226
15	Communication and information technology use in case preparation and presentation	235

PART III	**Opinion Writing**	**241**
16	Words and the barrister	243
17	Qualities of good writing	246
18	Plain English	253
19	Opinion writing	269
20	The use of law in an opinion	293
21	Getting started	302
22	Advice on evidence in a civil case	314
23	Advice on evidence in a criminal case	329
24	Checklist for opinion writing skills	347

Index   353

DETAILED CONTENTS

Foreword   v
Preface   vi
Acknowledgements   vii
Guide to using this book   viii

PART I   **Legal Research**   **1**

1   **Preparation: a forensic skill**   3

2   **Introduction to practical legal research**   5
2.1   What is 'practical' legal research?   5
2.2   The importance of legal research   6
2.3   Practical legal research and the pupil barrister   7
2.4   Legal research as a process   8

3   **Legal research methods and techniques**   9
3.1   Planning legal research   9
3.2   Analysing the problem   10
3.3   Researching the issues   12
3.4   Following through   16
3.5   Updating the law   17
3.6   Further research techniques   17
3.7   Applying the law to the facts   19
3.8   Recording your research   21
3.9   In conclusion   24

4   **Legal resources for the practitioner**   25
4.1   Introduction: using the law library   25
4.2   Legal commentary   27
4.3   Practitioner textbooks   27
4.4   Legal encyclopedias   30
4.5   Legal journals   32
4.6   Judicial dictionaries   33
4.7   Forms and precedents   33
4.8   Primary sources of law   34
4.9   Primary legislation: Public General Acts ('statutes')   34
4.10   Secondary legislation: Statutory Instruments   40
4.11   Case law and law reports   42
4.12   European Union legal documents   51
4.13   EU legislation   52
4.14   EU law reports   57
4.15   EU periodical literature   58
4.16   Current awareness: finding out about new developments   60
4.17   Key EU websites   60
4.18   Human rights documentation   60

4.19   The European Convention on Human Rights   61
4.20   Human rights law reports   61
4.21   Human rights serials   62
4.22   Key human rights websites   63

5   Using electronic resources for research   **64**
5.1   Electronic formats   64
5.2   Types of electronic database   65
5.3   Commercial legal databases   66
5.4   Free legal information on the internet   70
5.5   Search strategies using electronic resources   73

6   Researching words and phrases   **80**
6.1   Introduction   80
6.2   Checklist   80
6.3   Where to look for definitions   81
6.4   Foreign legal vocabulary   83
6.5   *Pepper v Hart* research: using *Hansard*   83

7   Reading and interpreting a case   **90**
7.1   Introduction   90
7.2   Judicial precedent   90
7.3   The *ratio* of a case   93
7.4   Some test questions   95
7.5   Analysing cases   97
7.6   *Batey v Wakefield* [1982] 1 All ER 61   98
7.7   *Lewis v Lady Rook* [1992] 1 WLR 662   104
7.8   Answers to test questions   114

8   Practical legal research: a summary   **117**
8.1   The purpose of this chapter   117
8.2   Notes to pupil supervisor   121
8.3   Summary   123
8.4   Criteria by which you may assess your legal research   123
8.5   A sample exercise in legal research   123
8.6   And, finally, some useful tips   124

9   Legal sources for the practitioner: a bibliography   **126**
9.1   Legal encyclopedias   126
9.2   Legal dictionaries   126
9.3   Law reports   127
9.4   Journals   127
9.5   Legal sources—by subject area   127

PART II   **Fact Management**   **139**

10   Overview of a civil case   **141**
10.1   Introduction   141
10.2   Stages in a civil case   141
10.3   Roles of solicitor and barrister   143
10.4   Pre-claim stage   148
10.5   Instituting proceedings   154
10.6   Interim stage: preparing the evidence   158

10.7	The trial: final preparation and hearing	164
10.8	Settlement during the process	168
10.9	Enforcement	169
10.10	Appeal	169
10.11	Costs	169
11	**Anatomy of a criminal case**	**171**
11.1	Introduction	171
11.2	Role of the defence barrister	171
11.3	Legal aid	172
11.4	Crown Prosecution Service	173
11.5	Stages of a criminal case: a thumbnail sketch	173
11.6	The stages in greater detail	175
12	**The fact management process**	**187**
12.1	Introduction to the fact management process	187
12.2	Starting from scratch: defining basic terms	188
12.3	The CAP approach	190
12.4	Stage 1: context	191
12.5	Stage 2: analysis of issues and evidence	205
12.6	Stage 3: the presentation of the case or argument	214
12.7	The client's choice: acting on instructions	218
12.8	Suggested charts	218
13	**Presentation for the practitioner: the CAP approach in action**	**223**
13.1	Applying the CAP approach	223
13.2	Instructions to counsel	223
13.3	Practising the skill	224
13.4	Criteria by which you may assess your own performance	224
13.5	Preparation: the common foundation to all your work	225
14	**Dealing with figures**	**226**
14.1	Introduction	226
14.2	Importance of numeracy	226
14.3	Relevance of figures in a barrister's practice	227
14.4	Risk assessment	230
14.5	Stages in a claim when you may need to deal with figures	231
14.6	Collecting evidence of figures	233
14.7	Statistics and graphs	233
15	**Communication and information technology use in case preparation and presentation**	**235**
15.1	Introduction	235
15.2	Modern practice	235
15.3	Essential skills	236
15.4	Data protection and security	239
PART III	**Opinion Writing**	**241**
16	**Words and the barrister**	**243**
16.1	Introduction	243
16.2	Tools of the trade	243
16.3	Speaking and writing	243
16.4	Communication	244
16.5	The spoken word and the written word	244

16.6   Standards   244
16.7   Good writing   245

17   Qualities of good writing   246
17.1   The qualities   246
17.2   Making choices   246
17.3   The English language   247
17.4   Clarity   247
17.5   A logical structure   248
17.6   Spelling   248
17.7   Grammar   248
17.8   Punctuation   249
17.9   Precision   249
17.10 Non-ambiguity   250
17.11 Conciseness   250
17.12 Completeness   250
17.13 Style   251
17.14 Appearance   251
17.15 The reader   251
17.16 Reading over   252

18   Plain English   253
18.1   Introduction   253
18.2   What is plain English?   253
18.3   Why use plain English?   253
18.4   What does legalese look like?   254
18.5   Why do lawyers write legalese?   257
18.6   What is being done to promote plain English?   258
18.7   Learning to write plain English   259
18.8   Basic rules of plain English   260
18.9   Bad words and phrases   262
18.10 Some exercises   264
18.11 Further reading   265
18.12 Suggested answers to exercises in 18.10   265

19   Opinion writing   269
19.1   Why learn to write opinions?   269
19.2   What is opinion writing?   269
19.3   The right mental attitude: the practical approach   271
19.4   The thinking process: preparing to write an opinion   273
19.5   The writing process: the opinion itself   279
19.6   How the opinion should be set out   281
19.7   Points of content   288
19.8   Style   291
19.9   Professional conduct   291
19.10 Further reading   292

20   The use of law in an opinion   293
20.1   Introduction   293
20.2   Dealing with the well-known principle of law   294
20.3   Only cite authorities on points of law   294
20.4   How to cite cases   295
20.5   Show the relevance of the case   297
20.6   Which case(s) to cite   297
20.7   Using statutory materials   298

20.8	Which sources to cite	299
20.9	Apply the law to the facts	299
20.10	Producing sound conclusions	300
20.11	Summary	300
21	**Getting started**	302
21.1	The problem	302
21.2	The analysis	303
21.3	Writing the opinion	311
22	**Advice on evidence in a civil case**	314
22.1	An approach to writing a civil advice on evidence	314
22.2	Sample advice on evidence	324
23	**Advice on evidence in a criminal case**	329
23.1	An approach to writing a criminal advice on evidence	329
23.2	Sample advice on evidence for prosecution	336
23.3	Sample advice for defence	341
24	**Checklist for opinion writing skills**	347
24.1	The purpose of this chapter	347
24.2	Language and style	347
24.3	Content	348
24.4	Conclusions and reasoning	349
24.5	Structure	350
24.6	Practicality	352
Index		353

Part I

Legal Research

1   Preparation: a forensic skill   3
2   Introduction to practical legal research   5
3   Legal research methods and techniques   9
4   Legal resources for the practitioner   25
5   Using electronic resources for research   64
6   Researching words and phrases   80
7   Reading and interpreting a case   90
8   Practical legal research: a summary   117
9   Legal sources for the practitioner: a bibliography   126

Preparation: a forensic skill

The image of successful barristers suggests that their success depends on the ability to think on their feet, to use words persuasively, to mesmerise by their fluency, and to impress by their very presence and charisma those whom they address. Certainly those skills help. However, the real basis for their confidence is effective preparation for the task they are undertaking so that they know the facts of the case thoroughly and, having considered the potential relevance of all the facts to their legal context, can respond effectively to any point made; and, having thought through and planned their argument beforehand, they can deliver it clearly and address in a convincing way all the relevant questions which must be decided.

The work of a barrister (more fully dealt with in **Chapters 10** and **11**), although more varied than many realise, is focused on answering one question. If the case came before a court, how likely is it that the client would win? The only way that this question can be answered is for the barrister to address the underlying question, which is: how can the case be presented so that evidence can be put before the court which will prove on the facts that the client is legally entitled to a finding in his or her favour? This is why case preparation is a forensic skill.

In order to answer this underlying question, the barrister will need to look closely at the facts of the case to see what the client's problem is and what the client hopes to achieve from any legal claim. The barrister will then need to research the law to see whether there is a legal principle which will give the client a right to the outcome being sought. The facts of the case will then need to be analysed to determine whether they can be presented in such a way that all the component parts of the legal principle can be shown to be fulfilled. The barrister will also need to consider whether there are witnesses who can be called to give evidence which, if believed, will prove the facts on which the argument is based and which, it is hoped, will persuade the court of the client's entitlement to a finding in his or her favour.

This analytical process can be demonstrated in graphical form as in **Table 1.1**.

Table 1.1 **Initial analysis of a case**

Legal framework	Facts in support	Evidence
Insert below each element of the crime, cause of action, and/or defences	Insert below in relation to each legal element facts which establish that element	Insert below in relation to each fact the evidence which proves that fact

By identifying every element of the legal principle which is relied on and the facts and evidence which support it, the barrister can test whether there is sufficient available evidence of the facts to establish the legal basis of the case. Even then the preparatory work will not be completed, for the barrister, before being able to advise on the likely success of a case, will have to consider all the arguments about fact and law which the other side might raise, and whether and how they can be countered. Only then will the barrister be able to answer, with any hope of that answer being justified, the question whether the client will win, or be able with confidence to present the case convincingly to the court.

The aim of this manual is to explain and demonstrate some methods of legal research and fact management which, in the context of the work of a barrister, will assist in developing effective case preparation skills.

Chapters 2 to **9** show how legal research can be made more efficient by increasing familiarity with the basic sources of information and by outlining some of the main techniques of research.

Chapters 10 and **11** provide an overview of the stages of first a civil and then a criminal case. The Bar is predominantly a referral profession and a barrister may be consulted at various stages of a case; therefore it is always important that any preparation is focused on the particular instructions that have been received. As particular aspects of the case may require different emphasis at different stages, it is always crucial to tailor one's preparation to the stage that the case has reached.

Chapter 12 describes the intellectual processes and the analytical skills which are required for effective fact management. The acronym CAP (Context, Analysis, Presentation) has been adopted to summarise the process by which the preparation of a case progresses from an initial understanding of the legal and factual context to a detailed analysis of the issues and the evidence, and finally to the construction of a persuasive and pertinent argument which can be presented to whatever audience is appropriate, be it the client or a tribunal.

The chapter also illustrates some of the possible techniques which can be used to ensure that the CAP process is carried out rigorously, and may help you to develop your own analytical skills. One technique has already been displayed above at **Table 1.1**. Once that table has been completed in relation to any set of facts it should provide both an overview and a detailed analysis of the interrelation of the law, facts, and evidence, issue by issue. This should make it possible not only to assess the likelihood of success in establishing your client's case but also to carry out your specific instructions more precisely.

For instance, if your advice is sought, whether in a conference or as a written opinion, the completion of **Table 1.1** should make obvious whether there is a prima facie case so that a preliminary assessment of potential success or advice on further steps necessary can be given. If the instructions are to draft a statement of claim, the centre column will have identified the material facts which should be included. Moreover, the inability to complete the table fully will, of itself, identify what further information may be needed.

If a similar analysis is also done of the case for the other side, this should assist—once the strength of all the available evidence has been considered—in providing the basis for planning any negotiation, for mediation or court advocacy, and in answering the basic questions: how likely is it that the client will win? How can the case be presented most effectively?

It comes as a surprise to some considering careers at the Bar that virtually every client will want to know 'how much?' in relation to some aspect or other of their case. **Chapter 14** provides guidance with dealing with figures. It will be less of a surprise that information and communication technology is becoming of increasing significance to practice at the Bar. **Chapter 15** presents the ways in which it is likely to be of most importance to you. Finally, for this part of the manual, **Chapter 15** presents the different ways in which case preparation may be applied to the different types of work that barristers may be instructed to undertake and indicates the other manuals in this series which assist you in those tasks.

Chapters 16–24 show you how to apply these research and preparation processes to the task of writing opinions: advising your client in writing.

Introduction to practical legal research

If you think that the highest function of the barrister is courtroom advocacy, think again. Barristers are 'learned' counsel. They have earned their traditional title, not by their in-court resourcefulness but by being the specialists of the legal profession, lawyers whom other lawyers consult. Barristers are sought for their knowledge and understanding of the law and their resourcefulness in applying it to the legal problem presented by their client.

The ability to provide counsel's opinion is based on effective legal research and is the first requisite of the barrister—first, because it comes long before advocacy or even the drafting of statements of the case. There is of course a close connection between all of these functions: the opinion given is one which the barrister knows he or she must be prepared to deliver in court. It must be well founded on thorough research, to which the advocacy skills of the barrister can then be applied. It is in their ability to find the law and their facility to adapt and apply it to their client's cause that the most able barristers can be recognised.

2.1 What is 'practical' legal research?

Practical legal research is not the same as academic legal research practised at law schools and universities. Students absorb essential legal knowledge and principles presented in textbooks and by their university tutors. They may have the opportunity to research specific areas of law in essays or dissertations, but the research required for academic purposes allows for the pursuit of interesting legal principles and points of law while articles and cases are quoted in support of broad legal arguments.

Practical legal research is 'applied' research and a much more focused discipline. The practising lawyer seeks the law he or she needs in order to answer very specific legal questions posed by a particular problem on which the client seeks advice. The barrister conducts legal research to meet the client's needs and so must be able to:

- identify the legal issues involved in a legal problem presented by a client;
- research those issues comprehensively while remaining focused on the problem itself;
- identify the primary sources (i.e. case law and legislation) on which an answer would depend;
- identify legal aspects which might pose problems for the client—and which act in favour of the case for the other side;

- formulate an accurate answer and a reliable opinion for the client; and
- research quickly, thoroughly, and effectively.

In some respects, this last point is the most important for the practising barrister. Research must be comprehensive and accurate—going to court poorly prepared and getting the law wrong can amount to negligence—but it must also be quick ('time is money').

2.2   The importance of legal research

We have already seen that barristers are legal experts, sought by clients for their knowledge and expertise. No lawyer, however skilful, experienced, or clever, can know the answer to every legal problem—but through effective legal research, they should be able to find a solution. The dangers of conducting poor legal research are amply demonstrated in the case of *Copeland v Smith & Goodwin* [2000] 1 WLR 1371, where three advocates took a case to the Court of Appeal only to find at the hearing that the Court of Appeal had decided exactly the same point of law several months previously. Counsel for the appellants had not researched their case law thoroughly enough and '. . . such failure had resulted in significant costs being expended on an appeal. It was essential that advocates should take steps necessary to keep abreast of all relevant reported cases.'

Similarly, specialist counsel in a divorce case came in for stinging criticism from Judge Horowitz QC in *Martin Dye v Martin Dye* [2006] 1 WLR 3448. Counsel challenged a division of marital assets by referring to statutory regulations that had been revoked four years previously. In addition to failing to update the legislation and direct the District Judge to the correct regulations, they had also failed to consult the relevant paragraphs of *Rayden & Jackson* (the leading practitioner's text on family law) where, it was pointed out in the judgment, there is set out a 'clear and complete statement of the required practice'. The cost of two wasted hearings was put at half a million pounds. Counsel have a duty to direct the judge to the correct law—they can only do so if they do their research properly and get the law right themselves.

Legal research skills are also important in their own right, to you as an individual and to your career. They are skills that will be utilised in whichever area of law you eventually practise. You may learn employment law as a student but never use it in a commercial law practice or for a career as a criminal barrister—but the ability to conduct legal research will be of fundamental importance in all areas of law, throughout your career. On a personal level, learning and practising your legal research skills will:

- widen your knowledge of the law;
- teach you to analyse legal issues;
- encourage you to think laterally, coherently, and independently;
- increase your ability to be accurate and concise; and
- teach you essential information-management skills.

Indeed, many employers in the legal world regard the ability to conduct efficient legal research and present it concisely and coherently as the most important skill a newly qualified lawyer should possess. The Bar Standards Board, in conjunction with chambers and pupil supervisors, takes the view that the ability to conduct legal research is an essential skill for pupil barristers. Consequently, all vocational law courses include practical legal research as an essential skill, pervasive to all other assessed subjects taught on the course.

2.3　Practical legal research and the pupil barrister

The skills needed for systematic legal research can be taught in law schools—and this manual presents a scheme for learning those skills—but it is no replacement for the experience of doing the research for yourself. If you ask any barrister how he or she learnt to research law, the chances are that they will say they learnt it 'on the job', by 'trial and error', or by 'jumping in at the deep end'.

To some extent, these comments reflect the informal network of assistance and support that has long been provided to new pupils by their pupil supervisors, fellow pupils, and barrister colleagues. New barristers also have access to the structured internal resources offered by the chambers themselves:

- access to printed legal resources (journals, case reports, court forms);
- subscriptions to legal databases;
- information-management databases with notes of legal research; and
- professional support for legal research—through updating services or, sometimes, a dedicated staff member.

The successful barrister will use both informal networks and structured access to a chambers' own resources, assistance, and advice to assist him or her in researching the law—but these are not replacements for sound legal research skills acquired through experience of researching the law using both printed and electronic sources.

Researching the law for your pupil supervisor on behalf of a client is likely to be one of the first tasks that you, as a new pupil barrister, will be given. On entering pupillage, it is difficult to make a significant contribution to chambers until you have acquired some experience, but legal research is one function that a new pupil can perform largely unsupervised. This means that chambers are generally attracted by the prospect of having an effective and reliable legal researcher to research the law for them. Earning a reputation as a good legal researcher is an attractive prospect for yourself and a good incentive for chambers—or, indeed, for any legal employer—to take on a new employee.

But what is actually required of a new pupil barrister researching the law?

Chambers expect pupils to be able to research a client's legal problem and to present a precise, accurate, and succinct summary of their findings, which could be used to advise a client. A pupil supervisor would expect pupils to have written a thorough record of how they have done the research, the sources they have consulted, and the issues they have addressed. The 'research note' allows the research to be checked, followed, and updated at a later date and is an essential part of the information-management process in chambers.

A pupil barrister is expected to carry out such a task from day one. A pupil's familiarity with practitioner texts and the way legal knowledge (statute law, case law, etc.) is organised in the law library and on electronic databases—how they cite the law, classify it, and cross-refer—is simply assumed and is regarded as part of the task. Research methods, techniques, how to analyse the issues and write the formal research note are not skills that are taught in chambers, and again it is assumed that the new pupil barrister already has these skills to some degree.

2.4 Legal research as a process

Successful legal research in chambers in preparation for a case is a process involving three essentials:

- *Analysis*—a succinct analysis of the law, which is focused on the client's legal problem.
- *Resources*—knowing what resources are available and how to use them, and using them effectively.
- *Method*—a research method that is comprehensive yet time-efficient.

These elements are interdependent: no amount of careful analysis will make up for a failure to identify key resources, while knowing your resources but failing to use them systematically will not produce a clear analysis of the issues.

The chapters that follow address each of these elements.

Chapter 3 considers the essential ingredients of successful legal research. It will look at planning your legal research, analysing issues, identifying keywords, and applying problem-solving techniques; and it goes on to outline some key techniques for researching the law comprehensively, yet quickly and effectively.

Chapters 4 and **5** will consider more closely the wealth of resources that are available to the legal researcher—printed resources and online legal databases—and how they might be used effectively: where to start and which to choose; how the law library is organised and the resources you will find there.

Chapters 6 and **7** deal with specific aspects of practical legal research which cause difficulty—the interpretation of words and phrases, interpreting legislative ambiguity, and the reading and interpretation of cases.

Chapter 8 provides a useful summary of those chapters that have gone before with a thorough worked-through example of a legal research problem.

Legal research methods and techniques

Practical legal research is an intellectual exercise that requires much more than a simple overview of the legal resources available to the practitioner. To prepare for a case, a barrister is expected to analyse the issues involved and, using a research method that is comprehensive and time-efficient, come up with solutions and answers that are tightly focused on the client's legal problems. When faced with a multitude of resources, a sequence of problems to resolve, and no clear starting point, this can seem a daunting and time-consuming task rather than a rewarding aspect of the barrister's work. In fact, even when carrying out the research itself, there can be practical problems to face and challenging issues to overcome. It can, for example, be difficult to:

- identify all the relevant legal issues with any certainty;
- access the resources that you need, when you need them;
- know where to start, particularly if the legal problem is itself unclear;
- know if the information you have found is relevant, reliable, and up to date;
- keep focused on the client's problem; and
- know when to stop researching, even if you find nothing.

Indeed, there is a need to be realistic about what legal research can actually achieve. Where facts are important to a case rather than the law itself, legal research is of limited use and analysis of those facts is far more important. Legal research can assist with finding and communicating principles of law to the client and determining how they have been applied and interpreted in the courts but, however thorough the research, it does not guarantee certainty; many cases come to court simply because the law is unclear.

Furthermore, there is no single 'correct' way to research the law; instinct and experience—making mistakes, misclassifying the law, and following 'false leads'—all play a part. Fortunately, however, there are methods and techniques that can be employed to improve your analytical skills and to develop your legal research abilities. The need to think about legal research strategically, to plan beforehand, to adopt an approach that is appropriate to the particular purpose, to research systematically, and to utilise your findings in a way that is meaningful to the client and the court, are all fundamental to your success as a legal researcher and a pupil barrister.

3.1 Planning legal research

Planning your legal research plays an important part in ensuring that you stay focused on the key problems, legal issues, and remedies that could lead to an answer to the client's legal problem. It can also help to find the elusive 'starting point'. Extensive 'background' reading, making notes, and collating photocopies are very unlikely to help and will only serve to confuse. In order to plan research effectively, we need to identify the essential steps in practical legal research that we might follow. A typical method might look something like this:

- assemble the facts and identify those that are most relevant;
- analyse the legal issues involved and identify the legal questions that need answering;
- research the legal issues;
- analyse and synthesise the facts and the law; and
- come to preliminary conclusions that can be used to prepare a research note.

In formulating a plan for legal research, the researcher might take each of these stages and consider the following:

- the resources that will be needed (printed and online);
- the steps to be taken—whether the research can be divided into more manageable tasks;
- the findings that need to be recorded; and
- the time it will take—how 'big' is the task? A few quick-reference searches or a time-consuming project?

Thinking about these issues helps to identify what needs to be done and when. It also allows the researcher to plan more systematically; it follows that the research itself is likely be more systematic too. Most legal issues involve legislation, case law, and rules of procedure and these can usefully be researched separately. Sometimes a legal question is very focused and so planning is much easier—for example, a trawl through case law to find likely damages for a personal injury claim. At other times, legal issues are unclear or more numerous and therefore require more research and analysis. It is important to assess this at the initial stages of research so that you can give yourself sufficient time, both to find the information you need and to analyse your findings. Legal research nearly always takes longer than you think it will.

3.2 Analysing the problem

Preparing a plan and a schedule for legal research is difficult without first having looked at the facts of the case and analysed the issues. Legal problems arrive in chambers in the form of papers outlining factual situations—letters, contracts, or statements from individuals. Translating the 'facts' that they contain into legal issues is one of the most difficult aspects of legal research but it is also central to the barrister's role. A man slips, falls, and is seriously injured on a building site—those are the facts, but what are the legal issues?

3.2.1 Factual analysis

Assembling the facts and analysing them carefully will help you to identify:

- the 'material' facts—those that are important and those that can be omitted;
- connections between the facts; and
- possible areas of law and legal issues to research.

Read the papers carefully and ask yourself:

- What is the case about?
- Which facts are relevant?
- What does the client want?
- What am I being asked to do?

In our example of a man falling at a building site and being seriously injured, we may learn from the facts that he was an employee working on scaffolding and was seen to be talking on a mobile phone just before he fell. These would be material facts. The fact that he had just had lunch is immaterial to his fall (unless he was seen to have drunk alcohol with his lunch).

Having read the papers before you and analysed the facts, you may find it helpful to write a succinct summary of the circumstances. An accurate précis of the information will help you to understand the client's situation. A summary should be concise and focused on the material facts. It is not an investigation of the facts themselves (which would, in any case, be impossible for the barrister to carry out). Avoid elaborating on the original facts but do take into account the client's wishes or needs, as well as facts that are unfavourable to your client (you will need to provide defences for those facts). Analysing and summarising the facts will help with the next stage—identifying the legal issues.

3.2.2   Legal analysis

By taking the facts of the case and analysing them more closely you can begin to identify legal problems or questions that need researching. Legal analysis is a preliminary identification of the legal issues involved in a case. It differs from factual analysis in that the researcher begins to apply his or her knowledge of legal principles to the facts in order to identify:

- possible legal issues in the case;
- key areas of law relevant to the facts; and
- specific points of law.

One way of building up a useful set of issues to research is to ask 'who, how, what, where, when, and why' questions of your facts and the client's situation and intentions. Questions you might ask yourself include:

- What essential areas of law are important to this case?
- What legal issues emerge from the material facts?
- How do these issues impinge on the facts of the case . . . and vice versa?
- What does the client want as a solution to their legal problem?
- How could they achieve their objectives and what are the alternatives?
- What facts might impede this outcome and how might they be overcome?
- What causes of action are available?
- Who is liable?

Not all of these questions will be relevant all of the time. In our example, health and safety legislation and the employer's duty of care towards employees are legal issues which will need researching. Who is liable here? Is it the employer or is there a contributory element to the fall on the part of the victim? In asking all these questions, be as specific as possible; this will make your research more focused, and the application of the law to your client's case more relevant.

Having analysed the facts, you should be able to draw up a list of questions, issues, and problems that it would appear (from the facts before you) that the court would need to determine. The questions should address the legal aspects of your client's case and the alternative outcomes. The questions posed should be capable of being answered through legal research; you do not have the option of investigating the facts themselves. Note, also, that the legal issues you identify are not the same as the client's original question or problem (which would be resolved by the court); they are simply those matters that need researching before you can even start to form an opinion on the solution to the client's original problem.

3.3   Researching the issues

Once you have sketched out a plan of research, analysed the client's problem, and produced a list of legal issues, think about approaching the sources and starting to research. But which issue would you research first and how?

Now that you have identified the legal questions that you need to answer, it would be useful to list them in order of importance and to research them in that order. Having done some research on the principal issues, you might find that some minor aspects of the legal problem prove irrelevant or perhaps do not need researching at the early stages when you are merely determining the strength of a case. At this point it is also useful to categorise the issues and identify the sources you might approach and the keywords you might use to search that source (whether it be a database or the contents list or index of a practitioner text).

3.3.1   Categorising legal issues

For each legal issue:

- establish if it is a civil or criminal matter;
- identify the principal area of law—this will become your subject heading (e.g. contract, tort, family law, offences against the person); and
- decide which aspects of the issue are substantive or procedural in nature.

Categorising the issues in this way will help to identify the principal areas of law you need to research (e.g. contract, tort, family law), which will assist in your selection of a legal commentary as your starting point. It will also help produce a few broad terms which then become subject headings in your research (e.g. negligence). These terms might be too broad to be of use in an index to a practitioner text but they can be used to search the table of contents.

3.3.2   Identifying keywords

Legal issues are researched using electronic databases or the contents list or index of a book. Selecting the 'best' keywords to access these resources will determine how successful your research will be. Formulating legal issues will itself lead you to keywords, while finding relevant keywords during your research will help you to think about legal issues.

Choose keywords that describe the legal issues most accurately, avoiding general terms (which would give too many references) and, indeed, terms that are too specific (which might be hidden away in a printed index under a broader term). Which words define the problem you are researching? These might be:

- words offered to you by your analysis of the legal issue itself;
- alternatives to those words (i.e. synonyms); and
- concepts behind those words.

EXERCISE 1   SIMPLE KEYWORD PROBLEMS

Example

A Bar students' magazine wants to run a competition for BPTC students. You are asked to advise the magazine on whether there are any restrictions or regulations applicable.

Analysis

Can there be any legal objection to this? What area of law would it be? It doesn't look like gambling; no money is involved. Nor is it a lottery with tickets. Competition law? Prize law? Surely they mean something quite different? But 'competition' or 'prize' would be good keywords to start with.

1. Must London taxis have meters?
2. Is endorsement of a driving licence obligatory for the offence of driving without insurance?
3. The author of a fraudulent misrepresentation thought that the representation was irrelevant or unimportant. Is this defence likely to succeed?
4. Is it true that barristers enjoy immunity from suit for alleged negligence in the conduct of civil proceedings when acting as advocates?
5. Does a witness who deliberately fabricates evidence in legal proceedings have immunity from suit in negligence in relation to the evidence given in court?

Think laterally about how the problem might be described; those who write practitioner texts and database content do not necessarily describe concepts in the same way. To make the best use of these resources, you may need to browse the contents of a text, look up several keywords in an index, or combine keywords when searching a database. In determining the keywords or phrases you might use, bear in mind:

- broader and narrower terms—words may appear in a printed index as a subdivision of a broader heading rather than a term itself (e.g. dismissal, unfair);
- alternative, interchangeable terms (e.g. drunkenness, intoxication; drugs, narcotics; pharmaceuticals, prescription drugs);
- terms dependent on context (e.g. forfeiture, of a lease or of the proceeds of crime?);
- concealed keywords—the relevant statute may contain a very precise word that we would tend to broaden or paraphrase in everyday language (see **Exercise 2**); and
- changes to the meanings of words—new words in legal parlance ('Part 20 claims'; the law relating to 'terrorism') and old ('employment law' was once known as 'labour law'). The 'labelling' of terms and their organisation within texts and on databases also varies between publishers.

In thinking about concepts you might also consider terms that relate to types of activity, actions, remedies, etc.:

Type of activity	Accident, slip, trip
Causes of action	Tort, negligence, contributory negligence
Remedies	Damages, conviction
Parties/subjects/relationships	Employer, employee, third parties
Things	Victims, hazards

Printed tables of contents and indexes are excellent resources in themselves for finding keywords, arranged as they are in a hierarchy from broad concepts to narrow, more specific terms. The index to *Halsbury's Laws of England and Wales* is perhaps the most useful, its encyclopedic nature meaning that it offers a wide range of keywords, including cross-references to alternative terms, 'preferred' terms and broader concepts, and a separate index of definitions of particular words and phrases. (See **4.4**.)

Choosing keywords to search on a legal database, however, is more problematic and subject to a greater degree of error. An awareness of alternative terms is particularly important, while terms such as 'duty of care' are simply too broad and will produce far too many results to be of any use; knowing how to combine terms and search correctly is crucial. Keywords should be specific enough to yield a manageable quantity of information but not so specific as to find no results at all. Database search techniques are dealt with in greater detail in **Chapter 5**.

Finally, look at your list of legal issues and identify at least one keyword for each issue you need to research. Now we can begin to identify the sources you might use and start the research itself.

EXERCISE 2   KEYWORDS AND LEGAL ISSUES

Example

Rita, employed by a large company, says that she was frequently bullied or ridiculed by fellow employees, that she became ill as a result, and had to give up her job. She now wants to sue her employers. They say that she gave no reason for leaving other than ill-health; that she never complained about her treatment; and that since any such alleged misconduct was never brought to their notice, they cannot be liable.

Analysis

There would no doubt be a conflict here on the facts. However, the legal issue is whether the employers could in principle be vicariously liable; and if so liable, for what? The missing keyword is 'harassment'.

1. Charles's house was badly damaged in a severe gale last night. The upper part is in danger of falling. Charles's surveyor says it must be pulled down and made safe without delay. Workmen are standing by to do the necessary work. But the house is a listed building and no authorisation has been obtained. Can Charles go ahead?

2. Fred Warmington, a travel agent, registered as a domain name 'Warmington.holidays.com'. The borough of Warmington-on-Sea, a well-known holiday resort, wishes to object to this as likely to confuse people looking for holidays there. Fred says he is entitled to use his own name. Advise the borough.

3. A firm of auctioneers are your clients. Their sale catalogue described a piece of furniture as Georgian. An experienced dealer purchased it at the auction. He says (and they now agree) it is Victorian and that this amounts to a false trade description. The auctioneers point out that their catalogue conditions state that, being merely auctioneers, they are not responsible for vendors' statements of authenticity, origin, date, etc., of any article. They also say that, anyway, the purchaser is himself an expert who did not rely on their description. They therefore say that they are not liable for false trade description. Are they right?

3.3.3   **Starting to research**

You should by now have a list of the legal issues, problems, or questions you wish to research and a list of relevant keywords to look up in a printed source or to use as search terms on a legal database. You may also have an idea of the relevant areas of law you need to cover and the case law, legislation, or procedure you need to look up. Often you will recognise the legal context (contract, tort, crime, procedure, etc.) even though you may not know the actual answer. If this is the case, then start researching those issues first; accessing the law you are familiar with will lead you to other relevant sources. If it isn't clear what area of law the problem falls into, then try classifying the problem: is it more likely to be civil or criminal litigation or health and safety law? Is the answer more likely to be found in legislation than in case law, or does the problem turn on a procedural point?

These questions all help determine which source you choose to use as your starting point for research. There will be a range of resources available to answer any legal question and you may need to use more than one to find what you need. Law sources are 'primary' (case law and legislation—the law itself) or secondary (expert opinion and commentary on the law). (See **4.1.3**.) These terms refer to their importance in the law rather than the order in which you should refer to them. Unless you are very familiar with the relevant case law or legislation, it is nearly always best to start your research with a secondary source (hereafter referred to as 'legal commentary')—why start trying to interpret case law or legislation, or to understand how the various legal principles fit together, when an expert has already done it for you?

3.3.3.1   Selecting a legal commentary

Use the list of practitioner texts, journals, and law reports arranged by subject in **Chapter 9** to identify a suitable text covering the area of law you need. You may need to use more than one legal commentary to feel sure you have a good grasp of the relevant law. Try to use the most appropriate source for the question, only moving on to another if the answer you find is unclear or is not detailed enough. An excellent starting point for almost any area of English law is the comprehensive legal encyclopedia, *Halsbury's Laws of England and Wales*. (See **4.4**.)

Knowledge of a range of legal resources, and how they work and relate to other sources, is not only useful but is a prerequisite for successful legal research. Take some time to learn how to use a practitioner text, including its table of contents, its index, its overall layout, and the methods used to update the text. (See **4.3**.) Similarly, you should be aware of how legal databases work, their contents, and how they update their material. (See **Chapter 5**.)

Commentary will help identify other legal issues relevant to your problem and will lead you to the relevant case law and legislation but, however well-regarded the source, most legal commentaries are not authoritative in court and are no substitute for researching the primary sources of law. When citing authority for a proposition of law, you should refer to statute law and/or case law, not to what is said in a textbook.

3.3.3.2   Locating primary sources

Primary sources are legislation (statutes and statutory instruments) and case law. You would rarely approach the primary sources directly unless the legal problem you face is fairly straightforward and simply involves finding a definition from a statute or reading the points of law established in a leading case, for example. Researching legislation is perhaps slightly easier and more finite an activity than researching case law, which can be very time-consuming. Commentaries on (or annotated versions of) statutes and statutory instruments (SIs) very often refer to cases, so providing a means of identifying some of the most important cases that may be relevant. The reverse is also true—reports of cases will cite relevant legislation which again provides a useful 'way in' to researching statute law. (See **4.8** for researching primary sources of law.)

3.4   Following through

Researching a legal problem in legal commentaries and finding relevant legislation and case law will start you off in legal research but it is rarely sufficient in itself, though this may not be immediately apparent. Further analysis of the material facts in the light of the information you have found will nearly always reveal legal issues you hadn't originally thought of and which will need investigating, and perhaps new keywords you could use to search the legal commentaries and databases. At this point you should return to your list of legal issues and the client's original problem. Here are a few tips and techniques for following through on your research:

Don't rely on your memory. You may have misremembered, or the law may have changed. Even if you think you know an area of law thoroughly and have some knowledge of the specific issue, you should always check your sources and ensure your law is up to date.

No source is comprehensive. You may need to look up the same keywords in several texts to gain both an overview of an area of law and sufficient detail on specific issues. *Halsbury's Laws* provides an excellent starting point for employment law, for example, but a specialist loose-leaf such as *Harvey's* is bound to go into more detail on specific issues. Conversely, the sources will also overlap; don't read through the same material twice unless you are looking for a different perspective on a particular legal issue or point of law.

Use your sources properly. Have you followed *all* the references the index referred to or only some of them? Failing to follow up references in an index or 'hits' on a database, is one of the most common errors in legal research, which can lead to crucial information being missed. Random browsing through a text using a table of contents is useful but it must be accompanied by a systematic approach to following up references in the index.

Stay focused on the legal issues, problems, and questions you are trying to answer. Avoid exploring interesting areas of law at the expense of the main issue. Keep referring back to the client's problem and reviewing your progress. Are you answering the question? Are you finding solutions to their problem? Your plan of research may change as new legal issues arise but this should be a matter of positive decision rather than the result of meandering research.

Lateral thinking. Sometimes there is a need to think around a problem and find a different angle on a complex legal issue, or an alternative source. If you are looking on a case law database for *Re M (a minor)* but find there are 20 cases of that name, you could read the headnotes of them all to find the particular case you need. Or, if you know the area of law covered by the case, you could approach a specialist text and use the table of cases, or search a full-text database using the case name and a keyword. If something is taking you too long, there is probably a more efficient way of doing it.

Know when to stop. Striking a balance between retrieving too much information and retrieving too little is one of the more difficult aspects of legal research. As practical legal research is a highly focused discipline, researching specific issues in depth is probably more useful than researching more widely (though if it is an unfamiliar area of law then wider research to acquire knowledge of the subject and a 'feel' for the issues, is probably justified). There is no 'right answer' in many cases, and too much research only serves to confuse and is counter-productive.

Finding nothing. This can be a worrying situation—where, despite a lot of research, you can find no relevant commentary on an issue, no legislation, and no case law, and have to face a demanding pupil supervisor with these results. It is worth trying to approach the problem from a different angle but it may simply be that there is no clear answer and no law to find. It is not necessarily a failure, provided you have researched thoroughly and updated your findings correctly. In some circumstances (especially in updating your research), finding nothing is perfectly 'normal'.

3.5   Updating the law

The distinction between the law as originally made and the law as amended and currently in force is fundamental to practical legal research. The law is not static but develops, and from the researcher's point of view we need to see how established law is affected by later legal developments; updating the law is therefore essential. As the law can change so quickly, printed texts obviously become out of date almost as soon as they are published and so most texts have some form of updating. For example, practitioner texts may have a supplement updating the commentary while legal encyclopedias have 'noter-up services', so called because the service volume 'notes-up' or updates the main volumes with later developments. (See **4.4.1.**) Similar 'noter-up' services operate for the primary sources of law and these are dealt with in more detail in **Chapter 4.**

Legal databases of case law and legislation are generally more up to date than printed equivalents but the commentary they contain is rarely more recent than the printed version. Most electronic sources started life as a published text and the contents have simply been transferred to a database with no repackaging for the electronic user; this can make them difficult to browse and read online but it also offers no advantage in terms of how up to date the text is. Updating legal sources online is dealt with in more detail in **Chapter 5.**

There are four principal ways in which primary law is amended:

- *Statutes affecting earlier statutes.* Check to see if a statute has come into force, if it is still in force (i.e. has it been repealed?) or if it has been amended. Also, bear in mind the possibility of statutory instruments amending statutes. (See **4.9.2** and **4.10.2.**)
- *Cases affecting earlier case law.* Check to see if a case has been applied, approved, followed, distinguished, or overruled. (See **4.11.4.**)
- *Cases interpreting statutes.* Check to see if a case has interpreted a statute. (See **4.11.4.**)
- *Statutes affecting earlier case law.* The best way of finding out whether the effect of a case has been reversed by statute is to look for the case in a textbook. (See **Table 4.9.**)

3.6   Further research techniques

The steps for researching the law outlined earlier and summarised at **3.6.1** are a well-established method of practical legal research. This is not the only approach, however, and there are several techniques that you can use in conjunction with these essential steps of legal research.

'Funnel' approach: broad to narrow. The importance of starting your research with a broad area of law and a corresponding legal commentary should not be underestimated. It is nearly always necessary to access unfamiliar areas of law through the context and meaning provided by a practitioner text, a legal encyclopedia, a loose-leaf, or an article. They provide assistance with finding and interpreting statutes and reported cases. However, the law exists in the primary authorities. Legislation and case law must always be read; it is these that you will use to advise the client and which you will rely on in court, not the legal commentaries.

Linear approaches. Use existing knowledge to link to other relevant information. If you know the name of a statute, you can locate an updated version of the Act, any subsidiary legislation, and cases referring to the Act. Similarly, if you know the name of a case you will be able to find other related cases and legislation referred to in the case.

Legal definitions. If a specific legal term is relevant to your research then a judicial dictionary will guide you to where the word or phrase is defined within the context of specific statues and cases. As such, they provide invaluable short cuts to the primary law. (See **Chapter 6**.)

Researching systematically. Build the techniques and methods described here into your research process. Updating the law, for example, is an essential part of the research process, not an afterthought. It takes little extra time and the updating material itself can be a useful source of information. Similarly, browsing contents tables to find key areas of law, checking all relevant references in the index and following through from practitioner text to case law and legislation are all signs of systematic legal research.

Checklists and flow charts. In planning your legal research you may find it helpful to create a checklist of sources to consult, keywords to use and steps to follow for each legal issue you have identified. These also serve as brief notes which can be used to prepare a more formal research note. (See **3.8.2**.) If you are a visual learner then use a flow chart instead of a checklist. Also, make good use of the tables within **Chapter 4**; they essentially operate as checklists for the types of information you need to look for within each source you use.

Brainstorming. Writing down everything concerning a legal issue is a useful starting point for thinking about keywords. Empathise with your client and try to think of issues from their point of view—then reverse the process and imagine it from the other side's point of view. This will broaden your thoughts on legal issues and keywords.

Asking questions. This was considered in the context of legal analysis (see **3.2.2**) and can also be usefully employed to think about keywords. In addition to 'who, what, why, how', etc., think about relationships (what caused . . . ? which came first . . . ?), comparisons (what is the opposite . . . ? is this similar to . . . ?), and evidence (what facts are there . . . ? is this possible . . . ?).

Thinking hats. De Bono's 'thinking hats' method explores ways of thinking about issues from different angles—without bias, without emotion, critically, positively, creatively, and finally the 'big picture'. This is particularly useful for thinking through more difficult legal research problems where there is no clear answer.[1]

Visual methods. For analysing issues, or communicating ideas such as 'mind mapping', or thinking in terms of processes or 'cycles', these can help break down issues into smaller segments and then connect them and chart the relationships between facts and issues.[2] This can, for example, help to identify cause and effect, or to understand complex contractual relationships.

---

1   E. de Bono, *Six Thinking Hats* (Penguin, 2000).

2   T. Hutchinson, *Researching and Writing in the Law* (LawBook, 2006).

3.6.1 Practical legal research—a '7-step method'

1. *Plan your legal research*. Identify the 'size' of the research, how long it might take, and where you might find the resources.

2. *Analyse the client's problem*. Summarise the material facts and identify potential legal issues and any questions of law that need to be answered. This will flesh out your initial plan of research.

3. *Categorise the legal issues and identify keywords*. Categorise to find broad subject areas and identify keywords that reflect specific aspects of the problems you need to research.

4. *Research the issues*. Choose as your starting point a legal commentary that covers the principal area of law. Follow through all references to your chosen keywords, then to other sources, and finally to primary sources. Establish legal authorities—statutes and case law—for a statement of law.

5. *Update your findings*. Check to ensure the statute has been brought into force, and whether it has been amended or repealed. Are your selected cases still valid law or have they been overruled or distinguished?

6. *Check back to your client's problem*. Look again at your list of legal issues, the original question, and your client's objectives, and check to ensure you have answered all the questions that arise. Have further issues arisen during your research? If so, look for other resources and issues, and then update.

7. *Analyse and summarise the law*. Apply the law to the facts of the case before you (see **3.7**). Only then are you ready to advise the client.

3.7 Applying the law to the facts

No amount of research will be of any use to your client if the law you have found is applied incorrectly to the facts before you. Practical legal research is a means to an end, not an end in itself. In order to ensure that your research is focused on finding the relevant legal principles to determine the issues which the court will have to decide, you should keep in mind and check your research regularly against the following:

- the client's problem and their objectives;
- the legal issues that would need to be determined by the court;
- the facts of the case before you;
- the potential persuasive arguments you could use to further your client's cause; and
- the potential persuasive arguments your opponent might use against you.

When you have found the relevant law, you should then:

- carefully reconsider and decide precisely what issues the court will have to determine;
- decide precisely what legal principle(s) you consider may be applied to EACH issue;
- determine whether your opponent is likely to argue either that these legal principles do not apply or that the court should determine differently what the legal principles are;

- apply the precise legal principles to the facts on EACH issue separately;
- be realistic in your application, noting gaps in the evidence and potential conflicts of fact; and
- set out your view on the conclusion the court is likely to reach: (i) on the facts (if possible); and (ii) on the legal issue.

In applying statutory provisions to the facts, you need to consider the precise wording of the provisions and the precise facts of your case. You need to ensure that you know the meaning the court will give to the relevant words:

- Is the word or phrase defined in an interpretation section?
- Is there case law interpreting it?
- Is the case law consistent on this, or are there conflicting judgments?
- Given the meaning of the relevant words, does the provision apply?
- How will the court apply it?
- What conclusion is the court likely to reach in respect of your client's case?

In applying case law to the facts, you need to consider the precise words of the legal principle(s) established by the case(s). If the legal principle is well established, you can rely on an accepted wording of it (for example, as set out in an authoritative practitioner text such as *Chitty on Contract* or *Clerk & Lindsell on Tort*). If the legal principles are not well established, you need to read the judgment(s) which have set them out and to identify the particular part of the judgment on which you will rely, to argue precisely what each legal principle is. You then need to check the facts of the case to determine whether or not your client's problem can be distinguished from those facts. You then need to formulate arguments to support a finding for your client on the issue, and to consider those arguments which your opponent is likely to formulate to persuade the court to find against your client. Then decide the likelihood that the court will be persuaded to find for or against your client on that issue.

It is the application of the law to the facts that forms the basis of the advice you will give to the client. It also informs the development of a persuasive argument and the preparation of a case for court. At this point you may find problems or issues emerge that require further research or clarification:

Inadequate factual information. It may not be possible to advise on some aspects of the client's problem simply because the facts, as presented, are unclear or questions arose during the research that you first need to clarify with the client. The client does not know the law; it is your job to find out the questions that need asking of the client to ensure that the court has all the relevant facts before it. Your opinion should advise the instructing solicitor on the further evidence which is required. (For more on this, see **Part III: *Opinion Writing*.**)

Insufficient analysis of the problem. Researching the law and applying the law to the facts without having a clear idea of the client's situation can lead to omissions in research, poor application of the law, and, consequently, bad or negligent advice. Empathise with the client's problem. What would be the best solution for you? Is it achievable within the facts before you or is there a suitable alternative?

Insufficient research. Advising your client on the basis of research using only secondary texts containing commentary and summaries of legislation and case law is flawed. The author of a practitioner text analyses the law from a perspective that is not necessarily analogous with your client's situation. If you have found relevant law, then you need to know *exactly* what it says—always research the law in the primary sources once you have exhausted the legal commentaries.

Ambiguity. You may find that the law is conflicting and it might not be possible to give a clear indication to the client of the likely outcome of a case. In such a situation, it will be up to the court to decide on the legal issues presented to it. However, when it comes to advising the client, you must still give advice on the approach that the court is likely to adopt (for example, expressing a view on how likely it is that the court will follow one line of authority in preference to another, or how the court is likely to construe a provision that has not previously been the subject of judicial interpretation). Ensure you have researched ambiguous case law thoroughly; a conflict in case law may, for example, have been commented on in journal articles or by judges in other cases. In applying the law to the facts, consider whether cases which are less favourable to your client's case might be 'distinguished' (and bear in mind that your opponent may try to distinguish authorities that are favourable to your client's case). If there is no relevant case law at all, then you should base your advice on appropriate general principles and hypothesise how these principles might be applied to your client's situation.

Disregarding the law. It may be tempting to outline a favourable outcome to a client when in fact the law does not support their position, or does so only partially. A false impression of a successful outcome when the application of the law to the facts says otherwise is both negligent advice and a disservice to a paying client.

3.8   Recording your research

As a pupil barrister, you are very likely to be conducting research for a more senior barrister. Your pupil supervisor will usually ask you to prepare a note of your research that will form the basis of an opinion. Keeping a thorough record of the legal research you have undertaken is crucial when it comes to preparing this formal note of legal research. The research note serves several purposes and may be used:

- as a means for the pupil supervisor to check the research you have carried out, and to ensure no legal issues have been missed and all findings have been updated;
- as a formal record of the research undertaken that would stay on a client's file and might be referred back to at a later stage in the proceedings;
- to advise a client verbally in a meeting or in writing through an opinion;
- in the preparation of a skeleton argument; and
- in the construction of legal argument where an issue in a case depends on a point of law.

The research note serves a multitude of purposes, each of which requires a different level of detail. Some clients, for example, may be more interested in the advice itself than in knowing the details of relevant legal sources, while a formal opinion would always contain references to key authorities. The research you carry out must be recorded in sufficient detail to be able to serve all those purposes; if it omits crucial information, then it could mean repeating some of your research at a later date or, at worst, an error going undetected, meaning deficient advice may be given to the client.

3.8.1   Taking notes during your research

The quality of the formal research note you prepare will depend to some extent on how well you have recorded your research as you were carrying it out. Careful note-taking will avoid trips back to the library to consult texts for a second time or further electronic searches to find legislation or case law that you referred to but failed to update. While carrying out research, record your progress so that you are clear as to the research you have completed and that which is still to be done. In researching printed sources you should note:

- the full reference of the sources consulted (and any sources that were unavailable; if you have a note of them, you can always check for them later in your research);
- the part of a book consulted (contents, indexes, tables);
- the keywords used in an index and the references given;
- paragraph numbers and footnotes referred to and the information they contain;
- full references for any legislation and case law referred to;
- any supplements or updating materials consulted; and
- a note of how up to date your findings are.

In using electronic sources, you would in addition need to take note of:

- the database you searched and any limitations in its scope which might require research elsewhere (e.g. case law only back to 1980 on *Lawtel*);
- specific sources within databases (e.g. Cases on *Lexis Library*, Crime Practice Area on *Westlaw*, or Legal Journals Index on *Lawtel*);
- the search terms (or keywords) you used and the exact search carried out on each database (it is very easy to search a database randomly, but without systematically planning your electronic searches, you will miss relevant information: see **Chapter 5**);
- how you updated the legislation or case law you found; and
- the date you carried out the electronic research (you may need to conduct the same electronic search at a much later stage to bring your research up to date).

Notes should be clear, well organised, and easy to follow, with sufficient detail to prevent the research having to be repeated. You may find it helpful to keep a checklist for each legal issue you research; sources consulted, keywords used, references to follow up, updating information, and so on. A checklist provides a useful format for keeping detailed notes and acts as a visual reminder of the stages in legal research you need to complete. In preparing the formal research note for the pupil supervisor, you may not need to use all the notes you have made but, if your notes are thorough, you will find it easier to distinguish the important information that you do need to include.

3.8.2 Preparing a formal research note

Your pupil supervisor will not usually require you to produce a full opinion, but rather the notes or a 'research route' which could form the basis for an opinion. Individual chambers and pupil supervisors will have different requirements and expectations of a formal research note but it would typically consist of:

- *A heading.* The client's name (or case name or subject heading) and reference to the issue under consideration. A pupil supervisor is likely to have several cases under way, so a heading will help to identify quickly the case your research note refers to.

- *A legal answer.* A succinct answer to the client's legal problem(s) outlining the application of the law to the facts of the case. If there is no clear answer, then the most likely solution should be set out with the principal reservations and likely alternatives.

- *The research route.* A clear, concise, and accurate record of how the legal authorities (legislation and case law) referred to in the answer were found and what steps were taken to ensure they were up to date.

The research note you produce should be accurate, comprehensive, and concise. It can be in note form provided the notes are intelligible to another reader. It should be structured in such a way that it is clear and easy to read, using headings and bullet points where necessary for clarity. It should not be an essay nor should it present your research findings in a partisan or emotive way.

The legal answer should address the legal issues and offer a succinct treatment of the law relevant to the client's problem. It should not assume facts for which there is no basis but it may helpfully identify the need for further information on specific issues. It should include where possible some indication of a course of action that would be most likely to produce a favourable outcome for the client.

The research route serves to support the legal answer by providing details of how you found the relevant authority (usually case law and legislation) and how you updated it. It should:

- contain only reference to statutes, cases, and legal commentaries that proved relevant to the answer; citing irrelevant authority only serves to confuse. You may have done some background reading on an unfamiliar area of law but this is irrelevant to the client's legal problem and is therefore not cited in the research route;

- show how the authority cited is relevant by relating it to the facts of the case; this demonstrates your legal reasoning, which will be checked by the pupil supervisor. Cite primary authority in preference to secondary. Reference to secondary authority might be justified where the law is ambiguous; practitioner texts should be quoted in preference to academic opinion in student textbooks;

- cite primary authorities correctly so that they can easily be found again, with full titles for legislative enactments (see **4.9**) and full citations (including neutral citations) for cases (see **4.11.7**); identify a specific dictum within a case by reference to the relevant paragraph number (or for older cases, page number) of a law report;

- set out key points from each relevant source, avoiding repetition of the same material from different sources and avoiding moving back and forth between sources. If the problem covers distinct subject areas or is otherwise complex, it may be helpful to reorganise the research route so as to deal with the legal issues separately;

- avoid cutting and pasting or otherwise copying verbatim quotations from statutes, case law, or legal commentaries. You should instead identify the specific parts that are relevant and paraphrase, quoting only short paragraphs or precise words that are crucial. Quoting verbatim lengthens a research note unnecessarily and demonstrates an inability to identify relevant legal issues and principles and apply them to the facts of a case;

- always include updating information—how you checked your sources to ensure the law was up to date—and the date when you completed the research; and

- include reference to law that does not support the client's case so that legal argument can be prepared to address the case put forward by the other side.

3.9   In conclusion

This chapter has provided an overview of methods and techniques that will equip you with the essential skills of practical legal research. By now you should have some idea of:

- how to analyse a client's problem, identify the material facts, and recognise legal issues;
- how to categorise legal issues and identify keywords;
- how to select a starting point for your research and where to look for an answer;
- the importance of 'following through' your research to ensure that you have covered all relevant legal issues;
- the need to think laterally and apply different research techniques when you face a 'dead end' in your research;
- the need ALWAYS to update the law you find;
- how to apply the law to the facts and keep your research tightly focused on the client's needs;
- how to record your research systematically in preparation for a formal research note; and
- how to prepare a clear statement of the law as it applies to the client's problem, for a pupil supervisor.

No amount of careful analysis will make up for a failure to identify key resources, and knowing your resources but failing to use them systematically will not produce a clear analysis of the issues. Your analysis and the research method you use are only as good as the resources you have available and how you make use of them. This chapter has mentioned a few key resources available to the researcher. **Chapter 4** deals with these legal resources in more detail—what they are and how to use them to research the law. **Chapter 5** considers legal databases and shows the researcher how to develop search strategies that will utilise these resources more effectively. Some of the specific problems that are often encountered in legal research (researching words and phrases and interpreting a case) are addressed in **Chapters 6** and **7**.

Chapter 8 returns to legal research method in the light of these chapters and offers a worked example of researching a legal problem and producing a research note for the pupil supervisor.

Legal resources for the practitioner

4.1 Introduction: using the law library

The law library is an excellent starting point for any legal research you do as a student or a pupil barrister. The 'library' might simply be a collection of practitioner texts and law reports in your own chambers or at court, the resources available online via a subscription service such as *Lexis Library*, or the much more substantial holdings of your Inn library. The Inn library, in particular, is a major resource that London-based barristers will make use of throughout their career at the Bar; but with such extensive holdings, its organisation is complex and it can take some time to find what you need. Before you even start in pupillage, you should become familiar with the materials your nearest law library holds, their layout, organisation, 'finding aids', and the databases they subscribe to. While the types of legal material that law libraries hold tend to be very similar, no two libraries are the same in terms of their holdings, arrangement, facilities, and software.

4.1.1 Formats of legal resources: printed or online

The online databases that your chambers or Inn library subscribes to will also vary. Most law schools subscribe to an extensive range of electronic resources, which would include all the major legal databases—*Westlaw*, *Lexis Library*, *Lawtel*, and *Justis*—as well as more academic resources such as *HeinOnline* and *JSTOR*. Larger academic institutions can afford these substantial resources and the subscriptions are obtained at academic discounts that are not available to chambers or commercial law libraries. This means few chambers can afford a full suite of resources and those that can are likely to confine themselves to a case law database, a full-text legislative service, and perhaps a suite of online resources for a 'practice area' (such as an employment law service). The Inn libraries will subscribe to rather more, but remember that their passwords are not available in chambers, making a trip to the library necessary.

At law school, your choice between printed and electronic resources (and most likely that of your tutors) will probably have been governed by personal preference and their easy availability and apparent ease of use. As a pupil barrister, your use of these online resources is likely to be governed by a wider variety of factors:

- the availability of PC facilities at the library and in court;
- technical hazards of passwords and online access at the time you need it;
- the availability of online subscriptions and the particular database content subscribed to;
- your own skills in searching databases—for example, you can't afford to miss cases through poor searching or fail to update legislation; and
- time—if *Current Law* is easily to hand, why log on to update a case?

4.1.2   Availability of legal materials

It is highly unlikely, then, that you will have all the resources you need for legal research either literally at your fingertips via an online subscription or easily to hand in your chambers' library. An essential part of legal research is knowing where legal materials are held, planning your use of these resources, and preparing to research. A new pupil barrister will need to be able to:

- identify the resources that will be required before starting the research;
- plan library visits and use of online facilities and passwords;
- know what resources are available and where to find them; and
- know how to use them and deal with issues that arise (or know how to find out or when to ask).

These skills become much more important in chambers when you need to complete your legal research quickly and effectively. This chapter will introduce the key printed resources that are available and provide some guidance on how to use them.

4.1.3   Types of legal material

The principal resources for practitioners' legal research can be classified into 'primary' and 'secondary' materials. Primary sources are 'the law' itself—legislation and case law precedent that form the raw materials a barrister calls upon to argue his case:

- statutes detail the law as passed by Parliament—either in its original form or as amended by later legislation; and
- law reports provide detailed analysis of individual cases.

Secondary sources (referred to as 'legal commentaries' hereafter) cannot be relied upon in court as a statement of 'the law', but they do offer opinion and interpretation of the law:

- legal encyclopedias such as *Halsbury's Laws*, *Current Law*, etc., are excellent and authoritative tools and a good starting point for legal research;
- practitioner texts and loose-leaf works (or their electronic equivalents) provide more in-depth coverage of the law and it is these texts that form the 'meat' of the practitioner's legal resources;
- journals offer discussion and analysis of the law and serve to inform and keep the barrister up to date—recent case law, legislation coming into force, and legal practice in general, or in specific subject areas; and
- legal dictionaries such as *Stroud's Judicial Dictionary* or *Words and Phrases Legally Defined* combine statutory and case law definitions of words in one reference work—a quick shortcut in legal research.

Most law libraries will take a mixture of these materials, allowing access to all types of material electronically or in print. Smaller collections may offer access to a limited range of legal commentaries in hard copy while providing access to primary sources only in electronic format.

4.1.4   Exercises

Familiarity with the printed and online legal resources and the efficiency with which you use them are skills that are acquired through practice and experience, not just by reading about them. A few exercises are included throughout this chapter to help you practise; doing these will help you tackle the longer research problem set out in **Chapter 8**.

4.2 Legal commentary

Legal commentaries often contain highly regarded expert opinion and interpretation of the law (and some leading texts are occasionally quoted in court). This makes them a useful starting point for legal research—why start trying to interpret the 'raw data' of legislation and case law when someone more expert has already done the work for you in a practitioner text or in a legal encyclopedia such as *Halsbury's Laws*? If, on starting to research your legal problem, you are sure of the area of law involved and have some knowledge of it, then it makes sense to go straight to a legal encyclopedia or to the appropriate practitioner textbook. Commentary from a legal text can provide:

- an overview of an area of law and contextual information;
- a summary of legal principles;
- definitions of terms;
- commentary on specific points of the law; and
- footnotes leading you to relevant case law and legislation.

4.3 Practitioner textbooks

Student textbooks such as *Street on Torts* or the popular *Nutshells* series are excellent guides to the law but they are rarely used in legal practice. The *Practical Approach to . . .* series and the more substantial and well-regarded academic textbooks such as *Treitel on Contract* are of more value to practitioners researching the law, but they are rarely authoritative enough to cite in court. The most useful texts are the more heavyweight (and expensive) legal tomes written for the profession by judges, barristers, and solicitors—titles such as *Chitty on Contract*, *Clerk & Lindsell on Torts*, *Archbold's Criminal Pleadings*, and *McGregor on Damages* are used on an almost daily basis in chambers and in court.

Practitioner texts in law are nearly always known by their author's name and for long-established titles running to many new editions, the original author's name has become part of the title even where the author or editor has changed. Many practitioner texts run to several volumes (*Stone's Justices' Manual* or *Rayden and Jackson on Divorce and Family Matters*, for example), while others, such as *Kemp & Kemp: Quantum of Damages*, come in a multi-volume, loose-leaf format and are updated with the issue of new sets of pages, several times a year. There is a complete list of practitioner textbooks by subject area in **Chapter 9**. If you know the area of law you wish to consult, then this listing will lead you to the most authoritative texts.

4.3.1 Using a practitioner textbook

The layout of a practitioner text differs from that of an ordinary student textbook. Their large size, complex layout, and specialist legal language proves daunting to most lay readers and can make them difficult to navigate even for those more experienced in their use. Spending some time with the text to learn how it works can avoid frustration and hours of wasted research. A few tips and techniques will help to ensure you make more effective use of them:

1. Ensure that you have all the volumes in a multi-volume work—including any supplements (see **4.3.2**); the contents or index may refer you to a volume you don't have to hand.

2. Start by using the general table of contents to find your broad subject headings. Tables of contents are particularly useful when you have broad terms for a less familiar area of law and need some context first before researching more specific issues.

3. Look up your chosen keywords in the index. You are more likely to find references to specific issues through the index than by browsing the table of contents. You could also make use of the tables of statutes and cases which again pinpoint specific issues within a text.

4. Be aware that there may be more than one index. *Halsbury's Laws* boasts three volumes of index, the last of which includes an additional index of legal definitions of words and phrases. *Stone's Justices' Manual* has a separate index to each of its four volumes, while encyclopedic loose-leaf works often have separate supplementary indexes.

5. References in contents and indexes are to paragraph numbers not pages; paragraph numbers are generally quoted in square brackets [ ] when you are taking notes.

6. Avoid reading large sections of text—the textbooks are laid out in short, titled paragraphs to facilitate browsing to the part you need. You should be able to scan to the most relevant part.

7. Read the footnotes carefully; useful commentary on case law and legislation is referred to here.

8. Follow cross-references and, after finding what you need, always check back to the index for further references to your keywords.

9. Update your findings *before* moving on to another source (see **4.3.2**)—you'll only forget and have to return to the library to do the research again.

10. Can't find what you need within the leading practitioner text on the subject?

    - Use different keywords, perhaps broader or more specific terms.
    - Try a different angle. If you know a relevant case, look for it in the table of cases; if you know the statute, look for it in the table of statutes.
    - No textbook is comprehensive and it may simply not cover the point you need (or that point may not exist)—try another text with the same keywords.

4.3.2 Updating a practitioner textbook

Books are out of date as soon as they are printed and most practitioner texts are not published annually. Always use the latest edition of any printed text and check to see if it has itself been updated by another publication. Publishers update their texts using a combination of one or more of the following:

- cumulative supplements: hardback volumes for legal encyclopedias such as *Halsbury's Laws, Atkin's Court Forms*, etc.; paperback supplements for practitioner works (e.g. first supplement to *McGregor on Damages*, fourth supplement to *Stroud's Judicial Dictionary*, etc.);

- loose-leaf noter-ups: loose sheets housed in a separate hardback binder (e.g. *Halsbury's Statutes*);
- loose bulletins, inserts, or newsletters (e.g. *Wilkinson's Road Traffic Bulletin*); and
- online updates and companion websites using an internet service (e.g. *Blackstone's Criminal Practice* companion website).

It is also important to know whether the law within the printed text is up to date. Consider the following:

- new editions and/or supplements: check for a statement 'the law is as stated at . . . [date]' or 'up to date to . . . [date]', usually located at the end of the preface or shortly after the title page;
- loose-leaf noter-up: look at loose-leaf issue numbers and dates printed on each individual page and check the filing record located at the front or rear of the first or last volumes in the set; and
- online updates: look for a statement when you log on to the publisher's web page.

Note that, if the commentary within the practitioner text or its update refers to legislation or case law, you may need to bring those authorities more up to date using an electronic database or another printed source.

4.3.3 Electronic versions of practitioner texts

Some of the leading legal practitioner works are available online in full text—for example, *Clerk & Lindsell on Torts* on *Westlaw*, or *Halsbury's Laws* on *Lexis Library*. These rarely offer many advantages over their printed equivalents, especially for the pupil barrister unfamiliar with the language and layout of the texts. Normally, the electronic publishers have simply transferred the practitioner text online, and only occasionally do they try to provide more sophisticated means for the text to be searched and viewed. In short, if a practitioner work is available in printed form, then you will generally find this quicker and easier to use than its online equivalent. You should also be aware that not all electronic services are updated as frequently as you might think; just because a text is online does not mean it is any more up to date than its printed equivalent. The merits and pitfalls of using and updating electronic resources are dealt with in more detail in **Chapter 5**.

EXERCISE 3   USING PRACTITIONER TEXTS

Archbold's Criminal Pleading, Evidence and Practice

1. What is the maximum penalty on indictment, in years, for taking indecent photographs of children? How many categories of material are there?
2. What is the maximum sentence on indictment for having a knife in a public place?

Stone's Justices' Manual or Blackstone's Criminal Practice

3. Does the fact that disqualification of a driver would make his disabled wife's life unbearable amount to 'special reasons'?
4. How many points may be endorsed on a driving licence for the offence of driving without insurance?

Clerk & Lindsell on Torts

5. Is a claim against a fast-food restaurant, claiming that it broke its common duty of care under the Occupiers' Liability Act 1957 by serving tea and coffee piping hot, likely to succeed?

6. Is it contributory negligence if a coach passenger injured in an accident failed to wear a seat belt?

Chitty on Contracts

7. Can mistakes in the grammar of a contract be disregarded if the intended sense is clear from the surrounding text? Are there any recent cases on this subject?

Kemp & Kemp: The Quantum of Damages

8. Find the details of a case of unwanted pregnancy following failed sterilisation. What was the award in this case and for what specific reasons were the damages awarded?

4.4   Legal encyclopedias

A multi-volume work such as *Halsbury's Laws, Halsbury's Statutes,* or *Atkin's Court Forms* is often described as a legal encyclopedia. A full listing of legal encyclopedias is provided in **Chapter 9**. Here, we are concerned with the leading encyclopedic commentary, *Halsbury's Laws,* which serves as an excellent starting point for nearly all areas of legal research.

Halsbury's Laws is the definitive encyclopedic treatise on the law of England and Wales. The law is arranged by subject across more than 50 volumes. Not only is the encyclopedia very comprehensive, covering every area of law currently in force, but each subject is also written by a leading expert in the field. Some subjects (such as employment law or crime) are covered in less detail than in dedicated practitioner texts but other subjects seldom encountered (such as ecclesiastical law) receive an in-depth treatment that would not be found in a regular textbook. The encyclopedia as a whole receives monthly updates and is available in full text electronically via the *Lexis Library* service.

Halsbury's Laws is particularly useful for those starting out in legal research simply because it is so comprehensive. Explore one point of law that you need and you will invariably find a reference to another area of law you had not thought of. The index is similarly thorough: look up one keyword in the index and it will guide you to other keywords and concepts you hadn't thought of. The printed index is an excellent companion to lateral thinking and keyword analysis (see **3.3.2**), and has recently become available within the electronic version of the text.

4.4.1   Using and updating legal encyclopedias

Most legal encyclopedias follow a similar format, so learning how to use *Halsbury's Laws* will help you to use the other encyclopedias more effectively. Updating *Halsbury's Laws* is crucial as individual volumes are published infrequently and are often many years out of date. Yet legal encyclopedias are amongst the most up-to-date commentaries available to the practitioner, by virtue of a system of updating that combines the use of:

*   *cumulative supplements:* hardback volumes issued annually, providing cumulative updates to the text of the main volumes (e.g. *Halsbury's Laws*) or

*   *paperback supplements:* issued monthly, providing cumulative updates to the text of the annual cumulative supplement (e.g. *Halsbury's Laws Current Service Noter-up and Monthly Review*); and

- *loose-leaf noter-ups:* loose sheets housed in a separate hardback binder issued monthly (or sometimes quarterly), providing updates to the text of the cumulative supplements (e.g. *Atkin's Court Forms*).

The electronic versions of printed encyclopedias have the advantage here, in that updates are either included within the text online (*Atkin's Court Forms*), or just underneath, or linked from, the text of the main paragraph (*Halsbury's Laws*). Note, however, that the online text is no more up to date than its printed equivalent; if you are updating using the printed *Halsbury's Laws*, there is no need to go online to view the electronic version for updates.

4.4.1.1   How to use *Halsbury's Laws*

Halsbury's Laws is an authoritative and comprehensive statement of the law of England and Wales, annotated with references to legislation, case law, judicial interpretation, and other works. Quick and easy to use, *Halsbury's Laws* offers convenient access to expert commentary on any area of law and is available online via *Lexis Library*. **Table 4.1** explains how *Halsbury's Laws* are arranged.

Table 4.1 ***Halsbury's Laws***

Volume	Arrangement	Frequency
1–52	The law is divided into subject areas defined by a *title*. Titles appear on the spine and the volumes are arranged alphabetically by title.	Irregular
53	*Consolidated Tables* . . . legislation, practice directions & European materials	Annual
54	*Consolidated Table of Cases*	Annual
55–57	*Consolidated Index*. An index of *words & phrases* appears to rear of volume 57.	Annual
	Cumulative Supplement Parts 1 and 2—updates the law in volumes 1–52.	Annual
Current Service	Two paperback supplements. The *Noter-up* notes developments in the law since publication of the *Cumulative Supplement* while the *Monthly Review* contains digests of recent case law and legislation.	Monthly

How do I use Halsbury's Laws?

- Choose keywords that define the problem you wish to research and look them up in the *Consolidated Index*. All references lead you to a volume number (in bold) and a paragraph number.

- Occasionally, using the indexes may lead you to an incorrect paragraph number because the main volume has been reissued since the *Index* or *Tables* were published. Where this occurs, check the reissued volume's own index or list of contents for the correct paragraph number.

How do I update Halsbury's Laws?

- Note down the volume number and paragraph number you are updating. Look them up in the hardback *Cumulative Supplement* and then in the monthly *Noter-up*. Volume numbers appear across the top of the page, page numbers down the side. Always check both *Cumulative Supplement* and *Noter-up*, as there may be changes in both: one does not supersede the other.

- You might also check the index to the *Monthly Review* for summaries of relevant cases or legislation. The references lead you to the paragraph of the relevant monthly review.

4.5 Legal journals

Legal journals offer discussion and analysis of the law and keep the practising lawyer up to date with developments in the legal world. The three legal weeklies, *New Law Journal*, *Solicitors' Journal*, and *Law Gazette*, for example, serve to inform the practising lawyer of recent case law, legislation coming into force, and legal news and practice in general. Long-established titles such as *Modern Law Review* or *Law Quarterly Review* offer more academic in-depth analysis of the law. More specialist titles (*Criminal Law Review*) offer substantial analytical articles or come as newsletters (*Corporate Law Update*; *Company Law Newsletter*) covering particular practice areas or aspects of the law. Some newsletters (*Archbold News*, *Kemp News*) 'update' practitioner texts of the same title; bulletins in loose-leaf texts serve a similar purpose.

A barrister would very rarely quote articles from legal journals in court but would consult articles that provided in-depth analysis of the law. For legal research purposes, you may have recourse to journal articles for:

- background information for an unusual area of law or legal issue;
- opinion on and discussion of new and unreported cases and forthcoming legislation;
- ideas to develop an argument in a case;
- current awareness—to keep up to date with the law; and
- updating specific practitioner texts (*Kemp News*) or areas of law (*Corporate Briefing*).

4.5.1 Finding legal journal articles

There are well over 400 legal journal titles and finding references to articles that are relevant and then finding a library that takes the specific journal (or otherwise getting hold of a copyright-cleared copy) can be difficult, time-consuming, and expensive—in terms of practical legal research, it may not be worth the pursuit. That said, a quick search on a legal journal's database can be very enlightening, revealing articles discussing very recent cases perhaps on the legal issue you're interested in, and alerting you to new legislation; it all serves as useful background information.

4.5.1.1 To find references to articles by subject

- *Lawtel's Articles Index* indexes articles from around 50 leading UK law journals from 1998, providing a short summary of the article with links to relevant case law and legislation.
- *Legal Journals Index* started in 1986 and is a much more comprehensive referencing service. Extensively indexed with abstracts of articles from over 400 UK, Irish, and European journals, it's available via the *Current Legal Information* (*CLI Online*) database and *Westlaw*. (See **Chapter 5**.)
- *Index to Legal Periodicals* is less comprehensive for UK articles but has a more international scope with articles from leading journals in English-speaking jurisdictions. It is useful for more historical legal research as it started indexing legal journal articles back in the 1920s.

4.5.1.2 To find references to very recent articles on a particular area of law

- *Halsbury's Laws Noter-up*: the Articles Index lists articles by subject area. Updated monthly and providing a cumulative list, it offers a quick and easy way to check what's new in a practice area.

- *Current Law Monthly Digest*: again, this is a cumulative list of recent articles appearing in leading UK legal journals, published monthly.

- Update services on electronic databases such as *Lawtel* and *Westlaw* alert you by email to recent articles published in a specific area of law.

4.5.1.3   To find the full text of an article for which you now have the reference

- Approach your Inn library—they have good journal holdings and are very likely to have it.

- Search a full text database such as *Westlaw* or *Lexis Library*. Both services hold the full text of many journals, though often retrospective coverage is poor. They offer the additional facility of being able to search for very specific items (company names, for example) throughout the entire journal rather than just in the titles of the articles.

- Contact your database provider—chambers subscribing to *Lawtel* or *Legal Journals Index* can often obtain copies of articles electronically or by fax through their subscription.

- Make use of a document delivery service such as the *DocDel* service from Sweet & Maxwell, or those provided by the Institute of Advanced Legal Studies or The Law Society (for solicitors).

4.5.1.4   To find leading journals on a particular area of law

Key journals in specific practice areas are listed under subject headings in **Chapter 9**.

EXERCISE 4   LEGAL JOURNALS

1. Find a journal article which discusses a case in which the court was asked to consider the scope of the exemption the driver of a police car has when driving dangerously at high speed.
2. Find the most recent article you can on: (a) *Romalpa* clauses; and (b) lawyer–client confidentiality.

4.6   Judicial dictionaries

Legal definitions (i.e. the meanings of words in statutes and statutory instruments and how they have been interpreted in case law) form a significant element of legal research. Legal dictionaries such as *Stroud's Judicial Dictionary* or *Words and Phrases Legally Defined* combine statutory and case law definitions of words in one reference work, which forms a quick shortcut in legal research. Researching words and phrases is studied in greater detail in **Chapter 6**.

4.7   Forms and precedents

Court forms and precedents of contracts, etc., are generally required for very specific procedural purposes. The two leading encyclopedic sources are *Atkin's Court Forms* and the *Encyclopaedia of Forms and Precedents*. Both sets run to more than 40 volumes apiece, with indexes and form-finding aids to provide easy access by keyword, and a loose-leaf updating service. The commentary that accompanies the forms and precedents is itself an unrivalled source of procedural law. Both are available online via *Lexis Library*.

Many court forms are also available on the HM Courts & Tribunals Service website (see **5.4.3**) and precedents can be found in the appendices of practitioner texts or in dedicated loose-leaf texts such as *Butterworths Civil Court Precedents*. You should, however, be aware that they will need updating.

4.8 Primary sources of law

Secondary sources and expert legal opinion are only a route to the primary sources. Having exhausted legal commentary, the researcher should have a list of primary sources to peruse—legislative enactments to analyse and interpret and cases to read and update. Occasionally, a researcher may approach the primary sources directly, but to do so without a confident knowledge of the area of law would be to run the risk of missing essential statutes, statutory instruments, or cases.

While legal commentaries are generally easier to approach in their printed form, the opposite is the case for primary sources. Databases are more suited to finding legislative data and case law quickly and easily, and provided the researcher updates the material found carefully, it is also usually slightly more up to date than equivalent printed sources.

4.9 Primary legislation: Public General Acts ('statutes')

Legislation in the UK uses the terms 'primary' and 'secondary'. Primary legislation denotes Acts (or 'statutes') passed by Parliament while secondary legislation is delegated—legislation made by government departments, agencies, local authorities, and other public bodies on behalf of Parliament and by the explicit authority of a specific Act.

Within these two general types there are other forms of enactment. Primary legislation includes Public General Acts, Local Acts, Personal Acts, Private Acts, and Church Measures, while secondary legislation includes Statutory Instruments, rules, and by-laws. Usually, the legal researcher will only be concerned with Public General Acts and Statutory Instruments; encounters with the other types are somewhat rarer and will not be dealt with here. **Table 4.2** introduces the principal resources available in the law library to the researcher tracing statutes and statutory instruments.

4.9.1 Finding statutes

In researching statute law, a barrister would need to distinguish between:

- The 'original' version of a statute—the form of wording used when the statute was passed by Parliament and received Royal Assent. It is this 'Queen's Printer's' version of an Act of Parliament which the barrister would need to cite and quote from in court.

- The 'amended' (or 'consolidated') version of a statute—the wording of a statute after the text from subsequent amendments, revocations, and repeals has been included. The consolidated version of a statute is far more useful than the original version to a barrister who needs to say what the law is, at the time he or she drafts an opinion or takes a case to court.

- 'Annotated' statutes—the original and/or amended version of a statute, with additional commentary by legal editors (on, for example, the legislative background to an Act), references to cases or regulations, and guidance on the interpretation of individual sections of the statute. This form of statute is of particular use to the barrister interpreting a statute and exploring the meaning of particular words and phrases. See **Chapter 6** for more details regarding researching words and phrases.

Modern statutes are denoted by a short title and calendar year (e.g. the Theft Act 1968), and a 'chapter' number (e.g. 1968 c 60). The short title and/or chapter number are key to finding the full text of a statute. This form of citation is used in tables of contents within practitioner texts, in alphabetical and chronological listings of statutes within collections such as *Halsbury's Statutes* and *Current Law Statutes*, and in online sources of legislation, such as *Westlaw* and *Lexis Library*. If you're not sure of the short title, calendar year, or chapter number, then you will need to approach the legislation by subject. While this can be done through most of the printed and electronic resources listed in this chapter, it may be quicker and easier to return to the practitioner texts or a legal encyclopedia such as *Halsbury's Laws* to find more specific references to the legislation you might need, or indeed to find the legislation itself. For example, *Harvey on Industrial Relations and Employment Law* provides ready access to most of the relevant employment statutes.

4.9.2 Updating statutes

The distinction between the law as originally passed and the law as amended and currently in force (including statutes that have not yet been brought into force and those that have been repealed) is fundamental to practical legal research. It poses three distinct questions:

- Has the statute come into force?
- Is the statute still in force?
- Was the statute in force at a particular point in time?

These questions can most easily be answered by searching a legislative database. Essentially, we are looking for details of commencement, repeal, and other amendments by subsequent legislation. *Westlaw* and *Lexis Library* provide consolidated, full-text versions of all UK legislation currently in force (including prospective commencements and repeals). Search for the statute by its short title and you will obtain the full text of the statute, as amended by later legislation (details of the amending statutes are provided) and including notes on dates of commencement and, if it is no longer in force, the date of its repeal. These notes are contained within the text of individual sections of the statute, however, so it would be a laborious process to check several sections; a table of legislative amendments such as that provided on *Lawtel* might prove more useful.

Table 4.2 **Resources for finding legislation**

Legislative service	Description and notes on use . . .
Current Law Statutes, Sweet & Maxwell. Includes: –*Statutes Annotated* –*Legislation Citator* –*Current Law Service*.	Printed reference work with the full text of all statutes from 1947 in their original form, including repealed statutes. Extensive annotations and detailed notes to assist with interpretation. Allows for more detailed historical legislative research. Accompanied by tables of legislative amendments in the form of a *Statute Citator (1947–)* and an *SI Citator (1993–)*; updated by *Current Law Statutes loose-leaf service*.
Halsbury's Statutes of England and Wales, 4th edn., Lexis Library.	Printed reference work for finding all statutes as amended and currently in force in England and Wales. Statutes are annotated with brief notes and details of commencement, repeals, amendments, etc. Updated by reissued volumes, cumulative supplement, and loose-leaf service. Separate *Statutes Citator* and *Is it in Force?*
Halsbury's Statutory Instruments, Lexis Library.	Printed reference work for finding all statutory instruments, from 1951, currently in force in England and Wales. Editors select SIs for fuller treatment, providing summaries of some and the full text of only a very few. Fully annotated. Updated by monthly loose-leaf *Noter-up* service.
Justis UK Statutes *Justis UK SIs*	Online subscription service or CD-ROM database containing the original, full-text version of all statutes from 1235 with notes of repeals. Statutory instruments from 1671 on a separate database.
Lawtel UK	Online subscription service containing the original full-text version of statutes (1984–) and SIs (1988–) with a linked *Statutory Status* table of legislative amendments and an *Index of Amended Legislation*.
Lexis Library Legislation	Online subscription service containing amended versions of all statutes (1236–) and SIs (1950–) currently in force throughout the UK. Includes some annotations from *Halsbury's Statutes*.
legislation.gov.uk <http://www.legislation.gov.uk>	Free website service. Acts from 1988 in original and revised form; revised texts taken from *UK Statute Law Database*. Selected earlier Acts from 1801–1988. Statutory Instruments from 1987 in full text (selected SIs 1948–1986), but these are not amended.
Practitioner texts	Legislation is often reproduced in full text in: –practitioner texts (e.g. *Family Court Practice*) –loose-leaf works (e.g. *Palmer's Company Law*) –handbooks (e.g. *Paterson's Licensing Acts*)
Westlaw Legislation	Online database containing amended versions of all statutes (1267–) and SIs (1948–) currently in force throughout the UK. Use the *Advanced Search* facility to find historical versions of statutes in the form in which they were in force at a particular date.

A quick reference, printed source for this type of query is the *Is it in Force?* volume of *Halsbury's Statutes*, updated with an *Is it in Force?* section within the loose-leaf *Noter-up*. If there is no commencement information, then it would be wise to check online. If you are using printed sources to update, you also need to check the citation of any statute that is repealing the Act under consideration—the repealing statute may not have been brought into force or may itself have been repealed.

4.9.3   How to use *Halsbury's Statutes*

Halsbury's Statutes contains an up-to-date version of the amended text of every statute currently in force in England and Wales. Each statute is annotated with amending and subordinate legislation, commentary, judicial interpretation, relevant leading case law, and other useful cross-references. As such, it is a leading source for tracing and interpreting legislation; there is no equivalent online source for the annotations.

4.9.3.1   How do I use *Halsbury's Statutes*?

- All references lead you to a volume number (in bold) and a page number in that volume. Where (S) is indicated after a bold volume number this refers to the *Current Statutes Service* binder. **Table 4.3** explains how to use *Halsbury's Statutes*.

Table 4.3 **How to use *Halsbury's Statutes***

To find a statute when you know . . .	Use the volume entitled . . .	Look up the . . .
. . . the title	*Consolidated Index*	Alphabetical list of statutes
. . . the subject area	*Consolidated Index*	Volume index (i.e. list of titles, to the front)
		OR use the word index
. . . its chapter number	*Consolidated Index*	Chronological list of statutes
. . . it's very recent	*Current Statutes Service* Binder A	Contents section: alphabetical, chronological, and subject lists

- If the statute is not listed, the title or date of the statute may be incorrect, the statute may have been repealed or not yet brought into force. *Halsbury's Statutes* only contains legislation currently in force. Check its status in *Halsbury's Statutes Citator* or *Is it in Force?*

4.9.3.2   How do I update *Halsbury's Statutes*?

- Note down the volume number and page reference of the statute you are updating. Look them up in the hardback *Cumulative Supplement* and then in the loose-leaf *Noter-up*. Volume numbers appear across the top of the page, page numbers down the side. Always check both *Supplement* and *Noter-up*, as there may be changes in both: one does not supersede the other.
- In both the *Cumulative Supplement* and the *Noter-up*, the update for a particular volume in the *Current Statutes Service* will follow the update for the main volume of the same name (e.g. the update to *Volume 12 (S) Criminal Law* immediately follows the update to *Volume 12[1–4] (2008 reissue)*.

Table 4.4 shows you how to research a statute.

Table 4.4 **How to research a statute**

Looking for . . .	Electronic services	Printed resources
The full text of a statute . . .		
The **original** version of a full text statute as enacted by Parliament	*Justis UK Statutes* *Lawtel* *<http://www.legislation.gov.uk>*	Queen's Printer's copy bound in: *Law Reports Statutes* *Public General Acts* *Statutes at Large* *Statutes of the Realm*
An **amended version of a full text statute currently in force**	*Lexis Library Legislation* *<http://www.legislation.gov.uk>* *Westlaw Legislation*	*Halsbury's Statutes* *Current Law Statutes Annotated*
Annotated statutes	Very limited annotations on: *Lexis Library Legislation* *<http://www.legislation.gov.uk>* *Westlaw Legislation*	*Halsbury's Statutes* *Current Law Statutes Annotated*
Alphabetical or chronological index to the statutes	Most online services provide the facility to browse an alphabetical or chronological list of statutes.	*Chronological Index to the Statutes 1235–1990* *Current Law Statutes Service* *Halsbury's Statutes*
Subject index to the statutes	All online services can be searched by keyword. See **Chapter 5** for further details.	*Chronological Index to the Statutes 1235–1990* *Halsbury's Statutes*
Repealed statutes in full text, possibly as amended by later enactments up to a particular date, but no longer in force	*Justis UK Statutes* *<http://www.legislation.gov.uk>* *Westlaw Legislation*—use Advanced Search for historical versions of statutes.	*Current Law Statutes Annotated* *Halsbury's Statutes*—use old editions for earlier statutes. *Law Reports Statutes* *Public General Acts* *Statutes at Large* *Statutes of the Realm*
A very **recent statute**	*Lexis Library Legislation* *<http://www.legislation.gov.uk>* *Westlaw Legislation*	*Current Law Monthly Digest* *Current Law Service* *Halsbury's Statutes Current Service Binders A–F + Noter-up*
Updating information . . .		
Commencement dates for statutes and sections of statutes including **forthcoming** dates –Is the statute in force? –Has the statute come into force?	*Lexis Library Legislation* *<http://www.legislation.gov.uk>* *Westlaw Legislation*	*Current Law Monthly Digest* *Current Law Statutes Citator* *Halsbury's Laws Noter-up* *Halsbury's Statutes—Is it in Force? + Noter-up*
Tables of amendments within an alphabetical or chronological **index** to statutes	*<http://www.legislation.gov.uk>* *Lawtel—Statutory Status Table*	*Chronological Index to the Statutes 1235–1990* *Current Law Legislation Citator* *Halsbury's Statutes Citator*
Cases under a section of a statute	*Lawtel* *Lexis Library Legislation* *Westlaw Legislation*	*Current Law Statutes Citator* *Halsbury's Statutes*

TABLE OF STATUTES   MAIN VOL   *OR* CURRENT STATUTES   CUMULATIVE   NOTER-UP
& GENERAL INDEX   & PAGE NO.   SERVICE BINDERS   SUPPLEMENT

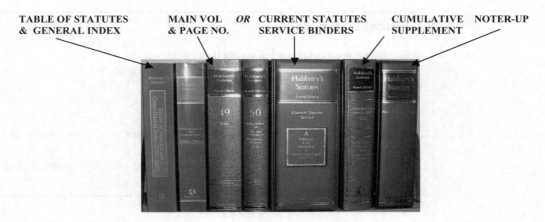

Figure 4.1   Correct sequence for using *Halsbury's Statutes.*

4.9.4 How to use *Current Law Statutes*

Current Law is a comprehensive legal information service covering all case and statutory developments from 1947 to date. **Table 4.5** sets out the structure of *Current Law Statutes* and **Table 4.6** shows you how to use the service.

Table 4.5 **Current Law Statutes**

Volume	Arrangement . . .
Current Law Legislation Citator: Statute Citator	Notes up statutes dating back to 1235. Amendments, cases, and subordinate legislation under an Act are listed from 1947. Arranged chronologically in chapter order and published in the following sequence of volumes: 1947–1971; 1972–1988; 1989–1995; 1996–1999; 2000–2001; 2002–2004.
*Current Law Statutes Annotated	Each bound volume incorporates the Public General Acts for the year in chronological order and by chapter and with annotations and commentary. This part of the service is published annually.
Current Law Statutes: Service Files	Volumes 1 and 2 update changes to the Public General Acts since publication of the last bound volume and are updated monthly.

* Current Law Statutes since 1994.

Table 4.6 **How to use Current Law Statutes**

To find . . .	Use the . . .
A statute where the name and date of the statute are known . . .	*Current Law Statutes* volume for the year; then update using the *Current Law Legislation Citator* for each subsequent year; then check the *Current Law Statutes Service* file for any recent changes.
Amendments to sections of a statute or the date an Act came into force . . .	*Current Law Legislation Citator* for the year of the Act and for each subsequent year then update with the relevant section of the *Current Law Statutes Service* file.
Commencement orders and statutory instruments . . .	
Cases brought under a section of an Act . . .	*Current Law Legislation Citator* for the year of the Act and for each subsequent year then update the case using the cumulative table of cases in the most recent *Current Law Monthly Digest.*

EXERCISE 5 STATUTES

1. What is the short title of the statute 1997 c 55?
2. What is the heading to Part VIII of the Law of Property Act 1925?
3. Are the following statutes currently in force?
   (a) Employment of Children Act 1973
   (b) Family Law Act 1996
4. Is s 1 of the Perjury Act 1911 still in force? Name two cases brought under this section. Does this Act extend to Scotland?
5. Find the text of ss 34A and 34B of the Enterprise Act 2002 and update them to find notes of amendments, repeals, etc.

4.10 Secondary legislation: Statutory Instruments

Statutory Instruments (SIs) account for the bulk of secondary legislation in the UK. Over 3,000 SIs are issued by government departments, agencies, and public bodies each year on behalf of Parliament and under the explicit authority of a specific Act of Parliament. SIs serve numerous functions and come in various forms, the most common of which are:

- rules and regulations regarding the technical detail of how a statute operates;
- commencement orders bringing statutes (or individual sections of statutes) into force; and
- regulations bringing European legislative enactments into force.

Of these, rules and regulations are of most use to the practitioner and SIs of this type feature in nearly all areas of law: employment law, landlord and tenant law, and financial regulation, to name a few. While a statute provides a broad framework outlining what the law should be, an SI provides the technical detail of how that law will operate. Thus, *The Civil Procedures Rules* SI 1998/3132 or *The Management of Health and Safety Regulations* SI 1999/3242 provide rules, regulations, and procedures that must be followed and statutory duties that need to be met.

The importance of SIs should not be overlooked. Relevant SIs should be referred to in advice to a client and may need to be quoted in court. The precise wording of a regulation is often important to a case (for example, for an alleged breach of employment regulations) and, unlike statutes, SIs can be challenged as *ultra vires*, where it is alleged that an SI has outlined the law to an extent or in a form that was not originally intended by the parent Act.

4.10.1 Finding Statutory Instruments

Like statutes, SIs are denoted by a short title, a calendar year, and a unique series number (e.g. *Criminal and Defence Service (Very High Cost Cases) Regulations* 2008/40). Often only the year and the number of the SI are quoted (e.g. SI 2007/3201) but this citation should be sufficient to find the SI in either a printed or an electronic source. On *Westlaw* and *Lexis Library*, the citation can simply be entered into the relevant fields on the search screen. With *Halsbury's Statutory Instruments*, make use of the indexes found in the loose-leaf volume which will refer you to the SI within a bound volume. Further details on finding SIs are provided in **4.10.2.**

4.10.2 Updating Statutory Instruments

While statutes are only occasionally repealed, SIs are frequently revoked and replaced, or amended. Updating them is crucial to practical legal research and the questions posed regarding statute law (see **4.9.2**) are just as pertinent for SIs. Again, electronic databases provide the easiest way of accessing the most up-to-date, full-text version of an SI. Search for a citation and you will obtain the full text of the SI, as amended by later SIs and including notes on the date when it came into force and, if it is no longer in force, the date of its revocation. *Justis UK SIs* and *Lawtel* are particularly adept at producing tables of SIs that have been amended or revoked by a subsequent SI. Using *Halsbury's Statutory Instruments*, update using the *Noter-up* section in Service Volume 1. **Table 4.7** shows you how to research a Statutory Instrument.

EXERCISE 6   STATUTORY INSTRUMENTS

1. What is the correct title and citation of an SI relating to maternity and parental leave issued in 1996?
2. The Football Spectators (Seating) Order affects certain football grounds. To which grounds has it been applied and what requirements does it impose?
3. The Terrorism Act 2000 lists 'proscribed organisations'. When was 'Jundallah' added to the list and how? (i.e. by which statute or statutory instrument?)

Table 4.7 **How to research a Statutory Instrument**

Looking for . . .	Electronic services	Printed resources
An SI . . . in full text or summary form		
An SI by its **title** or its series **number** . . . . . . within an **alphabetical** or **chronological** (i.e. numerical) **index** to the SIs	Most online services provide the facility to browse an alphabetical or chronological list of statutes; full text is mostly in original form	*Halsbury's SIs—vol 1*
An **amended** version of a full text SI currently in force	*Lexis Library Legislation* *Westlaw Legislation*	*Halsbury's SIs—an edited few are as amended and in full text; others have annotations of amendments*
Annotated SIs	Very limited annotations on: *Lexis Library Legislation* *Westlaw Legislation*	*Halsbury's SIs—a few are annotated* Practitioner texts by subject area
Repealed SIs	*Justis UK SIs* <*http://www.legislation.gov.uk*> *Westlaw Legislation*—use Advanced Search	*Halsbury's SI Citator*
A very **recent** SI	*Lexis Library Legislation* <*http://www.legislation.gov.uk*> *Westlaw Legislation*	*Current Law Monthly Digest* *Halsbury's SIs, vol 1 + Monthly Index* (to rear of Service volume)
A **Subject Index** to the SIs	Inadvisable to search for SIs by subject but all online services can be searched by keyword	Practitioner texts by subject area *Halsbury's SIs—Consolidated Index*
An SI **known by a different title** (e.g. Civil Procedures Rules, Insolvency Rules)	Available on most online databases but may be difficult to find	Practitioner texts by subject area—likely to include annotations and amendments

Updating information . . .

Tables of amendments within an **alphabetical** or **chronological** index to SIs	*Lawtel—Statutory Status Table*	*Current Law SI Citator* + Service file update
		Halsbury's SI Citator + *Noter-up*
To see if Regulations (i.e. SIs) have been **made under a statute** . . .	Look for annotations under a specific section of a statute on:	*Current Law Monthly Digest Current Law Statutes Citator* + Service file update
	Lawtel—Statutory Status Table	
	Lexis Library Legislation	*Halsbury's Laws Noter-up*
	Westlaw Legislation	*Halsbury's Statutes—Is it in Force?* + *Noter-up*
	<http://www.legislation.gov.uk>	
Cases brought under an SI or specific SIs **considered in cases**	*Lawtel*	*Current Law SI Citator* + Service file update
	Lexis Library Legislation	
	Westlaw Legislation	*Halsbury's SI Citator*
		Practitioner texts by subject area

4.11 Case law and law reports

Legal commentaries invariably lead the researcher to the relevant case law. References to cases relevant to an area of law or a legal issue are to be found in the footnotes of practitioner texts and legal encyclopedias such as *Halsbury's Laws*, within annotated statutes, or as links within the resources of a legal database. Should these materials not provide references to the case law that you are looking for, then it could be that there is no relevant case law or that no cases have dealt with that particular point of law in sufficient depth for it to be deemed fit to be reported. Only around five per cent of cases in the UK are actually reported at all. To merit reporting, a case might:

- modify or introduce a new principle of law;
- settle a doubt as to what the law should be; and
- interpret statute or case law precedent in a new way.

This principle is applied to the *Official Series* of law reports (see **4.11.2**) but is not always followed in the commercial series, and in fact many cases 'of interest', but which add nothing new to the law, are frequently reported.

Searching for case law with few leads from the legal commentaries, selecting relevant cases from a multitude of law reports, reading and interpreting the case, and determining which cases to cite in court can prove very time-consuming. Case law research should not be undertaken lightly. While legislative research is reasonably finite, the corpus of material available for case law means that researching case law is far less so. Before starting your search for relevant cases, plan your research strategically and determine:

- Do you need to search for cases at all? Many cases are determined by their facts, not by precedent.
- Are there any issues with which case law might help? Reported cases deal with points of law and there is no need to quote only loosely comparable cases.

- How much research and detailed reading of case law are justified by the issue you need to resolve? A case used simply to advise a client, by providing examples of other cases similar in fact, or to illustrate a point of law or the current approach of the courts, probably does not warrant extensive research. Cases (or 'authorities') chosen to be quoted in court and to assist the judge, however, should be chosen with great care. (See **4.11.6**.)

4.11.1 Legal citations and abbreviations

4.11.1.1 Printed law reports series

Having found a reference to relevant case law, the abbreviations used to describe the law report series must be deciphered. For unknown abbreviations, refer to the following:

- *Cardiff Index to Legal Abbreviations:* <http://www.legalabbrevs.cardiff.ac.uk>;
- Raistrick, *Index to Legal Citations and Abbreviations*;
- *Current Law Case Citator*;
- *Halsbury's Laws*—Volume 1; and
- *The Digest*—annual supplement volumes.

Both square and round brackets are used when citing the year of publication and these should be written correctly when citing a case:

- where the year is given in square brackets, e.g. [2001] 1 WLR 270, it is part of the reference and the year operates as a volume number;
- where a date appears in round brackets, it is useful information as to the actual year of the publication, but non-essential because the publishers have given each volume its own number in sequence in the set—for example, (1985) 80 Cr App R 117. This volume-number method is now mainly used for journals.

4.11.1.2 Online subscription services

Many case reports now appear on legal databases well before they appear in the pages of any of the standard series of reports. The use of these electronic sources in court has been officially approved but it calls for a system of 'neutral' citation, not only because citation by series, volume, and page number no longer applies but also because citations have to be uniform and recognisable, whichever medium or provider or publisher has been used for a particular report. So, when transcribed, each judgment is given a unique case number, with paragraph numbers instead of page numbers. See *Practice Note* [2001] 1 All ER 293, and *Practice Direction* [2002] 1 WLR 346.

The following citations are used:

- UKHL   House of Lords
- UKPC   Judicial Committee of the Privy Council
- EWCA Civ   Court of Appeal Civil Division
- EWCA Crim   Court of Appeal Criminal Division
- EWHC Admin   High Court Administrative Court
- EWHC   High Court

For example, *White v White* [2001] EWCA Civ 955 [1] indicates case number 955 in the Court of Appeal, first paragraph; *Lewisham LBC v Hall* [2002] EWHC Admin 960 [22] is case 960 in the Administrative Court, QBD, at paragraph 22.

4.11.1.3   Practice Directions

Practice Directions (also known as Practice Notes or Practice Statements) are not case reports but they are reported as such in law reports. As their title suggests, they give essential guidance on practice demanded by the court that must be followed. Numerous and often difficult to find, they are also subject to change and can be overruled or partially amended (for example, the 2001 Practice Note mentioned here has been amended in part).

4.11.2   Law reports

Today, an extensive range of law reports is available to the practitioner:

1. *The Law Reports* (known as the *Official Series*) from 1865 are preferred as the 'senior' series of law reports—checked by judges before publication and usually including a summary of counsels' argument, in addition to head notes, facts, and the judgment itself. Today, they comprise just four series (*Appeal Cases*, *Chancery*, *Queens Bench*, and *Family*) out of the original set and are accompanied by cumulative ten-year and latest-year 'Pink and Red' indexes. The entire series is available online in full text via *Justis*, *Lexis Library*, and *Westlaw*. (For a full list of titles in *The Law Reports*, see **Chapter 9**.)

2. *Weekly Law Reports* are the 'junior' official series, published, since 1953, within a month or so of a case having been decided. The entire series is available online in full text via *Justis*, *Lexis Library*, and *Westlaw*.

3. *All England Law Reports* from 1936 are a well-established commercial series and regarded as comparable in all respects to the *Weekly Law Reports*. The series is available online in full text via *Lexis Library*.

4. Specialist series of subject-based law reports have proliferated in recent years. Some, such as *Lloyd's Law Reports*, are a very well-established and authoritative series; others, such as *Road Traffic Reports*, are a little younger but very highly regarded. More recent creations, such as *European Human Rights Reports* or *Business Law Reports*, appear when specific issues become of more concern in the legal world; some survive, some don't. Many of these are available online via their respective publishers' legal databases. Thus, *Westlaw* makes its own *Road Traffic Reports* available but the researcher will need to subscribe to *Lexis Library* for access to the *Times Law Reports*. Law reports are listed by subject in **Chapter 9**.

5. Legal journals very often carry law reports either as brief summaries (*New Law Journal*, *Solicitors Journal)* or in more detailed reports that don't appear elsewhere (*Estates Gazette*). This is particularly useful as a source for very recent case law. The full text of many journals, including their law reports, is available online either free (*Law Gazette*) or via a fee-based legal database (*New Law Journal*) on the same basis as law reports.

6. Newspaper law reports are the most current form of law report and appear a few days after the case. The *Times Law Reports* are perhaps the most well-regarded

series and the newspaper has been publishing law reports since 1884. The reports are available online as part of *The Times* newspaper via *Lexis Library*.

7. Older reports are still valuable for legal research and are surprisingly well used:

- *Nominate reports.* Until *The Law Reports* were established in 1865, law reporting was left to individual judges and barristers, whose names came to be applied to published collections of cases spanning 350 years of law reporting. Recognised by the names and initials of the original reporters, these individual volumes are still available in older law libraries.

- *English Reports (ER).* In 1865, the nominate reports were collected into 176 volumes and reprinted as the *English Reports* with a two-volume index at the end of the sequence. This lists cases by name, citing the original reporters' names and the volume and page number. Available electronically via *Lexis Library, Justis* and *HeinOnline*.

- *Continuous Series.* Several journals in the nineteenth century included regular law reports and these were bound into volumes of cases: *Law Journal Reports (LJ)*, *Law Times Reports (LT)*, and *Times Law Reports (TLR)*.

- *Year Books.* The oldest anonymous law reports from 1235 to 1535, can be found in summarised form at <http://www.bu.edu/law/seipp>.

4.11.3 Finding case law

In researching case law for practical legal research, the barrister is likely to be looking for:

- cases in the same area of law;
- cases with similar facts and circumstances;
- cases covering one or more specific points of law;
- issues arising out of a point of law; and
- analysis and reasoning to assist in developing an argument.

In doing so, he or she is likely to need:

- A summary of the case. By reading a brief abstract of the case first, it is possible to assess how relevant it is to your research. For this reason, always read the 'head notes' to a reported case first; they give a concise account of the legal issues, what was 'held', and any statements on the law.

- A detailed law report for a closer analysis of the legal issues and argument.

- The judicial history of the case, to see where a case has been cited in later cases (see **4.11.4**).

The legal researcher is best served by legal databases for all three aspects. *Westlaw*, for example, provides a summary of the case with links to the full-text law report and the judicial history and subsequent citation. *Lexis Library* performs a similar function, though you need to restrict your search to 'head notes' to obtain a summary. *Lawtel* specialises in providing detailed abstracts so it is a particularly useful compromise where the full text of a report is not required.

This, however, does not render the printed sources obsolete. They are particularly useful for quick reference work, especially where you know the parties to the case and need to quickly find an abstract of a case and update it (while waiting in court, for example). Online databases are not always available (again, whilst in court) and there are problems with searching for case law electronically with keywords that are too broad, which can result in having too many cases to trawl through or too few that are actually relevant.

4.11.3.1   Search strategies for researching case law

As a pupil barrister, you may be asked to find all the case law in a particular subject area or, more specifically, involving a particular point of law. Practical legal research, where time is pressing, requires a systematic approach to researching case law. A few techniques:

1. Start with legal commentary to find references to relevant case law; it is easier to find a case when you know the parties and an approximate date. Following these and updating them will help identify possible legal issues, as well as leading to the other relevant cases.

2. If you need cases defining specific words and phrases then start with a judicial dictionary, which will outline all the cases where a particular definition has been considered in court.

3. Select your keywords carefully before searching a case law database, otherwise you are very likely to retrieve too many cases; this is a common problem with searching online services. See **3.3.2** for assistance with identifying keywords and **5.5** for search strategies using legal databases.

4. If you have specific legislation in mind, then search for cases under the relevant section of a statute or an SI, using a citator (see **4.11.4**).

5. Search more than one resource and know the contents of each resource. If your chambers only have a subscription to *Lexis Library*, a search will identify the leading cases on a particular legal issue but it will not be a comprehensive search. *Current Law* is the most comprehensive citator of case law since 1947 in the UK, and this is only available on *Westlaw*.

4.11.4   Updating case law

A case may have been overruled or indeed had its authority strengthened by a subsequent 'affirming' case at a higher court. This means you must take note of the 'judicial history' of a case—to see where a case has been cited in later cases—to ensure it is still 'good law'. A list of 'meanings' you will find online is given in **Table 4.10**. **Table 4.9** shows you how to research and update a case. However, there is one aspect of updating which is more difficult to ascertain—where statutes affect case law.

A well-established body of case law may have been overturned by recent legislation either deliberately, or as an incidental side-effect. Neither legal databases nor their printed equivalents (*Current Law Cases, The Digest*) indicate where this has occurred. There may eventually be an annotation in *Current Law Statutes Annotated*. In the meantime, if you have a suspicion that case law might have been overturned by a statute, search for a journal article on the subject or the particular case (see **4.5**), or if the case is referred to in a practitioner text, check for a supplement to the text or search for a more recent text on the same subject that might mention the case or relevant statute. **Table 4.8** introduces the principal resources for finding case law and **Table 4.9** explains how to research a case using those resources.

Table 4.8 Resources for finding case law

Case law service	Description and notes on use . . .
BAILII <http://www.bailii.org>	Free website service from the *British and Irish Legal Information Institute* offering access to transcripts of cases from the High Court and Court of Appeal, from 1996.
Casetrack <http://www.casetrack.com>	Online subscription service providing full-text transcripts of judgments from 1996.
HM Courts & Tribunals Service <http://www.courtservice.gov.uk>	Free website service. Database of selected High Court judgments; links to tribunals (many with their own judgments); full text of Practice Directions.
Current Law Cases, Sweet & Maxwell. Includes: –*Current Law Year Books* –*Current Law Monthly Digest.*	Printed reference work includes annual printed *Year Book* volumes containing brief digests of UK cases since 1947, taken from over 70 UK law report series. Accompanied by case citators, listing cases in alphabetical order with notes of where a case has been digested in the *Year Books,* where reported in law reports, and where it has been cited in later cases. Updated by cumulative table within latest issue of *Current Law Monthly Digest.* Particularly useful for quick reference work. Available online via *Westlaw Cases.*
Current Legal Information—Cases (*CLI Online*).	Online subscription service providing abstracts of cases from 1986 onwards. Owned by Sweet & Maxwell and coverage is approximately the same as *Lawtel UK.*
The Digest	Printed reference work for finding British, European, and Commonwealth cases.
Lexis Library	Selected cases are available online via *Lexis Library Cases.*
JustCite	A searchable archive of cases and their citations with links to full case reports in related *Justis* products.
Justis English Reports, The Law Reports, Times Law Reports, etc.	Online subscription service or CD-ROM. Separate databases offering access to individual series of law reports (see **4.11.2**).
Lawtel UK	Online subscription service providing abstracts of cases from 1980, many with links to full-text transcripts. Comprehensive coverage of decisions from HL, CA, PC, and High Court. *Lawtel PI* offers personal injury cases.
Lexis Library Cases	Online subscription service containing most of the text of *The Digest* and wide coverage of UK and EU case law with links to the full-text law reports of earlier and subsequent cases where available. The series of law reports it connects to are largely limited to those published by *Lexis Library.*
Westlaw Cases	Online subscription service containing the full text of *Current Law Cases.* Wide coverage of UK case law and includes brief digests of UK cases since 1947 with links to the full-text law reports of earlier and subsequent cases where available. The series of law reports it connects to are largely limited to those published by Sweet & Maxwell.

Table 4.9 **How to research a case**

Looking for . . .	Electronic services	Printed resources
A citation for a case where you know the name and/or the year . . .		
Cases **from 1980**	*CLI Online* *Lawtel UK* *Lexis Library Cases* *Westlaw Cases*	*Current Law Case Citator*—use citator for relevant year, or earliest citator if year unknown *The Digest*—Index
A very **old case, pre-1947**	*Lexis Library Cases*	*Current Law Case Citator* 1947–; *The Digest*—Table of cases in volumes for cases before 1947
A very **recent case** within the last year	*BAILII* *Lawtel UK* *Lexis Library Cases* *Westlaw Cases*	*Current Law Monthly Digest*—most recent monthly issue *Halsbury's Laws Monthly Review*
Alphabetical or **chronological** table of cases	Most online services provide the facility to browse a chronological or alphabetical table of cases	*Current Law Case Citator* *The Digest*—Index Practitioner texts by subject area
Subject index to the cases	All online services can be searched by keyword. See **Chapter 5** for further details.	*Halsbury's Laws* *Current Law Year Book* *The Digest*
The full text, digest, report, or transcript of a case . . .		
A **digest** or an **abstract** of a case	*CLI Online* *Lawtel UK Cases* *Lexis Library Cases* *Westlaw Cases*	*Current Law Cases* *The Digest*
The **full-text law report** of a case	*Justis* (by title) *Lexis Library Cases* *Westlaw Cases*	*Law Reports (Official Series)* *Weekly Law Reports* *All England Law Reports* *Individual series, etc.*
An **unreported** case or a **transcript** of a case	*BAILII* (1996–) *Casetrack* *CLI Online* *Lawtel UK Cases* (1993–) *Lexis Library Cases* (1980–)	HL, PC, CA (Civ) 1950–; CA (Crim) 1989–; Other courts–various years *Current Law Year Books* 1973–89 (summaries only)
Updating information . . .		
The **judicial history** of a case	*Lawtel UK Cases* *Lexis Library Cases* *Westlaw Cases*	*Current Law Case Citator* + most recent *Monthly Digest* *The Digest* + *Cumulative Volume* + *Quarterly Supplement*
Discussion of a recent case in a **journal article or commentary** on leading cases	*Lawtel UK's Articles Index* *Legal Journals Index*	*Current Law Monthly Digest* *Halsbury's Laws Noter-up*—Articles Index Practitioner texts by subject area
Cases brought **under a legislative enactment** (statute or SI)	*Lawtel* *Lexis Library Legislation* *Westlaw Legislation*	*Current Law Legislation Citator* *Halsbury's Statutes*
Cases overruled or otherwise **amended by statutes**	Look for articles or commentary discussing the case (see **Discussion . . .** above)	*Current Law Statutes Annotated*

Table 4.10 **Case law annotations**

Applied	The principle of law described in the earlier case has been applied to a new set of circumstances in the later case.
Approved	The earlier case has been deemed good law by the later case in a higher court.
Considered	The earlier case has been given careful consideration in the later case but gives no remarks on the quality of the case.
Digested	The case is summarised in a short digest at the reference provided. In *Current Law* this gives the Year Book and paragraph number, e.g. 05/634 = *Current Law Year Book* 2005, [634]
Distinguished	The earlier case is not necessarily doubted but an essential difference in facts or in law is highlighted between it and the later case.
Doubted	The court in the later case has found the earlier case to be inaccurate in some way, but has not gone to the length of stating that the case is wrong.
Followed	The same principles of law have been applied in both cases (though there may be a difference in facts or circumstances between the cases).
Overruled	The later case in a higher court has ruled that the judgment in the earlier case was wrong.

4.11.5 How to use *Current Law Cases*

Current Law Cases is a comprehensive legal information service covering all case and statutory developments from 1947 to date. **Table 4.11** explains how *Current Law Cases* is arranged and **Table 4.12** shows you how to use the service.

Table 4.11 *Current Law Cases*

Volume	Arrangement . . .
Current Law Case Citator	This part of the service consists of a number of index volumes listing both UK and Scottish cases in alphabetical order. They are published in the following sequence of volumes: 1947–1976, 1977–1997, 1998–2001, 2002–2004, 2005–
Current Law Year Book	The Year Books date back to 1947 and contain brief details of all cases cited. Published annually.
Current Law Monthly Digest	Paperback volume of the service which updates the case citator index with cases reported in the current year. It contains a subject index in alphabetical order and cumulative table of cases.

Table 4.12 **How to use *Current Law Cases***

To find . . .	Use the . . .
The full name of a case, a digest of the case, and where it has been reported	*Case Citator* covering the year of the case if known, or the earliest *Citator* if unknown. This directs you to a digest of the case in the relevant Year Book.
The judicial history of a case . . .	*Case Citator* covering the year of the case if known, or the earliest *Citator* if unknown. This provides details of later cases that have considered, applied, distinguished, etc. the earlier case.
	Update using each subsequent *Case Citator*, in chronological order, following references to the Year Book for a digest of any relevant cases.
	Complete the updating process using the cumulative table of cases in the most recent *Monthly Digest*.
Cases on a specific subject . . .	*Year Books* which lists contents by paragraph number under subject headings alphabetically. Some entries include summaries or *Digests* of a case as well as references to articles.
A recent case, including Scottish cases	Latest *Monthly Digest's* cumulative table of cases which includes a *Scottish Cases Citator*

4.11.6   Selecting cases: the importance of precedent

Having found a body of case law which seems relevant, you will need to read the law reports and interpret the cases. Only a detailed analysis of the case will enable you to identify the arguments that you will put forward on behalf of your client. Reading and interpreting a case is dealt with in more detail in **Chapter 7**. Here we are concerned with the preceding stage: identifying and selecting the cases you might use and cite in court. There are several aspects to consider:

- Determine if the case is meritorious. As noted at **4.11**, just because a case has been reported does not mean it adds anything new to the law—this is a matter for you to interpret through your reading of a case.

- Note which court made the decision. A Court of Appeal decision carries more weight than that of a county court. A decision in the county court is in any case of little relevance, even if the point of law is similar to that which you need. The rules on the application of precedent also vary from court to court, which means there may be different practices, depending on whether a court is operating in a supervisory or an appellate capacity. (See *Halsbury's Laws*, volume 26 [573]—judgments and orders section.)

- Obtain the fullest report available. It is not always clear from the law report exactly what the court decides—the *ratio decidendi*. Brief reports rarely carry sufficient detail of the judgment or analysis of the full reasoning and there may be incidental arguments that are of use. Relying on a short report instead of obtaining a fuller report is a poor use of case law.

- Determine if the case will be of use in court. A case may be of assistance to the judge if there is a clear legal issue to be considered and if the case itself can show the judge how similar facts have been dealt with or a point of law been interpreted, in another court.

- Cite the case correctly within rules prescribed by the court and with the correct legal abbreviation (see **4.11.1**).

4.11.7   Citation of cases in court

The growth in commercial law reporting and the much more extensive use of legal databases over the last decade led to a proliferation in the citation of legal authorities in court. This practice is now actively discouraged by the courts, and rules regarding the use of legal authorities in civil courts were laid out by the Court of Appeal in *Practice Direction (Citation of Authorities)* [2001] 1 WLR 1001. Lawyers are directed to:

- cite a case only if it clearly establishes a new principle of law, extends the law, or if its use can otherwise be justified;
- state the proposition of law that each case portrays;
- justify citing more than one authority for a given proposition of law; and
- justify the citation of any authority from outside England, the European Court of Justice, or the European Court of Human Rights.

If a case is to be quoted in court then the most authoritative series of law reports must be cited and there is a strict hierarchy of authority. Again, the correct procedure has been laid out by the Court of Appeal in *Practice Direction (Citation of Authorities)* [2012] 1 WLR 780. Cases must be cited from law reports in the following order:

- *The Law Reports* (Official Series) are preferred as the 'senior' series of law reports checked by judges before publication but notoriously slow to be published;
- *Weekly Law Reports* are the 'junior' official series; and
- *All England Law Reports* are regarded as comparable in all respects to the *Weekly Law Reports*.

Where a judgment is reported in the Official Law Reports ... that report must be cited. These are the most authoritative reports; they contain a summary of the argument. Other series of reports and official transcripts of judgments may only be used when a case is not reported in the Official Law Reports ...

If a judgment is not (or not yet) reported in the Official Law Reports but it is reported in the Weekly Law Reports (WLR) or the All England Law Reports (All ER) that report should be cited.

Where a case to be cited in court has not appeared in any of these series of law reports, then the lawyer may cite authoritative specialist series of subject-based law reports such as *Lloyd's Law Reports* or *Road Traffic Reports*. Very occasionally, where an unreported case is to be cited (insofar as it may be citable), the 2012 practice direction stipulated that the only acceptable version is the official transcript (available next day via *Lawtel* or the *Casetrack* service). In principle, every unreported case has the same value as a reported case but it is assumed that every judgment of any importance has been or will be reported, and so the restrictions on citation outlined in the 2001 practice direction have particular force with regard to unreported cases. i.e. 'an unreported case should not usually be cited unless it contains a relevant statement of legal principle not found in reported authority'

EXERCISE 7   CASE LAW

1. What do the following abbreviations stand for:
   (a)   ER
   (b)   RTR
   (c)   SJLB
   (d)   EHR
   Which of these law reports (if any) are in your nearest law library?
2. Where can I find a report of the case *Sachdeva v Sandhu*?
3. *Pepper v Hart* [1993] AC 593 is out of the library. Find an alternative citation.
4. Find the case cited as *Inglis v Mansfield*; identify the court which heard the case.
5. Find a summary of the case *Ashburner v Macquire* (1786).
6. Find a case where a local authority was held liable in damages for the conduct of its environmental officer.
7. Find the most recent cases in the library on:
   (a)   the attitude of courts to TV crews accompanying police operations; and
   (b)   whether the prosecution are obliged to reveal their witnesses' previous convictions to the defence.

4.12   European Union legal documents

European Union law forms a substantial part of the law of the UK. This is reflected by its prominence in law school syllabuses. Knowing how to look up an EU directive or trace a case heard by the Court of Justice is therefore a key skill for the practitioner.

The larger firms of solicitors and some chambers hold a range of EU materials and Middle Temple Library has an extensive collection. There are also European Documentation Centres (EDCs) throughout the UK and the rest of the EU which receive all EU official publications; to find your nearest EDC, see the Europe Direct website at <http://europa.eu/europedirect/meet_us/unitedkingdom/index_en.htm>.

The EU produces types of law corresponding broadly to the categories of UK domestic law: primary legislation, secondary legislation, and case law.

4.13   EU legislation

4.13.1   Primary legislation

The European Union's primary legislation consists of the founding treaties, subsequent amending treaties, and the accession treaties by which new Member States have joined over the years.

The founding treaties determine the structure and functions of the EU. The two key treaties are:

- *Treaty on the Functioning of the European* Union (TFEU), 1957. This has been heavily amended over the years and has had two title changes: it was originally the *Treaty Establishing the European Economic Community*; then, in November 1993, it was renamed *Treaty Establishing the European Community*. Its current title (*Treaty on the Functioning . . .*) dates from 1 December 2009. It is now cited as 'TFEU' (for example, 'article 253 TFEU'); previously it was cited as 'TEC' or 'EC' (and originally as 'EEC'). It is often known as the 'Treaty of Rome'.

- *Treaty on European Union*, 1992, otherwise known as the 'Maastricht Treaty', or 'EU Treaty'. It founded the European Union and is cited as 'EU' (or sometimes 'TEU').

The remaining primary legislation includes: the *Treaty Establishing the European Atomic Energy Community* (1957), the *Single European Act* (1986), the *Treaty of Amsterdam* (1997), the *Treaty of Nice* (2001), and the *Treaty of Lisbon* (2007).

Beware that the articles of the Treaty of Rome were renumbered by the *Treaty of Amsterdam* and then renumbered again by the *Treaty of Lisbon*. Correspondence tables giving the old and new numbers can be found in annexes to these amending treaties.

Primary legislation appears in its original form in the *Official Journal of the European Union*, usually in the C series (see **4.13.3**). Periodic consolidations of the *Treaty on the Functioning of the European Union* and *Treaty on European Union* can also be found in the C series.

There is a convenient collection of EU primary legislation—both original and consolidated versions—on the *EUR-Lex* website (see **4.17**). Although the treaties are also on subscription databases such as *Westlaw, Justis CELEX*, and *Lexis Library*, they are not presented there in such a user-friendly format. The treaties may also be found in UK publications, such as Sweet & Maxwell's *Encyclopaedia of European Union Law*.

4.13.2   Secondary legislation

EU secondary legislation consists of regulations, directives, decisions, recommendations, and opinions, as laid down by article 288 of the *Treaty on the Functioning of the European Union*. Recommendations and opinions are not binding, despite being classed as legislation.

Regulations, directives, and decisions are cited by their year and running number, for example:

- *Council Regulation (EC) No 44/2001 of 22 December 2000 on jurisdiction and the recognition and enforcement of judgments in civil and commercial matters;*

- *Directive 2003/88/EC of the European Parliament and of the Council of 4 November 2003 concerning certain aspects of the organisation of working time; and*

- *2001/145/EC: Commission Decision of 21 February 2001 concerning certain protection measures with regard to foot-and-mouth disease in the United Kingdom.*

4.13.3 The *Official Journal*

Legislation is published in the *Official Journal of the European Union*, the EU's official gazette. Before February 2003, it was called the *Official Journal of the European Communities*. It is divided into two main series, 'L' and 'C', cited as 'OJ L' and 'OJ C'.

Since 1 July 2013, the online edition of the *Official Journal*, not the print edition, has been the authentic version (Regulation 216/2013, [2013] OJ L69/1). Before this, the print edition was the authentic version. The print OJ ceased general publication at the end of 2013 (although it is still possible to order single print issues on an ad hoc basis).

The OJ L contains all secondary legislation. Primary legislation, on the other hand, is mostly found in the OJ C, although the Single European Act and the accession treaties are in the OJ L. Until 2002, proposals for legislation appeared in the OJ C, but from 2003 onwards they have only been published in the COM DOCS series (see **4.13.8**), which is available on the *EUR-Lex* website (see **4.13.4**). Much of the OJ C is taken up by non-legislative documents, such as case summaries and Commission notices. **Table 4.13** sets out the key contents of the *Official Journal*.

Table 4.13 **Key contents of the *Official Journal***

L series	C series
Secondary legislation	Most primary legislation
Some primary legislation (Single European Act, accession treaties)	Proposals for legislation (until 2002; now only found on EUR-Lex)
	Case summaries and court notices
	Notices from the European Commission
	European Parliament minutes
	Common positions of the Council of the EU

4.13.4 Finding secondary legislation

The quickest way to find a particular instrument is to use the EU's free legal database, *EUR-Lex* (<http://new.eur-lex.europa.eu/>), which has the authenticated online edition of the *Official Journal*, as well as the old, unauthenticated online edition. A new version of *EUR-Lex* was launched in 2013 and most, but not all, of the content has been uploaded to it, although the old *EUR-Lex* (<http://eur-lex.europa.eu/>) is still running in parallel to it at the time of writing. EU legislation can also be found on subscription databases such as *Lexis Library, Lawtel EU, Westlaw,* and *Justis CELEX*.

EUR-Lex and the subscription databases can be searched by keyword or instrument number. They will give the full text of the instrument, plus its OJ reference; you could then use the OJ reference to find the authentic printed text of pre-July 2013 instruments, if required. *EUR-Lex* also provides a browsable subject index of current legislation, the *Directory of Legislation in Force*, although this can be difficult to use. There is no overall printed index to the *Official Journal*, only monthly and annual ones, which are not cumulative. **Table 4.14** shows you how to research EU legislation.

Table 4.14 **How to research EU legislation**

Looking for . . .	Electronic services	Printed resources
Primary legislation, original text	*EUR-Lex* website (Treaties collection) *Westlaw* *Justis CELEX* *Lexis Library* *Lawtel EU*	*Official Journal* (get citation from EUR-Lex); does not include the original versions of the 1950s founding treaties
Primary legislation as amended	*EUR-Lex* website (Treaties collection) *Westlaw* *Justis CELEX* *Lexis Library* *Lawtel EU*	*Official Journal of the European Union*, C series
Secondary legislation, original text	*EUR-Lex* website (see 'Linked Documents' for amendments) *Westlaw* (see 'References' for amendments) *Justis CELEX* (see 'Amending Items' for amendments) *Lexis Library* (list of amendments towards top of each document)	*Official Journal*, L series
Secondary legislation, as amended	*EUR-Lex* website (N.B. consolidated amended texts may not be up to date—always check list of amendments) *Lexis Library* (but more recent consolidated texts may be available on *EUR-Lex*; and always check list of amendments before using consolidated text)	Encyclopedias and textbooks, such as *Gore-Browne on EU Company Law* and Sands (ed.), *Documents in European Community Environmental Law*

4.13.5 Is it in force?

When you search for EU legislation on a website or database, you will often be presented with the original text accompanied by a list of amendments (if any). On the new *EUR-Lex* and on *Lexis Library*, your search will also find one or more consolidated amended versions of the instrument. However, consolidated texts are provided by the EU for research purposes only and the EU institutions disclaim liability for their contents. Furthermore, consolidated versions are not available for all instruments, and those that are available are not always completely up to date. Consolidated versions are not available on *Westlaw* or *Justis CELEX,* and *Lexis Library* does not always have as complete a set of consolidated versions as *EUR-Lex*.

It is important to note that *consolidated texts will not always say if the instrument has been repealed:* for example, the original Working Time Directive (93/104/EC) was repealed by Directive 2003/88/EC, but the latest consolidated version makes no mention of the fact. This means that it is important to check for repeals in the list of amendments. On the new version of *EUR-Lex*, the list of amendments appears under 'Linked Documents', a tab attached to the original text of the instrument (on the old *EUR-Lex*, see 'Bibliographic Notice'). To find the list of amendments on *Westlaw*, click on 'References' and look under 'Modified by'; on *Justis CELEX*, click on 'Amending Items'; on *Lexis Library*, the amendments are given in a table towards the top of each document.

4.13.6 Implementation of directives

A directive sets out the result to be achieved and the date by which this must be done, but leaves each Member State to transpose its provisions into national law. This process is known as implementation or transposition. In the UK, almost all implementation is done by statutory instrument; only occasionally is an Act of Parliament required (e.g. the Consumer Protection Act 1987, which implemented the Product Liability Directive). At the other extreme, a directive relating to banking practice may need only an internal circular from the Bank of England to the clearing banks. And no implementing legislation is required at all where the government consider that the scope of a directive is already covered by existing UK law.

On the new *EUR-Lex*, the 'Linked Documents' tab for each directive gives details of implementation by all Member States under 'Display the national implementing measures' (on the old *EUR-Lex*, see 'Bibliographic Notice'). *Justis CELEX* and *Westlaw* also provide implementation data for all Member States, and the editors of *Justis* add details of implementing SIs that are missing from *EUR-Lex*. *Lawtel EU* only covers implementation by the UK. Be warned, however, that the implementation data on these databases is not always complete or up to date. If a database says 'No reference available' for a particular country, it is not safe to assume that the directive has not been implemented there; check several other sources (see later in the chapter) and ask any relevant contacts to make sure.

On *Lexis Library*, implementation data for England and Wales (not Scotland) can be found in *Halsbury's EU Legislation Implementator* (formerly *Butterworths EU Legislation Implementator*). *LexisNexis* also has a separate online service, *EU Tracker*, which provides detailed information about implementation by most Member States, although it only covers selected directives.

Printed sources of implementation data include *Current Law*, *European Current Law*, and *Halsbury's EU Legislation Implementator*. The latest monthly part of *Current Law* lists all of the present year's statutory instruments which have implemented directives in the UK; *European Current Law* covers implementation by most Member States; *Halsbury's EU Legislation Implementator* (part of *Halsbury's Statutory Instruments*) covers England and Wales only.

For a very recent directive, details of UK implementation can often be found on the website of the government department concerned; failing that, contact the department's legal section. There is even a multi-lingual gateway to the national legislation websites of Member States, *N-Lex* (see **4.17**), although it is rather difficult to use effectively. *N-Lex* is in fact best used to find the text of a foreign implementing instrument once you have got the title and reference from *EUR-Lex* or elsewhere. **Table 4.15** shows you how to trace the implementation of EU directives into national law.

Table 4.15 **How to trace the implementation of EU directives into national law**

First try . . .	
EUR-Lex website (old *EUR-Lex*—data not available on new *EUR-Lex* at time of writing)	Search for directive, then go into 'Bibliographic Notice' click on 'MNE'
or *Westlaw*	Search for directive, then click on 'National Measures'
or *Justis CELEX*	Search for the directive and scroll down
or *Lexis Library EU Tracker*	Covers most Member States, but selected directives only
If above sources say 'No reference available', check elsewhere . . .	
Government websites	Use Google Advanced Search to search specific web domains, e.g. .gov.uk or .fr
European Current Law	Covers most Member States, but not every directive
Current Law	Check latest monthly part; gives UK information only
Halsbury's EU Legislation Implementator	UK implementation information only
Commercial Laws of Europe (Sweet & Maxwell)	The annual volumes have tables of implemented legislation for all Member States (not cumulative)
Newsletters and journals	Search journals on *Westlaw* for articles about implementation of the directive
N-Lex website	Multi-lingual gateway to national legislation websites of most EU Member States. Can be searched in English, but the results are in the original language
If all else fails . . .	
Contact the relevant Directorate-General of the European Commission—see <http://ec.europa.eu/dgs_en.htm>	

4.13.7   EU draft legislation

Legislation is drafted by the European Commission and the first published version is known as a 'proposal'. The Commission's proposals, equivalent to parliamentary Bills in the UK, are published in the COM Documents (or COM DOCs) series, on the *EUR-Lex* website. Significant new proposals are reported in the various legal news sources, such as the 'Current Awareness' sections of *Lexis* and *Westlaw*.

When finally adopted, the instrument will appear in the *Official Journal* L series. The entire legislative process, from adoption of the original proposal to publication of the legislation in the OJ, can now be tracked in the *Legislative Procedures* section of the new *EUR-Lex* website, although the old legislation-monitoring websites, *PreLex* (produced by the European Commission) and the *Legislative Observatory* (produced by the European Parliament), are still available as well (see **4.17**).

EXERCISE 8   EU LEGISLATION

1. What is the latest available consolidation of the *Treaty on the Functioning of the European Union* on the (new) *EUR-Lex* website?
2. What is the official title of the *Maastricht Treaty*? What is the subject of Title III of the Treaty?
3. Find Regulation 44/2001 on *Westlaw*, *Lexis Library*, or *Justis CELEX*. What is the *Official Journal* reference? (Tip: to find EU legislation on *Lexis*, go to the main Legislation screen and click on the 'International Legislation' link on the left-hand side.)
4. Find Directive 97/33/EC on interconnection in telecommunications. Is it still in force?
5. Has the UK implemented the Airport Charges Directive (2009/12/EC)?

4.14   EU law reports

4.14.1   The *European Court Reports*

The European Union's judicial institution is officially called the 'Court of Justice of the European Union'. It consists, in fact, of three courts: the Court of Justice (often known as the 'European Court of Justice', or 'ECJ'), the General Court (previously called the 'Court of First Instance', but renamed by the Treaty of Lisbon), and the Civil Service Tribunal.

Decisions of the three courts are reported in an official printed series, *Reports of cases before the Court of Justice and the Court of First Instance*. This series is usually known as the 'European Court Reports' (ECR), but this is not its actual title. Although all cases formerly appeared in the ECR in full, since mid-2004 less significant cases, such as uncontested infringement proceedings, have either been omitted or are summarised at the back of the ECR rather than reported in full. These cases are available in full in the case database on the Curia website, but not always in English.

Part I of the ECR publishes Court of Justice decisions and Part II publishes Court of First Instance/General Court decisions. Civil Service Tribunal decisions appear in the sub-series, *European Court reports: reports of European Community staff cases* (ECR-SC).

New volumes of the ECR are slow to appear, but provisional case reports can be found on the Curia website on the day of the judgment (see **4.17**). Cases are also available on the *EUR-Lex* website and on subscription databases such as *Justis CELEX*, *Westlaw*, *Lexis Library*, and *Lawtel EU*.

4.14.2   CMLR

The best-known EU law reports published in the UK are the *Common Market Law Reports* (CMLR). They include relevant cases from courts in the UK and other Member States, as well as those of the ECJ. A noteworthy ECJ case will usually appear in the CMLR long before it comes out in the *European Court Reports*.

4.14.3   Finding EU cases

Searching online by party name alone can be difficult, since many EU cases have names which are so common as to be meaningless: for example, there are more than 100 cases involving the Commission and the UK.

If you know the number with which the case was originally registered, it will be easy to find on *EUR-Lex*. Case numbers are prefixed by a C for ECJ cases, a T for the Court of First Instance/General Court, or an F for the Civil Service Tribunal—for example, *European Parliament v Council of the European Communities*, C–65/90. If you do not have the case number, it is usually best to search by a combination of party names, year, and/or area of law.

Printed indexes which cover EU cases include the *Current Law Case Citator* and *European Current Law*.

Cases at the Court of Justice usually go through two stages: first, the Advocate General will deliver his or her opinion; then, a few months later, the judgment is given. The same case number is used for both stages and the opinion appears in the same printed and electronic sources as the judgment. General Court and Civil Service Tribunal cases only have one stage: the judgment.

All registered cases are listed on the Curia website (see **4.17**). They are arranged in case-number order, but the lists can be searched by party name using Ctrl-Find. It will say here whether a case has been heard, has been dropped ('removed from the register'), or is still pending. For hearing dates, see the Judicial Calendar in the Case Law section of the Curia website, which provides a schedule up to a few weeks in advance.

EXERCISE 9   EU CASES

1. What is the *European Court Reports* citation for *Arsenal Football Club plc v Reed*?
2. Use (new) *EUR-Lex* to find case number C-199/04. Which court heard it?
3. Use *Westlaw* to find the CMLR citation for *Salgoil SpA v Foreign Trade Ministry of Italy*. (Tip: use the main Cases screen, as the EU screen does not cover the CMLR.)
4. Use the Curia website to find out whether case T-629/13 is still pending, or whether it has been heard.
5. Use *Lexis Library*, *Westlaw*, or *Justis CELEX* to find EU cases concerning working time. (Tip: on Lexis, go to the main Cases screen and click on 'International cases'.)

4.15 EU periodical literature

Various law publishers have their own European journals, many of which are available online as well as in printed form. They include:

- *Common Market Law Review* (on *Kluwer Law Online* and *Proquest*);
- *European Law Review* (on *Westlaw*);
- *Journal of Common Market Studies* (on *Wiley Online Library* and *Business Source Premier*); and
- *European Intellectual Property Review* (on *Westlaw*)

To find journal articles on a particular topic, use the Journals section of *Westlaw*, which is more extensive than the *Lexis* Journals collection.

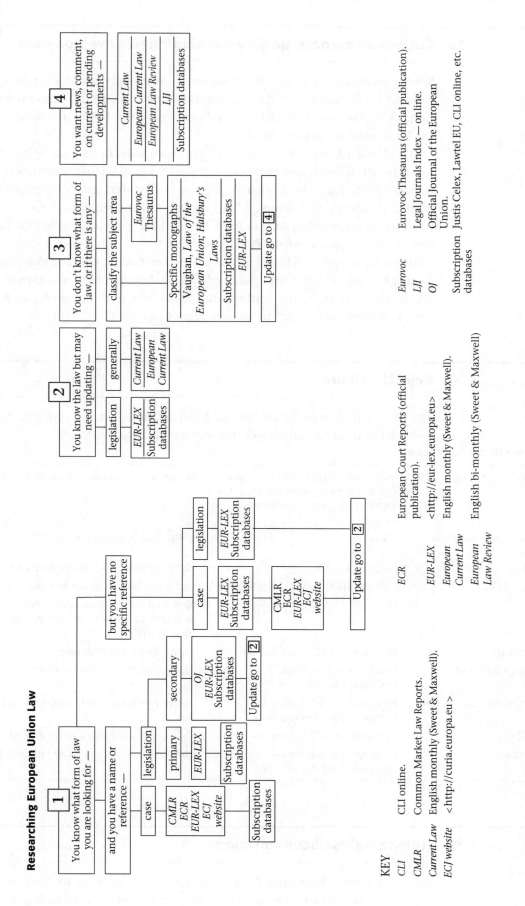

Figure 4.2 Researching European Union Law

4.16   Current awareness: finding out about new developments

Several publishers offer monthly, weekly, or even daily updates on paper and online. News of EU developments can be found on *Lawtel EU*, in the 'Current Awareness' sections of *Westlaw* and *Lexis*, and in the *Europolitics* e-newsletter (the latter is published by the European Information Service).

The EU website has a Newsroom (<http://europa.eu/newsroom/>) providing press releases on all subjects; and *EUR-Lex*, *PreLex*, or *Legislative Observatory* (mentioned earlier) can be used to track the legislative process. On Twitter, see the accounts of EU institutions and officials, for example @EU_Commission and @Europarl_EN.

Independent websites such as *EurActiv* and blogs such as *eutopia* (<http://eutopialaw. com>) are also useful (see **4.17**).

In print, EU legal developments are covered by *Current Law* and *European Current Law*. *Current Law* has a 'European Union' subject heading, but EU developments affecting the UK are digested under the appropriate UK law headings. *European Current Law* is valuable, as it covers every country in Europe, not just the EU.

4.17   Key EU websites

The principal sources for EU law are freely available on the internet. **Table 4.16** lists some of the most important websites you are likely to need.

Table 4.16 **Key EU websites**

Curia case index	Index with links to full text; gives status (pending, removed from the register, etc.); cross-references joined cases	<http://curia.europa.eu/jcms/jcms/ Jo2_7045/>
Curia cases database	All cases	<http://curia.europa.eu/juris>
EU Newsroom	EU press releases	<http://europa.eu/newsroom/index_en.htm>
EUR-Lex	EU legislation, cases, *Official Journal*, COM Docs, etc.	Old site: <http://eur-lex.europa.eu/en/index.htm>
		New site: <http://new.eur-lex.europa.eu/> (migration of content from old to new site in progress at time of writing)
EurActiv	Independent EU news website	<http://www.euractiv.com>
European Direct	Directory of European Documentation Centres	<http://europa.eu/europedirect/index_en.htm>
Legislative Observatory	Progress of legislation— European Parliament site	<http://www.europarl.europa.eu/oeil/home/home. do>
N-Lex	National law of EU Member States	<http://eur-lex.europa.eu/n-lex/index_en.htm>
PreLex	Progress of legislation— European Commission site	<http://ec.europa.eu/prelex/apcnet.cfm?CL=en>

4.18   Human rights documentation

Since the *Human Rights Act 1998* came into force, UK citizens have been able to use domestic courts to enforce the European Convention on Human Rights. However, the European Court of Human Rights (ECHR), the judicial institution of the Council of

Europe, is of course still very active. The human rights lawyer therefore needs to be familiar with both UK and ECHR legal sources.

Many ECHR publications are available on the internet. Printed materials can be found in major law libraries; Gray's Inn Library has a good human rights collection.

4.19 The European Convention on Human Rights

The 1950 European Convention on Human Rights is properly called the *Convention for the Protection of Human Rights and Fundamental Freedoms*. It was officially published as number five in the Council of Europe's *European Treaty Series* (ETS 005), but it is also reproduced in numerous human rights textbooks, and elsewhere. Several protocols have amended the Convention and these have also been published in the *European Treaty Series*.

Both the Convention and its protocols can be found on the Council of Europe (CoE) conventions website (<http://www.conventions.coe.int>).

For commentary on the Convention, see *Theory and practice of the European Convention on Human Rights*,[1] and *Jacobs and White: The European Convention on Human Rights*.[2]

4.20 Human rights law reports

4.20.1 Official printed series

The official printed series of European Court of Human Rights cases is *Reports of Judgments and Decisions* (cited as 'ECHR'). Before 1996, cases appeared in *Series A: Judgments and Decisions* (cited as 'ECHR' or 'Series A'). From 1960 to 1987, there was also *Series B: Pleadings, Oral Arguments and Documents* (cited as Series B).

The European Commission of Human Rights, now defunct, published its rulings in *Decisions and Reports* (cited as 'DR') from 1975 to 1998; before then, they appeared in the *Collection of Decisions of the European Commission of Human Rights* (cited as 'CD' or 'Coll. of Dec.').

Resolutions of the Council of Europe's Committee of Ministers in application of the Convention are published in *Collection of Resolutions Adopted by the Committee of Ministers in Application of Articles 32 and 54 of the European Convention for the Protection of Human Rights and Fundamental Freedoms*.

4.20.2 The HUDOC case database

The CoE's free HUDOC website (see **4.22**) aims to provide every ECHR judgment and decision, back to 1959, although there are some gaps. It also includes admissibility decisions and public reports of the European Commission of Human Rights back to 1986, and some of the Commission's older admissibility decisions, plus all the resolutions of the CoE's Committee of Ministers.

---

1   Pieter van Dijk, *et al.* (eds), *Theory and practice of the European Convention on Human Rights*, 4th edn (Intersentia, 2006).

2   Clare Ovey, *Jacobs and White: The European Convention on Human Rights*, 5th edn (Oxford University Press, 2010).

Each ECHR case has an application number, consisting of a serial number followed by the year it was lodged: for example, 21413/02. HUDOC can be searched or filtered by application number, party names, Convention Article number, key words, and many other criteria.

4.20.3   Other law reports

Selected ECHR cases are published in the *European Human Rights Reports* (EHRR) and UK human rights cases appear in the *Human Rights Law Reports* (HRLR); both series are published by Sweet & Maxwell and are also available on *Westlaw*. The EHRR series is particularly useful as a source of English versions of cases whose original language was French. *Butterworths Human Rights Cases* (BHRC) covers decisions from both national courts and the ECHR. It is on *Lexis Library* as well as being available in print. Further sources are listed in **Chapter 9**.

4.20.4   Finding human rights cases

If you are looking for an ECHR case but do not have a citation, the HUDOC website is the best tool to use (see earlier). Other sources include the *Lawtel Human Rights* database, *Westlaw*, and *Lexis Library*.

The printed versions of series such as EHRR have indexes. If all else fails, Barbara Mensah's *European Human Rights Case Locator 1960–2000* (Cavendish, 2000) is a useful resource for tracing older cases.

Several case digests are available. These include the six-volume *Digest of Strasbourg Case-Law Relating to the European Convention on Human Rights*, produced by the CoE's Directorate of Human Rights and the Europa Instituut at the University of Utrecht (Carl Heymanns, 1984–5); *A Systematic Guide to the Case-Law of the European Court of Human Rights*, edited by Peter Kempees (Martinus Nijhoff, 1996), which is arranged by Convention Article; and *Human Rights Case Digest* (Martinus Nijhoff, 1990–). Recent issues of the latter are on the *HeinOnline* database.

Information concerning forthcoming ECHR cases is available on the European Court of Human Rights website (<http://www.echr.coe.int>) under the heading 'Hearings'.

EXERCISE 10   ECHR CASES

1. What does DR stand for in a case citation?
2. Use HUDOC to find *Murray v United Kingdom* (application number 18731/91). Was it ruled that there had been a breach of Article 6-2, or not?
3. Use HUDOC to find cases on Article 12 of the European Convention on Human Rights.
4. Use *Westlaw* to find *Allenet de Ribemont v France (No. 2)* (1996) 22 EHRR 582.

4.21   Human rights serials

CoE serial publications include the *Yearbook of the European Convention on Human Rights* (prepared by the CoE's Directorate General of Human Rights and published by Martinus Nijhoff). It includes summaries of selected cases, lists and statistical analyses of cases, selected recommendations and resolutions of the Assembly, texts adopted by the Committee of Ministers, replies to the recommendations, and other information. Online, there is the free *Human Rights Information Bulletin*, which includes articles and case summaries (but ceased publication in 2012), and *Case-Law Information Notes*, consisting of case digests and statistics. The Bulletin is on the CoE website and the *Information Notes* are on the ECHR website (see **4.22**); a printed edition of the *Bulletin* is also available.

There are various commercially published serials, such as the *European Human Rights Law Review* (Sweet & Maxwell; available on *Westlaw* as well as in printed format), the *Human Rights Law Review* (Oxford University Press; available on *HeinOnline* and *Oxford Journals* as well as in print), and the monthly bulletin *Human Rights Updater* (LexisNexis).

4.22   Key human rights websites

The principal internet sources for researching European human rights law are listed in **Table 4.17**.

Table 4.17 **Key human rights websites**

Council of Europe Conventions	<http://www.conventions.coe.int>
European Court of Human Rights	<http://www.echr.coe.int/>
HUDOC case database	<http://www.echr.coe.int/Pages/home.aspx?p=caselaw/HUDOC&c=>
Human Rights Information Bulletin	<http://www.coe.int/t/dgi/publications/bulletin/index_bulletin_en.asp>
Case Law Information Note	<http://www.echr.coe.int/Pages/home.aspx?p=echrpublications/other&c=#n1347528850996_pointer>

5

Using electronic resources for research

This chapter offers a practical overview of the main strategies and techniques you will need to employ when researching legal problems using an electronic source. It does not give detailed instructions as to how to use each resource: mastering the mechanics of the databases is best achieved by reading the user guides available online or attending a training session or demonstration given by an experienced user (such as a law librarian).

When searching an electronic legal database you need to be aware of three major issues, all of which are dealt with in greater detail in this chapter:

(a) *Know the precise scope and content of the database you are searching.* The overviews of the major commercial legal databases given in this chapter provide a good starting point. This issue also applies to printed sources, but there is a temptation to assume that 'everything' is available on a database. This is not an assumption one would make with a book, nor is it one that applies to electronic sources.

(b) *Learn how to search the database.* The risk of failing to retrieve material simply because you don't know how to use the database correctly is much greater for the untrained user than it is when you use printed sources. The correct formulation of a search strategy is all-important.

(c) *Update your findings.* It is tempting to assume that information available electronically is always more up to date than any printed equivalent. Often this is the case but not always . . . and updated information is rarely incorporated into the main text on the database straight away. You need to learn how each database updates its material.

5.1 Electronic formats

There are two main methods of accessing electronic databases.

5.1.1 Internet

The internet offers database publishers the ability to combine sophisticated search mechanisms with a technology that allows them to remotely update their databanks on a daily basis. The currency of the information is particularly attractive to those producing and using legal databases. Commercial databases on the internet are usually made available on subscription under licence, with the cost of the licence varying, depending on the number of users, the type of organisation, and how the organisation uses the information retrieved. For example, a large commercial law firm would be charged more than an academic institution. Occasionally a 'pay-as-you-go' option is available, with a charge based on the number of results retrieved and viewed from a search. This is particularly useful for light users of databases but requires planning of individual searches to ensure searching is cost-effective.

There are disadvantages to using an internet-based database, however. It is not always clear what information a database contains or how often it is updated, and the search engines on many databases lack functionality and user-friendliness.

5.1.2 CD-ROMs

CD-ROMs remain a popular alternative to database provision via the internet. They offer limited storage capacity—they could never hold the *Westlaw* or *Lawtel* databases, for example—but searching is often much quicker and more sophisticated on a CD-ROM than it is on the internet. Users can search at their leisure as there are no hidden online charges and this makes them more suitable for in-depth legal research. These advantages could well be outweighed by their lack of currency, however—updated disks are generally supplied quarterly, or monthly at best. Providers often get round this by supplying the main database on CD-ROM but then allowing users to access updated material on the internet.

5.2 Types of electronic database

It is important that the user knows both the contents and type of database he or she is searching. Electronic legal databases fall into three broad categories.

5.2.1 Full-text services

The full text of a document is added to the database. *Lexis Library* contains the full text of law reports from *The Official Series*, for example. Full-text services offer the user the ability to conduct in-depth research at the desktop without needing to leave the database to search for another source. In this respect they offer greater flexibility and the possibility of thorough research. In practice, however, they require good search techniques and a sound knowledge of the database contents. Simply because of the size of these databases, the number of results that are returned tends to be unwieldy whilst the user can never be sure that he or she is not missing some relevant information. The need for refined search strategies and techniques rapidly becomes apparent on a full-text retrieval database.

5.2.2 Abstracting and indexing services

In these, law reports, journal articles, legislation, and other documents are summarised by professional indexers and the summaries placed on the database. Keywords identifying concepts are assigned to each abstract and links are provided to related summaries and sometimes to the full text of a document. When the user searches the database, he or she is searching the summaries and keywords rather than the full text of the document itself. This allows for much greater precision in searching, reducing the number of extraneous results. *Current Legal Information* and *Legal Journals Index* (available via *Westlaw* or as separate services) and *Lawtel* are all abstracting and indexing services.

5.2.3   Bibliographic services

Bibliographic services offer publication details only. The *Index to Parliamentary Papers* CD-ROM, for example, is a searchable bibliographical database which can help to locate relevant parliamentary Bills and Bill numbers when carrying out *Pepper v Hart* research (see **6.5**). Some bibliographic databases now offer links to the full text of documents and this greatly increases their value to the researcher even if the full text of the document itself is not searchable. The gateway website, *Official Documents* (http://www.gov.uk/government/publications), is an example of a searchable bibliographic database that links to the full text of many (though not all) of the documents it indexes.

5.3   Commercial legal databases

The databases listed here are the main competitors in the provision of electronic legal information in the UK. There are other legal database providers and the list does not aim to be comprehensive. All are commercial services usually available on subscription.

5.3.1   *Justis*

Justis is an online library of full-text services focusing on individual resources such as statutes or law reports. The resources are largely for the UK jurisdiction, but *Justis* also offer services covering Irish sources and European law. *Justis* databases include legislation, primary case law, and specialist law reports series including:

- *The English Reports*;
- *The Law Reports* (Official Series);
- *Times Law Reports* (from 1990);
- *Parliamentary Resources;*
- *Statutes* and *Statutory Instruments* (full text in their *original* form—statutes from 1235, SIs from 1671, and local and private acts from 1791); note that these are taken from the *Statutes at Large* series and are unofficial;
- *Justis EU*, including *CELEX* (the official database of the European Communities); and
- *JustCite*, an excellent web-based legal reference and citation search facility indexing around 2 million cases including transcripts and unreported judgments, and with extensive links to full-text material from online services such as BAILII, *Casetrack*, *Lexis*, and *Westlaw*.

5.3.2   *Lawtel*

An abstracting and indexing service for UK law, owned by Sweet & Maxwell. The strengths of the main *Lawtel UK* database lie in its coverage of unreported cases and the speed with which decisions are placed on the service. The main database, *Lawtel UK*, is supplemented by separate, specialist databases such as *Employment, Personal Injury, Kemp on Lawtel*, and *Lawtel Human Rights*. *Lawtel UK* databases include:

- Case law abstracts from 1980. Comprehensive coverage of more than 60,000 decisions from the House of Lords, Court of Appeal, Judicial Committee of the Privy Council, and Supreme Court, many with links to full-text transcripts.

- *Legislation*—full-text UK legislation in its *original* form. Statutes from 1984, statutory instruments from 1987. Tables of commencement, amendments, repeals, etc., but the text itself is not amended.

- *Articles Index*. Summaries of articles from over 50 legal journals, many of which discuss cases unreported elsewhere.

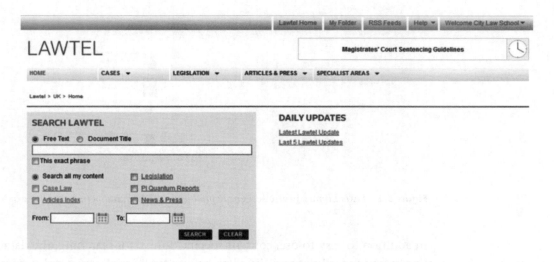

Figure 5.1 *Lawtel* front screen. *Reproduced with the kind permission of Sweet & Maxwell.*

5.3.3 *Lexis Library*

Lexis Library describe their flagship database as a 'library' of UK law and, indeed, its content is impressive. Extensive case law and legislation databases, both with updating facilities, cover the primary sources for legal research. Many of the publisher's leading publications are available in full text, including loose-leaf works, textbooks, journals, law reports, and legal encyclopedias such as *Halsbury's Laws* and *Atkin's Court Forms*. These commentaries can be searched independently of each other or as a group. In all, the system boasts over 32,000 sources with a 30-year archive of some journals and law reports. *Lexis Library* databases include:

- *Case Search*—case summaries with links to full-text law reports. Includes an archive of case law from 1502 taken from *The Digest*;

- *All England*—complete archive from 1936 and recent cases in advance of publication in the printed series;

- *Halsbury's Laws*—full text of the encyclopedia with cumulative supplement and monthly *Noter-up*;

- *UK Legislation*—full text of UK legislation in force, as amended by later enactments; and

- *Practice Areas*—subject-based services such as Employment, Family, and Property.

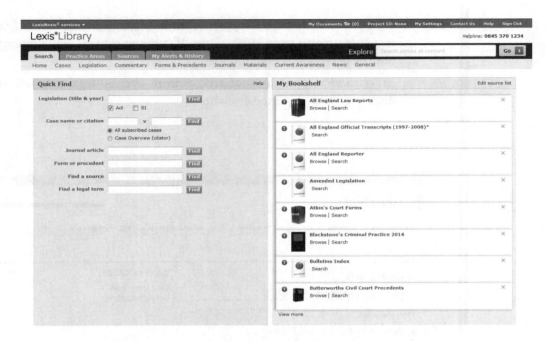

Figure 5.2   *Lexis Library* home screen. *Reproduced with the kind permission of LexisNexis.*

In addition to easy-to-use, content-specific 'forms' for searching, the database has extensive browsing facilities and also plays host to traditional search techniques using Boolean operators (see **5.5.2.4**). Combined with the ability to save favourite searches and customise groups of sources, this means that *Lexis Library* offers sophisticated access to its extensive materials, for the trained user. *Lexis Library* is not always an intuitive database to search with its plethora of links to various resources, and most users would need some guidance in its use. There is however an impressive range of guidance available online, including interactive tutorials.

5.3.4   *Westlaw UK*

A formidable full-text database that has very quickly established a leading market position in the UK to match that of its principal rival, *Lexis Library*.

The full text of many Sweet & Maxwell journals and loose-leaf works are available online. This service is available by subscription or on a 'pay-as-you-go' basis. *Westlaw UK* databases include:

- *Case Law*—databases of case law abstracts with links to the full text of many law reports and journals (though these are mostly limited to Sweet & Maxwell publications);

- *Legislation*—full-text statutes and statutory instruments currently in force, as amended;

- *Journals*—full text of around 125 Sweet & Maxwell journals, and many more abstracted and indexed titles. *Westlaw* incorporates the excellent *Legal Journals Index* service formerly hosted on *Current Legal Information (CLI) Online*.

Figure 5.3   *Westlaw UK* front screen. *Reproduced with the kind permission of Thomson Sweet & Maxwell.*

5.3.5   Practitioner texts, law reports, and journals on the internet and CD-ROM

Many legal publishers still produce some of their published works electronically, either as independent works on the internet or on CD-ROM. *Jordans* offers a full suite of family law publications, all its law reports, and some specialist practice area databases as separately packaged services on the internet. *Justis* also has a good selection of electronic versions of texts on CD-ROM (see **5.3.1**). Both internet and CD-ROM services are particularly useful for expanding a law collection piecemeal, without the need to buy and store printed copies or to pay an annual subscription for an expensive service such as *Lexis Library* or *Westlaw*. Some of these key services are mentioned in the list of works in **Chapter 9**.

Many CD-ROMs are still supplied free with the printed publications while others require separate annual subscriptions. Disks are usually supplied on a monthly or quarterly basis to update the work, or the user might download updates from a website with a password. Internet-based resources are usually updated more often than the CD-ROM versions.

Online and CD-ROM versions of texts vary considerably in scope and quality. Most allow you to search the texts using forms, and to browse using a 'contents tree'. *Jordans* products offer 'quick search', 'assisted search', and 'advanced search' facilities, as well as updates such as *Newsline* and *Newswatch*.

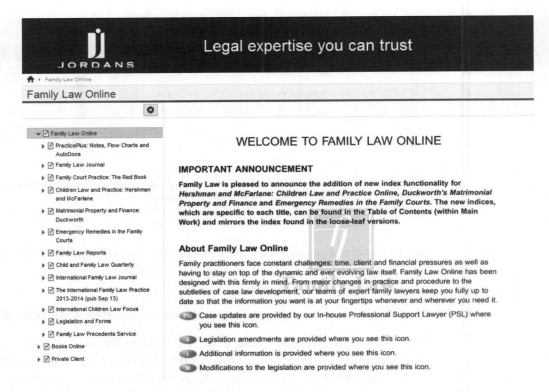

Figure 5.4   *Jordans Family Law Online* front screen. *Reproduced with the kind permission of Jordan Publishing Ltd.*

The software for CD-ROMs also varies considerably but searching can be faster than the internet and material can also be downloaded in a format suitable for word processing. Publications such as forms and precedents work well with CD-ROM technology for this reason, as users need to complete forms and precedents before printing them. Many CD-ROMs also offer additional interactive tools such as damages calculators and the ability to save searches, cases, and related data, and return to work with them at a later date.

5.4   Free legal information on the internet

The internet is a rich source of free legal information, with many websites offering a range of legal databases and documents of great use to practitioners. A few of the most useful websites are listed in the table at **5.4.3**. It is very tempting to see the internet as *the* source for all legal information. In fact, any websites you find on the internet should be used with extreme caution, particularly for legal information where currency and accuracy are so important—the quality of a website is crucial when using the internet for legal research. This makes it necessary to search in a controlled way for the information you need, and to evaluate every website you find in terms of the currency and quality of the information offered.

5.4.1   Searching the internet for legal resources

5.4.1.1   Search engines

These are best used when you want to search the internet for a specific resource: to find the Court Service home page for example, or to see if there is a transcript of a particular case available for free on the internet. Choose a UK-based search engine such as *Google UK* at <http://www.google.co.uk> rather than US versions.

5.4.1.2   Directories

These allow you to browse a list of categories and subcategories to narrow down the area of the search until you find what you are looking for. *Yahoo! UK & Ireland* at <http://dir .yahoo.com/> is a good UK-based directory search engine: click Social Science to access listings under Law.

5.4.1.3   Legal gateways

These offer links to good-quality legal resources on the internet and are of most use when you wish to browse the internet for authoritative websites. The more general legal gateways, such as the *Delia Venables Portal* (popular in practice as it offers CPD courses) or Inner Temple's *Access to Law*, offer a short description of the linked website, evaluating its contents for the quality and currency of information. City University's *Lawbore* <http://www.lawbore.net> offers resources principally for students on academic law courses, but the links to recent articles under practice areas and excellent online tutorials for learning how to research the law (via *Learnmore*, <http://learnmore.lawbore.net>) may also prove useful.

Other gateways offer links to resources in a particular area of law, such as employment law or company law, often combined with a free current awareness service or newsletter, and occasionally an additional database or priced services. Several legal gateways are listed in the table at **5.4.3**.

Figure 5.5 *Lawbore* home page: <http://www.lawbore.net>. *Reproduced with the kind permission of City University, London.*

5.4.2 Evaluating the contents of a website

Once you have found a website offering legal information, you must ascertain how good it is. Currency and accuracy are vital in legal research. When viewing any legal website, ask yourself the following series of questions:

- *WHO* is providing the information and *WHY*? Are they reliable and authoritative?
- *WHEN* was the website, or the database it hosts, last updated? How often is it updated? Does it include all amendments? Is it likely to be there tomorrow?
- *WHERE* is the website published? Which jurisdiction? UK law or US law? England or Scotland?

You may find the legal information you need on a website through a simple search—but whatever you find, you must check it on a more authoritative database. Why not use a legal database from the start? If you do use the internet for legal research, use well-established websites available through legal gateways or use the resource in the same way as you would use an encyclopedia: to find background information which you would then check with a more authoritative source.

5.4.3 Free legal information on the internet

Table 5.1 lists some of the legal materials available for free on the internet. It is not a comprehensive listing. Web addresses are subject to change but all these websites (and many others) can be found through a legal gateway such as the *Delia Venables Portal*.

Table 5.1 **Free legal information on the internet**

LEGAL GATEWAYS	*Gateway sites with links to free legal resources on the internet*	
Access to Law (Inner Temple)	An annotated links directory for legal resources online with concise abstracts detailing website content, from the Inner Temple library.	\<http://www.accesstolaw.com\>
Delia Venables	*Legal Sites and Resources in the UK.* Pages of links regularly updated by Delia Venables.	\<http://www.venables.co.uk\>
Lawbore	Primarily an educational resource but with some profession-facing content. Links to practitioner resources, recent articles, and through the sister site, *Learnmore*, useful online tutorials for learning how to research the law.	\<http://www.lawbore.net\>
Law Society	Latest offerings on policy, law reform, and education and links to legal resources in the UK, Europe, and abroad.	\<http://www.lawsociety.org.uk\>
CASE LAW	*Transcripts, law reports, and summaries of cases*	
BAILII	UK portal, the *British and Irish Legal Information Institute*, offering access to transcripts of cases from the High Courts and Court of Appeal, from 1996.	\<http://www.bailii.org\>
Court Service	Database of selected High Court judgments (full-text transcripts from 1998 and links to tribunals, many with their own judgments); full text of Practice Directions from July 2000; extensive array of Court forms, leaflets, and guidance.	\<http://www.justice.gov.uk/about/hmcts\>
European Court of Human Rights—*HUDOC* database	Full-text judgments and decisions from 1959. Aims to be comprehensive but there are omissions. Includes pending cases, text of European Convention, and Rules of the Court.	\<http://www.echr.coe.int\>

European Court of Justice	Full-text judgments of the European Courts of Justice from 1954 and First Instance from 1989, added on day of delivery.	<http://curia.europa.eu/jcms/jcms/j_6/>
House of Lords	Full-text transcripts of all judgments delivered from 14 November 1996 to 30 July 2009. See also Supreme Court, later in the table.	<http://www.parliament.uk>
Recent, Current and Forthcoming Law Reports (ICLR)	Summaries of cases in *The Law Reports*, *Weekly Law Reports*, and *Industrial Cases Reports*. Also access to *Daily Law Notes*, offering briefs of forthcoming cases.	<http://www.lawreports.co.uk>
Supreme Court	Decided cases, latest judgments and current cases in the Supreme Court. See also House of Lords.	<http://www.supremecourt.gov.uk>
Swarbrick Law Index	Index of *c*.29,000 cases principally from the *Times* and *Law Society Gazette* abstracts. View by date, legislation, subject, or court.	<http://www.swarb.co.uk>
LEGISLATION	*Acts, SIs, Parliamentary and government material, EU legislation, etc.*	
EUR-Lex	Full text of all EU legislation, preparatory legislation, consolidated texts, and treaties. *Official Journal* (C and L series), from 1998.	<http://eur-lex.europa.eu/en/index.htm>
Government Information	Links to central and local government departments, agencies and services and to some NGOs.	<http://www.gov.uk>
Legislation	Comprehensive legislative service covering UK jurisdictions; full text but in their *original* form with long delays to tabulated annotated amendments.	<http://www.legislation.gov.uk>
Parliament	Full-text of parliamentary materials including Bills, *Weekly Information Bulletin*, recent *Hansard* debates, etc. from 1997.	<http://www.parliament.uk>
PUBLICATIONS	*Online versions of major publications*	
Bar Code of Conduct	. . . and other Rules and Guidance.	<http://www.barcouncil.org.uk>
Crown Prosecution Service	Publications including *Code for Crown Prosecutors*, the *Victims and Witnesses Charter*, and recent CPS reports.	<http://www.cps.gov.uk>
Electronic Law Journals	Gateway to UK law journals, electronic and paper. Some with links to full text, abstracts, and contents pages.	<http://elj.warwick.ac.uk>
Law Commission for England and Wales	Click Publications for summaries or full text of recent reports, consultation papers, annual reports, and *Law Under Review*.	<http://www.lawcom.gov.uk>
Legal Hub	Collated official directories of barristers, in-house lawyers, and expert witnesses; searchable by barrister or chambers.	<http://www.legalhub.co.uk>
Official Documents	Links to full text of UK official documents, including White Papers, Command Papers, research briefs, etc. Search by title, date, publishing department, or category.	<http://www.official-documents.co.uk>

5.5   Search strategies using electronic resources

5.5.1   First principles

Searching an online legal database requires a slightly different approach to that which many users employ when searching the internet. On the internet we tend to type any combination of keywords into the search box and click *Search*. In fact, 80 per cent of searches carried out on the internet use just one keyword. Another common approach is to type a sentence into the search box, much as you would when using the 'natural language' search engine, *Ask*.

We adopt this approach because, whatever we search for on the internet, we nearly always obtain a large set of results: *recall* is very high. We often find, however, that the *relevance* of many of these results is actually very low. If we were to search again using slightly different keywords, we would be very likely to find other websites that did not appear when we first searched: our original search has not been very *precise*.

When conducting legal research we need to adopt a more accurate and controlled approach to searching electronic legal sources; we cannot afford to miss any relevant results but nor do we have time to plough through a large set of results to find what we need. To do this, we need to devise a search strategy that uses carefully selected keywords combined in such a way as to maximise *recall*, *relevance*, and *precision*.

5.5.2 Basic search strategies for electronic sources

Legal research technique is dealt with in more detail in **Chapter 3**. What follows here relates more specifically to searching electronic databases.

5.5.2.1 Analyse the problem: what exactly are you looking for?

Spend some time identifying clearly the information you are trying to find. Is the solution likely to be found in case law or in legislation, or is it a procedural matter? This will help you to decide which database to search and the keywords you might use.

5.5.2.2 Choose which database you are going to search

It is very important to know the contents of the legal databases you have access to. There is little point in searching for a case dating from 1977 on *Lawtel*, for example, as the case law database began in 1980. Similarly, if you want the full text of a law report in *Criminal Appeal Reports* you will only find it on *Westlaw* as Cr App R is a Sweet & Maxwell publication and will not appear on a *Lexis Library* product.

Which database is the best one to use? It depends on what you need. A good method for finding out which database to use is to ask yourself what *type* of question you are faced with. Is it legislative or procedural? Might it involve finding case law? If you are faced with a very general problem and you don't know where to begin, then use a general source. An encyclopedia of law such as *Halsbury's Laws* is an excellent starting point.

EXAMPLE

When, during the year, does the law prohibit one from shooting snipe?

The word 'prohibit' hints that the answer is probably to be found in legislation and we might therefore use a legislative database but as there may be case law or procedure involved, it is probably best to start with a general source such as *Halsbury's Laws*.

5.5.2.3 Select the keywords

Search engines will find all occurrences within the text of the words you enter into the search box. If you enter a word that does not exist on the database or you misspell a word, you will get no results. If you enter too common a word, you will get too many results. Selecting the correct combination of keywords is crucial.

Which words define the problem you are researching? From our example, these might be:

- words offered to you by the problem itself (*shooting, snipe*);
- alternatives to those words (*shoot, bird, wild bird*); and
- concepts behind those words (*game, close season, licensing*).

Search engines are good at finding facts, names, and concrete entities; they are poor at classifying problems into concepts. Try to convert the problem into equivalent concrete keywords—the name of a case, the title of a statute, etc.

5.5.2.4 Combine the keywords in a 'controlled' search

After selecting our keywords, we need to combine them in a search that will maximise *recall*, *relevance*, and *precision* (see **5.5.1**). To do so we make use of a range of tools. **Table 5.2** explains how to use Boolean operators ('connectors') to refine our search.

Table 5.2 **Boolean operators (or 'connectors') AND, OR, and NOT**

Search phrase	*. . . will find . . .*	*Use it to . . .*	*Notes*
shoot AND *snipe*	. . . records containing the words *shoot* and *snipe*	. . . combine keywords, **narrowing** the search	Many databases assume an AND if no connector is entered (e.g. *close season* will find *close* AND *season* rather than the phrase *close season*).
shoot OR *game* OR *bird*	. . . records containing the words *snipe* or *bird* or *game*	. . . search for alternative key-words, **widening** the search	Useful for searching for alternative concepts (e.g. *copyright* OR *patents* OR *designs* OR *intellectual property*).
snipe NOT *bird*	. . . records containing the word *snipe* provided they do *not* contain the word *bird*	. . . exclude key-words, **narrowing** the search	Use rarely and with caution as it excludes records that may actually prove relevant.

Most databases allow several operators to be combined into one search. Brackets may be needed to group complex phrases and refine the search even further.

> e.g. *shoot AND (snipe OR bird)*
>
> e.g. *shoot AND (snipe NOT bird)*

Wild card characters/truncation

Wild cards, such as the asterisk * or the exclamation mark ! allow the user to search for different permutations of a word ending. Most databases use an asterisk * but some use other characters such as an exclamation mark !, a question mark ?, a percentage sign %, or a dollar sign $. Conveniently, *Lawtel, Lexis Library* and *Westlaw* all use an exclamation mark !.

5.5.2.5 Ensure the search form is completed correctly before clicking *Search*

Database providers have made their products easier to search by providing search forms but one of the most common user errors is not completing the form correctly, or entering incorrect truncation on keywords. **Table 5.3** explains certain truncations and how to use them.

Table 5.3 **Truncations**

Search phrase	. . . will find . . .	Use it to	Notes
licen!	. . . records containing the words *licence, licensing, licensed, licensee, etc.*	. . . replaces one or more letters, searching for alternative keywords, **widening** the search	Particularly useful for obtaining plurals to words (though some databases do this automatically).
licen*e	. . . records containing the words *licence* or *license*	. . . search for alternative keywords, **widening** the search	Allows for uncertain spelling (US v UK English, in this example). Might also be used where a hyphen may appear in the text, e.g. *self* incrimination.*

5.5.2.6   Display a list of results . . . and search again!

After performing a search, databases usually display the results as a list of 'hits' with links to the full text of the record. If the result list you have retrieved is too big (or too small) or you cannot find the information you need, you should go back and search again. Think about your keywords:

- too many results? *Narrow* your search—add another keyword using an AND;
- too few? *Widen* your search—think of alternative keywords the text might use and add them using an OR;
- results not relevant? Find a result from the list that is relevant, select keywords from that record, and combine them in a new search.

5.5.3 Updating your findings

After finding an answer on the database, you must check that the information you have found is up to date. Changes to legislation, case law, and commentary are rarely incorporated into the online text immediately and you are usually required to check elsewhere on the screen for updating information. The availability of updates also varies from one database to another and it may be necessary to 'migrate' to a different source to check that the law is current. You need to consider:

(a) *How the service actually displays updated material.* Is the updated information included in the text (*Lawtel UK* case database) or do you need to scroll to the bottom of the text (*Halsbury's Laws*)? Do you need to click an update button (*Lexis Library*) or a coloured flag (*Westlaw*)?

(b) *How often the service is updated.* If the database is updated daily, does this apply to the WHOLE database or just a part of it? Case law on *Lawtel UK* is updated daily, for example, but articles are added on a weekly basis.

As a general rule, case law and legislation are usually updated on a daily basis or regularly (i.e. 'within a few days') on an online service. Practitioner texts and loose-leaf works available online are usually only updated when the printed text is published. The online service may offer frequent *commentary* but this does not form part of the text of the work and it does not mean that the online version is more up to date.

CD-ROMs are updated infrequently. Check the front screen when you first log on for information about when the disk was last updated.

EXAMPLE

How do you go about changing a child's surname when the name was first registered incorrectly and where the divorced parents are in dispute as to what the correct form should be? **Table 5.4** works through the stages of legal research to answer this question.

Table 5.4 **Stages of legal research: questions and answers**

Stage of legal research: the question	The answer . . .
1. Analyse the problem: what *exactly* are you looking for?	The *procedure* for changing a minor's surname. Any relevant *legislation* and *case law*. The question assumes we *CAN* change the name but we must check *IF* we can.
2. Choose which database you are going to search.	The procedure may involve *legislation* and *case law*. Faced with such a general question, *Halsbury's Laws* online might be best placed to offer an answer . . .
3. Select keywords. What words most accurately define the problem you are researching? (i) words offered to you in the written text (ii) alternatives to those same words (iii) concepts behind those keywords	Keywords we could search on here might be: (i) child, changing, surname (ii) children, change, changes, name, forename (iii) registration of names; divorce
4. Join keywords using appropriate connectors and wild cards . . .	Join keywords with AND connector to narrow the search down; use a wild card to search for variations on the keywords: *child! AND chang! AND name!*
5. Ensure search form is completed correctly before clicking *Search*.	Ensure *Halsbury's Laws* is selected as the source to search and check all relevant keywords are entered.
6. Display a list of results . . . narrow and search again! (i) too few results? (ii) too many results? (iii) not relevant?	Around 170 results are returned in the 'hit list'. Narrow by topic (e.g.: *Children*) working through the results to find relevant results. You could also: (i) widen the search by using the OR connector in place of an AND; or search on fewer keywords by removing one (ii) narrow the search by adding another connector and keyword, e.g. *AND parent!* (iii) choose keywords from results that are more specific or more relevant and search again
7. Update your findings.	Scroll to the bottom of the paragraph or click UPDATE: the update information for *Halsbury's Laws* appears at the bottom of the screen and incorporates the text of the *Cumulative Supplement* and monthly *Noter-up*. The service is updated monthly.

5.5.4 More advanced searching

5.5.4.1 Fields

Databases are made up of 'records'—for example, a case summary on *Lawtel* or the full text of a law report on *Lexis Library*. Usually, those records are further divided into 'fields' (such as case name, citation, etc.) that are themselves searchable. If you retrieve too many results searching the full text, try *narrowing* your search by confining it to a specific field (such as the 'catchwords' field for case law or the statute title field for legislation) where the words would only appear if they were pertinent to the main text.

5.5.4.2   Proximity searching

Searching for several keywords joined by an AND can be a problem on a full-text database, as one keyword might appear at the beginning of the record and the other, in an entirely different context, right at the end. Proximity searching allows the user to define how close together the keywords should be, thereby *narrowing* the search. On *Lexis Library*, to find the phrase 'close season' in close proximity to 'snipe', enter the search: "close season" w/n snipe, where 'w' is for 'within' and 'n' is the number of words.

5.5.4.3   Phrases

Databases vary in how they search for phrases. If you were to enter *close season* into *Lexis Library* or *Justis*, it would find records containing the exact phrase. On *Lawtel* it would search for *close* AND *season*, unless you specified otherwise. Other databases may assume an OR between the words. Each search produces different results, so if you wish to search for a phrase (or an exact word and no other variations of it), always use double quotation marks " " around the keywords. For example, *"consumer protection"* finds only documents in which these two words appear next to each other rather than anywhere within the text of a database record.

You can also combine the use of the exclamation mark! wild card, and double quotes to search for derivatives of words next to each other—*"unfair! dismiss!"* finds *unfair dismissal* and/or *unfairly dismissed*. (See **Table 5.5**)

5.5.5   **Problematic searches**

There are a few situations in which you should be aware of the limitations of electronic searching and the foibles of the particular database you are searching.

5.5.5.1   Hyphenated words

Databases vary as to whether they treat a hyphen as a space or a character. Use an OR to ensure you retrieve all variations, e.g. *trademarks* OR *trade marks* OR *trade-marks*.

5.5.5.2   Stop words

Most databases will not search for very common words such as *the*, *is*, *of*, or *have*. Thus, *breach of confidence* will produce an error or too many results; use double quotation marks around the phrase, i.e. "breach of confidence".

5.5.5.3   Section numbers

When searching for a particular section of an Act, it is usually better to search on a specific field. If you must search the full text, avoid using the word 'section' or the abbreviation 's'. Those terms may or may not be used in the text and inputting the section number alone will suffice. Trying to specify subsections is similarly counterproductive. Use proximity searching, as the section number might appear before or after the title of the Act, e.g. *employment* w/4 *1998* w/15 7) to find s 7 of the Employment Act 1998.

5.5.5.4   Capital letters

While many databases are not case-sensitive, some do retrieve different results if you enter your keywords entirely in capital letters. This can be useful for organisation names and abbreviations but is otherwise confusing. It is good practice to enter keywords in lower case and the Boolean operators AND, OR, and NOT in capitals. You can then see immediately if you've entered your search terms and connectors incorrectly.

5.5.5.5   Boolean truncation and wild cards

Table 5.5 **Boolean truncation and wild cards**

	Lawtel	*Westlaw*	*Lexis Library*
Distinguish between search phrase with and without AND? (e.g. *firearms offence or firearms AND offence*)	No (assumes AND)	No (assumes AND)	Yes
Connectors allowed	AND, OR, NOT	AND, OR, NOT, w/n	AND, OR, NOT, w/n
Assumes plural? (e.g. looks for *vehicles* as well as *vehicle*)	No	Yes	Yes
What wild cards are used?	* at start or end of word (e.g. **legal* would search for illegal, legality, etc.) ? replaces single character " " allows exact phrase searching, e.g. *"professional negligence"* () e.g. (*dog OR animal*), (*firearm AND ammunition*)	* replaces single character ! truncates word " " allows exact phrase searching	* replaces single character ! truncates word " " allows exact phrase searching
Possible to search for words in proximity?	No	Yes. w/n (where n is a number) searches for terms within that many words of each other e.g. *alcohol w/4 bloodstream*	Yes. w/n (where n is a number) searches for terms within that many words of each other, e.g. *alcohol w/4 bloodstream*

6

Researching words and phrases

6.1 Introduction

Sometimes, a legal problem comes down to the precise meaning of a word or words. The uncertain words may be in an Act or regulations; or they may occur in a contract, insurance policy, lease, etc. Conversely, you may be drafting a document and trying to find an expression which will have the legal effect you want without any risk of unwanted side effects.

You will already know something of the interpretation of statutes and documents, the various approaches (literal, mischief, etc.) and subrules *(eiusdem generis*, etc.). Those may be needed if all your research fails to resolve the ambiguity. However, the initial question is whether the law has already defined the term used, giving it an authoritative interpretation.

6.2 Checklist

There are a number of questions to bear in mind:

(a) Does the Act or document provide its own definitions? If the expression is defined, does any uncertainty remain?

(b) Does the Interpretation Act 1978 help? It lays down some very basic clarifications (e.g. masculine includes feminine, etc.), but it only applies to statutes.

(c) Has any other statute or case provided a definition? Check specialist dictionaries and other sources—see **6.3**. If you find a definition, is it applicable to your problem? A definition of, say, 'child' in an Act dealing with succession is unlikely to be thought applicable to the construction of the same word in a statute on, say, employment conditions or education. On the other hand, Acts on the same subject (e.g. tax) have to be read together, including their definitions, so that, for example, 'income' has consistent meaning throughout. But two Acts on different subjects may sometimes be arguably on legally comparable subjects; if so, their definitions may be worth borrowing for the purposes of your argument.

(d) Would ordinary dictionaries help? They are quite often produced in court—see **6.3.7**.

6.3   Where to look for definitions

6.3.1   Dictionaries of words and phrases

These are multi-volume compilations, with updating supplements, which aim to include every word or phrase that has been judicially or statutorily defined. They give detailed citations and cross-references, examples of usage, and other helpful information. The two key works are:

(a) *Stroud's Judicial Dictionary*, published by Sweet & Maxwell; gives numerous entries for each word or phrase, mostly in just a line or two, with citations; and

(b) *Words and Phrases Legally Defined*, published by LexisNexis; gives fewer entries for each term, but gives them fully in the context of the judgment or other authoritative statement, with citations.

It is advisable to consult both works to ensure that you have not missed anything; make sure you also look at their updating supplements.

6.3.2   *Halsbury's Laws* Index

The final Index volume of *Halsbury's Laws* contains not just an ordinary index but also a substantial section devoted to words and phrases. These sometimes include a phrase missed by the legal dictionaries mentioned earlier. If you find your term here, once you have looked up the reference in the relevant subject volume, check for updates in the annual cumulative supplement and then in the *Current Service*.

The *Halsbury's Laws* index is on the *Lexis Library* database, linked separately in the Sources directory. Alternatively you can run a search across the whole work for definitions of your word or phrase. You would not want to retrieve every occurrence of what might be a fairly common word or phrase, but you could try to focus the search by asking for permutations of the various words that mean 'define' within ten or so words of the term you are trying to interpret (see **6.3.5**).

6.3.3   *The Law Reports* Pink and Red Indexes

The five- and ten-year cumulated index and current year's index to *The Law Reports* (see **4.11.2**) have a section of words and phrases as defined in any cases in the many report series covered. It is located under the letter 'W' for 'Words and phrases'. It makes it possible to trace the interpretation of a particular expression over the years or decades, which could be helpful.

6.3.4   *Current Law*

Current Law is a good source for very recent definitions. The latest monthly part of *Current Law Monthly Digest* cumulates all the words and phrases for the year so far; for previous years, check the *Current Law Year Books*.

6.3.5   Online sources

Westlaw has a new module, *Index of Legal Terms*, which is available for an additional charge. It supplies definitions from *Jowitt's Dictionary of English Law*, *Stroud's Judicial Dictionary*, and *Osborn's Concise Law Dictionary*. There is also a *Statutory Definition* search box on the ordinary *Westlaw* Legislation page.

Lexis has a *Find a legal terms* search facility on its home page, which finds statutory and/or judicial definitions and related commentary.

It is also possible to use *Westlaw* or *Lexis* to search the full text of every available statute or law report for statutory or judicial definitions. To reduce the number of irrelevant search results, try the following as the basis of your initial search strategy, adding or excluding further words as required:

- on *Lexis*: [the word] w/10 construe! OR defin! OR mean! OR interpret!
- on *Westlaw* the 'w' is not required: [the word] /10 construe! OR defin! OR mean! OR interpret!

There is one obvious pitfall in these examples: they exclude the word 'construction', which can refer to the interpretation of a word, but of course more usually refers to building work. So they will exclude building law cases, but might also miss cases in which the word 'construction' is used to mean interpretation of a word or phrase.

6.3.6   General law dictionaries

These provide general definitions of legal terms and concepts, including lawyers' Latin, rather than authoritative legal definitions with citations to case law and statute. They include *Jowitt's Dictionary of English Law* and the *Oxford Companion to Law*.

6.3.7   Ordinary dictionaries

As has already been mentioned, legal interpretation might eventually depend on the general dictionary definition if nothing more authoritative can be found. This definition can be used to establish the accepted meaning of a word, on the assumption that Parliament (or the parties) had that meaning in mind. An example is *R v Fulling* [1987] QB 426, which shows this can be done even where there is a definition in the statute, provided the definition is not exhaustive. The *Oxford English Dictionary* is the standard source.

EXERCISE 11   WORDS AND PHRASES

1. Find the most recent judicial explanations of:
   (a) 'car park';
   (b) 'grievance';
   (c) 'family life'.
2. An Act requires a notice to be 'displayed outside' premises. Is it sufficient to stick it to the inside of the window of the building so that it is visible outside but remains inside?
3. What do *'purger une hypothèque'* and *'Übertragung einer Schuld'* mean in foreign legal documents? (See **6.4**.)
4. Peter insured his factory against damage from 'flood, bursting or overflowing of water tanks, apparatus or pipes'. While moving some office furniture, his employees dropped a heavy metal cabinet onto a water pipe, which fractured, flooding the office and causing extensive damage to the firm's records. Peter's insurers say this loss is not within the insured perils. Advise him.

6.4   Foreign legal vocabulary

Nowadays, lawyers may be expected to have to translate legal terms from and to other European languages. There are professional legal translators who specialise in this work for big transactions, court documents, and so on. However, where it is just a term or concept in, say, a letter to or from an overseas lawyer, it may suffice to refer to a foreign legal dictionary. Most law libraries have such dictionaries, covering at least the major European languages.

The European Union's official multilingual thesaurus, EUROVOC, gives equivalents of terms used in EU law in more than 20 European languages, including English. It is on the internet at <http://eurovoc.europa.eu/>.

6.5   *Pepper v Hart* research: using *Hansard*

Since the House of Lords decision in *Pepper v Hart* [1993] AC 593, it has been permissible, subject to limitations, to cite in court what was said in Parliament during the passage of a Bill as an aid to statutory interpretation. Researching *Hansard* is a task which you may well be asked to do as a pupil. As it is a topic for which it is not feasible to provide practical training during the BPTC, you may well feel unprepared when asked to do it—even experienced practitioners who have not done it before can find themselves at sea. This short section can do no more than highlight some of the practicalities. But help will be at hand: if you are based in London you will almost certainly have to use Lincoln's Inn Library, which holds the specialist Parliamentary collection on behalf of the four Inn libraries, and whose experienced staff are always willing to offer expert guidance. Even if you are based outside London, they are happy to offer help over the phone.

The practicalities covered answer the following frequently asked questions:

- When might I or should I do it?
- What materials do I need to do it?
- Can I do it online?
- Where can I get the necessary hard-copy materials?
- How long does it take?
- How much do I need to know about Parliamentary procedure?
- What is the best way to get started?
- Are there any tips for finding my way around *Hansard*?
- If I cannot find any debates on the section, am I going wrong?
- If I find any relevant material, are there any formalities for putting it before the court?

6.5.1   When might I or should I do it?

Lord Browne-Wilkinson in *Pepper v Hart* (at p. 640) set out three criteria which have to be met if recourse to *Hansard* is to be taken:

- legislation is ambiguous or obscure, or leads to an absurdity;
- the material relied upon consists of one or more statements by a Minister or other promoter of the Bill, together, if necessary, with such other Parliamentary material as is necessary to understand such statements and their effect; and
- the statements relied upon are clear.

Once there is the possibility of the first criterion being met, then it will almost always be necessary to carry out *Hansard* research. It may indeed be professionally negligent not to do so. However, this research can be time-consuming (see **6.5.5**). If a matter is urgent and there is not time to do it, any advice involving statutory interpretation given in an opinion or in a conference should make that clear.

Pepper v Hart has since been considered by the House of Lords on several occasions, and you should be aware that its applicability has been qualified in some circumstances. The following are some of the leading cases:

- *Melluish (Inspector of Taxes) v BMI (No. 3) Ltd* [1996] 1 AC 454 (relevance of adjacent provisions);
- *R v Secretary of State for the Environment, Transport and the Regions, ex p Spath Holme Ltd* [2001] AC 349 (consolidation Acts, and enabling provisions to make Statutory Instruments);
- *R (Westminster City Council) v National Asylum Service* [2002] 1 WLR 2956 (use of Explanatory Notes on the Bill);
- *Wilson v First County Trust (No. 2)* [2004] 1 AC 816 (Human Rights Act compatibility cases);
- *McDonnell v Christian Brothers Trustees* 1 [2004] AC 1101 (overruling pre-*Pepper v Hart* cases);
- *Harding v Wealands* [2007] 2 AC 1 (latest HL general discussion); and
- *R v JTB* [2009] 1 AC 1310 (illustration of the weight of debate on unsuccessful amendments).

6.5.2   What materials do I need to do it?

Typically, you will need the following materials:

- A copy of the Act in question *as it was originally passed* (*Current Law Statutes* is best—its annotations may help before you even start; otherwise, from the official Stationery Office (Queen's Printer) copies).
- For Acts passed from 1984 to 2010, a copy of the relevant *House of Commons Sessional Digest* is useful since it gives the dates for each stage of the Bill, and lists the prints of the Bill. (It is no longer published but equivalent information is also available on the Parliament website.)
- The Bill, as reprinted, incorporating amendments during its passage—usually two complete prints for the Commons and three for the Lords.
- The Explanatory Notes accompanying the Bill (one for the Commons and one for the Lords) and for the Act—these were first provided in Parliamentary session 1998–1999.
- House of Commons *Hansard*.
- House of Commons *Standing Committee Debates* (since session 2006–2007 called *Public Bill Committee Debates*).
- House of Lords *Hansard*.

You may also need the following materials that precede the Parliamentary debates on the Bill, either as general background on the Bill or because they are referred to in the debates:

- any Law Commission report, or reports from Royal Commissions or official inquiries;

- Departmental consultation papers (green papers) and government white papers; and
- Draft Bills and Select Committee reports on Draft Bills: many Bills now receive 'pre-legislative scrutiny' by a Select Committee of the Commons or of the Lords, or by a Joint Committee; the procedure was first introduced in 1998.

Such materials can often be identified in the general note or annotations on the Act in *Current Law Statutes*.

6.5.3   Can I do it online?

Pepper v Hart research is one area of legal research where undoubtedly using the printed materials is considerably more convenient than using the material on screen. For the novice researcher in this area, using the printed materials also tends to give much greater confidence that nothing has been missed. However if you want to do it online, you can. For Acts passed from 1998 to 2006 you could do it online but only with significant added difficulty. For most Acts passed before 1998 you must use printed material.

All of the materials listed at **6.5.2** are only available online (free of charge on the Parliament website <http://www.parliament.uk>) in complete form from session 2006–2007 onwards, i.e. in relation to Acts passed from 2007 onwards. This was the first session in which all the Bills and their amendments were put up and retained on the website. Although *Pepper v Hart* research can be done without the benefit of having the Bills, it is even more time-consuming (see **6.5.5** and **6.5.7**). If you did need or want to research an Act before 2007 online, the availability of the *official* version of the debates on the Parliament website is as follows: Commons *Hansard* from 1988–1989, Lords *Hansard* from 1995–1996, and *Standing Committee Debates* from 1997–1998. The start date of the last category thus in effect limits this resource to research on Acts passed after 1997— research omitting the Commons committee stage would be dangerously incomplete. There is also now a separate '*Historic Hansard*' database available on the Parliament website. It does cover the main *Hansard* back to 1801, but again not the *Standing Committee Debates*. This database has two further significant drawbacks. The first is that in its current state of development it is far from easy to use for this type of research. Secondly, the text is merely digital and does not take the form of PDFs of the printed volumes, so would not be appropriate to produce for use in court (see **6.5.10**).

6.5.4   Where can I get the necessary hard-copy materials?

In London, Lincoln's Inn Library (which is open to barristers of any Inn) has a complete set of all the Parliamentary materials, except that its run of *Standing Committee Debates* only starts with session 1983–1984; they can advise on the best place to go if earlier ones are needed. All the other Inn libraries do have the main Commons and Lords *Hansard*, and Inner and Middle Temple libraries have some of the Bills, but it will usually be necessary to go to Lincoln's Inn to complete the research, if you do not go there in the first place.

Outside London, only the largest central public reference libraries and official publications collections in university libraries are likely to hold the necessary materials. Again, Lincoln's Inn Library can advise.

6.5.5 How long does it take?

Not all pupil supervisors may have had to do this for themselves. They may have unrealistic expectations as to how long it might take. If, as is typical, you only need to research a single section in a single Act, then the main factor is the size of the Act, since that dictates the volume of debates that have to be trawled. As a very rough guide: for a very short Act with only, say, half a dozen sections, an hour may be enough; for a very large Act, such as the Planning or Housing or Insolvency Acts, you should allow at least half a day. But other complications can arise: you may need to search more than one section, or there may be related provisions in successive Acts; also bear in mind that if the Act is before 1984 and you are planning to use Lincoln's Inn Library, you may well have to go off to another unfamiliar library for the *Standing Committee Debates*.

6.5.6 How much do I need to know about Parliamentary procedure?

There are numerous complications and exceptions, some rare, others less so, but you need to know at least the basic pattern of Parliamentary stages for a typical government Bill. A Bill may start in either House. If the Bill starts in the Lords (it will have 'HL' after its title in the prints for both Houses), the following applies *mutatis mutandis*:

- Commons first reading: purely formal, no debate;
- Commons second reading: general debate on the principle of the Bill, usually on a single day—no amendments at this stage;
- Commons committee stage: detailed clause-by-clause consideration, usually off the floor of the House in a Standing Committee (from 2006–2007 a 'Public Bill Committee'), over several days;
- Commons report stage: also known as the 'consideration stage'—further amendments, often more than one day;
- Commons third reading: usually purely formal with no debate—even if there is a debate, no further amendments would be made;
- Lords first reading: as for the Commons;
- Lords second reading: as for the Commons;
- Lords committee stage: not taken by a 'committee' as such, but by the whole House, usually on the floor of the House, or sometimes elsewhere physically in another room (a 'Grand Committee')—otherwise as for Commons;
- Lords report stage: as for the Commons;
- Lords third reading: unlike the Commons, a substantive stage with further amendments, but usually only one day;
- Commons consideration of Lords amendments: usually a brief stage when the Commons have to approve any amendments made by the Lords—usually last stage, but if disagreement with the Lords, then:
- 'Ping-pong': Lords will usually withdraw offending amendment.

6.5.7 What is the best way to get started?

Is it a consolidation Act?

Before starting, check whether your Act is a consolidation Act: such an Act will have as its long title at its head, for example, 'An Act to consolidate the Badgers Act 1973, the

Badgers Act 1991 and the Badgers (Further Protection) Act 1991', or 'An Act to consolidate the enactments relating to company insolvency . . . '. Such Acts, designed to tidy up the statute book, do not change the law and go through a special Parliamentary procedure, during which there are no further debates on their substantive provisions. You will need to trace the derivation of your section back to the Act in which it originally appeared, and then direct your researches to the debates on that Act.

Has the provision been inserted by a later Act?

If you have been using a version of the Act that presents the text in amended form, e.g. *Halsbury's Statutes*, check that the relevant provision has not been inserted by a later Act—if so, it will appear in square brackets or have a capital-lettered section number, e.g. 17A. Look then at the notes to see which Act inserted it, and research that.

Look at the Bills

The next step is to look at all the prints of the Bill—usually five in all. Note the clause number for the provision ('sections' in Acts are 'clauses' in Bills) in each print and the stage to which it relates—it may not start out as the same number as the section in the Act, and may change as the Bill is amended. Knowing the clause number at each stage makes it easier to find any debate on the provision when leafing through *Hansard* for that stage. At the same time, check whether there are any material differences in the text of the provision in the successive versions of the Bill as compared to the Act. If there is a change, you will know there must have been an amendment, so there must have been debate. But if the text is identical to the Act throughout, that does not mean there was no debate—there may have been debate on an *unsuccessful* amendment, and sometimes what a Minister says in moving the rejection of an amendment is more conclusive than what is said in proposing an amendment that is carried.

6.5.8   Are there any tips for finding my way around *Hansard*?

Running order

The sessional indexes to *Hansard* will give all the references to the debates. Even if you just have the dates of each stage, e.g. from *House of Commons Sessional Digest*, the debates for each stage can readily be found. The *Standing Committee Debates* are arranged by Bill in the first place. The difficulty, particularly when a stage lasts several days, is finding when your clause was reached, especially if, as often can happen, the clauses are not taken simply in sequential order. In the Commons, look at the very start of the debate at the stage in question; there is usually a motion on the order of consideration of clauses, which gives the running order. The official bound volumes of *Standing Committee* debates (cream-coloured volumes) have a clause index. In the Lords, the Bills come with 'marshalled lists of amendments', which are reprinted each day of the stage; from this you can see the running order and on which day your clause was reached, as well as seeing, before you get to *Hansard*, whether any amendments were indeed tabled.

Note that, other than at the second readings in each House, debates are entirely generated by amendments (or at committee stage a motion that a clause be omitted): if no amendments to the clause in question are tabled then there is no debate on it. Note also that entirely fresh clauses may be inserted as amendments at any stage, right up to the Lords' third reading.

If from looking at the Bills an amendment is known to have been made

If when looking at the successive prints you found the Bill had been significantly amended at a particular stage, look first at the debates for that stage—all may become clear. However, you may still need to look at all the earlier and later stages, too. Even if

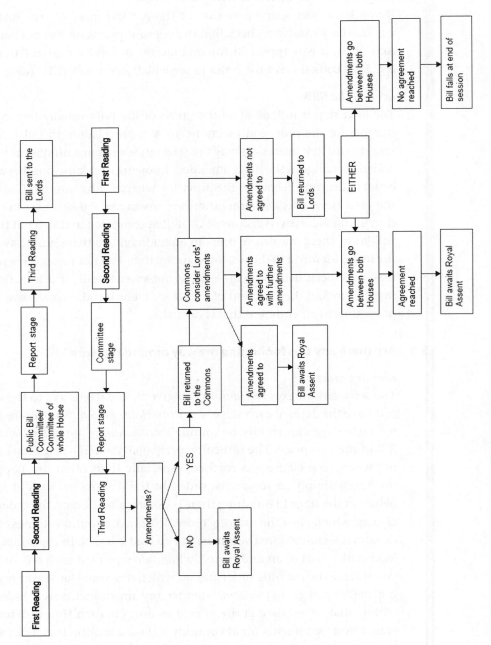

Figure 6.1   Example of a Bill originating in the Commons.

the provision is in its final form at that stage, there might have been debate on an earlier unsuccessful amendment, or there may be a later unsuccessful attempt to overturn the amendment, generating debate.

Ministerial statements

Remember that you are looking for *Ministerial* statements (the second criterion in *Pepper v Hart*). If you are uncertain whether the person speaking is a Minister, look back until you find when the person first spoke in the debate—at that point, *Hansard* will identify the speaker as a Minister (e.g. the 'Secretary of State' or the 'Under-Secretary of State'). There is also a list of Ministers at the front of each bound volume of *Hansard*. In the case of second reading debates, look first at the start when the Minister introduces the Bill, and then at the very end when the Minister (often a different Minister) winds up the debate. You only need to look at the debates in between if you need to elucidate something the Minister says in the winding-up speech.

6.5.9   If I cannot find any debates on the section, am I going wrong?

Provided you are satisfied that you found the debates at each stage and have examined them systematically, the answer is almost certainly no. At the committee stage, each clause has to be agreed, even if there are no amendments and so no debate. So you should at least find one line when the clause in question was approved (e.g. 'Ordered that Clause 25 stand part of the Bill' in the Commons; simply 'Clause 25 agreed to' in the Lords). At the other stages, other than second reading, if there were no amendments tabled to the clause, there will be no debate. It is very common, especially in large Acts, for provisions to be enacted with no debate whatsoever. You should also realise that even if debate is found, it may well be of no assistance to you, still less to the court. Cases where what has been found in *Hansard* has been decisive to the outcome, are rarer still.

6.5.10   If I find any relevant material, are there any formalities for putting it before the court?

In criminal cases, there is provision for this in the *Consolidated Criminal Practice Direction* (<http://www.justice.gov.uk/courts/procedure-rules/criminal/pd_consolidated> and as an appendix to *Blackstone's Criminal Practice*)—at para II.20 for the Court of Appeal and para IV.37 for the Crown Court. This stipulates the number of copies, on whom and by when to be served, and so on. It also mentions that copies must be from the 'Official Report', i.e. *Hansard* itself, though rarely could it be otherwise. It does not mention that the copies should be from the official *bound* volumes as issued by the Stationery Office, rather than from the daily or weekly parts. The bound volumes contain revisions (editorial rather than substantive) and there are adjustments to the column numbering.

In civil cases, there is no longer equivalent express provision in the practice directions accompanying the Civil Procedure Rules (CPR). The editors of *Blackstone's Civil Practice* (2014 edn, para 74.52) merely suggest that reasonable advance notice must be given to the other parties and the court. In the Court of Appeal, the extracts will need to be included in the bundle of authorities in accordance with PD 52, para 15.11.

7

Reading and interpreting a case

7.1 Introduction

This chapter is about case law. Its chief purpose is to give guidance to the reader on how to read a case in order to identify, extract, and where necessary apply its *ratio decidendi*. All those training for the Bar have in theory read many cases at the academic stage, and so have learned to do this. But you might not ever have given much analytical thought to the process of reading a case, or to identifying exactly what the *ratio* of it is. Also, anecdotal evidence suggests that there are some students who have got by to a very large extent using case books, which contain only digests of cases, or simply by reading the headnote of a case, which contains a short statement of what the reporter considers to be its *ratio*, but which may or may not be accurate, particularly after the case has been interpreted by a court in a later case.

Yet a barrister who is arguing a point of law before a judge, or seeking to persuade the judge to distinguish or to apply a case, needs to be able to analyse case law more deeply than that. Only a detailed study of a case and exactly what the judge(s) said in that case will enable you to identify and express clearly the arguments based on that case that you will put forward on behalf of your client. The *ratio* of a case is often found only through a very careful study not just of what the judge said, but of what he or she must be taken to have meant in the light of previous decisions, and the particular facts of the case.

So, with apologies to those who are already well versed in the art of case reading, let us take it through in stages.

7.2 Judicial precedent

It is not possible to think about finding the *ratio* of a case, or especially applying or distinguishing it, without being aware of the doctrine of judicial precedent. This is another matter that almost everyone picks up at the academic stage, but a quick reminder will do no harm.

7.2.1 The doctrine

The doctrine of judicial precedent is often stated in a Latin principle: *stare decisis*—to stand by what has already been decided. This means that once a court has decided a point of law, other courts are bound to follow it, unless they have the power to alter it by overruling, or unless they are permitted to reach a different conclusion (more on this later). So a decided case becomes a precedent, and that precedent is almost certainly binding on any court that is equal or lower in the hierarchy. A judge cannot make a correct decision on a point of law without first examining case law in order to determine whether there is a precedent which is binding on him or her. This doctrine is self-imposed by the courts; it has never been legislated.

7.2.2 The hierarchy

7.2.2.1 The European Court of Justice

A decision of the European Court of Justice on the interpretation of EU legislation, and the validity and interpretation of EU regulations, is binding on all English courts.

7.2.2.2 The House of Lords and the Supreme Court

A decision of the House of Lords was binding on all lower courts, and it was not bound by the decision of any lower court. But the House of Lords was not bound by its own previous decisions. It did not, however, overrule its previous decisions as a matter of course; it only did so rarely and after very careful consideration. The Supreme Court, which took over from the House of Lords in September 2009, has effectively stepped into the House of Lords' shoes. Although the Supreme Court has not yet pronounced on this question, it is safe to assume that it will apply exactly the same principles as the House of Lords, and regard itself as free to reverse its own decisions and those of the House of Lords where appropriate. This rule ensures that mistakes can be rectified, and that the common law can keep pace with the needs of society, without the need for legislation.

7.2.2.3 The Court of Appeal

The Court of Appeal is bound by any decision of the House of Lords or the Supreme Court, unless it can distinguish it, or unless it was reached *per incuriam* (by carelessness or mistake, for example by failing to take account of a relevant precedent). However, in an interesting development, the Court of Appeal decided in *R v James; R v Karimi* [2006] 1 All ER 759 that it should regard itself as bound by a decision of the Privy Council rather than a conflicting decision of the House of Lords, because the composition of the Privy Council had been nine law lords, who were clearly intending to overrule their own previous decision in the House of Lords.

Whether the Court of Appeal is bound by its own decisions is less clear. It decided in *Young v Bristol Aeroplane Co Ltd* [1944] KB 718 that it will normally be so bound except in three circumstances:

(a) the previous decision was reached *per incuriam*;

(b) there are previous decisions which conflict with each other (this does happen, although in theory it should not); and

(c) its previous decision has been overruled expressly or implicitly by the House of Lords (or now, the Supreme Court).

The Court of Appeal also allowed an additional, very narrow exception to the rule in the recent case of *Actavis UK Ltd v Merck & Co Inc* [2009] 1 All ER 196. The exception relates to European patent law. However it opens the door to a possible wider exception, namely that the Court of Appeal should not consider itself bound by a previous decision of its own which conflicts with European law.

Also, the Court of Appeal retains a discretion in criminal cases to refuse to regard a previous decision as binding, which it will exercise occasionally.

7.2.2.4   The High Court

A High Court judge is bound by the Court of Appeal, the House of Lords, and the Supreme Court. If faced by conflicting decisions, he or she must follow that of the higher court or, if they are of equal status, the later in time. A decision of a High Court judge at first instance is binding on all lower courts, but not strictly on another High Court judge. It is therefore possible and not uncommon to get conflicting decisions at first instance. However, the decision of another High Court judge is strongly persuasive, and a judge will not readily decline to follow it.

7.2.2.5   The Upper Tribunal

Since April 2009 all the various tribunals have been reconstituted into a single organisation, which broadly consists of first-tier tribunals and the Upper Tribunal. In *R (Cart) v Upper Tribunal* [2010] STC 493 it was held that the Upper Tribunal is in effect the alter ego of the High Court. What this must mean is that a decision of the Upper Tribunal has the same status as a decision of the High Court at first instance, and so the rule in **7.2.2.4** must apply.

7.2.2.6   Lower courts

The decisions of all judges in higher courts are binding on all lower courts, including a circuit judge sitting in the Crown Court or the county court, magistrates' courts, and first-tier tribunals.

7.2.3   When is a case binding?

A case is only binding to the extent that it decides a point of law. No court is bound by any other court's decision on a pure question of fact. The extent to which a case is binding depends on identifying and extracting its *ratio decidendi* (or *ratio* for short). There is more on this in **7.3**. Any part of a court's reasoning that is not part of the *ratio* is known as an *obiter dictum*—something said 'by the way'. *Obiter dicta* are not binding, though they may be persuasive.

7.2.4   Overruling and reversing

When a decision of a lower court is altered by a decision of a higher court on appeal in the same case, then that decision is said to have been reversed.

When a decision of a lower court is altered by a higher court in another case, so that it is no longer binding precedent, then it is said to have been overruled.

When a decision is overruled, the effect is retrospective. That is to say, the previous decision is taken never to have been the law, rather than to have been the law up to this point. This makes it possible for the higher court to reach the opposite conclusion on the facts of the case before it. However, the decision in the overruled case stands.

7.2.5   Distinguishing

The chief way in which a court avoids being bound by a precedent is by distinguishing it. If a case contains a decision on a point of law, the court will probably have first decided a principle and then made a decision on the facts of the case by applying that principle. The decision on the principle is undoubtedly binding law, assuming the case has then been decided by applying it. But if in the end the court decided the case without applying that principle, then what the court had to say remains *obiter*. A previous decision is, however, only binding if it is indistinguishable on the facts from a later case. If the two cases have some significant factual differences, the judge in the later case may be able to distinguish the former case. He or she is then saying that the previous case, although it contains a binding point of law, does not bind him or her on the facts of this case, and so he or she is free to establish a new precedent.

For example, in a previous case a court was faced with the question 'is the defendant liable to the claimant in these circumstances?' It held that facts A, B, and C existed, and concluded that when facts A, B, and C exist, the answer will as a matter of law be 'Yes'. In the present case, if the judge, faced with the same question, finds that facts A, B, and C exist, he or she will be bound. But if he can find that facts A and B exist, but not C, he will not be bound. He or she may then decide that the answer is 'No'. He or she will also not be bound if he or she decides that facts A, B, C, and D exist, D being a fact that did not exist in the previous case, and a fact which makes a difference.

Alternatively, the judge may find that facts A, B, and C exist, but that, on closer examination, there are two kinds of fact B: B1 and B2. In the previous case, facts A, B1, and C existed, but in this case, facts A, B2, and C exist. If B1 and B2 are significantly different, then again he or she is not bound and may decide that the answer is 'No'.

7.2.6 Persuasive precedents

A precedent may not be binding, but that does not mean it can be ignored. Many non-binding precedents are nevertheless highly persuasive. A non-binding decision by the House of Lords or the Supreme Court on a point of law is, for example, so strongly persuasive that it will be very difficult indeed to persuade the Court of Appeal, let alone a judge, to depart from it. Courts will take into account *obiter dicta*, decisions of lower courts, decisions of Commonwealth courts, dissenting judgments, and give them such weight as they see fit. The Court of Appeal will not infrequently be persuaded to a decision by the *obiter dicta* of a lower judge.

7.3 The *ratio* of a case

7.3.1 What is the *ratio* of a case?

There are differing views on what the *ratio* of a case actually means. The strict view is that the *ratio* of the case is to be found only in any decision and reasoning on a pure point of law, and no case is binding to the extent that it decides a question of fact. However, very few cases turn entirely on a question of law, just as very few turn entirely on a question of fact. The great majority involve points of mixed law and fact, and it is very difficult to persuade a judge to decide a case differently to a reported case when it is almost identical on the facts, even if there is not a fully binding point of law.

So it is submitted that for practical purposes it is best to consider the *ratio* of a case to be the reasoning that has led to the conclusion. If the Court of Appeal, for example, has interpreted a piece of legislation in a certain way, and has applied this interpretation to the facts of the case before it to reach a conclusion on those facts, then that interpretation is part of the *ratio* and is binding on a lower court in a subsequent case. But if the Court of Appeal has then managed to decide the case without relying on its interpretation, so that it would have reached the same conclusion even without that interpretation, then that interpretation is not part of its *ratio* and is not binding on any lower court.

7.3.2   Discovering the *ratio* of a case

It is often quite difficult to discover the *ratio* of a case. It may need close examination and analysis. This is because the judge rarely sets the *ratio* out expressly. He or she is concerned with deciding the case before the court and giving reasons. He or she has little thought to helping judges in subsequent cases. Even if he or she does attempt to state it, the correct view is that the *ratio* of a case is what a later court decides it to be, not what the judge who decided the case perceived it to be. The *ratio* has to be dug out from all the dicta and reasoning contained in the judge's judgment. Some of what he or she says will be *ratio*, some will be *obiter*.

Let us take another example. A court in a previous case was again faced with the question 'is the defendant liable to the claimant in these circumstances?' It found that facts A, B, C, D, and E existed, and decided that in all the circumstances the answer was 'Yes'. It may be tempting to assume that all of facts A, B, C, D, and E must be present before the answer can as a matter of law be 'Yes'. But it might be that, on closer analysis of the judge's reasons, only facts A, B, and C were required as a matter of law to reach the eventual conclusion, and facts D and E were no more than persuasive on the particular facts of the case. Then what the judge had to say about facts D and E is *obiter*, and the *ratio* is only that facts A, B, and C must be present before the answer will be 'Yes'. Alternatively, the judge might have said that although facts A, B, C, D, and E existed, he or she did not think fact D was essential. It would be tempting then to assume that only facts A, B, C, and E must be present before the answer can as a matter of law be 'Yes'. But a later court, on closer analysis, might conclude that the judge did in fact give more weight to fact D than he said he did, and that the *ratio* is really that all five facts must be present before the answer is 'Yes'.

It can therefore often be important, when reading a case, to separate those facts which truly form the *ratio* of the decision, because the decision would not have been the same without them, from those which were merely persuasive, and pointed the judge in the direction of the decision, but in the end have not resulted in that decision.

7.3.3   Altering the *ratio* of a case

Sometimes the *ratio* of a case may be altered by another case. For example, a judge decides that facts A, B, C, and D are present and that the answer is therefore 'Yes'. In another case, a judge finds that facts A, B, and C are present, but not D. Nevertheless, he or she does not distinguish the first case, but decides that the answer is still 'Yes'. The law is now that only facts A, B, and C need be present before the answer will be 'Yes'.

It is not unusual for the Court of Appeal to be faced with previous decisions of lower courts, or maybe even of its own, which at first sight seem to be in conflict with each other. What it will often then do is to reconcile the conflicting decisions, by discovering a common principle which was not clearly enunciated by the previous judges, and by applying it so as to produce a valid distinction which justifies all the previous decisions and the differences between them. The *ratio* of all previous decisions must now be read in the light of the Court of Appeal's 'explanation'.

7.3.4   The *ratio* when there is more than one judgment

If a case is decided in the Court of Appeal, the House of Lords, or the Supreme Court, there may well be more than one judgment. If every member of the court says the same thing in different words, then the *ratio* of the case is clear. But what if they do not?

First, if the court does not reach a unanimous conclusion, then the *ratio* will only be found in the judgments of those in the majority. If the minority judge(s) agree with the reasoning on any issue with the majority, what they have to say is still *obiter*, because it is not what has led them to their individual conclusion.

If two or more judges reach the same conclusion but for different reasons, then only the reasoning of the majority can form the *ratio* of the case. If all three members of the Court of Appeal come to the same conclusion, but two of them reach that conclusion for reason A, and the other for reason B, then the *ratio* is based on reason A. If there are three different reasons, then the case has limited value as a precedent, because there is no binding *ratio*. If the House of Lords decides a case by a majority of three to two, but only two of the majority decide as they do for the same reasons, then again there is no clear *ratio* in the case. There must be a majority of the whole court on the *ratio* before there is a binding precedent.

It is not uncommon for judges in the Court of Appeal and the Supreme Court to give a single judgment of the whole court. There is then only a single *ratio* and this is as good as three or five separate judgments, each giving the same reasons. But it is also not uncommon for judges in the Court of Appeal, the House of Lords, and the Supreme Court to give separate judgments, some of which consist only of the words 'I agree'. This strictly means that the judge agrees only with the conclusions of his colleagues, not necessarily with their reasons. The *ratio* may then be hard to determine, or there may be none. If, however, he or she says 'I agree with Bloggs LJ for the reasons he gives', then there is no problem.

Sometimes a judge says 'I agree and would just like to add . . .'. He or she then addresses certain issues only. His or her reasoning on those issues may help to determine the *ratio*, but on issues which he does not address, his judgment is of no help.

7.4 Some test questions

Try these questions to see if you are able to apply the principles explained in the previous paragraphs. The answers and their explanations are given at the end of this chapter.

7.4.1 Question 1

A High Court judge is deciding a case which involves a point of law on which there is no binding authority. Which of the following statements is correct?

[A] He or she should always follow a decision of a High Court judge rather than an *obiter dictum* of the Court of Appeal.

[B] He or she should follow the decision of a fellow High Court judge if he or she can find no good reason to differ.

[C] If there are conflicting Court of Appeal decisions he may choose which he prefers.

[D] He should follow an *obiter dictum* of the Supreme Court rather than an *obiter dictum* of the Court of Appeal.

7.4.2 Question 2

A High Court judge is deciding a case involving a point of law which has previously been dealt with in a Court of Appeal decision. In which of the following circumstances will he or she be bound by that decision?

[A] The Court of Appeal decision is just about distinguishable.

[B] The Court of Appeal decision was later reversed by the House of Lords.

[C] The Court of Appeal decision was later changed by an Act of Parliament.

[D] The Court of Appeal decision was regarded as highly dubious by the House of Lords in a later case.

7.4.3   Question 3

You are advising a client on a matter involving a point of law and you come across several Court of Appeal cases which include persuasive *obiter dicta* in favour of your client's position, but also one High Court case which seems to decide the point against your client. You should:

[A] See if you can distinguish the High Court case making use of the Court of Appeal dicta.

[B] Ignore the High Court case and advise on the basis of the Court of Appeal cases.

[C] Advise your client that his case is unarguable.

[D] Advise your client that in the light of the Court of Appeal dicta his case is strong.

7.4.4   Question 4

A judge is deciding a case on a point of law which has previously been considered by the Court of Appeal and the House of Lords in different cases. The Court of Appeal decided that the defendant was liable to the claimant because facts A, B, and C existed. The House of Lords decided that the defendant was liable because facts A, B, and D existed and doubted that fact C was relevant. In which of the following circumstances is the judge NOT bound by previous precedent?

[A] He or she finds facts A, B, C, and D exist.

[B] He or she finds facts A, B, and C exist, but not D.

[C] He or she finds facts A, C, and D exist, but not B.

[D] He or she finds facts A, B, and D exist, but not C.

7.4.5   Question 5

In 2014, a circuit judge is deciding a case on a point of law which has previously been considered as follows:

(1) In 2009, the Court of Appeal decided in favour of the claimant because facts A and B existed.

(2) In 2010, a High Court judge decided in favour of the defendant because facts A, B, and C existed.

(3) In 2011, a High Court judge decided in favour of the claimant because facts A, B, C, and D existed.

(4) In 2012, the Court of Appeal decided in favour of the claimant because facts A, B, and C existed.

(5) In 2013, a High Court judge decided in favour of the defendant because facts A, B, C, D, and E existed.

In which of the following circumstances should the judge find in favour of the defendant?

[A] He finds facts A and B exist.

[B] He finds facts A, B, and C exist.

[C] He finds facts A, B, C, and D exist.

[D] He finds facts A, B, C, and E exist.

7.4.6   Question 6

In a case involving the interpretation of the Unfair Liability Act 2013, the Supreme Court ruled in favour of the defendant. The Judges were unanimous that the claimant could only succeed if he could show that for the purposes of the Act a warehouse was a 'workshop' but a forklift truck was *not* a 'vehicle' and a portacabin was *not* a 'building'. The Judges decided as follows:

Lord Able SCJ: a warehouse is a workshop, a forklift truck is a vehicle, a portacabin is not a building.

Lord Boot SCJ: a warehouse is not a workshop, a forklift truck is a vehicle, a portacabin is not a building.

Lord Cobbler SCJ: a warehouse is a workshop, a forklift truck is a not a vehicle, a portacabin is a building.

Lord Dupe SCJ: agreed with Lord Cobbler SCJ for the same reasons.

Lord Egg SCJ: agreed with Lords Able and Boot SCJJ 'for the reasons they give'.

Which of the following interpretations of the Unfair Liability Act has been decided as a matter of law?

[A] A warehouse is a workshop.

[B] A forklift truck is a vehicle.

[C] A portacabin is not a building.

[D] All of these.

7.5   Analysing cases

We are now going to take two short cases and analyse them, looking at the reasoning of the judges, working out what the *ratio* of each case is, and understanding the distinction between them. As it happens, they are tax cases, but do not be put off by that. There are no points of specialist tax law involved. In fact, they both turn on a judicial examination of the concept of 'a dwelling house' and what those words mean in a certain context. The cases are *Batey (Inspector of Taxes) v Wakefield* [1982] 1 All ER 61 and *Lewis (Inspector of Taxes) v Lady Rook* [1992] 1 WLR 662, and both are in the Court of Appeal. Only the judgments are printed; the facts and the relevant law are all included in the judgments, so you need no more. After each case there appears a commentary. Because of the need to refer in the commentaries to particular sections of the judgment, the format of the judgment has been altered, and they are given paragraph numbers in the modern neutral citation style. In the original reports, of course, you would have to refer to passages by page numbers and marginal letters.

7.6   *Batey v Wakefield* [1982] 1 All ER 61

Batey v Wakefield was heard in the Court of Appeal on 22 June 1981. Judgment was delivered on the same day.

7.6.1   The judgments

FOX LJ:

[1] This is an appeal from a decision of Browne-Wilkinson J relating to capital gains tax. Mr Wakefield, the taxpayer, purchased about one-and-a-half acres of land in 1957 near Marlborough in Wiltshire. At that time there were various buildings on the land; they consisted of, or included, brick loose boxes, a forage store, and a garage with a room above. Those buildings were sold off by the taxpayer not long after he acquired the land. As a result of those and further sales, the amount of land which was owned by the taxpayer from 1966 to 1974 was about 1.1 acres.

[2] In about 1959, the taxpayer built a dwelling house called 'Paddocks' on the land; that dwelling house consisted of about eight rooms. The house was built for occupation by the taxpayer and his family. Because of the demands of his work, the taxpayer was not originally able to live at Paddocks all the time; during the week he lived in a flat in London with his wife and daughter. Paddocks was therefore left unattended, except at weekends when the taxpayer and his family lived there.

[3] There were a number of burglaries in the neighbourhood, and Paddocks itself was burgled once. So the taxpayer decided that since he and his family were not living in the house during the week, he must have a caretaker at Paddocks to look after it. He therefore employed a caretaker-gardener, together with his wife as a housekeeper.

[4] For them, in 1966, he built on part of the 1.1 acres a chalet-bungalow called Paddocks Lodge, which had one main bedroom; precisely what the other accommodation was, I am not certain. Paddocks Lodge had a detached garage of its own, and access from a different road from that giving access to Paddocks itself. It was separated from Paddocks by about the width of a tennis court and by a yew hedge which had been established before the building of Paddocks Lodge. Paddocks Lodge was occupied free of rent and rates by the caretaker-gardener and his wife and son, in return for work done at Paddocks. The General Commissioners found that the occupation of Paddocks Lodge was intended to enable the caretaker and his wife to perform the duties of their employment with the taxpayer.

[5] By 1974 it was no longer necessary for the taxpayer to live in London, so he took up full-time residence at Paddocks. The need for the caretaker therefore no longer existed.

[6] In about March of 1974, the taxpayer sold Paddocks Lodge with about 0.2 of an acre of land, for some £18,000, which gave rise to a capital gain of some £11,895. Since the sale of Paddocks Lodge the taxpayer and his family have continued to live in Paddocks. The properties had always been separately rated.

[7] For completeness, perhaps I should mention that in 1967 the taxpayer made an election under the statute to treat Paddocks as his main residence. The Crown claims capital gains tax on the gain of £11,895 on the sale of Paddocks Lodge.

[8] I come now to the statutory provisions. Section 29(1) and (2) of the Finance Act 1965, which is the material statute for the purposes of this transaction, provides as follows:

'(1) This section applies to a gain accruing to an individual so far as attributable to the disposal of, or of an interest in—(a) a dwelling-house or part of a dwelling-house which is, or has at any time in his period of ownership been, his only or main residence, or (b) land which he has for his own occupation and enjoyment with that residence as its garden or grounds up to an area (inclusive of the site of the dwelling house) of one acre or such larger area as the Commissioners concerned may in any particular case determine, on being satisfied that, regard being had to the size and character of the dwelling-house, the larger area is required for the reasonable enjoyment of it (or of the part in question) as a residence.'

'The gain shall not be a chargeable gain if the dwelling-house or part of a dwelling-house has been the individual's only or main residence throughout the period of ownership, or throughout the period of ownership except for all or any part of the last twelve months of that period.'

[9] Then I should mention sub-s (5), which deals with the case of a dwelling house part of which is used for the purposes of trade; sub-s (8), which deals with the position of a husband and wife, and provides that where they are living together there can only be one residence for both; sub-s (12) deals with apportionments of consideration where a person disposes of a dwelling house, only part of which is his only or main residence. Subsection (10) deals with what were referred to as 'granny flats'; it does not determine the question which is in issue in the present case.

[10] The decision of the commissioners, so far as material, was as follows:

'We . . . found that a dwelling house could consist of more than one building on the same site not being contiguous buildings. "Paddocks Lodge" was occupied in conjunction with "Paddocks" having been built specifically for staff purposes. It could equally have been occupied by the children or aged parents of the family. We were satisfied that 1.1 acres was a reasonable area of land for a dwelling house of the character of "Paddocks". We were satisfied that the taxpayer's intention was to make additional accommodation available for his staff or the better enjoyment of his own dwelling house. We found that by building "Paddocks Lodge" for the caretaker/gardener and housekeeper the taxpayer was doing no more than increasing his reasonable enjoyment of his residence. We found that the disposal of "Paddocks Lodge" was a disposal of part of [the taxpayer's] dwelling house which had been his only or main residence throughout the period of ownership and that the gain which he made on the sale of "Paddocks Lodge" was therefore exempt from capital gains tax . . . '

[11] The Crown appealed from that decision. Browne-Wilkinson J upheld the decision of the commissioners and dismissed the appeal.

[12] In effect, the argument of the Crown is this, that one must ascertain whether what has been disposed of is part of a dwelling house. The lodge is quite a separate physical dwelling, actually used as a separate dwelling house by a separate family; it cannot, therefore, be part of another dwelling house, namely Paddocks. It is said that an independent dwelling house used by a separate household, like Paddocks Lodge, cannot be part of another dwelling house; and it is said, therefore, that the decision of the commissioners must be bad on the face of it.

[13] I do not for myself feel able to accept that. In approaching these matters, there are two propositions which seem to me to be correct. First, it seems to me that in the ordinary use of English, a dwelling house, or a residence, can comprise several dwellings which are not physically joined at all. For example, one would normally regard a

dwelling house as including a separate garage; similarly it would, I think, include a separate building, such as a studio, which was built and used for the owner's enjoyment. Indeed, I think a living room could be in one building and bedrooms in another; that might be inconvenient, but I see no reason why they should not together constitute a single dwelling house for the purposes of this statute.

[14] Secondly, if a dwelling house contained a staff flat which is self-contained and with, for example, its own access, I see no reason why that cannot accurately be called part of the larger dwelling house. It seems to me that that is exactly what it is; it is physically part of the dwelling house and its user is for the purpose of serving the dwelling house as a residence.

[15] What, then, is the position of a building which is itself a house but which is physically separate from the dwelling house of which it is said to form a part? That is Paddocks Lodge in the present case. The fact that it is physically separate from what I might call the main dwelling house, Paddocks, seems to me to be irrelevant. As I have indicated, separate buildings can together form the residence; similarly, a self-contained residence may form part of a dwelling house. I can see no logical reason why a house which is physically quite separate should not form part of another residence or dwelling house. For example, a flat over a coach house in a stable yard which is occupied by servants is, I think, none the less part of the main dwelling house even though it is physically separate from it and I think that, as a matter of the ordinary use of English, it would be so described as being part of the main dwelling house.

[16] I do not think that one can approach the matter in a piecemeal way; a dwelling house can consist of more than one building. I agree with the judge that what one is looking for is the entity which in fact constitutes the residence of the taxpayer. I can see no difference in principle between a coachman's flat in the stable yard used for the purpose of serving the main house and a bungalow such as Paddocks Lodge, built on the comparatively small area of land held with Paddocks for the purpose of serving Paddocks. It is, it seems to me, a question of degree in each case. The question is what are the true constituents of the residence which is in question?

[17] The judge, in his judgment, said this ([1980] STC 572 at 577):

'On the commissioners' findings, the lodge was built and occupied to provide services and caretaking facilities for the benefit of the main house. The lodge was occupied by the taxpayer through his employee, who was employed for the purpose of promoting the taxpayer's reasonable enjoyment of his own residence. In those circumstances, bearing in mind the fact that the buildings are very closely adjacent, it seems to me proper to find that the lodge was part of the residence of the taxpayer . . . '

I agree with that. What has to be determined is the identity of the dwelling house. The fact that it comprised separate accommodation in which staff, or children, or guests may be accommodated does not, in my view, determine conclusively that such accommodation is not part of the dwelling house. It may be a factor, but it is no more. It is, as I have indicated, a matter of degree in every case whether a separate building does or does not in truth form part of the residence in question. That question is one for the commissioners to determine. The court can only allow an appeal from the commissioners if their decision is shown to be wrong in point of law. I see no reason for saying that the commissioners misdirected themselves in law in the present case, and I am quite unable to say that no reasonable tribunal, properly directed, could have reached the conclusion which they did.

[18] Therefore, despite the very helpful and able argument of counsel for the Crown, I do not feel able to interfere with the determination of the commissioners. I think the judge reached the right conclusion, and I would dismiss the appeal.

OLIVER LJ:

[19] I entirely agree and do not feel that I can usefully add anything.

STEPHENSON LJ:

[20] I also agree.

7.6.2 Commentary

If we work through the judgment of Fox LJ, we can see how it is put together.

7.6.2.1 The facts

In paragraphs [1] to [7], the judge is setting out the facts. This is not of course necessarily a statement of all of the facts—they have been selected by the judge. But that is useful for two reasons: you can avoid having to read unnecessary factual material, and you know which facts the judge regards as relevant. These are likely to be the facts that have led him to his conclusion, or which were persuasive. You may in due course decide that they are part of the *ratio* of the case.

Do not, however, assume that this statement of the facts will *only* contain relevant facts, nor that you will not find relevant facts elsewhere in the judgment. Where, as here, the judge is delivering the judgment *extempore*, perfection in this respect cannot be expected of him!

7.6.2.2 The law

The judge then sets out the relevant statute law in paragraphs [8] and [9].

The law is simply contained in section 29(1) of the Finance Act 1965, and as we shall see, the case turns on the construction of this section, or more accurately, two words in this section: 'dwelling house'. The rest of it turns out to be material only insofar as it determines the undisputed outcome of the case once this point of law has been resolved.

7.6.2.3 The commissioners' decision

Then in paragraph [10] the judge sets out the decision of the commissioners by quoting from their written decision. Note that only their conclusions are set out here—this passage does not contain any reasons, or the full *ratio* of their decision. At this point the judge makes no comment on it, as he might do in some cases. He is still continuing to set out all the relevant background material before he starts to say what he thinks.

7.6.2.4 The appeal

There is then a very short paragraph [11] in which the appeal route is stated. Note that Fox LJ is the third judge to consider the case. The decision of Browne-Wilkinson J is not referred to further at this point; we discover that he reached the same conclusion as the commissioners, but not whether he did so for the same reasons. Some of his reasons appear later in paragraph [17].

7.6.2.5 The Crown's argument

In paragraph [12] Fox LJ then outlines the argument on behalf of the Crown (the Inland Revenue). The Crown seems to have adopted an all-or-nothing argument: that an independent household in a separate building can never be part of another dwelling house. It had to put its case this way, as it can only appeal on a point of law, not on a question of fact. It must therefore seek to show that the original decision was wrong in law.

7.6.2.6   The conclusion and reasons

Fox LJ then starts to set out his conclusion and reasoning. This begins at paragraph [13] and continues to the end of the judgment at paragraph [18]. Note that we are now about two-thirds of the way through the judgment, and everything said so far is simply by way of introduction. We know therefore that the decision and the *ratio* of the case will be found exclusively in the few paragraphs still to come.

The judge makes his decision clear in three short statements:

(a) The first sentence of paragraph [13]—'*I do not feel able for myself to accept that*'.

(b) The sentence '*I agree with that*' in paragraph [17]. The judge is adopting the reasoning of Browne-Wilkinson J.

(c) The final paragraph [18].

The rest of this section contains the judge's reasons, and within it you will find both the legal proposition decided by this case and its *ratio*.

This section, however, subdivides. In paragraphs [13]–[16], the judge is dealing with his conclusions and reasons on the issue of law. In paragraph [17], he is dealing with his conclusions and reasons on the facts.

7.6.2.7   The legal issue and conclusion

The question of law in this case was 'What is a dwelling house?'; or more specifically, 'Can a dwelling house consist of more than one building?' The answer was 'yes'.

This conclusion is not of course a complete definition, but a partial definition: the case decided as a matter of law that a 'dwelling house' for the purposes of the statute could consist of more than one building, even if each building was in its own right a dwelling house.

The court did not of course decide that a dwelling house *must* consist of more than one building. Nor did it decide that more than one building will *always* amount to a single dwelling house. There is a further question of fact to be decided—whether the separate buildings in any given case do or do not amount to a single dwelling house.

7.6.2.8   The *ratio*

The legal *ratio*, that is the reasoning that led to the conclusion on the point of law, is found in paragraphs [13] to [16].

There are four propositions mentioned by the judge:

(1) A dwelling house, or residence, can comprise several dwellings which are not joined:

[13] . . . First, it seems to me that in the ordinary use of English, a dwelling house, or a residence, can comprise several dwellings which are not physically joined at all. For example, one would normally regard a dwelling house as including a separate garage; similarly it would, I think, include a separate building, such as a studio, which was built and used for the owner's enjoyment. Indeed, I think a living room could be in one building and bedrooms in another; that might be inconvenient, but I see no reason why they should not together constitute a single dwelling house for the purposes of this statute.

(2) A self-contained staff flat within a single dwelling house can be part of that dwelling house:

[14] Secondly, if a dwelling house contained a staff flat which is self-contained and with, for example, its own access, I see no reason why that cannot accurately be called part of the larger dwelling house. It seems to me that that is exactly what it is; it is physically part of the dwelling house and its user is for the purpose of serving the dwelling house as a residence.

(3) There is no logical difference between that and a staff residence in a separate building:

[15] . . . I can see no logical reason why a house which is physically quite separate should not form part of another residence or dwelling house. For example, a flat over a coach house in a stable yard which is occupied by servants is, I think, none the less part of the main dwelling house even though it is physically separate from it and I think that, as a matter of the ordinary use of English, it would be so described as being part of the main dwelling house.

(4) What one must look for is the entity which in fact constitutes the residence of the taxpayer, and its true constituents:

[16] I do not think that one can approach the matter in a piecemeal way; a dwelling house can consist of more than one building. I agree with the judge that what one is looking for is the entity which in fact constitutes the residence of the taxpayer . . . The question is what are the true constituents of the residence which is in question?

Propositions (1), (2), and (3) are steps in the judge's reasoning process, and contain the reasoning that led to the conclusion that a dwelling house can in law consist of more than one building. But proposition (4) is also important. In effect here, the judge states as a matter of law the approach that must be adopted when determining the factual issue in each case. This is therefore also part of the *ratio*. The judge says the same thing again in slightly different words in paragraph [17]: '*What has to be determined is the identity of the dwelling house.*' The judge doubtless meant to say the same thing, but he changed 'residence' to 'dwelling house', which is a slip that is picked up in the later case of *Lewis v Lady Rook*.

7.6.2.9   The decision on the facts

There is no appeal to the Court of Appeal on a question of fact, only on a question of law. So the issue to be decided was *not* 'Is Paddocks Lodge part of the dwelling house?' but 'Was the decision that Paddocks Lodge was part of the dwelling house open to the commissioners?' The court can only overturn their decision if:

(a) it was wrong in law, that is because they reached it through a misunderstanding of the concept of a dwelling house; or

(b) it was wrong in law because they applied the wrong test; or

(c) it was irrational, that is because no reasonable tribunal, properly directed, could have reached the conclusion which they did.

Here, the Court upheld the decision on the facts.

7.6.2.10   The *ratio* on the facts

There can be no binding *ratio* on the facts because the Court did not decide the factual issue. However, if one can identify the facts which were persuasive to the commissioners and those which the Court believed were relevant, what the Court said about them will be sufficiently persuasive to need distinguishing in any subsequent case in which the decision is different.

Here one might well say that the following facts were persuasive:

(1) The buildings were very closely adjacent (paragraph [17])—separated by about the width of a tennis court and a yew hedge (paragraph [4]).

(2) Paddocks Lodge was occupied by an employee (paragraph [17]).

(3) The employee paid no rent (paragraph [4]).

(4) The employee was employed for the purpose of promoting the taxpayer's reasonable enjoyment of his own residence (paragraph [17]).

7.6.2.11 *Obiter dictum*

Anything that is not part of the *ratio* is strictly *obiter*, but there is a good example of an *obiter dictum* in paragraph [17], when the judge says that the fact that there is separate accommodation for staff or guests does not determine conclusively that that accommodation is not part of the dwelling house but then adds that '*it may be a factor but it is no more*'. The implication is that in other cases, the separateness of the accommodation may tend to point away from its being part of the dwelling house.

7.6.2.12 Agreement by the other judges

Oliver and Stephenson LJJ agree with Fox LJ. There is potential to argue that they agree with the conclusion but not necessarily the reasons. But in the light of the issues to be determined in this case it is highly probable that they can be taken to agree with everything Fox LJ said, and so the *ratio* of his judgment is the *ratio* of the whole Court of Appeal's decision.

7.7 *Lewis v Lady Rook* [1992] 1 WLR 662

Lewis v Lady Rook was heard in the Court of Appeal on 30 January 1992. Judgment was reserved and delivered on 19 February 1992.

7.7.1 The Judgments

BALCOMBE LJ:

[1] This is an appeal by the Crown from a decision of Mervyn Davies J [1990] STC 23 dated 5 December 1989 affirming a decision of the General Commissioners for Sevenoaks that the respondent taxpayer was entitled to relief from capital gains tax on the disposal by her of 1 Hop Cottages, Newlands, Crockham Hill, Kent, on 30 August 1979.

[2] The facts as found by the General Commissioners are set out in para 5 of the case stated as follows:

'(1) On 6th June 1968 the taxpayer purchased the property known as Newlands, Crockham Hill, Kent for £34,501. (2) Included in the purchase were two cottages known as Nos 1 and 2 Hop Cottages (formerly an oasthouse) on the south boundary of the property. (3) The total acreage of the property owned by the taxpayer on 30th August 1979 was 10.5 acres. The distance between the nearest points of No 1 Hop Cottages and Newlands is approximately 569 feet (175 metres). (4) The main house Newlands has a large hall, an imposing landing, a very large dining room, a drawing room, a playroom, a further reception room making four in all, eight bedrooms, one used as a billiard room, a kitchen, a pantry, a scullery and a silver room. (5) No 1 Hop Cottages comprised a dining room, a lounge, a kitchen, two bedrooms and a bathroom. No 2 Hop Cottages next door had similar accommodation. (6) Before the taxpayer purchased Newlands and Nos 1 and 2 Hop Cottages, No 1 Hop Cottages had been occupied by Mr and Mrs Foster. Mr Foster worked in the garden of the main house and Mrs Foster helped in the main house. When the taxpayer was on the point of completing the purchase of Newlands Mr Foster died. Mrs Foster remained at No 1 Hop Cottages after the purchase but never worked for the taxpayer. (7) Mrs

Foster paid the taxpayer a contribution of £1.12 per week which was the amount she had always paid ever since the taxpayer purchased the property. She paid this in respect of No 1 Hop Cottages and in respect of No 2 when she moved. She was 75 years of age at the time of the appeal hearing. (8) In early February 1973 Mrs Foster vacated No 1 Hop Cottages and moved into No 2 Hop Cottages. Since purchasing Newlands, the taxpayer had renovated No 2 Hop Cottages (which at the date of purchase had no bathroom and outside sanitation). In February 1974 the taxpayer's gardener moved into No 1 Hop Cottages. In February 1978 the gardener vacated No 1 Hop Cottages. (9) By contract dated 30th August 1979 the taxpayer sold No 1 Hop Cottages for £33,000. The sale proceeds helped to finance the conversion into residential accommodation of the Coach House which was immediately adjacent to the main house and which had previously been used for storing hay in the loft with two garages below. After vacating No 1 Hop Cottages the taxpayer's gardener moved in the Coach House. The taxpayer was elderly, lived alone in the main house and needed someone close at hand; hence the reason for the gardener's move. (10) The greenhouses, tool shed and compost heaps used in connection with the main house garden were situated between the main house and No 1 Hop Cottages and convenient to No 1 Hop Cottages. The greenhouses and the potting shed were located approximately half way between No 1 Hop Cottages and the main house. (11) During the taxpayer's ownership of it, No 1 Hop Cottages had never been screened from the main house so that the taxpayer could see the lights in the cottage and could flash a light if she needed help. She also had a ship's bell which she could ring and which could be heard from the cottage which she would use if she needed help. This had happened more than once. It was very convenient to come up through the garden to the house and it was not convenient by the road.'

[3] The relevant statutory provisions are to be found in ss 101 and 102 of the Capital Gains Tax Act 1979 (the 1979 Act). Section 101, so far as relevant, is in the following terms:

'(1) This section applies to a gain accruing to an individual so far as attributable to the disposal of, or of an interest in—

   (a) a dwelling-house or part of a dwelling-house which is, or has at any time in his period of ownership been, his only or main residence, or

   (b) land which he has for his own occupation and enjoyment with that residence as its garden or grounds up to the permitted area.

(2) In this section "the permitted area" means, subject to subsection (3) and (4) below, an area (inclusive of the site of the dwelling-house) of one acre.

(3) In any particular case the permitted area shall be such area, larger than one acre, as the Commissioners concerned may determine if satisfied that, regard being had to the size and character of the dwelling-house, that larger area is required for the reasonable enjoyment of it (or of the part in question) as a residence.'

Section 102, so far as relevant, provided at the material date:

'(1) No part of a gain to which section 101 above applies shall be a chargeable gain if the dwelling-house or part of a dwelling-house has been the individual's only or main residence throughout the period of ownership, or throughout the period of ownership except for all or any part of the last twelve months of that period.

(2) Where subsection (1) above does not apply, a fraction of the gain shall not be a chargeable gain, and that fraction shall be . . . '

The rest of s 102 is concerned with the calculation of the amount of the relief and that is not in issue on the present appeal.

[4] The issue is whether No 1 Hop Cottages formed part of a dwelling house which was the taxpayer's only or main residence.

[5] The General Commissioners' findings are contained in para 9 of the case stated as follows (at 26):

'We the Commissioners who heard the appeal, having considered the parties' contentions and the evidence before us, found that No 1 Hop Cottages formed part of the entity which comprised the dwelling-house of Newlands. We considered that during Mrs Foster's residence at No 1 Hop Cottages the exemption should not apply and we found that accordingly an apportionment should be made and a figure of £2,855.10 of tax paid . . . '

[6] The judge upheld the commissioners' findings, although on grounds which formed no part of the commissioners' decision. His conclusions are contained in the following passage from his judgment (at 31):

'I now look at the facts of this case with a view to deciding whether or not No 1 Hop Cottages is within the entity constituting the taxpayer's residence. There are the following considerations: (i) The cottage is about 190 yards from Newlands House. (ii) The cottage is rated separately from Newlands House. (iii) At a relevant time it was occupied by a gardener employed by the taxpayer. (iv) His work took him up the path from the cottage to the lawn and vegetable garden, the boundaries of which were less than 100 yards from the cottage: see in this connection para 10 of the case stated [at 26] as quoted above [at 27]. (v) The taxpayer, elderly and living alone, placed reliance on a presence in No 1 Hop Cottages: see the case stated [at 26] para 11 as quoted above [at 27]. Taking these considerations into account it seems to me that the entity constituting the taxpayer's residence included No 1 Hop Cottages because the taxpayer's way of living embraced use not only of Newlands House itself with its gardens but also of the cottage of the gardener who attended to the gardens. That the cottage is about 190 yards distant from the house is, to my mind, not of paramount importance in the context of the Newlands set-up; that is, of the way of life led by the taxpayer. It is a matter of degree. In these circumstances I do not feel able to say that the commissioners came to an unsound determination.'

[7] The Crown maintains that no reasonable tribunal of fact, properly directing itself, could have reached the conclusion that No 1 Hop Cottages (the cottage) and Newlands together formed one dwelling house which was the taxpayer's residence.

[8] It is to be noted that s 101(1)(a) refers to 'a dwelling-house . . . which is . . . his . . . residence'. The Crown would wish to argue from the reference to a dwelling house (in the singular) that the buildings which form a taxpayer's dwelling house under s 101(1)(a) cannot include buildings apart from the taxpayer's main house which themselves form a separate self-contained dwelling house. Mr Warren, counsel for the Crown, accepted that this argument was not open to him before us because of the decision of this court in *Batey v Wakefield* [1982] 1 All ER 61, although he reserved the right to argue the point in a higher court.

[9] Since *Batey v Wakefield* is the first of three reported cases in which a question arose similar to that in the present case, it will be convenient to consider those cases before turning to the arguments in the present case.

[10] In *Batey v Wakefield* the main house (Paddocks) was a four-bedroomed house set in 1.1 acres of land. On a part of that land the taxpayer built a chalet bungalow (Paddocks Lodge) for occupation by a caretaker/gardener. Paddocks Lodge had one main bedroom, its own garage and separate access from the road. It was separated from Paddocks by the width of a tennis court and a little more. It was built behind an established yew hedge. The taxpayer subsequently sold Paddocks Lodge which sale gave rise to a capital gain and the question was whether that gain was exempt from capital gains tax under the provisions of the Finance Act 1965 corresponding to ss 101 and 102 of the 1979 Act. The General Commissioners decided that the gain was exempt. The Crown appealed. The appeal was dismissed, both at first instance by Browne-Wilkinson J (1980) 55 TC 550 and by this court (Stephenson, Oliver and Fox LJJ) [1982] 1 All ER 61. Browne-Wilkinson J said, 55 TC 550, 556:

'The difference between the two sides depends on whether one stresses the words "a dwelling house", as the Crown suggests, or the words "a residence", as the taxpayer suggests. In the ordinary use of the words, if one looks at a man's residence it includes not only the physical main building in which the living rooms, bedrooms and bathroom are contained, but also the appurtenant buildings, such as the garage and buildings of that kind. One is looking at the group of buildings which together constitute the residence. It is true, as the Crown says in this case, that s 29 [of the Finance Act 1965] draws a distinction between a dwelling house, which is dealt with by sub-s (1)(a), and the land occupied and enjoyed with the residence as its garden or grounds, which is separately dealt with by sub-s (1)(b). Therefore the dwelling house referred to in sub-s (1)(a) does not include the whole of its curtilage. But in my judgment sub-s (1)(a) is including in the dwelling house some other buildings which are appurtenant thereto; for example, the garage, the potting shed and the summer house, which otherwise would not come within s 29 at all . . . In my judgment the commissioners were right in saying that what one has to look at and discover is: what was the residence of the taxpayer? For that purpose, you have to identify the dwelling house which is his residence. That dwelling house may or may not be comprised in one physical building; it may comprise a number of different buildings. His dwelling house and residence consists of all those buildings which are part and parcel of the whole, each part being appurtenant to and occupied for the purposes of the residence. The Crown does not go so far as to maintain that a building separate from the main can never be part of the dwelling house. If that be so, then it seems to me that the commissioners directed themselves rightly in seeing whether the lodge was itself appurtenant to and occupied for the purposes of the building occupied by the taxpayer. On the commissioners' findings, the lodge was built and occupied to provide services and caretaking facilities for the benefit of the main house. The lodge was occupied by the taxpayer through his employee, who was employed for the purpose of promoting the taxpayer's reasonable enjoyment of his own residence. In those circumstances, bearing in mind the fact that the buildings are very closely adjacent, it seems to me proper to find that the lodge was part of the residence of the taxpayer, and accordingly the gain falls within the exemption in s 29(2).'

[11] Fox LJ, with whom the other members of the court agreed, said [1982] 1 All ER 61, 64:

' . . . what one is looking for is the entity which in fact constitutes the residence of the taxpayer. I can see no difference in principle between a coachman's flat in the stable yard used for the purpose of serving the main house and a bungalow such as Paddocks Lodge, built on the comparatively small area of land held with Paddocks for the purpose of serving Paddocks. It is, it seems to me, a question of degree in each case. The question is what are the true constituents of the residence which is in question? . . . What has to be determined is the identity of the dwelling house. The fact that it comprised separate accommodation in which staff, or children, or guests may be accommodated does not, in my view, determine conclusively that such accommodation is not part of the dwelling house. It may be a factor, but it is no more. It is, as I have indicated, a matter of degree in every case whether a separate building does or does not in truth form part of the residence in question. That question is one for the commissioners to determine.'

[12] The next case in the sequence is *Markey (Inspector of Taxes) v Sanders* [1987] 1 WLR 864. There there was a main house with outbuildings in 12 acres of land. The taxpayer built a detached three-bedroomed bungalow some 130 metres away from the main house and separated from it by a paddock. The bungalow, which was occupied rent-free by staff, had its own garden, and was also screened by trees and separated by a ha-ha from the main house. The issue was whether the main house and the bungalow together formed a dwelling house which was the taxpayer's residence. The General Commissioners held that they did. This decision was reversed by Walton J on appeal. He considered *Batey v Wakefield* [1982] 1 All ER 61 and said [1987] STC 256 at 263, [1987] 1 WLR 864 at 869:

'The way in which it was put by the Court of Appeal, therefore, was that one had to look to see whether the separate building was one which was "very closely adjacent"; and so I think one can lay down fairly simply the conditions which have to be satisfied before a taxpayer can claim that a building which is not the part of his main residence where he himself ordinarily resides does for the purposes of the Capital Gains Tax Act 1979 fall within that description. The first condition is that the occupation of the building in question must increase the taxpayer's enjoyment of the main house. That is a necessary but clearly not a sufficient condition. The second condition, and again I take this at the moment straight from the Court of Appeal, is that the other building must be "very closely adjacent" to the main building; and, once again, that is a necessary but not sufficient condition.'

Then, after rejecting a test based on the words 'curtilage' and 'appurtenant' as used by the judges in *Batey v Wakefield*, he said at pp. 870–2:

'Now I myself would prefer to ask: looking at the group of buildings in question as a whole, is it fairly possible to regard them as a single dwelling house used as the taxpayer's main residence? I prefer to put it in that way because the concept of "very closely adjacent" does not of itself indicate that the scale of the buildings must be taken into consideration, which appears to me to be fairly obvious: for what would be "very closely adjacent" were one dealing with the sale of no 7 Paradise Avenue, Hoxton, might very well be quite different from what those words would mean if one were considering the sale of Blenheim Palace. Of course, those are two absurd examples at either end of the scale, but the fact that buildings can vary as much as those two vary indicates quite clearly that "very closely adjacent" is perhaps in itself too imprecise, whereas if one takes the test that I suggest, which I think is fully in line with the spirit of the decision of the Court of Appeal, it becomes very much easier to see what one is really talking about . . . What is said by counsel for the taxpayer, who has taken every conceivable argument on the part of the taxpayer, is that the test of "very closely adjacent" is an elastic test and that it is one which must be left to the commissioners to determine. I entirely agree that it is an elastic test, but merely because it is an elastic test does not mean that the commissioners are entitled to apply it absolutely regardless of the facts. Following up his way of putting it, there comes a time when the elastic snaps and the court is entitled to say, "You have gone too far." It is no use the commissioners describing in great detail what is clearly recognisable as an elephant and then concluding that it is a giraffe: it just does not work. So it seems to my mind that something has gone wrong here, but I am totally unable to determine precisely what it is . . . Whilst I do not put it in the forefront of my reasons, it does strike me that it would be a very curious circumstance indeed that where a house, including the ground on which it stands, is allowed (as it were) free of capital gains tax up to one acre (and there has been no determination by the commissioners that any area greater than one acre would be proper in this case, although I understand that the Revenue is prepared to concede that the gardens, which do exceed the one acre, do qualify for relief) a house which is sited well over an acre's worth of land away from the main residence and separated from it by a paddock which is not part of the ground so allowed could nevertheless be deemed to be part of it. It seems to me that that really is a totally absurd conclusion.'

[13] The last case in the series is *Williams (Inspector of Taxes) v Merrylees* [1987] 1 WLR 1511. In that case, a lodge some 200 metres from the main house was held by the General Commissioners to be part of a dwelling house which was the taxpayer's residence, being 'within the curtilage of the property of and appurtenant to' the main house. Vinelott J dismissed an appeal by the Crown, although expressing doubts that he would himself have reached the same conclusion. He considered both *Batey v Wakefield* [1982] All ER 61 and *Markey v Sanders* [1987] 1 WLR 864. He doubted whether it was possible to spell out of the decision of the Court of Appeal in *Batey v Wakefield* [1982] 1 All ER 61 two distinct conditions each of which must be satisfied before a separate building can be considered part of a dwelling house.

[14] I have to say that I do not find the current state of the authorities very satisfactory, and it is hardly surprising that different sets of General Commissioners have reached conclusions which are not always easy to understand.

[15] In these circumstances, it is necessary to go back to the words of the statute. What has first to be determined is what in the particular case constitutes the 'dwelling house'.

This is an ordinary English word of which the definition in the *Shorter Oxford English Dictionary*, 3rd edn (1944), rev. 1973, is 'a house occupied as a place of residence'. That dwelling house can, following the decision of this court in *Batey v Wakefield*, consist of more than one building and that even if the other building itself constitutes a separate dwelling house. Nevertheless, I agree with what Vinelott J said in *Williams v Merrylees* [1987] 1 WLR 1511, 1519:

'What one is looking for is an entity which can be sensibly described as being a dwelling house though split up into different buildings performing different functions.'

[16] How, then, can that entity be identified in any given case? First, attention must be focused on the dwelling house which is said to constitute the entity. To seek to identify the taxpayer's residence may lead to confusion because where, as here, the dwelling house forms part of a small estate, it is all too easy to consider the estate as his residence and from that to conclude that all the buildings on the estate are part of his residence. In so far as some of the statements made in *Batey v Wakefield* suggest that one must first identify the residence they must, in my judgment, be considered to have been made *per incuriam*.

[17] In all the cases to which I have referred, there has been an identifiable main house. Where it is contended that some one or more separate buildings are to be treated as part of an entity which, together with the main house, comprises a dwelling house, Mr Warren submitted for the Crown that no building can form part of a dwelling house which includes a main house, unless that building is appurtenant to, and within the curtilage of, the main house.

[18] At first I was inclined to the view that this introduced an unnecessary complication into the test, even though this was the way in which Browne-Wilkinson J approached the problem in *Batey v Wakefield*, 55 TC 550. On reflection I have come to the conclusion that this is a helpful approach, since it involves the application of well-recognised legal concepts and may avoid the somewhat surprising findings of fact which were reached in *Markey v Sanders* [1987] 1 WLR 864, *Williams v Merrylees* [1987] 1 WLR 1511 and, indeed, in the present case. In *Methuen-Campbell v Walters* [1979] QB 525, 543–44 Buckley LJ said:

'In my judgment, for one corporeal hereditament to fall within the curtilage of another, the former must be so intimately associated with the latter as to lead to the conclusion that the former in truth forms part and parcel of the latter. There can be very few houses indeed that do not have associated with them at least some few square yards of land, constituting a yard or a basement area or passageway or something of the kind, owned and enjoyed with the house, which on a reasonable view could only be regarded as part of the messuage and such small pieces of land would be held to fall within the curtilage of the messuage. This may extend to ancillary buildings, structures or areas such as outhouses, a garage, a driveway, a garden and so forth. How far it is appropriate to regard this identity as parts of one messuage or parcel of land as extending must depend on the character and the circumstances of the items under consideration.'

[19] That passage was cited with approval by all the members of this court in *Dyer v Dorset CC* [1989] QB 346, all of whom emphasised the smallness of the area comprised in the curtilage. This coincides with the close proximity test to which the other cases refer: 'very closely adjacent' in *Batey v Wakefield* 55 TC 550, 551 *per* Browne-Wilkinson J, approved in the same case by Fox LJ [1982] 1 All ER 61, 64, and adopted by Walton J in *Markey v Sanders* [1987] 1 WLR 864.

[20] This approach also avoids the difficulty to which Walton J referred in the final passage cited from his judgment in *Markey v Sanders*. Since under Section 101(2) and (3)

the 'permitted area' of garden and grounds which is exempt from capital gains tax is limited to one acre or such larger area as the commissioners may determine as required for the reasonable enjoyment of the dwelling house as a residence, it does seem to me to be remarkable that a separate lodge or cottage which by any reasonable measurement must be outside the permitted area can nevertheless be part of the entity of the dwelling house.

[21] If the commissioners in the present case had applied what in my judgment was the right test: 'Was the cottage within the curtilage of, and appurtenant to, Newlands, so as to be a part of the entity which, together with Newlands, constituted the dwelling house occupied by the taxpayer as her residence?'—I do not see how they could have reached the decision which they did. The fact that the cottage was 175 metres from Newlands, that Newlands was on the northern boundary and the cottage on the southern boundary of the 10.5 acre estate, and that they were separated by a large garden with no intervening buildings other than the greenhouses and tool shed (as is apparent from the commissioners' findings and the plans and photographs which were before us as they were before the commissioners) leads me to the inescapable conclusion that the cottage was not within the curtilage of, and appurtenant to Newlands, and so was not part of the entity which, together with Newlands, constituted the taxpayer's dwelling house.

[22] In my judgment, Mervyn Davies J also adopted an incorrect test when he referred to 'the entity constituting the taxpayer's residence' as Mr Milne QC for the taxpayer conceded. However, for present purposes it is sufficient to say that, if the commissioners had properly directed themselves, they could not have reached the conclusion that the cottage and Newlands together formed one dwelling house which was the taxpayer's residence.

[23] Accordingly I would allow this appeal.

RALPH GIBSON LJ:

[24] I agree that this appeal should be allowed for the reasons given by Balcombe LJ to which I can add nothing.

STUART-SMITH LJ:

[25] I also agree.

7.7.2 Commentary

We will start by working through the judgment of Balcombe LJ. We can see that once again the other members of the Court of Appeal have agreed with him, so his is the only judgment which carries the decision and the *ratio*.

7.7.2.1   The facts

The judge begins with the appeal history (paragraph [1]), then goes on to the facts, this time taking them from the decision of the commissioners (paragraph [2]). This is logical, because it is the commissioners who have found the facts: neither the judge nor the Court of Appeal have heard any evidence, so they are in no position to make any new findings of fact. The commissioners' statement of the facts is the most authoritative statement there can be.

7.7.2.2   The law

Then the statutory provisions are set out in paragraph [3]. This time the relevant section is section 101(1)–(3) Capital Gains Tax Act 1979, which is a successor to section 29(1) Finance Act 1965; it is not identical, but has the same effect.

7.7.2.3   The issue

A very short paragraph [4] setting out the factual issue to be determined comes next.

7.7.2.4   Commissioners' decision

Next, in paragraph [5], the judge sets out the commissioners' conclusion: simply the basic decision, with no reasons.

7.7.2.5   The judge's decision

Then the conclusion of the judge is set out a little more fully in paragraph [6], quoting from his judgment, and giving some of his reasons, as well as his overall conclusion on the issue. The judge reached the same conclusion as the commissioners but for different reasons. His *ratio* has therefore overridden theirs as far as precedent is concerned. He says that the distance between the cottage and the main house is not of paramount importance; rather, it is the taxpayer's way of living that should be the determining factor, and on the facts found by the commissioners, the taxpayer's way of living embraced both the main house and the cottage.

7.7.2.6   The Crown's contention

In paragraphs [7] and [8], the judge sets out the Crown's contention. It is important to note that the Crown did not argue that the commissioners were wrong in law. They were bound by *Batey v Wakefield*, as indeed was the judge, and as also are the Court of Appeal. So the Crown indicated that it would like to argue that the law was wrong in the House of Lords, but for now was bound to contend either that the commissioners applied the wrong test, or that their decision was wrong on the facts. As we shall see, these two arguments are linked. Once the Court decides the correct test, it can consider what conclusion the commissioners would have reached on the facts if they had applied it, and reverse their decision if necessary.

7.7.2.7   Case law

At this point, the structure of the judgment differs substantially from that in the previous case. In *Batey* no other cases were considered, but here the judge reviews three previous decisions: *Batey v Wakefield* (paragraphs [10] and [11]), *Markey v Sanders* (paragraph [12]), and *Williams v Merrylees* (paragraph [13]). The first is a Court of Appeal decision and so will be binding on any issue of law; the other two are first instance decisions, but are nonetheless persuasive, and the judge will try hard not to overrule either of them.

We will consider the judge's reasoning later, but this part of a judgment always needs to be looked at carefully. The cases that are reviewed will contain *ratio* and dicta, all of which might well be incorporated into the judge's reasoning in this case, and form part of its *ratio* in due course. It is important to look at the judge's review of these cases to see what he says about each of them. When advising a client, this part of the judgment is also the most fertile for finding arguments in support of your client's case.

In each of the first two cases, the judge states the facts (or an abbreviated version of them) and then quotes substantial sections of the judgments. He does not, however, go on yet to indicate any of his own views about them. He is simply setting out more law, by way of preliminary material which he will draw upon to reach his conclusions and give reasons. This is rather unusual. In most judgments a judge will comment on the cases he is referring to as he goes along.

7.7.2.8   *Batey v Wakefield*

We have already studied the decision of the Court of Appeal in *Batey v Wakefield*, but it is worth noting that the judge gives rather more weight to the reasoning of Browne-Wilkinson J at first instance than he does to Fox LJ. Note, too, that Browne-Wilkinson J used the word 'appurtenant', which does not appear in Fox LJ's judgment. We shall see the significance of this word shortly.

Let us remember too the outcome in *Batey v Wakefield*: the lodge was distant from the main house by the width of a tennis court and a hedge (perhaps 30 metres?) and was held to be part of a single dwelling house.

7.7.2.9   *Markey v Sanders*

The separate bungalow in this case was 130 metres away from the main house and was held on appeal not to be part of a single dwelling house comprising both buildings. The judge reversed the decision of the commissioners, so he had to explain why they were wrong in law or reached a decision that could not be justified on the facts as found.

We can see that the judge was looking for a test to help determine when a separate building could be part of another dwelling house. He rejected a test based on the words 'curtilage' and 'appurtenant', and instead attempted to find more law in *Batey v Wakefield*. He came up with two conditions to make a single dwelling house of two buildings: first, the occupation of the building in question must increase the owner's enjoyment of the main house, and, secondly, it must be very closely adjacent to it. The first test was doubtless satisfied, but applying the 'very closely adjacent' test, he came to the conclusion that the commissioners reached a conclusion on the facts which no reasonable commissioners could have reached. He accepted that this was an elastic test, but (maintaining the metaphor) decided that the commissioners had stretched the elastic to breaking point. He therefore reversed their decision. In other words, *Batey v Wakefield* was distinguished.

7.7.2.10   *Williams v Merrylees*

In this case, the lodge was 200 metres away from the main house. The commissioners concluded that it was part of a single dwelling house, applying a test of whether it was 'within the curtilage of and appurtenant to it'. But this time the judge felt unable to reverse their decision as being irrational, though he doubted it. He also rejected the approach of the judge in *Markey v Sanders*.

7.7.2.11   Comment of the judge

After this review of the cases, the judge for the first time comments in paragraph [14]. Not surprisingly, he finds the state of the law unsatisfactory. Different judges have approached similar factual situations in different ways, and their conclusions on the facts are hard to reconcile. In particular, the judge in *Williams v Merrylees* reached a decision similar to that in *Batey v Wakefield*, doubting the *ratio* of *Markey v Sanders*, yet on facts which might have seemed more similar to those in *Markey v Sanders*, and the judge in this case had adopted a different approach to any of those three cases, using the test of the taxpayer's way of living.

7.7.2.12   The legal conclusion and the *ratio*

Next, Balcombe LJ comes to the point and sets out his decision on the law (paragraphs [15] to [20]). He is faced with cases which conflict in their reasoning and seem to have produced inconsistent decisions on the facts. So he is seeking a legal *ratio* which can justify all the previous decisions; in other words he is seeking to reconcile them.

Batey v Wakefield decided that a dwelling house can be more than one building, but gave little guidance as to *when* a dwelling house can comprise more than one dwelling. What is needed is a test, which can be applied in any future case (including this one) and which will not be inconsistent with any of the previous cases (if possible). This is what the judge attempts to provide.

So the question of law to be decided is: 'When is a dwelling house that consists of more than one building or household a single dwelling house?'

The judge answers the question with three propositions:

(1) That there must be an identifiable main house (see paragraph [17]). The law that he is about to propound is only applicable in such a situation. A further test will need to be developed in the future when the two buildings said to comprise a single dwelling house are of equal status.

(2) No building other than the main house can form part of a dwelling house unless it is appurtenant to, and within the curtilage of, the main house:

[17] . . . Where it is contended that some one or more separate buildings are to be treated as part of an entity which, together with the main house, comprises a dwelling house, Mr Warren submitted for the Crown that no building can form part of a dwelling house which includes a main house, unless that building is appurtenant to, and within the curtilage of, the main house.

[18] . . . On reflection I have come to the conclusion that this is a helpful approach, since it involves the application of well-recognised legal concepts . . .

(3) In applying this test to the facts, it is necessary to focus attention on an entity which can be described as the taxpayer's dwelling house, and *not* his residence:

[15] . . . I agree with what Vinelott J said in Williams v Merrylees *. . .*

'What one is looking for is an entity which can be sensibly described as being a dwelling house though split up into different buildings performing different functions.'

[16] How, then, can that entity be identified in any given case? First, attention must be focused on the dwelling house which is said to constitute the entity. To seek to identify the taxpayer's residence may lead to confusion . . . In so far as some of the statements made in Batey v Wakefield *suggest that one must first identify the residence they must, in my judgment, be considered to have been made* per incuriam.

These, therefore, are the points of law to be derived from this case and which constitute its legal *ratio*.

However, the judge goes on to give some further explanation on the meaning of curtilage. He does this by citing a passage from *Methuen-Campbell v Walters*, in paragraph [18]:

. . . for one corporeal hereditament to fall within the curtilage of another, the former must be so intimately associated with the latter as to lead to the conclusion that the former in truth forms part and parcel of the latter. . . . How far it is appropriate to regard this identity as parts of one . . . parcel of land as extending must depend on the character and the circumstances of the items under consideration.

This passage was further cited with approval in another case, *Dyer v Dorset CC*, referred to in paragraph [19], and both cases emphasised that the area comprised within the curtilage is small. Balcombe LJ is then able to use this point to reconcile the cases which used the 'curtilage and appurtenant' test with those which used the 'very closely adjacent' test, by pointing out that it is likely to come to much the same thing. This enables him to avoid overruling any previous case.

7.7.2.13   The decision and *ratio* on the facts

Having formulated a test, Balcombe LJ then looks at what happens when it is applied to the facts, in paragraphs [21] and [22]. This naturally leads to the judge setting out his conclusion on the facts.

In this case, the Court of Appeal did decide that the commissioners' decision had been wrong in law. Balcombe LJ says in paragraph [20] that if they had applied the test he has now established, they could not reasonably have come to the conclusion they did. This therefore entitles the court to reverse the decision on the facts, and find for the Crown.

The *ratio* on the facts is clearly set out. It must be noted that certain facts are in common with those in *Batey v Wakefield*:

(1) The cottage was occupied by an employee.

(2) The employee was housed there to promote the taxpayer's reasonable enjoyment of her own residence.

It is not clear on the given facts whether the gardener paid rent or not. But none of the preceding facts would justify any distinction being made between this case and *Batey*.

However, there were several identified facts on which the judge felt able to distinguish *Batey*:

(1) The distance of the cottage from the main house—175 metres.

(2) They were at opposite boundaries of the estate.

(3) They were separated by a large garden with few intervening buildings. The judge clearly identified this as a persuasive fact, the implication being that open space between them links them less closely than a series of other buildings would.

There was a further persuasive fact on which the judge expressed a view *obiter*, namely that . . . 'it does seem to me remarkable that a separate lodge or cottage which is outside the permitted area can nevertheless be part of the entity of the dwelling house.' (Paragraph [20].)

7.7.2.14   Agreement by the other judges

This time there can be no doubt that there is a *ratio* to be found in the decision of the Court of Appeal as a whole, because Ralph Gibson LJ expressly agrees for the same reasons as Balcombe LJ, and so at least two have adopted the same *ratio*. So, too, probably has Stuart-Smith LJ, even though he does not actually say so.

7.8   Answers to test questions

For the questions, see **7.4**.

7.8.1   Question 1

The correct answer is [B]. Although the decision of another High Court judge is not binding, nevertheless it is sufficiently persuasive that there must be a good reason to differ. Answer [A] is wrong because neither the decision of the other judge nor the *obiter dictum* is binding, and so neither will *always* take precedence. Answer [C] is wrong: in this case the judge must follow the later decision. Answer [D] is wrong: the judge might well prefer an *obiter dictum* of the Supreme Court, but he does not have to.

7.8.2   Question 2

The correct answer is [D]. It does not matter how dubious the House of Lords felt the Court of Appeal decision to be; if they did not overrule it, it is still binding law. The words 'just about' in answer [A] are a red herring; if the case is distinguishable, it is distinguishable. Answers [B] and [C] are wrong because in each case the Court of Appeal decision is no longer good law.

7.8.3   Question 3

The correct answer is [A]. This is what you should do in the circumstances. Answer [B] is wrong because the High Court case is binding law and cannot be ignored. Answer [C] is wrong because it is too pessimistic and probably involves a breach of your duty to do the best you can for your client. Answer [D] is wrong because it is too optimistic and you would be misleading your client.

7.8.4   Question 4

The correct answer is [C]. Answer [A] is wrong because the judge is bound both by the House of Lords and by the Court of Appeal: facts A, B, C, and D or A, B, and D will lead to the same result. Answer [B] is wrong because the judge is bound by the Court of Appeal. Answer [D] is wrong because the judge is bound by the House of Lords. Only in answer [C] is there a factual difference, the absence of fact B, sufficient to enable the judge to distinguish the other decisions.

7.8.5   Question 5

The correct answer is [D]. We need first to track the legal effect of the five decisions. The judge in 2010 distinguished the decision of the Court of Appeal in 2009. The judge in 2011 distinguished the decision of the judge in 2010. The Court of Appeal in 2012 overruled the decision of the judge in 2010. Therefore, as the law now stands, the claimant wins if facts A and B exist, or facts A, B, and C, or facts A, B, C, and D. It follows that facts C and D are no longer relevant. The judge in 2013 distinguished the decision of the Court of Appeal in 2012.

So, answers [A], [B], and [C] are wrong because in each case the judge is bound by the Court of Appeal decision in 2012 to find in favour of the claimant. Only in the situation described in answer [D] should the judge find in favour of the defendant, because facts C and D being irrelevant, he should follow the judge in 2013, and hold that adding fact E to facts A and B is sufficient to distinguish all the earlier decisions.

7.8.6   Question 6

The correct answer is [B]. We are looking for the overall *ratio* of the Supreme Court decision. We can observe quite easily that the Judges ruled unanimously in favour of the defendant. Only if they found for the claimant on three issues out of three would the decision go the claimant's way. Each Judge found for the defendant on at least one issue.

So we now look to see whether any three of them ruled in favour of the defendant for the same reason.

Lords Able SCJ, Cobbler SCJ, and Dupe SCJ all agreed that a warehouse was a workshop, but that was a decision in favour of the claimant, so cannot be part of the *ratio*. Answer [A] is therefore wrong. Lords Able SCJ, Boot SCJ, and Egg SCJ all agreed that a portacabin was not a building, but that, too, was a decision in favour of the claimant, so answer [C] is wrong. Lords Able SCJ, Boot SCJ, and Egg SCJ were also all agreed, however, that a forklift truck was a vehicle. That was a decision in favour of the defendant, and produced the overall result in favour of the defendant, so that is the *ratio* of the case, and is binding law. Answer [B] is therefore correct. Answer [D] is wrong by default.

Practical legal research: a summary

8.1 The purpose of this chapter

This chapter is intended to summarise some of the key points about practical legal research.

8.1.1 What is 'practical' legal research?

The important hallmarks of legal research carried out by a practitioner are these:

(a) A practitioner may start the research with a textbook, but will base the advice to the client on primary sources (cases, statutes, or statutory instruments), unless there is no primary source which adequately answers the question.

(b) Research carried out by a practitioner has a very narrow focus: the practitioner will search only for the law which is needed to answer the specific questions which have to be answered in order to deal with the specific matters on which the client needs advice. For the practitioner, the law is a means to an end, not the end itself.

(c) A practitioner's research must be quick ('time is money'), but it must also be accurate (since getting it wrong might well amount to negligence).

8.1.2 Identifying the issues

The first step is, of course, to digest the facts of the problem. Once you have done this, the next step is to identify the issues which need to be researched. In some cases, your instructing solicitor will already have done this, and your instructions will contain a series of questions for you to answer. Even if this is so, you should consider whether there are any other questions which the solicitor should have asked you so that the lay client receives complete advice. In other cases, the solicitor will seek general advice and so you will have to identify the specific questions yourself.

Remember that some problems with which you may be faced might involve basic principles of law and so need little or no legal research (though you may still need to check that there have been no significant changes in the law of which you are unaware), or else the problems might raise purely factual or evidential questions which involve no law (and so require no legal research).

8.1.3 What sources should I use?

If the problem is one where you need to do some legal research, you must first decide what source(s) you are going to use.

In most cases, there will be more than one starting point to solving the problem. All libraries have lists arranged according to subject matter of the titles they hold. There is also the list of practitioner books in **Chapter 9**.

8.1.4 Textbooks

If you are unfamiliar with the area of law in question, you will probably want to start the research process by using a textbook. You should use textbooks written for practitioners, not those written for students. For example, *Chitty on Contracts, Clerk & Lindsell on Torts, Charlesworth on Negligence*, or 'loose-leaf' works (such as *Harvey's Industrial Relations and Employment Law* and *Butterworths Family Law Service*). The latter may look rather off-putting at first, but they function in exactly the same way as ordinary textbooks. If you cannot identify an appropriate practitioner text, or the one you want is not available, *Halsbury's Laws of England* is often a good starting point.

Unless you are looking for commentary on a particular case or a particular statutory provision (in which case, you will use the table of statutes or table of cases in whichever book you are using), the best starting point in any textbook is the index. This is the essential tool which enables you to find the part of the book you are looking for. To use an index you need to be able to formulate the question which you are trying to answer by using words which are likely to be found in the index. This involves identifying 'keywords'. If you cannot find the word(s) you are looking for, try to reword the question. To take a rather trite example, you might have to look for 'taxi' instead of 'cab'. In many practitioner textbooks, there is also a detailed table of contents (towards the front of the book) which can be a useful aid to navigation within the text. We have already seen that practitioners base their answers on primary sources, and so the use of textbook(s) at the start of the research process must be seen merely as a means of locating the appropriate primary sources.

8.1.5 Primary sources

In some instances, you might want to bypass textbooks and go straight to the 'primary' sources (in other words, statutes, statutory instruments, or cases). You might know, for example, that the basic law governing a particular subject is statutory, and so the statute is likely to provide the starting point you need. For example, the statutory provisions relating to unfair dismissal are in the Employment Rights Act 1996, so you might decide to start your research there. However, you should only start the research process with primary sources if you are already familiar with the area of law in question; if you are not, it is much better to start with a textbook, which will help you to understand the particular topic you are researching by putting it into context.

If you want to find a statute in a printed version (rather than online), you should ideally choose an annotated version, since this will give you assistance in interpreting the Act. *Current Law Statutes Annotated* contains commentary written when the statute was first enacted (including *Hansard* references to Parliamentary debates for *Pepper v Hart* research). However, *Halsbury's Statutes* has two advantages over *Current Law*. First, the volumes are periodically reissued; this means that where the statute has been amended, the amended version is shown, and the footnotes take account of cases decided after the enactment of the statute. Second, there is a very useful *Cumulative Supplement*, which gives up-to-date information about the statutes printed in the main volumes and in the loose-leaf binders which contain more recent statutes.

When you are trying to find your way around a statute, remember that the list of sections (headed 'Arrangement of Sections') at the start of each Act will help you to find the section(s) you need. Many textbooks also reprint particular sections of statutes, although the commentary will often be in the main body of the text and not in the form of annotations to the statute itself.

If you are looking for case law, the starting point for finding relevant cases will often be to use a textbook. When reading the cases themselves, it is best to use the official law reports published by the Incorporated Council for Law Reporting (the *Weekly Law Reports*, the *Appeal Cases*, etc.) or the *All England Law Reports*. However, do not forget that there are several very useful 'specialist' series of law reports. For example, the *Industrial Relations Law Reports*, the *Family Law Reports*, the *Criminal Appeal Reports*, and the *Justice of the Peace* reports.

8.1.6 Electronic resources

You should also be aware of the range of electronic databases available for legal research. Quite a lot of information is available free of charge on the internet. This includes statutes and statutory instruments (<http://www.legislation.gov.uk/>); House of Lords decisions from 1996 to July 2009, when the Supreme Court came into existence, (<http://www.publications.parliament.uk/pa/ld/ldjudgmt.htm>); and decisions of the Supreme Court (<http://supremecourt.uk/decided-cases/index.shtml>). Judgments from the Civil and Criminal Divisions of the Court of Appeal, and from the High Court, are available on the BAILII (British and Irish Legal Information Institute) database (<http://www.bailii.org/>). There are also various online subscription services, such as *Lexis Library* (which includes an electronic version of the *All England Law Reports*, *Halsbury's Laws of England*, and *Halsbury's Statutes*), *Westlaw*, and *Lawtel*.

If you know the name of the case or statute you are looking for, you can simply enter that name into the database (or the citation, if it is a case); otherwise, you have to decide what words you are going to ask the computer to search for. Each database has its own rules regarding how searches should be phrased, but all search engines perform the same basic function of looking for words or phrases. Some databases allow the use of a 'wild card', which may be a ! or a *: if you search for negligen!, or negligen*, the results should include 'negligent', 'negligently', 'negligence'.

Searching for combinations of words will also make your research more focused. For example, if you are trying to find cases on sentencing in theft cases, you will get far too many hits if you just look up 'theft' or if you just look up 'sentencing'. If you search for <theft AND sentenc!>, you should get a far more manageable number of hits.

Another way of defining your electronic search to get a more manageable number of hits is to look for words within a specified distance of each other. For example, if you are looking for cases involving theft in breach of trust, you could ask the computer to look for 'theft' within ten (say) words of 'trust' (this might be written as <theft w/10 trust>). On some databases it is also possible to use a 'w/p' connector to find documents in which the words sought appear within the same paragraph (for example, <retirement w/p pension> would find all the instances where 'retirement' occurs within the same paragraph as 'pension'); similarly, the 'w/s' connector finds documents where the words sought are in the same sentence.

8.1.7 Finding relevant material

Once you have found the law you are looking for, you must be able to sort through it. You will generally find more law than you need in order to answer the particular question you are dealing with. You therefore have to be able to distinguish between what is relevant and what is irrelevant. The acid test of relevance is whether the source you have found actually helps you to answer the question or whether it is merely background material.

If, when you are giving your advice, you cite a case, it must be clear what proposition you derive from it. It is a mistake to cite cases without making it clear what proposition of law is to be derived from each one.

8.1.8   Interpreting the law

In some cases, the law will be so clear that only one interpretation is possible. However, this will not always be so.

When reading a statute, you should always look to see if there is a definition section which gives specific definitions to particular words or phrases used in the statute. Such definitions may appear within the particular section you are reading; sometimes you will need to find a separate definition section. You should also look for relevant case law which interprets that section.

In an area governed wholly or mainly by case law, you may well have to distil the relevant legal principles from dicta in a series of cases.

When you have found relevant case law, it may be necessary to consider whether the facts of the case upon which you are advising can be distinguished from the facts of the authorities you have found. If there are conflicting authorities, it may be necessary to predict which is more likely to be followed.

If you cannot find a clear answer to the problem you are researching, it may well be that you can find a case (or series of cases) setting out a narrow principle which you can then use to establish a wider principle.

A good starting point for such research will be a textbook, since textbooks will often show how various authorities relate to each other (for example, summarising the effect of a line of cases), pointing out any inconsistencies and suggesting ways in which apparently conflicting case law can be reconciled.

8.1.9   Following through between sources

You must be able to 'follow through' from one source to another. For example, if a textbook sets out a proposition of law which seems to answer the question you are researching, and the book cites a particular case as authority for that proposition, you should ensure that the case really does say what the textbook asserts. It is rarely sufficient (although very tempting!) to rely on what textbooks say about primary sources.

8.1.10   Updating

For the practitioner, one of the most important stages of the legal research process is the updating stage. Giving advice to a client, or making submissions to a court, based on out-of-date law may well amount to negligence on the part of the researcher. It is therefore essential that you take all reasonable steps to ensure that your answer is current.

For example, where you have found the primary sources upon which your answer is based through use of a textbook, check how up to date the textbook is and whether there is a supplement to it (this will give you an idea of the period which your subsequent updating should cover).

If your answer is based on a statute, make sure that the statute was in force at the relevant time (i.e. that, at the relevant time, it had been brought into force and had not been repealed) and that it has not been amended. If you are doing paper-based research in *Halsbury's Statutes,* it is important to remember to check not only the hardback annual *Cumulative Supplement* but also the loose-leaf *Noter-up* service binder.

If your answer is based on case law, it is important to check the 'status' of the case(s) on which your answer is based (e.g. that the case on which your advice is based has not been overruled, or distinguished in a case that is similar to the one in which you are advising). If you are doing the research using paper sources, you can check *Current Law* and/or the 'Cases Judicially Considered' section of the *Law Reports Index.*

If you are doing research electronically, remember that you still have to do some updating. Exactly what you have to do depends on how up to date the particular source is and whether it contains an updating facility. The online version of *Halsbury's Laws* is updated regularly and contains all the text that is in the annual *Cumulative Supplement* and in the loose-leaf *Noter-up* service binder which updates the supplement. The legislation database on *Lexis Library* is kept up to date, showing the amended version of statutes and statutory instruments quite soon after the changes are enacted; there is a 'stop press' button which gives brief information about any changes which have not yet been incorporated into the database.

A useful electronic source for checking the currency of case law is *Westlaw.* The 'case analysis' section of the summary often includes details of cases which cite the case you are currently looking at: this includes references to cases in which the present case has been considered, applied, distinguished, or even overruled. It is important to carry out such checks even if you are using a source that is regularly updated, such as *Lawtel* (which has new cases added quickly but does not usually indicate in a case summary whether that case has subsequently been applied or overruled).

8.1.11 Using the law that you have found

Once you have done all this, you need to be able to summarise the relevant law, and apply it to the facts of the case you are dealing with, so that you can give clear, accurate and succinct advice to your client.

A barrister does not carry out abstract legal research. The purpose of the research is to give the best advice you can to your client, or to ensure that the strongest possible case is put before the court on behalf of your client. You must therefore apply the law to the facts of the case in a realistic and practical way. Your advice must not be an essay on the law: it must be specific to the case in which your advice is sought.

You must attempt to answer all the questions or issues raised in your instructions. It may or may not be possible to give a definite answer. If you are unable to give a categorical answer, you must try to assess the likely result and the degree of probability that the court will come to the conclusion you suggest.

Each answer you reach must be 'satisfactory', in the sense that it has a reasonable prospect of being upheld by the court.

8.2 Notes to pupil supervisor

In most cases, your pupil supervisor will not require you to produce a full opinion, but rather the notes which could form the basis for an opinion or part of an opinion. The notes must be clear, concise, and accurate. The following guidelines may help you:

(a) You may write in note-form (rather than writing complete sentences which conform with the rules of grammar) if you wish to do so, but do remember that the result must be intelligible to another reader (in this case, your pupil supervisor).

(b) Your answers must be 'satisfactory', in the sense of being sustainable given the present state of the law which applies to the question(s) you are answering.

(c) Your answers must be supported by relevant authority (usually, statutory or case law):

   (i)   Only cite *relevant* authority, as the citation of irrelevant sources adds to the length of your notes and tends to create confusion. Something is relevant only if it makes a difference to your answer.

   (ii)   Show *how* the authority you cite is relevant. This will involve relating that authority to the facts of the case in which you are advising. When you are citing precedent, you will often find it easier to show its relevance by referring to a particular dictum rather than simply referring to the case as a whole. If you do not set out your legal reasoning, your pupil supervisor cannot check the soundness of your reasoning.

   (iii) Correct citations must be given for each primary source to which you refer. For example, a statutory instrument should be cited thus: the Data Revenue and Customs Appeals Order 2012 (SI 2012/533). A case should be given its full citation, for example *Hashwani v Jivraj* [2011] UKSC 40; [2011] 1 WLR 1872. Where a particular dictum is referred to, it should be located: for example, 'per Elias LJ at para 13'; in older cases, where there is no 'neutral citation' (i.e. the first half of the citation used in the example), the dictum is located by reference to the page number of the report being referred to. If you do not give the correct citation for the authority which supports your conclusion, and the relevant passage(s) of the judgment(s), your pupil supervisor will not be able to find that material quickly.

   (iv)   Verbatim quotation of statutes and judgments should be kept to a minimum. If the passage upon which you wish to rely is very short, or the precise words are crucial, then you will have to write it out in full. Otherwise, you should simply distil the essentials, which will involve paraphrasing the material rather than copying it out. You should, of course, still cite the source, even if you are paraphrasing it rather than copying it out.

   (v)   You should always base your advice on 'primary' sources (i.e. statutes, case law, etc.) in preference to 'secondary' sources (textbooks, articles, etc.). However, if there is no authority, or there are conflicting authorities, then it may be appropriate to cite academic opinion. In that case, you should wherever possible refer to a source which could be cited in court (i.e. a textbook written for practitioners rather than students, or an article in a publication which is aimed, at least in part, at practitioners).

(d) Finally, some guidance on the incorporation of background detail in your notes. If you are unfamiliar with an area of law, it may well be that you will have to do a certain amount of background reading before you can put the question(s) which you have to answer into context. However, your notes should contain only reasoned answers to the questions which are posed (expressly or by implication) in your instructions. Otherwise, you will find that you are writing a legal essay, not the notes which form the starting point for an opinion.

8.3 Summary

To summarise, these are the basic steps of legal research:

(a) Analyse the issues raised by your instructions so that you can identify what questions of law (if any) have to be answered.

(b) Classify the questions (e.g. magistrates' court procedure, contract, tort, highways). This will help you to decide what source(s) to look for. Remember that if the source you want is unavailable, there is almost certainly another one that you could use.

(c) Decide what word(s) you are going to look up in the index or on the database ('keywords' or 'catchwords'). To do this, you must be able to formulate the question(s) you are trying to answer and then see what keywords appear in that formulation. If the word you are looking for is not in the index or database, try to think of another one.

(d) If you have found what you are looking for, distil what you have found. Set out the statement of law and the authority for that statement.

(e) Ensure that the law you have found is up to date. Is the statute in force? Has the statute been amended? Has the statute been repealed? Has the case you have found gone on appeal to a higher court? Has the case been considered, followed, distinguished, or overruled by a later case?

(f) Check that you have answered the question(s) completely. If not, look for other relevant sources, distil the contents, and check that what you have found is up to date.

(g) Summarise the relevant law, apply it to the facts of the case you are dealing with, and advise the client.

8.4 Criteria by which you may assess your legal research

To assess the standard of your performance in carrying out a legal research exercise, you may use or adapt the following basic criteria. In carrying out legal research, you should be able to:

- identify the specific issue(s) of law involved;
- identify appropriate primary and, where appropriate, secondary source(s) for resolving those legal issues, citing the source(s) correctly;
- ensure that your answer is up to date; and
- apply the law correctly to resolve all legal issues contained, explicitly or implicitly, in the question.

8.5 A sample exercise in legal research

There is no single 'right' way of conducting legal research. However, to give you an opportunity to practise your legal research skills, here is an exercise for you to have a go at. A worked-through answer is available on the online resource centre (but you should bear in mind that is suggests one way of approaching a particular exercise: it is not the only approach that is possible).

RE JOHN AND JANE HAYWARD

Instructions to Counsel to Advise

Counsel is instructed on behalf of Mr and Mrs Hayward. They recently purchased the freehold of a plot of land in Kent. This land has been used as an apple and pear orchard for over 100 years. Together with their two children (Emily and Rachael), they moved into a large mobile home which they brought onto the land.

Shortly after the mobile home was moved into the orchard, the local authority wrote to Mr and Mrs Hayward saying that this represented a change in the use of the land (by introducing a residential element onto land which should be used for wholly agricultural purposes). However, Mr and Mrs Hayward have refused to remove the mobile home. They say that they could not afford to buy a house as well as the orchard and so they have no choice but to live in the orchard.

The local authority have now issued proceedings in the County Court seeking an injunction requiring Mr and Mrs Hayward to remove the mobile home from the orchard.

Counsel is instructed to appear at the hearing of this application and to use best endeavours to prevent the granting of the order being sought by the local authority.

8.6 And, finally, some useful tips

You might find this non-exhaustive list of tips helpful in carrying out your legal research. You may like to add to the list as you do your own research and discover for yourself useful shortcuts.

8.6.1 Paper sources

(a) If you are unfamiliar with an area of law, it is often best to start with a paper source rather than an electronic source: it is generally easier to browse through a paper source to get an overview of a subject.

(b) Once you have formulated the legal question(s) you are trying to answer and you have found an appropriate textbook, it is usually best to start with the index at the back of the book rather than the contents pages at the front, unless the contents pages are very detailed.

(c) Do not forget to go through the updating process: e.g. check to see if the textbook you are using has a supplement. Remember that even if there is a supplement, it is likely to be at least a little out of date, so check the supplement to see when it was issued and update from then; similarly, even loose-leaf publications can be out of date, so check when the publication was last updated.

(d) If your answer is based on a statute or statutory instrument, check that it was in force at the relevant time.

8.6.2 Electronic sources

(a) Remember that in most databases you can make your search more efficient by the use of 'Boolean searches', i.e. using connectors such as AND, OR, NOT.

(b) Sometimes the use of brackets is needed in a search, e.g. '(transfer OR transaction) AND illegal' if you are not sure whether the appropriate noun is 'transfer' or 'transaction'.

(c) You can narrow your search by using 'proximity searching', e.g. looking for one word within (say) ten words of another word, e.g. <solicitor w/10 negligence>.

(d) Truncation (use of 'wild cards') enables you to look for words with a common stem; with some databases, the symbol to use is an asterisk (*), with others it is an exclamation mark (!). For example, neglig* would find negligent, negligently, negligence.

(e) If you want to find out whether a particular word appears in the file you have currently opened, click on 'edit'—'find' and type in the word you are looking for.

(f) Be aware that you can find links to useful sites containing legal information from sites such as <http://www.venables.co.uk/sites.htm>, <http://www.kent.ac.uk/library/subjects/lawlinks//>, or the City Law School site <http://lawbore.net/>.

(g) If you want to copy information from the internet into a word-processed document, highlight the text you want to copy by dragging the cursor over the relevant text with the left-hand mouse button held down; then you have three options: click on 'edit', then 'copy', and then go to your word-processed document and click on 'edit', then 'paste' (or click on the paste icon); or press 'ctrl' and the letter 'c' simultaneously, then go to your word-processed document and press 'ctrl' and the letter 'v' simultaneously; or press the right-hand mouse button, highlight 'copy' and click with the left-hand mouse button, and when you are in your word-processed document, press the right-hand mouse button, highlight 'paste', and click with the left-hand mouse button. If you want to eliminate formatting from the text you are copying (e.g. you want to remove hyperlinks) you can select 'edit'—'paste special'—'unformatted text'. Remember to provide a citation for any material that is copied or paraphrased from another source (failure to attribute such material amounts to plagiarism).

(h) Remember that a case reported in one set of reports may be referred to in a later case that is not reported in the same set of reports: *Westlaw* or *Lawtel* are good sources for tracking down recent cases.

9

Legal sources for the practitioner: a bibliography

The list of books, law reports, journals, and electronic sources that follows offers a subject guide to some of the leading sources within each field of law. It is by no means a comprehensive list and there are many excellent practical legal works that are not listed here.

Works usually updated by one or more supplements before the publication of a new edition are indicated in the text. Most of the loose-leaf works referred to are available through an online subscription or sometimes on CD-ROM—more details can be obtained direct from the publisher. The main commercial legal databases are described in more detail in **Chapter 5** at **5.3**; a guide to free legal resources on the internet is at **5.4.3**.

9.1 Legal encyclopedias

Atkin's Encyclopaedia of Court Forms in Civil Procedure, 2nd edn (LexisNexis). Updated by reissued volumes and loose-leaf noter-up.

Current Law Cases and *Current Law Statutes* (Sweet & Maxwell). Includes *Yearbooks* and *Citator*. Updated by *Current Law Monthly Digest*. Available online via *Westlaw*.

The Digest: Annotated British, Commonwealth and European Cases, 3rd edn (LexisNexis). Updated by regular reissued volumes, annual *Cumulative Supplement*, and quarterly *Survey*.

The Encyclopaedia of Forms and Precedents, 5th edn (LexisNexis). Updated by reissued volumes and loose-leaf noter-up. Available online via *Lexis Library*.

Halsbury's Laws of England, 5th edn reissue (LexisNexis). Updated by regularly reissued volumes, annual *Cumulative Supplement*, and *Current Service Noter-up and Monthly Review*. Available online via *Lexis Library*.

Halsbury's Statutes of England and Wales, 4th edn (LexisNexis). Updated by regular reissued volumes, annual *Cumulative Supplement*, and monthly loose-leaf *Current Service Noter-up*.

9.2 Legal dictionaries

Stroud's Judicial Dictionary of Words and Phrases, 8th edn (Sweet & Maxwell, 2012). Updated by supplement.

Words and Phrases Legally Defined, 4th edn (LexisNexis, 2007). Updated by supplement.

9.3 Law reports

The principal series of 'general' law reports are listed here. For a more detailed analysis of the key series of law reports, refer to **Chapter 4** at **4.11.2**. Other law reports are listed by subject matter at **9.5**.

All England Law Reports, 1936– (LexisNexis).
The Law Reports (The Incorporated Council of Law Reporting for England and Wales), also known as *The Official Series*. For details of individual series, see **Table 9.1**.

Table 9.1 **The Law Reports**

The Law Reports	Citation	The Law Reports	Citation
Admiralty & Ecclesiastical	LRA & E	Exchequer Division	Ex D
Appeal Cases	AC	Family Division	Fam
Chancery Appeals	Ch App	King's Bench	KB
Chancery Division	Ch D	Privy Council	LR PC
Common Pleas	CP	Probate & Divorce	LR P&D
Common Pleas Division	CPD	Probate Division	PD
Crown Cases Reserved	LR CCR	Probate Division	P
English & Irish Appeals	LR HL	Queen's Bench	QB
Equity	LR Eq	Queen's Bench Division	QBD
Exchequer	LR Ex	Scotch & Divorce Appeals	Sc & D

Weekly Law Reports, 1953– (The Incorporated Council of Law Reporting for England and Wales).

9.4 Journals

Key journals of a general legal nature will keep the reader up to date with legal news and current legal issues. Other journals are listed by subject matter at **9.5**.

Counsel: Incorporating Bar Council and Bar Standards Board News (Bar Council).
The Law Society Gazette (Law Society). Available online at <http://www.lawgazette.co.uk>.
The Lawyer. Available online at <http://www.thelawyer.com>.
Legal Week (Legal Week). Available online at <http://www.legalweek.com>.
New Law Journal (LexisNexis). Available online at <http://www.newlawjournal.co.uk> and via *Lexis Library*.
Solicitors' Journal (Sweet & Maxwell). Available online at <http://www.solicitorsjournal.com>.

9.5 Legal sources—by subject area

Administrative Law
See also: **Civil Litigation**

See also: **Criminal Litigation**

Administrative Court Digest, law reports (Sweet & Maxwell).

Fordham, *Judicial Review Handbook*, 6th edn (Hart Publishing, 2012).

Lewis, *Judicial Remedies in Public Law*, 5th edn (Sweet & Maxwell, 2014). Updated by supplement.

Supperstone & Goudie, *Judicial Review*, 5th edn (LexisNexis, 2014).

Wade & Forsyth, *Administrative Law*, 10th edn (Oxford University Press, 2009).

Woolf, Jowell, & Le Sueur, *De Smith's Judicial Review*, 7th rev edn (Sweet & Maxwell, 2012). Updated by supplement.

Agency

Bowstead & Reynolds, *Law of Agency*, 19th edn (Sweet & Maxwell, 2010). Updated by supplement.

Arbitration

Arbitration Law Monthly, journal (Informa Publishing).

Lloyd's Arbitration Reports, law reports (Lloyd's).

Mustill & Boyd, *The Law and Practice of Commercial Arbitration in England*, 2nd edn (Butterworths, 1989). Updated by companion volume (2001).

Redfern & Hunter, *The Law and Practice of International Commercial Arbitration*, 5th rev edn (Sweet & Maxwell, 2009). Available online via *Westlaw*.

Banking

Elliott, *Byles on Bills of Exchange and Cheques*, 29th edn (Sweet & Maxwell, 2012).

Encyclopaedia of Banking Law, loose-leaf (LexisNexis). Available online via *Lexis Library*.

Guest, *Chalmers & Guest on Bills of Exchange*, 17th edn (Sweet & Maxwell, 2009).

Hapgood, *Paget's Law of Banking*, 13th edn (LexisNexis, 2006). Available online via *Lexis Library*.

Bankruptcy and Personal Insolvency

Bankruptcy and Personal Insolvency Reports, law reports (Jordans).

Dennis, *Insolvency Law Handbook,* 3rd edn (Law Society, 2013).

Muir Hunter on Personal Insolvency, loose-leaf (Sweet & Maxwell).

Totty & Moss, *Insolvency*, loose-leaf (Sweet & Maxwell). Available online via *Westlaw*.

Building

Construction Law Journal, journal (Sweet & Maxwell).

Construction Law Reports, law reports (LexisNexis).

Emden's Construction Law, loose-leaf (LexisNexis).

Furst, *Keating on Construction Contracts*, 9th rev edn (Sweet & Maxwell, 2013). Updated by supplement.

Charities

Tudor, *Tudor on Charities*, 10th edn (Sweet & Maxwell, 2014). Updated by supplement.

Children

See also: **Family Law**

Child & Family Law Quarterly, journal (Jordans).

Childright, journal (University of Essex).

Clarke, Hall & Morrison on Children, loose-leaf (LexisNexis). Available online via *Lexis Library*.

Hershman & McFarlane, *Children Law and Practice*, loose-leaf (Jordans). Available online via *Jordans*.

Civil Litigation
See also: **Administrative Law**
See also: **Costs**
Blackstone's Civil Practice, annual (Oxford University Press). Updated by supplement.
Blake, *A Practical Approach to Effective Litigation*, 7th edn (Oxford University Press, 2009).
Bullen & Leake & Jacob's Precedents of Pleadings, 17th edn (Sweet & Maxwell, 2011). Updated by supplement. Available online via *Westlaw*.
Butterworths Civil Court Precedents, loose-leaf (LexisNexis). Available online via *Lexis Library*.
The Civil Court Practice ('The Green Book'), annual (LexisNexis). Updated by supplement and regular reissues. Available online via *Lexis Library*.
Civil Procedure ('The White Book'), annual (Sweet & Maxwell). Updated by supplement and regular reissues. Available online via *Westlaw*.
Lawtel Civil Procedure, online service (Lawtel/Sweet & Maxwell).
Practical Civil Court Precedents, loose-leaf (Sweet & Maxwell).
Rose, *Pleadings without Tears: A Guide to Legal Drafting under the Civil Procedure Rules*, 8th edn (Oxford University Press, 2012).
Westlaw UK Civil Procedure, online service (Sweet & Maxwell).

Company and Commercial Law
See also: **Sale of Goods and Consumer Law**
All England Law Reports: Commercial Cases, 1996– (LexisNexis).
British Company Law and Practice, loose-leaf (CCH).
British Company Cases, law reports (CCH).
Butterworths Company Law Cases, law reports (LexisNexis).
Butterworths Company Law Service, loose-leaf (LexisNexis).
Butterworths Corporate Law Service, loose-leaf (LexisNexis). Available online via *Lexis Library*.
Company Lawyer, journal (Sweet & Maxwell).
Gore-Browne on Companies, 45th edn, loose-leaf (Jordans). Available online via *Jordans*.
Journal of Business Law, journal (Sweet & Maxwell).
Palmer's Company Law, loose-leaf (Sweet & Maxwell). Available online via *Westlaw*.
PLC Competition, Corporate, Property, database services (Practical Law for Companies).
PLC Magazine, journal (Practical Law for Companies).
Roberts, *Law Relating to Financial Services*, 8th edn (Financial World Publishing, 2014).
Westlaw UK Corporate Business, online service (Sweet & Maxwell).

Competition Law
Bellamy & Child, *European Community Law of Competition*, 8th edn (Oxford University Press, 2012).
Butterworths Competition Law, loose-leaf (LexisNexis).
European Competition Law Review, journal (ESC Publishing).
Korah, *An Introductory Guide to EC Competition Law and Practice*, 9th edn (Hart Publishing, 2007).
Sweet & Maxwell's Encyclopedia of Competition Law, loose-leaf (Sweet & Maxwell).
Whish, *Competition Law*, 7th edn (2011).

Conflict of Laws

Cheshire, North, & Fawcett, *Private International Law*, 14th edn (LexisNexis, 2008).

Dicey & Morris, *Conflict of Laws*, 15th rev edn (Sweet & Maxwell, 2012). Updated by supplement.

Contract

Chitty & Beale, *Chitty on Contracts*, 31st edn (Sweet & Maxwell, 2012). Updated by supplement. Available online via *Westlaw*.

Goff & Jones, *The Law of Unjust Enrichment*, 8th edn (Sweet & Maxwell, 2010). Updated by supplement.

Conveyancing

See also: **Real Property**

Emmet & Farrand, *Emmet on Title*, loose-leaf (Sweet & Maxwell).

Encyclopedia of Compulsory Purchase, loose-leaf & CD-ROM (Sweet & Maxwell).

Fisher, *Fisher & Lightwood's Law of Mortgage*, 14th edn (LexisNexis, 2014). Updated by supplement.

Ruoff & Roper, *Law and Practice of Registered Conveyancing*, loose-leaf & CD-ROM (Sweet & Maxwell).

Silverman, *The Law Society's Conveyancing Handbook*, annual (Law Society).

Sweet & Maxwell's Conveyancing Practice, loose-leaf (Sweet & Maxwell).

Coroners

Matthews, *Jervis on Coroners: with forms and precedents*, 13th edn (Sweet & Maxwell, 2014). Updated by supplement.

Costs

See also: **Civil Litigation**

See also: **Criminal Litigation**

Butterworths Costs Service, loose-leaf (LexisNexis).

Cook on Costs, annual (LexisNexis).

Criminal Litigation

See also: **Administrative Law**

See also: **Costs**

See also: **Sentencing**

Anthony & Berryman, *Magistrates' Court Guide*, annual (LexisNexis).

Archbold, *Criminal Pleading, Evidence and Practice*, annual (Sweet & Maxwell). Updated by supplement. Available online via *Westlaw*.

Blackstone's Criminal Practice, annual (Oxford University Press). Available online via *Lexis Library*. Updated by *Bulletin* and online companion website.

Criminal Appeal Reports, law reports (Sweet & Maxwell).

Criminal Law Review, journal (Sweet & Maxwell).

Stone's Justices' Manual, annual (LexisNexis). Available online via *Lexis Library*.

Westlaw UK Crime, online service (Sweet & Maxwell).

Wilkinson's Road Traffic Offences, annual (Sweet & Maxwell). Updated by supplement and regular *Bulletin*.

Damages

See also: **Personal Injury**

Allen, *APIL Guide to Damages*, 3rd edn (Jordans, 2013).

Bell, *Guidelines for the Assessment of Damages in Personal Injury Cases*, annual (Judicial Studies Board/Oxford University Press). Available online via *Lawtel*.

Kemp & Kemp: The Quantum of Damages in Personal Injury and Fatal Accident Claims, loose-leaf & CD–ROM (Sweet & Maxwell).

Lawtel Personal Injury, online service (Lawtel/Sweet & Maxwell).

McGregor, *Damages*, 19th edn (Sweet & Maxwell, 2014). Updated by supplement.

Personal Injury and Quantum Reports, law reports (Sweet & Maxwell).

Wilde, *Facts and Figures: Tables for the Calculation of Damages*, annual (Professional Negligence Bar Association/Sweet & Maxwell).

Data Protection

Carey, *Data Protection: A Practical Guide to UK and EU Law*, 4th edn (Oxford University Press, 2014).

Jay, *Data Protection: Law and Practice*, 4th edn (Sweet & Maxwell, 2014).

Encyclopedia of Data Protection, loose-leaf (Sweet & Maxwell).

E-Commerce
See: **Information Technology**

Ecclesiastical Law

Hill, *Ecclesiastical Law*, 3rd edn (Oxford University Press, 2007).

Education

Farrington & Palfreyman, *The Law of Higher Education*, 2nd edn (Oxford University press, 2012).

The Law of Education, loose-leaf (LexisNexis). Available online via *Lexis Library*.

Employment Law
See also: **Health and Safety**

Encyclopedia of Employment Law and Practice, loose-leaf (Sweet & Maxwell).

Employment Law Journal, journal (Legalease).

Harvey on Industrial Relations and Employment Law, loose-leaf (LexisNexis). Available online via *Lexis Library*.

Industrial Cases Reports, law reports (Incorporated Council of Law Reporting).

Industrial Relations Law Reports, law reports (LexisNexis).

Environmental Law

Encyclopedia of Environmental Health Law and Practice, loose-leaf (Sweet & Maxwell).

Encyclopedia of Environmental Law and Practice, 2nd edn, loose-leaf (Sweet & Maxwell).

Environmental Law Reports, law reports (Sweet & Maxwell).

Garner's Environmental Law, loose-leaf (LexisNexis). Available online via *Lexis Library*.

Equity and Trusts

McGhee, *Snell's Equity*, 32nd edn (Sweet & Maxwell, 2010). Updated by supplement.

Underhill & Hayton, *Law of Trusts and Trustees*, 18th edn (LexisNexis, 2010).

European Union Law
See also: **Competition Law**

All England Law Reports: European Cases, 1983– (LexisNexis).

Common Market Law Reports, law reports (Sweet & Maxwell).

Common Market Law Review, journal (Kluwer).

Encyclopedia of European Community Law, loose-leaf (Sweet & Maxwell).

European Court Reports, law reports (European Court of Justice). Available online via Eur-Lex <http://eur-lex.europa.eu/en/index.htm>.

European Law Review, journal (Sweet & Maxwell).

Official Journal of the European Union, journal (Office for Official Publications of the European Union). Available online via Europa <http://eur-lex.europa.eu/>.

Vaughan, *Law of the European Communities*, loose-leaf (LexisNexis).

Evidence

Cross & Tapper, *Evidence*, 12th edn (LexisNexis, 2010).

Dennis, *The Law of Evidence*, 5th edn (Sweet & Maxwell, 2013).

Keane, *The Modern Law of Evidence*, 10th edn (Oxford University Press, 2014).

May, *Criminal Evidence*, 6th edn (Sweet & Maxwell, 2014).

Phipson, *On Evidence*, 18th edn (Sweet & Maxwell, 2013). Updated by supplement.

Family Law

See also: **Children**

Bird, *Financial Remedies Handbook*, 9th edn (Jordans, 2013).

Butterworths Family Law Service, loose-leaf (LexisNexis). Available online via *Lexis Library*.

Family Court Reports, law reports (LexisNexis).

Family Law, journal (Jordans). Available online via *Jordans*.

Family Law Reports, law reports (Jordans). Available online via *Jordans*.

Jackson, *Matrimonial Finance and Taxation*, 9th edn (LexisNexis, 2012). Available online via *Lexis Library*.

Practical Matrimonial Precedents, loose-leaf & CD-ROM (Sweet & Maxwell).

Rayden & Jackson's Divorce and Family Matters, 18th edn, loose-leaf (LexisNexis, 2005). Available online via *Lexis Library*.

Forms and Precedents

See also: **Civil Litigation**

See also: **Criminal Litigation**

See also: **Individual subject areas**

Atkin's Encyclopaedia of Court Forms in Civil Procedure, 2nd edn (LexisNexis). Updated by reissued volumes and loose-leaf noter-up. Available online via *Lexis Library*.

The Court Service, online service at <http://www.hmcourts-service.gov.uk> (Court Service).

The Encyclopaedia of Forms and Precedents, 5th edn (LexisNexis). Updated by reissued volumes and loose-leaf noter-up. Available online via *Lexis Library*.

Kelly, *Kelly's Draftsman*, 19th edn (LexisNexis, 2006). Updated by supplement.

Health and Safety

See also: **Employment**

Encyclopedia of Health and Safety at Work Law and Practice, loose-leaf (Sweet & Maxwell).

Ford, *Redgrave's Health and Safety*, 8th edn (LexisNexis, 2012). Updated by supplement. Available online via *Lexis Library*.

Housing Law

Arden & Partington, *Housing Law*, 2nd edn, loose-leaf (Sweet & Maxwell).

Dowding, *Dilapidations: The Modern Law and Practice*, 5th edn (Sweet & Maxwell, 2013).

Encyclopedia of Housing Law and Practice, loose-leaf (Sweet & Maxwell).

Housing Law Reports, law reports (Sweet & Maxwell).

Human Rights

Emmerson, *Human Rights and Criminal Justice*, 3rd edn (Sweet & Maxwell, 2012).

European Human Rights Reports, law reports (Sweet & Maxwell).

Human Rights Practice, loose-leaf (Sweet & Maxwell). Available online via *Westlaw*.

Lester & Pannick, *Human Rights Law and Practice*, 3rd edn (LexisNexis, 2009). Available online via *Lexis Library*.

Immigration Law

Butterworths Immigration Law Service, loose-leaf (LexisNexis). Available online via *Lexis Library*.

MacDonald, *Immigration Law and Practice*, 9th edn (LexisNexis, 2014). Updated by supplement. Available online via *Lexis Library*.

Information Technology

Computers and Law, journal (Society for Computers and Law).

Encyclopaedia of Information Technology Law, loose-leaf (Sweet & Maxwell).

Journal of Information Law and Technology, journal (University of Warwick). Available online at <http://www2.warwick.ac.uk/fac/soc/law/elj/jilt>.

Rowland & MacDonald, *Information Technology Law*, 4th edn (Taylor & Francis, 2011).

Insolvency

See: **Bankruptcy and Personal Insolvency**

Insurance

Birds, *Birds' Modern Insurance Law*, 9th edn (Sweet & Maxwell, 2013).

Encyclopedia of Insurance Law, loose-leaf (Sweet & Maxwell).

Leigh-Jones, *MacGillivray on Insurance Law*, 12th edn (Sweet & Maxwell, 2012). Updated by supplement.

Lloyd's Law Reports: Insurance and Reinsurance, law report (Informa).

Intellectual Property

Copinger & Skone James on Copyright, 16th edn (Sweet & Maxwell, 2010). Updated by supplement. Available online via *Westlaw*.

Cornish, *Intellectual Property Patents, Copyright, Trademarks and Allied Rights*, 8th edn (Sweet & Maxwell, 2013).

Encyclopedia of United Kingdom and European Patent Law, loose-leaf (Sweet & Maxwell).

Fleet Street Reports, law reports (Sweet & Maxwell).

Kerly's Law of Trade Marks and Trade Names, 15th edn (Sweet & Maxwell, 2009). Available online via *Westlaw*.

Laddie, *Modern Law of Copyright and Designs*, 3rd edn (Butterworths, 2000). Available online via *Lexis Library*.

Merkin & Black, *Copyright and Designs Law*, loose-leaf (Sweet & Maxwell).

Terrell on the Law of Patents, 17th edn (Sweet & Maxwell, 2010). Available online via *Westlaw*.

Landlord and Tenant

See also: **Housing**

Garner, *A Practical Approach to Landlord and Tenant*, 7th edn (Oxford University Press, 2013).

Hill and Redman's Law of Landlord and Tenant, loose-leaf (LexisNexis). Available online via *Lexis Library*.

The Landlord and Tenant Factbook, loose-leaf (Sweet & Maxwell).

Landlord and Tenant Reports, law reports (Sweet & Maxwell).

Woodfall's Law of Landlord and Tenant, loose-leaf (Sweet & Maxwell). Available online via *Westlaw*.

Legal Profession

The Bar Handbook, annual (LexisNexis).

Boon & Levin, *The Ethics and Conduct of Lawyers in England and Wales* (Bloomsbury, 2008).

Camp, *Companion to the Solicitor's Code of Conduct*, 2nd edn (Law Society, 2009).

Cordery on Solicitors, loose-leaf (LexisNexis).

Paterson & Ritchie, *Law Practice and Conduct for Solicitors* (Sweet & Maxwell, 2014).

Solicitors' Accounts Manual, 12th edn (Law Society, 2011).

Solicitors' Code of Conduct 2011 (Law Society, 2011).

Legal Research

Burton & Watkins, *Research Methods in Law* (Routledge, 2013).

De Bono, *Six Thinking Hats* (Penguin, 2009).

Holborn, *Butterworths Legal Research Guide*, 2nd edn (Butterworths, 2001).

Legal Skills

Beardsmore, *Opinion Writing and Drafting in Tort* (Taylor & Francis, 2003).

Bennion, *Statutory Interpretation: A Code*, 6th edn (LexisNexis, 2013). Updated by supplement.

Blake, *A Practical Approach to Effective Litigation*, 7th edn (Oxford University Press, 2009).

Fridd, *Basic Practice in Courts, Tribunals and Enquiries*, 3rd edn (Sweet & Maxwell, 2000).

Hyam, *Advocacy Skills*, 4th edn (Blackstone, 1999).

Munkman, *The Technique of Advocacy* (Universal Law Publishing Co. Ltd, 2003).

Libel

Carter-Ruck, *Libel and Slander*, 6th edn (LexisNexis, 2009).

Gatley on Libel and Slander, 12th edn (Sweet & Maxwell, 2013). Updated by supplement.

Licensing

Entertainment and Media Law Reports, law reports (Sweet & Maxwell).

Hyde, *Licensing Procedures and Precedents*, loose-leaf (Sweet & Maxwell).

Pain, *Licensing Practice and Procedure*, 9th edn (Callow, 2008).

Paterson, *Paterson's Licensing Acts*, annual (LexisNexis).

Local Government

Bailey, *Cross on Principles of Local Government Law*, 3rd edn (Sweet & Maxwell, 2004).

Cross on Local Government Law, 8th edn, loose-leaf (Sweet & Maxwell).

Encyclopedia of Local Government Law, loose-leaf (Sweet & Maxwell).

Encyclopedia of Rating and Local Taxation, loose-leaf (Sweet & Maxwell).

Lawtel Local Government, online service (Sweet & Maxwell).

Ryde on Rating and the Council Tax, loose-leaf (LexisNexis). Available online via *Lexis Library*.

Maritime Law

Baughen, *Shipping Law*, 5th edn (Cavendish, 2012).

Benedict on Admiralty, 7th edn, loose-leaf (Bender).

Carver on Bills of Lading, 3rd edn (Sweet & Maxwell, 2012).

Hill, *Maritime Law*, 6th edn (LLP, 2003).

Lloyd's Law Reports, law report (Lloyd's).

Lloyd's Maritime and Commercial Law Quarterly, journal (Informa).

Lorenzon, *CIF and FOB Contracts*, 5th edn (Sweet & Maxwell, 2012).

Scrutton on Charterparties and Bills of Lading, 22nd edn (Sweet & Maxwell, 2013).

Thomas, *Modern Law of Marine Insurance* (LLP, 2002).

Medical Law

Grubb, *Principles of Medical Law*, 3rd edn (Oxford University Press, 2010).

LS Law Medical, Law Report (Informa).

Malsher, *Medical Records for Lawyers* (EMIS, 2002).

Montgomery, *Health Care Law*, 3rd rev edn (Oxford University Press, 2014).

Palmer, *Medicine for Lawyers* (Royal Society of Medicine, 2005).

Mental Health

Gostin on Mental Health Law, loose-leaf (Shaw & Sons).

Heywood & Massey, *Court of Protection Practice*, loose-leaf, 13th edn (Sweet & Maxwell).

Journal of Mental Health Law, journal (Northumbria Law Press).

Cretney, *Cretney & Lush: Lasting and Enduring Powers of Attorney*, 7th edn (Jordans, 2013).

Negligence

See: **Torts**

Partnership

Encyclopaedia of Professional Partnerships, loose-leaf (Sweet & Maxwell).

Lindley & Banks, *Lindley & Banks on Partnership*, 19th rev edn (Sweet & Maxwell, 2010). Updated by supplement.

Personal Injury

See also: **Damages and Road Traffic Law**

Bingham and Berryman's Personal Injury and Motor Claims Cases, 13th edn (LexisNexis, 2010). Updated by supplement.

Buchan, *Personal Injury Practice: The Guide to Litigation in the County Court and High Court*, 6th edn (LexisNexis, 2014).

Butterworths Personal Injury Litigation Service, loose-leaf (LexisNexis). Available online via *Lexis Library*.

Curran, *Personal Injury Pleadings*, 5th edn (Sweet & Maxwell, 2014).

Journal of Personal Injury Law, journal (Sweet & Maxwell).

Lawtel Personal Injury, online service (Lawtel/Sweet & Maxwell).

Middleton, *Personal Injury Practice and Procedure*, 11th edn (Sweet & Maxwell, 2004).

Personal Injury and Quantum Reports, law reports (Sweet & Maxwell).

Planning Law

Butterworths Planning Law Service, loose-leaf (LexisNexis). Available online via *Lexis Library*.

Encyclopedia of Planning Law and Practice, loose-leaf (Sweet & Maxwell).

Estates Gazette Law Reports, law reports (Estates Gazette). Available online via *Lexis Library*.

Estates Gazette Planning Law Reports, law reports (Estates Gazette).

Journal of Planning and Environmental Law, journal (Sweet & Maxwell).

Property, Planning and Compensation Reports, law reports (Sweet & Maxwell).

Rating
See: **Local Government**

Real Property
See also: **Conveyancing**

Butterworths Property Law Service, loose-leaf (LexisNexis).

Encyclopedia of Compulsory Purchase, loose-leaf (Sweet & Maxwell).

Estates Gazette Law Reports, law reports (Estates Gazette). Available online via *Lexis Library*.

Megarry & Wade, *The Law of Real Property*, 8th edn (Sweet & Maxwell, 2012).

Property Planning and Compensation Reports, law reports (Sweet & Maxwell).

Sara, *Boundaries and Easements*, 5th edn (Sweet & Maxwell, 2011). Updated by supplement.

Road Traffic Law
See also: **Personal Injury**

Bingham & Berryman's Personal Injury and Motor Claims Cases, 13th edn (LexisNexis, 2010). Updated by supplement.

Butterworths Road Traffic Service, loose-leaf (LexisNexis). Available online via *Lexis Library*.

Encyclopedia of Highway Law and Practice, loose-leaf (Sweet & Maxwell).

Encyclopedia of Road Traffic Law and Practice, loose-leaf (Sweet & Maxwell).

Road Traffic Reports, law reports (Sweet & Maxwell).

Wilkinson's Road Traffic Offences, annual (Sweet & Maxwell). Updated by supplement.

Sale of Goods and Consumer Law

Atiyah, *Sale of Goods*, 12th edn (Pearson/Longman, 2010).

Benjamin, *Sale of Goods*, 9th edn (Sweet & Maxwell, 2014). Updated by supplement.

Butterworths Law of Food and Drugs, loose-leaf (LexisNexis). Available online via *Lexis Library*.

Butterworths Trading and Consumer Law, loose-leaf (LexisNexis). Available online via *Lexis Library*.

Encyclopedia of Consumer Credit Law, loose-leaf (Sweet & Maxwell).

Encyclopedia of Consumer Law, loose-leaf (Sweet & Maxwell).

Goode, *Consumer Credit Law & Practice*, loose-leaf (LexisNexis).

Miller, *Product Liability and Safety Encyclopaedia*, loose-leaf (LexisNexis). Available online via *Lexis Library*.

O'Keefe, *Law of Weights and Measures*, loose-leaf (LexisNexis). Available online via *Lexis Library*.

Sentencing
See also: **Crime**

Criminal Appeal Reports (Sentencing), law reports (Sweet & Maxwell).

Magistrates Bench Handbook: A Manual for Lay Magistrates, loose-leaf (Waterside).

Thomas, *Current Sentencing Practice*, loose-leaf (Sweet & Maxwell). Available online via *Westlaw*.

Thomas, *Sentencing Referencer*, annual (Sweet & Maxwell). Available online via *Westlaw*.

Wasik, *A Practical Approach to Sentencing*, 5th edn (Oxford University Press, 2014).

Shipping
See: **Maritime Law**

Social Security and Welfare Law
Encyclopedia of Social Services and Child Care Law, loose-leaf (Sweet & Maxwell).

Journal of Social Welfare and Family Law, journal (Routledge).

Wikeley & Ogus, *The Law of Social Security*, 5th edn (Butterworths, 2002).

Taxation
See also: **Local Government**

Bramwell, *Taxation of Companies and Company Reconstructions*, loose-leaf, 9th edn (Sweet & Maxwell).

British Tax Review, journal (Sweet & Maxwell).

De Voil's Indirect Tax Service, loose-leaf (LexisNexis). Available online via *Lexis Library*.

Foster's Inheritance Tax, loose-leaf (LexisNexis). Available online via *Lexis Library*.

Simon's Direct Tax Service, loose-leaf (LexisNexis). Available online via *Lexis Library*.

Sumption, *Capital Gains Tax*, loose-leaf (LexisNexis).

Taxation, journal (LexisNexis).

Tolley's Orange Tax Handbook, annual (LexisNexis).

Tolley's Yellow Tax Handbook, annual (LexisNexis).

Whiteman & Sherry, *On Capital Gains Tax*, 5th edn, loose-leaf (Sweet & Maxwell, 2008).

Whiteman & Sherry, *On Income Tax*, 4th edn, loose-leaf (Sweet & Maxwell, 2009).

Torts
Charlesworth & Percy on Negligence, 12th edn (Sweet & Maxwell, 2010). Updated by supplement. Available online via *Westlaw*.

Clerk & Lindsell on Torts, 20th edn (Sweet & Maxwell, 2010). Updated by supplement.

Jackson & Powell on Professional Liability, 7th edn (Sweet & Maxwell, 2011). Updated by supplement.

Lloyd's Law Reports: Professional Negligence, law reports (LLP/Informa).

Powers and Harris, *Clinical Negligence*, 4th edn (LexisNexis, 2008).

Wills, Probate, and Succession
Biggs & Gaudern, *A Practitioner's Guide to Probate and the Administration of Estates*, 3rd edn (Wildy, Simmonds & Hill, 2012)

Butterworths Wills, Probate and Administration Service, loose-leaf (LexisNexis). Available online via *Lexis Library*.

Griffin & Walker, *Administration of Estates*, 3rd edn (Financial World Publishing, 2008).

Sherrin, *Williams on Wills*, 10th edn (LexisNexis, 2014). Updated by supplement.

Theobald on Wills, 17th edn (Sweet & Maxwell, 2010). Updated by supplement.

Tristram & Coote, *Probate Practice*, 31st edn (LexisNexis, 2014). Updated by supplement.

Williams, Mortimer, and Sunnucks, *Executors, Administrators & Probate*, 20th edn (Sweet & Maxwell, 2012). Updated by supplement.

Part II

Fact Management

10 Overview of a civil case   141
11 Anatomy of a criminal case   171
12 The fact management process   187
13 Presentation for the practitioner: the CAP approach in action   223
14 Dealing with figures   226
15 Communication and information technology use in case preparation and
    presentation   235

Fact Management

Overview of a civil case

10.1 Introduction

This chapter outlines the different contexts in which you will be working and what may be required of you at the different stages of a case by setting out the main stages in a civil case, explaining the different roles of the solicitor and barrister, the work done by the solicitor at each stage, the stages at which the barrister will generally be consulted, and the work done by the barrister at each of these stages.

10.2 Stages in a civil case

10.2.1 Introduction

Civil disputes cover a broad range of cases including those involving general common law, family matters, insolvency, Chancery claims, and claims to statutory tribunals such as employment tribunals. The steps set out here relate to those in the most common types of common law case taken in the High Court and County Courts, e.g. suing for debts and damages in tort and contract. This is not a civil litigation manual and does not cover the detailed rules but rather the main stages in a civil case and the work to be done by the lawyers at each stage. The Woolf reforms, implemented as the Civil Procedure Rules 1998 (CPR) in 1999, made major changes to the terminology used and procedure followed in both courts, simplifying them and attempting to cut the cost and delay of litigation in many cases. This was done by introducing the 'overriding objective' of the civil justice system, to deal with cases justly—and also the concept of 'proportionality' by which the court attempts to balance the need for disputes to be resolved as quickly and as cheaply as possible, with the need for cases to be properly prepared and fairly heard.

Further reforms of civil litigation procedures and costs which took place in 2013 ('the Jackson reforms') have now included proportionality as part of the overriding objective, by stating that cases must be dealt with justly and at proportionate cost. Further details of these reforms can be found in S Sime and D French, *Blackstone's Guide to the Civil Justice Reforms 2013* (Oxford University Press, 2013).

Although the changes have altered what is required or possible at any particular stage of a case, the main stages in the preparation of a case remain the same.

10.2.2 Main stages

The conduct of a civil case through the courts can be divided into seven main areas of work from the time the client first sees a lawyer, to the closure of the client's file:

(a) *Before action:* involves analysis of the case and decisions by the client and the lawyer, in particular as to whether court action is proportionate and how the costs will be paid. In some cases, some urgent action may need to be taken, e.g. a tenant claiming to have been unlawfully evicted may seek an injunction to be reinstated, pending determination of his or her right to remain by a full trial.

A big change introduced by the Woolf reforms in certain standard cases is the introduction of the concept of 'pre-action protocols', which requires parties to exchange a fair amount of information before initiating proceedings. A number of such 'protocols' have been implemented for specific areas of work, e.g. personal injury and clinical negligence. It is envisaged that such 'protocols' will be written for as many standard types of case as possible. In areas where no protocol exists, parties are expected to follow the guidance and procedure set out in section III of the Practice Direction—Pre-Action Conduct. The idea is to break down the present adversarial and secretive approach and promote settlement as early as possible.

(b) *Initiating proceedings:* involves deciding which court to use, the drafting and issue of proceedings, and exchange of statements of case by the parties.

(c) *Interim:* involves all the intermediate steps between the exchange of statements of case and the trial, some taken automatically and some requiring applications to the court. These steps are largely concerned with determining what issues will be fought and collecting the evidence to support the allegations by both sides.

(d) *Trial:* involves the preparation immediately before the trial and the actual day(s) of the trial.

(e) *Enforcement:* involves the winning party taking formal steps to force the losing party to obey the order of the court where there is any failure to do so.

(f) *Appeal:* involves any party dissatisfied with the court's judgment or order considering whether an appeal is possible and appropriate and taking the formal steps necessary to appeal.

(g) *Payment of costs:* involves ensuring all costs of the litigation have been assessed, where appropriate, and been paid to the relevant person or authority.

Clearly, the first four of these areas of work occur in succession. However, the parties may decide not to proceed further or to discontinue the case at any time during the process, for example if the parties agree to settle the case. A case may not involve enforcement or appeal. Payment of the various costs of litigation occurs throughout the process.

10.2.3   Civil Procedure Rules

The Civil Procedure Rules 1998 and the Jackson reforms set out in some detail how cases are to be conducted and prepared for trial. Important concepts introduced by these rules and reforms which affect the work of both barristers and solicitors are:

(a) The 'overriding objective', which the court and parties must bear in mind throughout. One of the principal concepts is that of 'proportionality' by which the court, parties, and lawyers must, throughout the case, deal with the case expeditiously and efficiently and keep the preparation and costs involved proportionate to the value and importance of the case.

(b) The use of pre-action protocols (see (a) in **10.2.2**). These result in the costs of a case being incurred earlier, as much of the information will have been exchanged before proceedings are even issued. It also sometimes means that barristers are more involved in cases before proceedings are issued (see **10.3.5**).

(c) Case management by the courts. The idea behind this is that the control of the timescale and costs of the litigation should be vested in the courts. This is done partially through tracking of cases (see (d)), where the steps and costs allowed in preparation are kept commensurate with the value and importance of the case. 'Procedural' judges are required take an active and robust role by keeping an eye on cases and, where necessary, having case management hearings with the lawyers to ensure that the case is proceeding in a way which is efficient and cost-effective.

(d) Tracking of cases. There are three tracks, each with its own set of rules to ensure that the cost and speed with which the case comes to trial are proportionate to the value and importance of the case. The three tracks are:

(i) Small claims (basically, where the value of the claim is £10,000 or less, with some exceptions). The way in which cases are dealt with in the small claims track is very different from the fast track. The procedure is very simple. The hearing is informal and strict rules of evidence do not apply. A party who wins his or her case will not have his legal costs paid. Such cases are therefore frequently conducted by litigants in person.

(ii) Fast track (basically, where the value of the claim is between £10,000 and £25,000). This is a slightly more detailed procedure with limited steps to ensure sufficient disclosure of documents, witnesses, and expert evidence (where relevant), and a trial date set for 30 weeks after the case has been allocated to this track. In addition, the time for the trial will be limited to one day. These rules attempt to ensure that the case comes to trial as quickly as possible and the costs of preparation are controlled.

(iii) Multi-track (basically, where the value of the claim is more than £25,000). This is a more detailed procedure, which allows for more detailed disclosure and preparation of evidence to reflect the greater complexity of the case. In addition, judges are more likely to become actively involved in managing the case through procedural hearings such as 'case management conferences' (held early on to determine the main issues, steps to be taken in preparing the case, etc.), 'listing hearings' (to assist the parties and court in the decisions necessary for fixing the date for trial), and 'pre-trial reviews' (to set out how the actual hearing will be conducted, e.g. the length of time for speeches, witnesses, etc.).

Thus, the amount of work involved in the interim and trial stages (see (c) and (d) in **10.2.2**) will vary depending on the 'track' to which the case is allocated and the specific requirements of the individual case.

10.3   Roles of solicitor and barrister

10.3.1   The Bar is a referral profession

There are now some cases where clients have direct access to barristers. These clients are either other professionals such as accountants under the Licensed Access Rules and Recognition Regulations, or the general public for some areas of work under the Public Access Rules. (These regulations were formerly annexed to the old Bar Code of Conduct. They can now be found in the new and revised code at section D2: 'Barristers undertaking Public Access and Licensed Access Work'). However, the Bar is largely a referral profession, which, generally, gets its work from solicitors. A solicitor will use counsel for specialist advice or advocacy, either because the solicitor lacks the relevant expertise or rights of audience, or because it is more cost-effective for the solicitor to use a barrister than to do the research or advocacy personally. The solicitor decides when to use a barrister, and if he or she fails to instruct counsel when it is necessary, the solicitor may be liable to the client in negligence.

10.3.2 Solicitors' work

The level of expertise and specialisation of solicitors' firms varies enormously, from a firm which offers a broad range of legal services, from drafting wills to acting for defendants in criminal cases, to one which specialises, e.g. doing largely personal injury work. In any firm, work will be done by the partners (who must be solicitors unless the firm is authorised as an Alternative Business Structure (ABS) by the Solicitors' Regulation Authority under the Legal Services Act 2007, Part 5), employed solicitors, and paralegals who are often qualified legal executives. Most firms will assign the contentious and non-contentious work to different people. The litigation department may also be divided into criminal, family, and civil, with solicitors specialising in one or two areas, e.g. personal injury and housing. In many firms, the litigation department has people with expertise in numerous areas ranging over commercial, landlord and tenant, employment, family, financial services, etc. Paralegals usually do the more routine aspects of civil litigation such as service of documents or sitting behind counsel and taking notes in a hearing.

Technically, a client instructs a firm of solicitors to act. All correspondence and instructions or briefs to counsel will be in the firm's name. Once the other side has been notified that solicitors are acting, it is improper for any other lawyer to communicate with the client directly (although there is nothing wrong with the parties dealing with each other directly). When court proceedings are issued, the firm (but not the individual solicitor) is on the record at court as acting for the client in the particular proceedings and will remain so until this is altered, or the case is concluded, or withdrawn. Although the firm as a whole technically acts for the client, an individual solicitor will usually conduct the case. Most firms will try to ensure that the solicitor who first sees the client takes the case on and sees it to completion.

The individual solicitor with conduct of the case will decide when to consult a barrister. Within the seven areas of work set out earlier, barristers will frequently be involved in pre-action, initiating proceedings, interim work, the trial, and appeals. In addition, they need to be able to justify costs where the court assesses costs summarily at the end of the hearing rather than doing a detailed assessment later. This is likely to happen where interim applications are made prior to the hearing. Barristers are rarely involved in enforcement.

10.3.3 Dealing with costs

Prior to taking any steps, including instructing counsel, the solicitor must explain the costs of litigation to the client and ascertain how they will be paid.

10.3.3.1 Ascertaining the costs

The bulk of the costs will be the fees to cover the work done by the solicitor and any barrister involved. The bulk of the solicitor's fees will usually be calculated on the basis of an hourly charge, with even small firms charging at least £100 an hour. Barristers' fees are usually calculated on a piecework basis, for a particular opinion, or statement of case, or court appearance. The level of the fee depends on the seniority of the barrister doing the work and its complexity, and is agreed between the solicitor and the barrister's clerk, but the minimum charge even for a junior barrister on a short application would be £100. In addition to the 'legal fees', expenses are incurred such as court charges and the costs of obtaining expert reports. The client must be made aware of the fact that every consultation with the solicitor, and every step taken in the case, adds to the costs. The solicitor must also make clear that, if the case is lost, the client may be liable for the other side's costs because the general rule is that costs 'follow the event' and the loser will be ordered to pay the winner's costs. However, the court rarely orders the loser to pay all the winner's costs. The solicitor should therefore also advise the client that, even if he or she wins, he or she is likely to be liable for some costs.

10.3.3.2 Methods of payment

The methods of paying costs in civil litigation have been radically changed by the Jackson reforms. The client may simply pay privately, i.e. pay the costs from his or her own pocket. He or she may be asked to pay 'on account' (i.e. a sum up front, calculated to cover a certain amount of work) and/or pay as he or she receives the invoices for work done by the solicitor. Expenses other than solicitors' fees (e.g. barristers' fee, court fees, experts' fees, etc., called 'disbursements') are paid by the solicitor and the money recouped from the client. If the client wins his or her case, the other side may be ordered to pay his or her costs. However, this might not be ordered, so the client might still be liable for all of his or her own costs, and in any event will almost certainly have to pay some of his or her own costs.

Alternatively, the client and solicitor may enter a conditional fee agreement (CFA) whereby, if the client loses, no legal fee will be charged by the solicitor, but if the client wins, the solicitor is entitled to payment of the usual rate plus a success fee. Under the Jackson reforms, if the client wins he will be unable to recover the success fee from the losing defendant. Such agreements with the solicitor will cover only the solicitor's fee and not 'disbursement' costs such as an expert's fees or the barrister's fees, which the client will pay in the normal way. A client conducting litigation on a conditional fee basis remains potentially liable for the other side's costs if the claim is unsuccessful, but this liability can often be covered by insurance. Some people have legal expenses insurance whereby the costs are met by the insurance company. This is called 'before the event' insurance, and is increasingly common as part of motor and household insurance policies. Even if no such insurance has been arranged before the event that results in litigation, 'after the event' insurance is available and increasingly popular. It can be obtained even during the litigation process. The premium payable will depend on the risk taken by the insurance company (i.e. the amount of cover sought and the strength of the case). In personal injury cases unsuccessful claimants are afforded protection from having to pay the winning defendant's costs in a new regime introduced by the Jackson reforms called 'qualified one-way costs shifting' (QOCS). This may remove the need for such claimants to take out litigation insurance.

The Jackson reforms now permit Damages-Based agreements (DBAs), whereby the client agrees to pay a percentage of any damages that he recovers to the solicitor. If the client loses the claim the solicitors will not receive their legal fees.

Finally, some people may qualify for public assistance (legal aid) by way of the Community Legal Service. This is now available in a reduced number of civil cases, as the Jackson reforms have abolished legal aid in cases such as clinical negligence and private family law (with exceptions). Firms must be contracted to undertake any new civil publicly funded work. This contract enables the firm to conduct publicly funded work on the basis of being paid from public funds for each case taken on. There are different forms of assistance with criteria to determine whether or not the client and the case qualify for assistance (for further details see the Civil Legal Aid (Merits Criteria) Regulations 2013).

10.3.4   Instructing and briefing counsel

The solicitor with conduct of the case will also decide which barrister to consult and when 'booking' the barrister will officially deal through the clerk to the barrister's chambers. Most solicitors build up a 'stable' of several barristers in any one field of work whom they use regularly because they are good, fast, efficient, get on well with clients, or with whom they have a particularly good rapport. Solicitors new to litigation or a particular area of work without such a 'stable' will select on the basis of recommendations of those working in the firm, solicitors working in the same field or, possibly, the clerk of a set of chambers which the solicitor has used. Lacking such recommendations, a solicitor may select on the basis of the specialisation of the chambers, which can be obtained from the various directories.

A solicitor will use a range of barristers, from very junior barristers for fairly simple matters, generally because it is cost-effective, to very senior Queen's Counsel for their highly specialist knowledge and advocacy skills on particularly complex cases. The cab-rank rule (see rule C29-30 in the new revised Code of Conduct for the Bar, which can be found in Part Two of the new *Bar Standards Board Handbook*) requires barristers not to refuse to do work except for specified reasons which include lack of expertise, in-adequate time and opportunity to prepare, and lack of proper fee. Within the rule, when taking on work for the barristers in their set, clerks do try to take into account the work preference of the barristers. However, in early years of practice most barristers have no particular area of expertise and will usually take a broad range of cases.

10.3.5   The barrister's involvement

A barrister's involvement in any civil case is limited to doing specific tasks as requested by the solicitor. The three types of task which solicitors will usually ask a barrister to undertake are:

- advising on:
    — merits and/or quantum,
    — difficult or obscure points of law,
    — evidence;
- drafting documents, e.g. statements of case, statements of truth; and
- advocacy at:
    — interim hearings,
    — trial.

The solicitor consults the barrister separately on each specific step. Most solicitors will want continuity of barrister throughout a case and will, for example, ask the same barrister who advised on the merits at the beginning to draft the statement of case and do the advocacy at the trial. However, if the solicitor is not satisfied with the work done at any stage, he or she may ask someone else or decide to do the work personally. A solicitor may also use barristers of different call for different aspects of the same case, e.g. one of very junior call for simple interim hearings but a more senior barrister for advising on evidence and the trial. Finally, briefs for interim hearings or for trial may pass from one barrister to another because the original barrister briefed is not available, e.g. when he or she is 'double-booked' because a case is taking longer than expected.

The solicitor is responsible for paying any fee charged by a barrister. The solicitor pays the barrister's fee and recoups the money from the client. If the barrister's fee is not paid, the barrister pursues the solicitor and not the lay client. The traditional way in which a barrister charged the fee was on a piecework basis (e.g. a fee for an opinion or a fee for the advocacy at an interim hearing). However, barristers now also enter CFAs (see 10.3.3.2) with solicitors, which operate on the same basis as CFAs between lay clients and solicitors (i.e. no fee if the case is lost but an additional success fee if the case is won). Such an agreement can cover all areas of work done by the barrister or be limited to specific areas of work. This means that the barrister has to do a 'risk assessment' when deciding whether or not to accept instructions from a solicitor. Doing such an assessment can be very complicated and further consideration of this is beyond the scope of this manual.

10.3.6   Form and content of instructions or brief

Although solicitors may consult counsel by phone on occasion, it is more usual for them to consult in writing or by email. Technically, a solicitor 'instructs' counsel to advise or draft documents and 'briefs' counsel to attend hearings. The solicitor will send a fresh set of 'instructions' or 'brief' each time the barrister is consulted. Instructions or briefs from solicitors should include copies of all relevant documents, follow a fairly standard format, and include:

(a) The heading, which sets out the names of the prospective parties if proceedings have not yet been issued or the title of the case as drafted if proceedings have been issued.

(b) The party for whom counsel is instructed or briefed.

(c) A list of the documents enclosed.

(d) The name of the instructing firm and the name, reference, and extension of the particular solicitor conducting the case within the firm.

(e) A brief summary of the case, which should identify the relevant issues, information, and documents, and explain the solicitor's opinion, advice given to the client, and the steps taken to date.

(f) Specific directions as to what work the barrister is instructed or briefed to do, for example to advise on merits and quantum, or represent a client at a hearing.

(g) A 'back sheet' which contains the heading, the barrister's name and chambers address; the solicitor's firm name, address, telephone number, fax number, and email address; the reference or name of the individual solicitor dealing with the case; and the words 'Community Legal Service' if the client is publicly funded, or counsel's fee where briefed to appear on a hearing for a private client. If counsel is instructed on a conditional fee basis this will be noted in the brief.

10.3.7   Returning the work and endorsing the brief

The barrister does the work as instructed or briefed and returns the instructions or brief to the solicitor with all the enclosed documents and an endorsement on the back sheet of the work done, the date, and the fee. The endorsement is important as it is the statement of the work done. Where an opinion or draft is enclosed with the returned brief, the endorsement merely signifies the work done, the date, and the counsel who did it. Where court hearings are attended, it is important to ensure that the endorsement fully and accurately sets out the order made or the settlement reached. It should contain all the relevant details, including the date, the judge, and the order made, and be signed by counsel. Writing a full attendance note for the solicitor can be very useful and may impress him or her.

The barrister usually retains none of the papers once the work under any particular set of instructions or brief has been completed. When solicitors instruct or brief counsel they should include any previous instructions or briefs, together with their enclosed documents, and any written advice or opinion. However, it is important for a barrister to keep a copy of any written work done for the solicitor and a note of any relevant detail about the case, e.g. factual analysis of the case or legal research done, for future reference, as the barrister may be instructed again on the case.

10.3.8   Solicitors and barristers as client's agent

Solicitors and barristers act as the client's representatives and as such the rules of agency apply. The actual authority of the solicitor conducting the case will depend on the instructions of the client and the solicitor should obtain specific instructions from the client before taking any step. The actual authority of the barrister at any stage will be limited to the work required by the current set of instructions or brief. Both solicitor and barrister may be liable to the client if they act outside their actual authority.

The apparent authority of solicitor and barrister to bind the client may be wider or narrower than their actual authority. The solicitor's apparent authority will extend to accepting service on behalf of the client and progressing the case to trial. It will also extend to making admissions and, in certain circumstances, compromising or settling the case. The barrister's apparent authority extends to speaking for the client in court and may also extend to making admissions and settlements on behalf of the client. If either the solicitor or barrister bind their lay client by acting within their apparent authority but beyond their actual authority, they will be in breach of their professional duty to the client and will be liable to them.

10.4   Pre-claim stage

10.4.1   The barrister's involvement

A barrister's involvement at this stage is usually confined to being:

- instructed to advise on merits and/or quantum; and
- briefed to appear in court to obtain pre-action orders.

In both situations, the solicitor will have dealt with the legal costs and how these will be paid. The solicitor will almost invariably have interviewed the client, and should have obtained full details of all relevant matters, and sent instructions or a brief to counsel, including all the relevant information and documents.

10.4.2   Opinion on merits and/or quantum

10.4.2.1   Generally

The solicitor will seek counsel's opinion if he or she wants a second opinion on the case or feels further legal research or a more expert view is required to assess it; or if this is required, e.g. by the insurance company where the client has legal expenses insurance.

Prior to seeking counsel's opinion, the solicitor should have obtained full information from the client on personal details, the problem, details of any loss suffered, and the solution the client is seeking. The solicitor should have discussed with the client what the best course of action is, given the remedy the client is seeking, taking into account all the relevant factors including:

- the solicitor's provisional view on the merits of the client's case;
- the position of the potential defendant(s) (e.g. easily located, in the country, financially good for the sum to be claimed, likely to pay up if proceedings are issued);
- the time it will take to bring proceedings to trial if necessary; and
- whether some other alternative, such as mediation or complaint to an ombudsman, might be more appropriate.

Having reached a provisional view that litigation is at least worth investigating, the solicitor may then seek counsel's opinion by sending instructions setting out clearly all the relevant information, the solicitor's own view and advice to the client to date, and any steps already taken: for example an attempt may have been made to mediate or settle the case, which has failed. The instructions should set out clearly what advice is sought from counsel.

The date of receipt of instructions in chambers will be noted on the instructions. Once the barrister has written the opinion, which should be signed and dated by counsel, it will be returned to the solicitor, together with the original instructions to counsel with the back sheet properly endorsed with the fee and the date the work was completed. One of the criticisms of barristers is the time taken to return written advice. It is important, therefore, to ensure you develop efficient methods which enable you to achieve a reasonable turnaround time. With ever more efficient methods of communication being used (e.g. fax, email) what is a 'reasonable' turnaround time gets shorter and shorter.

Although the instructions to counsel will rarely be shown to the lay client, solicitors frequently do either give or show a copy of counsel's opinion to the lay client. The client will then make a decision on whether or not to issue proceedings. Depending on the type of case and client, the solicitor may call the client in for an interview and give or show the client a copy of the opinion. Alternatively, a copy of the opinion may just be sent to the lay client, with a covering letter setting out the solicitor's view and seeking the client's decision.

10.4.2.2 Case analysis: advising on the merits and/or quantum

Context

Even where you are asked to advise before proceedings have been issued, your analysis is focused on what will happen at trial: what issues will be fought and what is the likelihood of success (i.e. will your client win and, if so, get the remedy he or she is seeking?).

When advice is being sought at this preliminary stage, the solicitor will have been conscious of not taking any steps which might cost the client and be wasted because the advice is not to proceed. Thus, the instructions may not contain, for example, expert reports, all the necessary documentation, or much in the way of evidence, e.g. proofs from witnesses. The solicitor may also have felt that, in the circumstances, despite the additional cost to the client, a conference with counsel might be advisable prior to any written advice being given. However, if the instructions do not suggest a conference, counsel should advise on the basis of the information in the brief. Clearly, if essential information has not been provided, counsel could contact the solicitor to obtain this before advising.

Consider the stage the case has reached. Is there any urgency? For example, is the limitation period about to expire? If it is a case where a pre-action protocol applies, has this been followed? From the tone of the instructions, how knowledgeable about civil procedure is your instructing solicitor? In addition to advising on the merits and quantum, what procedural aspects should you also include in your advice?

Analysis

Your analysis should be focused on the allegations which will be included in the client's statement of case, any possible counter-allegations by the potential defendants, and how these allegations will be proved in court. On the basis of this analysis, you must evaluate the client's case and form an opinion on the likelihood of the court finding in your client's favour.

You should be considering in as much detail as possible:

(a) What cause(s) of action will form the basis of the client's claim and what facts will be used to support the cause(s) of action? Thus, for example, if the claim is based on negligence, what precisely will you allege are the breaches? In addition, you must consider how the potential defendant is likely to defend the case, e.g. will he or she simply deny the breaches or also plead contributory negligence by your client? You are thinking forward to how you will draft your client's statement of case, which issues are likely to be disputed in the defence, and therefore the issues which the court will have to decide.

(b) What evidence exists to support or counter the allegations which will be contained in the statements of case? Your analysis of the evidence must be thorough, detailed, and precise. You need to be clear what evidence the solicitor has already identified and what further evidence should be collected. It is essential that your analysis is firmly focused on the allegations which are likely to be disputed and will need to be proved.

Having done this analysis, you then need to evaluate the case. Consider the allegations which need to be proved. Who bears the burden of proof? How likely is it that the court will find for your client on the allegations? How difficult and/or expensive will it be to collect the evidence? What remedy is your client likely to get if he or she wins?

Finally, consider any procedural points which need to be highlighted for your instructing solicitor, given your analysis and evaluation of the case.

Presentation

The opinion must be practical and accessible to the reader. The lay client will want to know his or her chances of succeeding and what the court will award if he or she does win. The solicitor will want to be able to understand quickly what your conclusions are, why you have reached those conclusions, and the action you advise be taken. This means that your opinion must be structured and written in language which clearly sets out:

- *your conclusions:* on the case overall and on the individual issues which will be fought;
- *your reasoning:* identifying the cause(s) of action, the allegations of fact, and the evidence on which you have relied in your evaluation of the case;
- any advice on further evidence to be obtained; and
- any procedural steps of which the solicitor should be advised.

For more information on writing opinions, see Part III on *Opinion Writing*.

10.4.3   **Making applications before issue**

There are a variety of orders which can be obtained prior to issue. Most of these are done by application to the court for a hearing at which the matter can be determined on the basis of written evidence. Although solicitors may have the right to appear on such an application, counsel is frequently instructed. The more common of these orders are set out as follows.

10.4.3.1   Injunctions

A client may require an immediate court order to be protected from an alleged wrong. Thus, for example, the client's neighbour may be doing building work which is undermining the client's house and an application is made to court to order the neighbour to cease the building work until the case can be determined at trial. Another client may fear that property relevant to his claim (e.g. a pirated DVD) held by the wrongdoer might be destroyed, and a search order will be sought to permit the client to search and seize the property pending trial. A third client, who fears that the wrongdoer will dissipate assets or transfer them out of the country so as to render judgment hollow, may seek a freezing injunction to freeze those assets.

10.4.3.2   Orders to assist collection of evidence

In order to ascertain whether or not a client has a sufficiently good case to issue proceedings, it may be necessary to obtain documents or inspect property which is in someone else's possession. If access is refused, an application can be made in certain circumstances for a court order that inspection be given.

10.4.3.3   Making the application

In these situations, particularly where injunctions are sought, counsel may receive extremely short notice of the hearing (e.g. an hour), and very little written information from the solicitor (sometimes only the back sheet). The written evidence which forms the basis of the application is that of the client but will be drafted by the barrister or the solicitor. Counsel may be asked to make the application on the basis of the written evidence drafted by the solicitor. Alternatively, counsel may also be instructed to advise in conference (where time is short, the whole thing may be done in one telephone call) and/or draft the written evidence (faxed to the solicitor's office). If time is very short, the written evidence may be drafted outside the court door. Indeed, the matter may be so urgent that a telephone application can be made for the injunction.

Where a detailed order is also sought (e.g. an injunction), counsel should have a draft order ready to present to the court. Again, this might have been prepared by the solicitor or by counsel. Clearly, care must be taken in the drafting of the order to ensure that it gives the client the protection sought and is within the court's powers.

Those attending court should, in theory, include the barrister, the solicitor, and the lay client. However, often the solicitor will not attend. If the case is sufficiently straightforward there may be no representation from the solicitor's firm. Alternatively, the solicitor may send an 'outdoor clerk', i.e. a file carrier from the solicitor's office who may be extremely bright and *au fait* with the client and the case, or a part-timer who has no idea about the case and very little, if any, legal knowledge. In addition, there is strictly no need for the client to attend, as he or she will have no role to play in the hearing (the evidence being that contained in the written statement). However, if possible, it is desirable for the client to attend in case something unexpected arises. Thus, the barrister at the hearing may have access to fairly comprehensive information where both the solicitor and the lay client attend. However, he or she may equally have to rely solely on information from the brief including the written evidence.

At court, there may be attempts to settle the matter, either just the immediate application or the whole matter. Although the solicitors might have been negotiating prior to this, once at the court door, negotiations will usually be between counsel. Thus, the barrister needs to be aware of the wider context of the case and be ready to receive and process information very quickly indeed. If a settlement is reached, the barrister should ensure that he or she knows exactly what has been agreed and that it is within the client's instructions. Clearly, this will be extremely difficult, if not impossible, where the client is not present and the solicitor is represented by an uninformed 'outdoor clerk'.

10.4.3.4   Case analysis: pre-issue applications

Context

As explained earlier, when instructed on a pre-issue application, you may be requested to draft the documents which form the basis of the application, or be required to make the application on the basis of documents drafted by someone else. In either case, you need to ensure that all the relevant documents are available for the hearing. What precisely should be included depends on the urgency of the application and whether or not it is being made without notice to the other side. You need to check the relevant CPR as to what documents are required. For most applications, even those made without notice to the other side, the applicant (as the prospective claimant) is obliged to have a claim form, particulars of claim, application notice, evidence to support the application (either a witness statement or affidavit, depending on the type of application), and a copy of the draft order sought in the proper format. Sometimes, e.g. for injunctions, the draft order is also supplied on disk or USB so that it can be readily adapted by the court.

If you are briefed to make the application on the basis of documents drafted by someone else, check that copies of all relevant documents are included in your instructions, and that they are in the required format. If you are instructed to draft relevant documents, ensure you are clear what documents must still be drafted. Generally, you will be instructed to draft the order and possibly witness statement/affidavit. However, you may also be instructed to draft the particulars of claim.

Whether you are instructed just to make the application or have also been instructed to draft the documents, you will need to be clear what the application is for and why it is being made now, what your client's case is, and what, if any, previous contact there has been with the (proposed) defendant(s). The instructions may contain minimal evidence about the case as a whole at this stage, e.g. just that contained in the witness statement or affidavit and exhibits, for much the same reasons as set out earlier (see **10.4.22**). The information and evidence in the instructions will be focused mainly on that required for the particular application.

Analysis

Your analysis should cover both:

(a) *THE case:* you need to be clear what cause(s) of action your client is relying on, who the defendants are, what facts are alleged by your client which support the cause(s) of action against each defendant, and what evidence there is at this point to prove those facts. All these should be clear from the particulars of claim, the witness statements (or affidavits), and the exhibits, if already drafted. If these have not yet been drafted, the information should be contained in the instructions from the solicitor and documents enclosed (e.g. statements from the client taken in interview). The extent to which the court will focus on the merits of the main case depends on the type of application being made and the test which the court applies in determining that type of application (see (b)). However, whatever the application, you must understand why your client's case is pleaded as it is (i.e. what the allegations of fact are and how they support the cause of action) and the evidence currently available.

(b) *THIS application:* you need to be clear about what the client is seeking; what test the court will apply in determining whether or not to grant the application; whether the application is opposed or not; what, if any, notice has been given to the other side and the reasons why no notice or short notice has been given; and what evidence is available to the court in the witness statements or affidavits and the exhibits on which to determine the application. This should be clear from the witness statements or affidavits and the exhibits, and the draft order, if already drafted. If these have not yet been drafted, the information should be contained in the instructions from the solicitor and documents enclosed (e.g. statements from the client taken in interview).

Once you have done this detailed analysis, you must formulate the arguments which can be used both for and against the granting of your client's application. In doing this, you must focus on the issues that will concern the court in determining the application. This will include considering every element of the test that the court will apply, and being clear which aspects will be disputed and which will be of most concern to the court and will therefore require more attention in your argument. In addition, you need to consider the precise wording of the order very carefully as you will be required by the court to justify the order as drafted.

You also need to evaluate the arguments, ensuring that you are focusing on your strongest arguments and ready to deal with any weaknesses in the case. If necessary, consider what your 'fall-back' position will be (i.e. if you cannot persuade the court to grant the order as drafted, what amendments might you suggest to get the most for your client?).

If the application is without notice to the other side, you need to consider carefully your duty of full and frank disclosure and ensure that you have identified any matters which professional conduct requires you draw to the court's attention in the absence of the defendant (see the ***Advocacy*** manual and the ***White Book***, CPR part 25 and PD 25A on this).

Finally, ensure that you are prepared to deal with costs if this is necessary. What are the rules on costs in this type of application? Have you all the relevant information from the solicitor (e.g. a schedule of costs, if this is required)?

Presentation

Ensure you know the order in which the judge will hear the submissions and tailor your submission accordingly. Thus, for example, if you are instructed for a defendant to oppose an application for an interim injunction, the judge will hear the applicant first. You need to be ready both to respond to the applicant and to make any additional points you feel are important to raise on behalf of your client.

Judges deal with numerous applications, often in a very short time. You must therefore ensure that you present your case clearly and concisely, focusing on the decisions that the judge has to make in the order he or she will make them. Thus, for example, if the application is made without notice to the other side, the court will want that issue addressed first in order to determine whether or not the application should proceed in the absence of the defendant(s). Only then will the court be interested in considering the test to be applied in determining the application.

Consider which matters may be of concern to the judge and which you wish to draw to the judge's attention and ensure you focus on these. Take very careful note of the arguments which are raised by your opponent and be ready to counter them with your strongest arguments. Alternatively, be clear when a strong argument by your opponent cannot be rebutted and where acknowledging this will add credibility to the other arguments on which you do rely.

Skeleton arguments are required in many instances. In any event, a skeleton argument is a useful tool to assist you. If you have time, draft a skeleton argument and have a copy ready to hand to the judge (for further advice on drafting skeleton arguments, see the *Drafting* manual).

Ensure that you have all the papers in order, suitably marked so that you can refer to specific documents quickly.

Once the judge has heard the submissions and states his or her decision on the application, if an order is granted, you must note the precise wording, and check that it is within the power of the court to make, and is enforceable. You must also make sure that the costs of the application have been dealt with and (where necessary) that a certificate for counsel has been granted. You should also be clear who must draft and serve the order.

Once outside court, you should ensure that the solicitor (or whoever attended from the office) and the lay client (if attending) understand exactly what has been ordered, both in terms of the substantive order and as to costs. The brief should be properly endorsed (see **10.3.7**).

10.5 Instituting proceedings

10.5.1 Introduction

If the client decides to take proceedings on the basis of the solicitor's advice or counsel's opinion, any of the requirements of a relevant pre-action protocol not already satisfied should be completed before issue. Even in cases where no pre-action protocol exists, the spirit of these protocols must be followed (see (a) at **10.2.2**). Failure to follow a particular protocol or the spirit of protocols may result in the client, even if he or she wins in the end, having to pay costs incurred by the other side which would not have been incurred if the protocol had been followed. At a very minimum, a 'letter before claim' should be sent to the proposed defendant or his or her solicitors, warning that proceedings will be issued if the client's claim is not satisfied. The client will have to pay court costs if no such letter is sent and the defendant satisfies the claim on receipt of the court documents, arguing that he or she would have done this if warned of the impending proceedings. The proper court documents must also be drafted, served, and, where necessary, filed with the court.

A barrister will rarely be involved in writing the 'letter before claim', but may be consulted on satisfying the pre-action protocol, and will frequently draft court documents. In addition, there are a variety of orders which may be sought early in the litigation process and the barrister may be briefed to obtain these (as noted earlier).

10.5.2 Court documents

10.5.2.1 The claimant's case

Claims are commenced by issuing a 'claim form' and 'particulars of claim'. The claim form always contains basic information such as the name and address of solicitors acting for the claimant. The particulars of claim set out the facts (but not generally the law or evidence) of the claimant's case sufficient to inform the defendant of the nature of the case which has to be met. The particulars of claim may be set out on the claim form or in a separate document. Whether or not a separate document is needed depends on the complexity of the case: generally only simple cases do not require a separate document.

It is vitally important that the statement of the claimant's case (the particulars of claim) is properly drafted as it sets out the issues which the claimant wishes the court to consider and the remedies being sought. It is usual to instruct counsel to draft the particulars of claim. The instructions from the solicitors should contain all the relevant information and documents. If counsel has already advised on the merits and/or quantum, the instructions seeking this advice, and the advice given, should be included in the instructions to draft the statement of the claimant's case.

When counsel has drafted the particulars of claim, his or her clerk will then arrange for the instructions together with the draft document to be returned to the solicitor. The solicitor (or a clerk in the firm) will then complete the formal documentation. This includes completing the claim form and the client or solicitor signing a 'statement of truth' verifying the content of the particulars of claim. The solicitor will also arrange for sufficient copies to be sent or taken to the court where they are stamped (the date of issue). Service on the defendant will be arranged by the court or by the solicitor by posting or personal delivery (by clerk or process servers).

Once served, the defendant will have a set period of time to respond by serving a defence. If the defendant fails to respond within the period, the claimant can get 'judgment in default' (i.e. of the defendant responding). This is a routine step in which the barrister will not be involved. A defendant who does respond might also consult a solicitor, who in turn may instruct counsel to draft the statement of the defendant's case.

10.5.2.2 The defendant's case

Counsel instructed to draft a response to particulars of claim should receive a proper set of instructions with all the relevant documents and sufficient information for the drafting of a defence and, where appropriate, a counterclaim (where the defendant, in addition to a defence, has a claim against the claimant), and/or an additional claim against another person (where the defendant alleges someone else is wholly or partly responsible for any damages which the claimant may obtain against the defendant). The barrister will return the instructions with the relevant documents which have been drafted to the solicitor, who will serve them on the relevant parties. Strict time limits apply and counsel must ensure that the necessary work is done in sufficient time for the solicitor to keep to those limits.

10.5.2.3 Reply by claimant

Where the defendant makes a counterclaim, which is relatively common, the claimant must serve a defence to that claim. If the defendant merely serves a defence, the claimant only needs to serve a 'reply' if the defence raises a good answer to the claimant's claim. The need for a 'reply' is rare. The barrister who drafted the initial statement will almost invariably be instructed to draft the subsequent responses. Again, there are time limits for these to be served.

10.5.2.4 The statements of case

The particulars of claim, defence, counterclaim, defence to counterclaim, and any reply constitute the 'statements of case'.

If any of the parties considers that the statement of case served on them does not give sufficient information to enable them to prepare their case properly, he or she may request further information. The further information provided will be available at trial.

10.5.2.5 Case analysis: drafting statements of case

Context

The statements of case set out the issues to be determined by the court, and the parties are confined to arguing the issues in dispute as set out in those statements. Although all statements of case can be amended throughout the litigation process, there are limits on the amendments which can be made and there are cost implications for a party seeking amendments. Thus, it is very important that counsel draft the statements of case carefully.

Analysis

In drafting particulars of claim, you must ensure that you have done sufficiently detailed and precise analysis to enable you to draft both the statement of the client's case and the relief sought as strongly and clearly as possible. The analysis is much the same as that set out in **10.4.2** (opinion on merits and/or quantum). Consider whom to join as parties, in particular whom should be joined as defendants, and how all the parties should be named on the particulars. Ensure that you have considered all possible cause(s) of action (e.g. the claim might be brought in contract *and* tort), and determined which should be pleaded, and the allegations of fact to be included to prove each element. Check that you have included all the remedies desired by and available to your client (e.g. if damages and an injunction are sought, both of these are included). Check that all the requirements on content contained in the CPR are satisfied (e.g. if your client is seeking aggravated or exemplary damages, the particulars of claim must include a statement to that effect and the grounds for claiming them).

In drafting defences, you must ensure that you have identified each and every allegation made in the particulars. You must then consider very carefully what your client's version of events is. You then need to consider each allegation in turn and decide how the defence will respond to it: admit it (where it is clear from your instructions and the evidence that it is true); deny it (where it is within your client's knowledge that it is not true and he or she has a positive case to the contrary); or require the claimant to prove it (where it is not something on which your client can comment because it is outside his or her knowledge or any evidence to the contrary). Finally, you must consider very carefully your client's positive case (i.e. his or her alternative version of events to that which appears in the particulars of claim) and ensure that you include any additional facts on which the defendant intends to rely. Check that all the requirements on content contained in the CPR are satisfied (e.g. if your client is relying on the expiry of any limitation period, details must be set out in the defence).

When acting for a defendant, your client may also contend that he or she has a counterclaim or that someone else is wholly or partially responsible for the claimant's losses. Drafting a counterclaim against the claimant or a claim against a new person (a 'third party') is the same as drafting particulars of claim (see earlier). If the counterclaim also amounts to a set-off, this must be included in the defence.

Presentation

Any statement of case, whether it be particulars of claim, defence, counterclaim, or claim against a third party, must be set out clearly and concisely and comply with the CPR both in the content and format. Your draft statements of case must be signed and dated by you before you return them to the solicitor. The solicitor must then have the statements of case verified by a statement of truth signed by the lay client or solicitor.

Detailed consideration of this is beyond the scope of this manual and you are referred to the **Drafting** manual.

10.5.3   Applications to the court

10.5.3.1   Introduction

In any civil proceedings, there is a variety of applications which the parties can make to shorten the process or obtain payment or some form of court order without having to wait for the full hearing. Although some of these can be used at any stage in the proceedings, they will more commonly be employed relatively early in the process and before much of the evidence has been collected.

Applications are usually heard by judicial officers known as Masters (in the High Court in London) and District Judges (in a County Court and the High Court outside London). Although solicitors have rights of audience in these matters, they often instruct counsel. The hearing will generally be in public but often in a smaller room than a courtroom, with counsel being invited to sit rather than stand. The Master or District Judge will hear argument from counsel for both parties on the basis of the statements of case served to date and written evidence. Counsel may have drafted the statements of case and also have been instructed to draft the written evidence for the hearing. However, applications often have to be made on the basis of statements of case and written evidence drafted by someone else, whether it be the solicitor or another barrister. The most common of the applications in which counsel may be involved are set out as follows.

10.5.3.2   Summary judgment

The claimant may apply to the court for 'summary judgment' where there is no real prospect the defence will succeed and therefore no real need for trial. The defendant may also apply for summary judgment where the claimant's case has no real prospect of success. The purpose of this process is to dispose of the case without the expense and delay of a full trial. In drafting the written statements and doing the advocacy at the hearing, counsel will need to balance the need to present the best case for the client with the fact that, as the purpose is to dispose of the case without extra expense, the application will be made at a stage before much of the evidence has been collected.

10.5.3.3   Interim payments

Although there are now procedures to attempt to bring cases to trial much faster than in the past, the interim payment procedure recognises that even this delay may cause hardship to a claimant and allows an application for early payment of at least some of the money being claimed. An interim payment will be ordered only where it is clear that the claimant will be at least partially successful and it would be unjust to delay immediate payment of that entitlement.

10.5.3.4   Security for costs

A defendant who considers he or she has a strong case may be worried that, though he or she will win at trial, the claimant will be unable to pay his or her costs. In certain circumstances, a defendant can apply to the court for an order that the claimant give 'security for costs', usually by paying a specified amount into court. There is no general right to obtain such security merely because an individual is impecunious. The applicant must satisfy the test in the CPR (see the **White Book**, CPR 25.12–15).

10.5.3.5   Other orders

The orders which can be sought prior to issue can equally be sought after issue and before the full hearing (see **10.4.3**).

10.5.3.6   Case analysis: applications to court

Context

Given that proceedings have been issued and served, the defendant(s) will be aware of the claim against them and the remedies sought by the claimant. The context varies according to the purpose of the application, which range from seeking to stop the claim in its tracks (summary judgment), through to getting money up front before the trial (interim payment), and to ensuring the claimant can pay the costs if the defendant wins (security for costs). It will also depend on the point in the litigation process at which the application is made. Although most of these applications will be made early on in the process, when little if any evidence has been collected or exchanged, they may also be made later in the process when much more of both sides' cases has been revealed.

Analysis

The process of analysis for these applications is much the same as for those made pre-issue (see **10.4.2.2**). Generally, the only difference will be that you are likely to have more information about the case.

Presentation

The considerations in respect of presentation for these applications are much the same as for those made pre-issue (see **10.4.2.2**). The only difference will be that, generally, a court file will exist which contains documents already filed and served. There will be no file available in a hearing before a Queen's Bench Master.

10.6   Interim stage: preparing the evidence

10.6.1   Introduction

Once statements of case have been exchanged, the issues between the parties have been defined and they now move to collecting and preparing their evidence for trial, including any relevant documents, real evidence (e.g. goods which are claimed to be faulty), expert reports, and witness statements.

    The evidence at trial is that of all the parties, and the solicitor for each party must ensure that he or she collects all the evidence relevant to his or her client's case and exchanges evidence and information with the other parties where mutual disclosure is required or appropriate.

10.6.2   Obtaining information from other parties

There are formal steps by which all parties are obliged to exchange information about their evidence. This will be done by the solicitor, sometimes with counsel's assistance. The steps involved include the following.

10.6.2.1   Disclosure

This is the process by which the parties exchange information about the potential documentary evidence which they hold. All parties are obliged within a set time period to make a list of all relevant documents (even those they themselves do not intend to use at the trial) which are or have been in their possession, custody, or power and serve the list on the other parties, who then have the right to inspect all those still in possession and for which privilege is not claimed. In cases on the multi-track (other than personal injury) the courts will consider a menu of disclosure orders, which can range from no disclosure at all to other options such as disclosure on an issue by issue basis, and the courts will select the most cost-effective option. Inspection may be by exchange of copies of documents or actual inspection at the solicitors' offices. From this exchange of lists and inspection, both sides collect the documents and information contained in them which may form evidence for or against them. The process, which it is essential to carry out carefully, can be extremely tedious and, fortunately, counsel is rarely involved in it, unless problems occur. Frequently, the process is done by each side sending photocopies of their relevant documents to the other side. Theoretically, the costs of the copying are borne by the side receiving them. However, to avoid unnecessary bureaucracy, it is also common for each side to undertake to pay these costs and, if the cost is low or comparable on either side, the parties then waive the right to enforce the undertaking.

10.6.2.2   Requests for further information

A party can request 'further information' from other parties on matters which are reasonably necessary and proportionate to enable the party to understand the case he or she has to meet or to assist in the preparation of his or her case. The request could be for clarification of or further information on the statements of case (see **10.5.2.4**) or other matters, such as witness statements. The requests and answers form part of the bundle of documents used at trial and counsel is likely to be involved in drafting both.

10.6.2.3   Notice to admit facts

The length and cost of trial will depend to a degree on the number of disputed issues which need to be determined. The statements of case limit the issues to those which the defendant denies or does not admit (i.e. put the claimant to proof). A party may attempt to limit the issues further by seeking admissions from the other side through the formal process of serving a notice to admit. A party who fails to admit facts in response to such a notice may have to bear the cost of proving them at trial. Counsel may be asked to draft notices and replies.

10.6.2.4   Exchange of witness evidence

Within a set period, parties must simultaneously exchange both witness statements and expert reports of all those they intend to call and are basically confined at trial to the evidence in the statements and reports exchanged. The actual wording of them is therefore very important and counsel will frequently be involved in the drafting of them. The solicitor then arranges the exchange with the other parties.

10.6.3   Advising on evidence

10.6.3.1   Generally

The solicitor may seek counsel's advice on evidence at any stage in the litigation process, either through formal instructions seeking written advice or through a conference with counsel, with or without the lay client. Even where this is done in conference, counsel is frequently asked to confirm the advice in writing. Counsel's involvement in collecting and preparing the evidence for trial is usually confined to advising on the strengths and weaknesses of the evidence and what further evidence should be collected.

10.6.3.2   Case analysis

Context

As explained earlier, you may be asked to advise on evidence at any stage in the proceedings and this will dictate the amount of information you have and the period which the

solicitors have to act on your advice. Generally, the disputed issues will have been identified and there will be some information on which to gauge the overall strength of the
case. Documents may have been inspected and expert reports and witness statements
obtained. At this point, you are focusing on precisely what evidence will be used, i.e.
which documents to include in the court bundle, whether any additional witnesses are
needed, and the precise content and format of witness statements and expert reports.

Analysis

Check that the solicitor has sent you all the relevant materials to enable you to advise
properly. From the statements of case, you should determine precisely what issues are
disputed and on whom the burden of proof lies to prove the various allegations of fact
on those issues. Consider whether any of the issues could be clarified or narrowed by
the use of requests for further information or notices to admit. Consider whether any
amendments are necessary to the statements of case in light of the evidence.

You then need to review the evidence available on each issue and decide what evidence to tender on each of those issues. It is helpful to make a list of the issues at this
point and, in respect of each issue, consider the evidence available. Are there any gaps?
In particular, identify the matters on which it is essential that evidence is tendered on
your client's behalf to make out your case, and ensure there are no gaps. Consider what
form the evidence will take on the various issues (witnesses of fact, expert opinion, documentary, and/or real evidence) and any formalities which need to be fulfilled to be able
to tender the evidence in this form.

In respect of potential documentary evidence, consider whether full disclosure has
been given by both sides. Do you want the authenticity of any document challenged?
Consider which documents relate to which issues. Where documents or real evidence
are to be relied on, consider who will produce them.

Consider what matters call for expert evidence. Check that the expert instructed has
the relevant expertise to give opinion evidence on these matters and that the report
contains relevant evidence, including copies of any articles, literature, etc., on which
the expert relies for his or her views. Check that the directions in respect of experts have
been followed (e.g. if a meeting was directed, has this happened?) and that the report
complies with the CPR on content and format. Whether there is a single joint expert or
an expert report from the other side, are there matters on which it might be useful to put
written questions to the expert?

Consider what witnesses of fact need to be called. Go through the proofs of each witness,
checking the issues on which he or she can give useful evidence. Note any gaps where the
proof does not cover matters on which it appears the witness could give evidence. When
you have considered all the proofs, check whether there are any issues on which there is
no or insufficient oral evidence. Consider whether or how these gaps can be filled (e.g. by
other existing witnesses or a new witness). Note if there are any particular difficulties in
respect of any of the witnesses (e.g. reluctant to give evidence or may be confused when
giving evidence). The solicitor, having taken the original statements from the witnesses,
may be in a better position to gauge this than you. Where you have been provided with
witness statements, ensure they comply with the CPR on content and format. Check that
any directions have been fulfilled (e.g. witness statements exchanged).

Having considered what is available, you need then to decide what evidence should
be tendered. For example, there may be several witnesses who can give evidence on the
same facts. Consider whether all of them are needed and, if not, which should be called.
Similarly, check which documents should be put before the court and what advice you
might give on the preparation of the bundles for use at trial.

When advising on the evidence to be collected and the evidence to be available for the hearing, you should be acutely aware of the overriding principle of 'proportionality' (see (a) at **10.2.3**). This involves two aspects. First, the amount of time involved and difficulty in obtaining the evidence. The actual work of collecting the evidence falls to the solicitor who will interview witnesses to obtain statements, ensure all the relevant documents and items of real evidence are assembled, and, where necessary, instruct and obtain a report from an expert. You must weigh up the need to have all relevant evidence available for the hearing with the feasibility of the solicitor actually being able to produce it in the time available. Second, collecting and preparing the evidence increases the client's costs. The solicitor charges for any work done on the case. In addition, there will be 'disbursement costs' incurred which will be passed on to the client where a charge is made to the solicitor to obtain information, copy documents, advice, etc., from others. Experts will charge for their work, as will counsel. You must therefore also weigh up the need for the evidence against the cost of obtaining it.

Presentation

An advice on evidence must be practical and accessible to the solicitor. He or she will want to be able to understand readily what further evidence needs to be collected and why it is needed. He or she will also want to be able to identify readily what evidence you advise should be tendered at court and the reasons for your decisions. This means that your opinion must be structured and written in a way which clearly sets out:

- what further evidence needs to be collected;
- what evidence should be tendered at trial;
- any formalities which must be satisfied to ensure the evidence can be tendered; and
- any procedural steps which should be followed.

For more information on writing opinions, see Part III on *Opinion Writing*.

10.6.4   Drafting witness statements

10.6.4.1   Generally

Until recently, all witnesses except expert witnesses gave evidence orally at trial. The solicitor drafted statements (or 'proofs' as they were sometimes called) for use by the advocate in court as the basis for questioning in examination-in-chief. These statements or proofs were not revealed to the other side and the evidence of the witness-in-chief was what was said orally at the trial. Any errors or omissions in the statements or proofs could therefore be rectified by counsel's careful questioning in court.

In virtually all cases now, witness statements must be in a particular format and exchanged prior to the hearing. The statements themselves stand as the bulk of the witness's evidence-in-chief. The actual wording of the witness statements is therefore incredibly important. The witness signs it as an acknowledgement that he or she accepts the truth of its contents and the solicitor should, therefore, ensure that the witness has the opportunity to check and amend the contents prior to signing and exchange.

10.6.4.2   Case analysis

Context

Although the witness statement is technically that of the witness, it is usually drafted by the solicitor or barrister. The Bar's Code of Conduct (para C9) prohibits 'witness coaching' and sets out some guidance for discussing the evidence with witnesses.

Generally, you will be instructed to draft statements on the basis of the solicitor's instructions and enclosed documents, including records of interviews with the client, letters, client files, and attendance notes by the solicitor. Alternatively, you may be instructed to 'polish' a statement drafted by the solicitor.

Analysis

The statement represents the witness's evidence-in-chief and should cover all the issues in the statements of case on which this witness can give evidence. You therefore need to determine from the statements of case precisely what issues are in dispute and the allegations of fact made by each side. You then need to consider each witness in turn and determine which allegations of fact they can deal with in their evidence. In addition, clarify what first-hand evidence the witness can give and what evidence is hearsay. Although hearsay evidence is now admitted in civil cases and can be included in the witness statement, the source of it should be set out in the witness statement and you should be conscious that it will be given less weight than first-hand evidence. Finally, consider what, if any, documents or real evidence support this witness's evidence and ensure that reference to these is included in the statement. Check that appropriate formalities have or will be fulfilled, e.g. hearsay notices served on the other side where appropriate.

Presentation

At trial, the witness statement will become the witness's evidence-in-chief. It is therefore written in narrative form in the first person, as if written by that witness. Getting the style or tone of the language right in a witness statement can be difficult as, while technically it is supposed to be the words of the witness, generally the language used is slightly more formal than the language many witnesses would use when questioned. Any documents or real evidence which the witness will produce must be formally marked and exhibited to the witness statement. The witness statement must also fulfil the formal requirements as to form and content. For further guidance on drafting witness statements, see the *Drafting* manual.

10.6.5 Experts and their reports

10.6.5.1 Generally

The success of many cases will depend on the expert evidence. Thus, for example, in personal injury cases, the court will usually determine the extent of the claimant's injuries on the basis of medical evidence. In building disputes, the parties may rely on the opinion of surveyors, e.g. as to the extent of disrepair and what is required to rectify it. Expert evidence is basically opinion evidence of a suitably qualified or experienced person. Experts can differ in their opinions. In order to prevent the trial disintegrating into the swapping of numerous expert opinions, parties are usually each confined to a certain number of experts, frequently one or two. In addition, the procedure has for a number of years encouraged the parties to limit as far as possible the need for experts to be called at trial, by directing exchange of expert reports and meetings of experts to attempt to limit the issues and have the reports agreed if possible. The Woolf reforms have increased the limitations on numbers of experts, including requiring the appointment of a single joint expert's report (i.e. no oral testimony) in fast-track cases generally.

Obtaining expert evidence can be a complicated task which requires great skill to choose the right experts, instruct them properly, and ensure that their evidence is well presented.

A barrister's involvement in obtaining expert evidence will depend on the level of expertise of the instructing solicitor. The solicitor may be new to this area of work and look to the barrister for advice throughout, including seeking advice on which expert to instruct. However, most solicitors who specialise will have a 'stable' of experts on which they can rely, and will be sufficiently *au fait* with the area to instruct them. The solicitor will obtain the report and the barrister will have no involvement with the expert prior to the evidence being given in court. The only exception to this is where the expert evidence is complicated or in an area not known to the barrister. In such a case, a conference may be held with the expert for the barrister to ensure that he or she has sufficient understanding of the evidence to deal with it properly at court.

The basis of expert evidence is the reports which the experts will write themselves. The report will be considered by the solicitor, who may also seek the barrister's view of it, to ensure that it covers all relevant matters and does not include irrelevant ones. If an expert report is not favourable, the lawyer (solicitor or barrister) can discuss the contents of the report with the expert. Clearly, there are professional conduct issues in the lawyers becoming too involved in the drafting of the report and attempting to 'rework' the opinion of the expert. If the expert's view is genuinely not favourable to the client, the lawyers need to decide whether or not to seek the opinion of another expert. The report of the first expert remains privileged and will not be shown to the other parties. However, if the other parties have discovered that the expert has been consulted, there is nothing to stop them from calling that expert to give evidence.

10.6.5.2   Case analysis

Context

As can be seen from the previous discussion, the contexts in which you may be instructed to deal with experts and expert evidence are many and varied. The two main areas on which you are likely to become involved are advising on the report and questioning experts in court.

Analysis

In either situation—advising on an expert report or preparing to question an expert in court—you need to: (a) check precisely what issues call for expert opinion evidence; (b) ensure that the expert has the relevant expertise (qualification and/or experience) to give the evidence; and (c) ensure that the report does cover the issues on which expert opinion is required. You also need to understand fully and in detail what the expert opinion is and the expertise on which it is based. This includes understanding all technical terms used and any diagrams or plans. It also includes understanding the basis of the expert's expertise (i.e. his or her experience and any other sources which inform his or her view such as journals, custom in the trade, etc.) and why he or she has the opinion he or she does in respect of this case.

To assist you in dealing with experts, keep information or ensure easy access to information on areas of expertise common to your practice, for example copies of relevant books; websites; and diagrams to assist in deciphering reports, e.g. medical dictionaries, surveying terminology, etc.

Once you thoroughly understand the expert evidence, identify any gaps and ambiguities in the report and the issues to which they relate. Check that any directions of the court in respect of experts have been or will be fulfilled and that the report satisfies the requirements of the CPR on both form and content.

Presentation

Advice on an expert report will usually be contained in an advice on evidence generally. See the earlier comments on this. Dealing with experts at trial will form part of preparation for trial. See comments in **10.7** on this.

10.7 The trial: final preparation and hearing

10.7.1 Introduction

Having gone through the stages of exchanging statements of case to define the issues to be tried and collecting and exchanging the evidence as required by the rules, the final preparations for trial involve ensuring that all the parties, witnesses, and lawyers attend court properly prepared and that the evidence is put into a format which is convenient for all, including the judge.

10.7.2 Trial dates and timetables

Cases assigned to the small claims and fast tracks will almost invariably be given trial dates when allocated to that track. In cases where no trial date has been given (in multi-track cases and some fast-track cases), a trial date will have to be obtained from the court. In addition, in both fast-track and multi-track cases, a few weeks before the trial date, the court will make directions as to the evidence to be called, the documents to be used (see **10.7.4**), how the trial should be conducted (trial timetable which will include limitations on the amount of time for each step in the trial), and any other matters it considers are required to prepare the case for trial. Where it is intended that counsel act as advocate, he or she should be involved in providing the information to the court on which decisions as to trial date and directions for trial are made (whether done in writing or by way of a procedural hearing at court).

10.7.3 Witnesses

It is the solicitor's duty to ensure that the witnesses attend court on the hearing day. The solicitor should therefore make sure that all the witnesses (and the client, if not also a witness) are given as much information as possible about likely hearing dates and, when it is actually fixed, the precise date. If there is any likelihood that a witness will not attend, the solicitor should consider compelling attendance by issuing and serving a witness summons.

10.7.4 Trial bundles

The claimant's solicitor must, within a set number of days before the date fixed for the trial, prepare and lodge with the court copies of all the documents which will be used or referred to at the trial by the claimant or defendant (the defendant's solicitor having given notice to the claimant's solicitor). The division of labour becomes more complicated where there is a claim and counterclaim (i.e. the defendant taking on the role of claimant in respect of the counterclaim).

The purpose of preparing and lodging the bundles of documents is to ensure that they have been put into a usable format for the court; the CPR sets out the number and format (e.g. paginating) of bundles to be lodged. The principal documents lodged include:

- the claim form and all statements of case;
- a case summary and/or chronology where appropriate;
- all requests for information and the answers;

- all witness statements with an indication of whether the contents are agreed;
- all expert reports with an indication of whether the contents are agreed; and
- all other documents which any of the parties wish to have before the court.

The claimant's solicitor will arrange for sufficient copies of the bundles to be provided for all parties (the other parties paying a reasonable fee for their copies). Each party will usually have three or four copies: one for the solicitor, one for counsel, one for the witness, and, possibly, one spare.

Ensuring that the bundles contain all the relevant documents and are compiled in accordance with the rules is an extremely important but tedious task. Fortunately, counsel's only involvement in this will be to advise on which statements, reports, documents, etc., are to be included.

10.7.5 Briefing the advocate

10.7.5.1 The brief

Where the solicitor has decided not to do the advocacy personally, his or her choice of counsel will depend on a variety of factors, including the type of case, its complexity, and whether counsel has been involved in the preparation stages. Whoever the solicitor decides to use should be properly briefed (see **10.3.6** for general format), and the brief should include copies of the following:

- any bundles lodged at court;
- all previous advice and opinions of counsel; and
- any additional proofs of evidence from witnesses (i.e. updating their statements).

The detail in the brief will depend on counsel's previous involvement. Thus, where counsel has been actively involved, and the documents enclosed include previous opinions and advice, the brief itself may be relatively short as counsel is *au fait* with all the detail.

10.7.5.2 The brief fee

The barrister's fee for the case will depend on his or her standing and the complexity of the case. It is agreed on the basis of a 'fee' of £x for the first day (a sum which includes preparation time) and a 'refresher' of £y (a lower sum than the fee, a daily charge) for subsequent days. Although technically the full fee is payable once the brief is delivered even if the case settles or folds before then, in practice many barristers agree to accept no fee if, for example, the case settles before a deadline date which is calculated to give them time to prepare.

Where a CFA has been made between the barrister and solicitor, the brief will be so marked.

10.7.5.3 Delivery of brief/acceptance by counsel

Ideally, where the trial is of any substance, briefs should be delivered to counsel at least two weeks before the hearing date.

While some solicitors are very professional and do ensure counsel has the brief in adequate time, some more often than not deliver it very late. On the reverse side of the coin, barristers who have been booked to do the hearing may become unavailable, e.g. because of being 'part heard' (i.e. in the middle of a case which has overrun its estimated time). Counsel's clerk should notify the solicitor as soon as the problem arises so the solicitor can choose another barrister to take the brief. Some chambers are very good at notifying solicitors and some delay the notification, hoping the barrister will in the end be free. The clerk may suggest someone else in chambers to take over. The advantage of this is that counsel taking over has more opportunity to discuss the case with counsel who was initially briefed.

10.7.5.4 Preparation for trial by the advocate: case analysis

Context

The brief you receive from the solicitor should contain all the documents set out in **10.7.5.1**. In addition, your instructing solicitor should confirm that all the witnesses and experts have been warned and, where necessary, witness summonses have been issued to compel attendance.

The focus of your preparation is on your submissions, in particular your closing submission and your questioning of the witnesses. If you are familiar with the case, and in particular have given an advice on evidence just prior to trial, you can build on the analysis done at that stage. In addition, you will at this stage have all the evidence on which the opponent relies, which you may not have had when you gave the advice on evidence. If you are not familiar with the case, you will need to do the analysis from scratch.

Analysis

Check that you have received all the relevant documents. The analysis will follow much the same lines as that set out in **10.6.3.2, 10.6.4.2,** and **10.6.5.2,** but this time it will also include consideration of the other side's evidence (i.e. identifying the strengths and weaknesses of their evidence).

You must ensure that you are clear which issues the court will have to determine, i.e. the issues in dispute and the factual allegations by each side on those issues, and the evidence which will be used by you and your opponent on those issues. Evaluate the strengths and weaknesses of your case on the basis of this analysis.

From your analysis and evaluation, the important areas of the case will have emerged. You then need to work out how you are going to present the case, focusing on the relevant issues, using the strengths, and avoiding or neutralising the weaknesses. This is often called developing a 'theory of the case'. Basically, it is your client's 'story' told through your submissions and the evidence of the witnesses which gives a logical and convincing account of how the events in the case are likely to have happened in a way which is favourable to your client's case. It must be plausible and firmly based on the legal principles and evidence. However, it will rely on inferences and generalisations to fill the gaps which always exist in cases (given they are generally based on what people remember of an event which occurred sometime in the past). You need to be clear what inferences you wish the court to draw and the generalisations (premises which rest on the general behaviour of people or objects) on which you rely to persuade the court to accept your explanation.

For example, you might have a case where your client, a 65-year-old woman, fell while in a fast-food hamburger restaurant just after a 19-year-old employee had washed the floor. She alleges that she slipped on a wet floor. The restaurant alleges that she was not paying attention to where she was going. The case turns on whether or not the floor was wet and whether this caused the fall. One could use the 'generalisations' that washing floors is a routine task and that most 19-year-olds would find it boring and that when someone finds a task boring they may not do it properly. The inference you would be seeking the court to draw is that the floor was not dried properly in this case.

The 'theory of the case' must be a coherent story which is consistent with the legal principles and all the evidence which will be heard by the court. It should include consideration of both the overall story and the 'characterisation' of any relevant witnesses (as done in the earlier example).

Having developed a 'theory of the case', you then need to consider the contents of your closing speech, the issues which will concern the court and how you will use your 'theory of the case' to persuade the court to find for you. You then need to consider each witness in turn and determine what you must draw out in questioning, both in examination-in-chief of your own witnesses and in cross-examination of the opponent's witnesses. You must also consider at what point documents and real evidence will be introduced.

Presentation

Determine what speeches are allowed by counsel, e.g. if you are for the defendant, will you be allowed an opening and a closing or just a closing speech (more likely)? Decide the contents of both, keeping your submissions/arguments for the closing speech.

Counsel should consider whether a skeleton argument is required. This might have been included in the case management directions, or it may be required by a specialist court guide. Skeleton arguments are generally required for trials and in the Court of Appeal, for interim applications in the High Court and increasingly in the County Court. Otherwise, it is a matter of professional judgement based on the complexity of the issues. Skeletons should be served on the other side and filed at court 24 or 48 hours before the hearing (except for the Court of Appeal, when they must be lodged early on in the process).

As witness statements generally stand as evidence-in-chief, oral examination-in-chief is severely restricted in civil cases. You will need the court's permission if you wish to expand or introduce new matters which have arisen since the exchange of witness statements. You will also need to inform your opponent. Knowledge of the general practice of the particular court is helpful on this as some courts are more restrictive in allowing oral examination than others.

Consider the witness statement of each of the opponent's witnesses. First consider whether or not you should cross-examine that witness. If there is no purpose to it, don't do it! You must 'put your case'. You must challenge all material parts of the evidence given by a witness which your client (or his or her witnesses) does not accept. Be clear which points you must 'put' to the witness. Then identify the evidence on which you can build (i.e. is helpful to your case or neutral and may support your theory of the case) and the areas on which the witness is damaging (e.g. evidence which directly contradicts your theory of the case). Then plan the order in which you will cross-examine, building on the favourable before moving on to the aspects with which the witness is likely to disagree.

Finally, consider how you will 'tab' the bundle (mark the documents for easy access by you in the trial). Make notes as appropriate to assist you both in the submissions and in the questioning. This may include highlighting the witness statements, documents, expert reports, etc. Also plan how you will take notes during the trial, e.g. during questioning of witnesses, to ensure that you can cross-examine or re-examine effectively and precisely.

10.7.6 The trial

When counsel is instructed as the advocate at trial, there may or may not be a representative of the instructing solicitor's firm present. The representative may be the solicitor, where the case or the client is worth a reasonable amount, or a 'file carrier' who may or may not know anything about the case or the law.

At trial, the advocate has control of and responsibility for the conduct of the case. There are numerous matters which require some attention immediately before going into court, e.g. there may be last-minute checking of information, updating of statements, reassuring witnesses who are nervous, ensuring the court has the advocate's name, etc. It is the advocate's duty to ensure the smooth running of the case—that all the witnesses are present, all the documents are before the court and available for those who need them, e.g. witnesses when giving evidence, etc. It is also important to make sure that witnesses have read their statements before giving their evidence.

Once the hearing has started, the advocate will be fully occupied either addressing the court or dealing with witnesses. It is an important part of the barrister's duty to take careful notes during the trial even where the attendant solicitor (or representative) is also taking notes. It is the barrister's own notes on which he or she will rely if questions arise later as to precisely what happened. The barrister may cross-check with the solicitor. However, it is not possible to turn constantly to the solicitor (or representative) for their notes and the quality of their notes varies enormously.

Once all the evidence has been called and the closing speeches given, the court will deliver judgment. This might be done immediately or, where the case has been long or complex, may be reserved by an adjournment to the next day or to a much later date where the judge requires more time to consider it. Counsel should take a full note of the judgment and endorse the brief properly (see **10.3.7**). Counsel should also check that any orders are within the court's power, the details are accurate, and that he or she understands the judgment or order in detail.

The advocate for the successful party will ask for costs. It is important that the court makes orders on all the costs before it, including any which are outstanding from interim hearings. In addition, the court should deal with the summary assessment of costs if it is a fast-track trial, or make an order for detailed assessment, including the detailed assessment of any public funding costs.

The judgment and/or order of the court cannot be enforced until it is formally drawn up. This will usually be the task of the court. Counsel must ensure that his or her notes and endorsement are sufficient for the solicitor to check that the court has done the task properly before serving the order on the party against whom it has been made.

10.8   Settlement during the process

A very high percentage of cases never get to trial but settle at some stage along the way. Although there is nothing preventing the parties themselves from negotiating a settlement, once proceedings are issued, negotiations are usually conducted through the lawyer, usually the solicitor. Counsel may be involved in negotiations, most frequently at the court door prior to the full trial or possibly at interim hearings. All such negotiations should be conducted on a 'without prejudice' basis which means that they cannot be revealed to the court if settlement is not reached.

A defendant who wishes to put some pressure on the claimant to settle can make a Part 36 offer. Under this procedure, the defendant makes an offer in writing and gives the claimant no less than 21 days to accept it ('the relevant period'). If the claimant accepts the offer then this ends the matter, or if he or she refuses the offer then the case will still go to court. However, if the claimant does not win more than the amount offered, he or she will have to pay the defendant's costs from the end of the relevant period. There is no longer a requirement for the defendant to make a payment of the money into court. A claimant can also make a Part 36 counter-offer. The contents of the letters cannot be revealed at trial prior to judgment. Counsel may be asked to advise on the level or format of the offer or its acceptance.

There is a growing use of alternative dispute resolution procedures, such as mediation, designed to facilitate the settlement of cases.

10.9   Enforcement

Many parties against whom judgments are given or orders are made comply with them without any further steps being required. However, if a party fails to comply, further formal steps are required to force compliance, e.g. the issue by the court of a warrant for possession to instruct the bailiffs to evict a person whom the court has ordered to deliver up possession, or a warrant of execution to instruct the bailiffs to seize goods and sell them to obtain money a person has been ordered to pay. All of this falls to the solicitor and the barrister is rarely, if ever, involved.

10.10   Appeal

A party may wish to appeal a decision of the court, e.g. because judgment has been given against them or because, although an order has been made in their favour, they disagree with the terms set by the court. Counsel will frequently be involved both in advising on whether or not to appeal and in drafting the grounds of appeal.

10.11   Costs

The costs incurred which form the subject of a costs order include court fees, lawyers' fees, and other costs such as photocopying costs and expert witness fees. Although the general rule is that 'costs follow the event', which means that the losing party is ordered to pay the winning party's costs, this is not always the case and the court may refuse to make the order, e.g. where there has been a Part 36 offer which has not been exceeded at trial.

Even where a costs order is made, the winning party will rarely have all of his or her costs paid by the loser. There are three different methods for determining the actual amount which the loser must pay:

(a) Under 'agreed' costs the parties agree how much of the winner's costs the loser will pay.

(b) 'Summarily assessed' costs are used in fast-track cases where, immediately after giving judgment, the court assesses and states the costs payable.

(c) 'Detailed assessed' costs are used where the solicitor whose client's costs are being paid submits a bill of costs to the court and a court officer decides the costs which should be allowed, reduced, or disallowed on either a 'standard' or 'indemnity' basis. The 'standard' basis is the usual basis used and allows a reasonable sum in respect of all costs reasonably incurred, any doubts being resolved in favour of the paying party. The 'indemnity' basis, under which all costs are allowed except insofar as they are unreasonable, is far more generous and is ordered against the loser only in exceptional cases.

The solicitor has overall responsibility for keeping a record of all the costs incurred, including the barrister's fees, paying the various expenses, including the barrister's fees, having the bill assessed where a costs order is made, and getting payment from the paying party and/or the client and/or the Community Legal Service.

Where a costs order is made, the winning party still has to pay his or her solicitor the full amount of the bill and is reimbursed by the losing party paying what was agreed or assessed. However, the winning party may feel that the bill is too high and have it assessed (which may be done on the indemnity basis). Only the amount allowed on assessment is payable. Counsel's brief fee will generally be what was agreed between the clerk and the solicitor. Although technically still payable by the solicitor to the barrister, the solicitor will only recoup from the client what was assessed as reasonable. In light of this, the barrister needs to decide whether or not to press for the full amount or the assessed amount, particularly where these solicitors regularly instruct the barrister.

A barrister who has entered a CFA with the solicitor will be paid in accordance with that agreement—generally nothing if the case is lost and a success fee if the case is won.

Anatomy of a criminal case

11.1 Introduction

The purpose of this chapter is not to act as a textbook on criminal procedure, nor as a guide to criminal advocacy. Rather, its function is to set out the stages of a case in which counsel may be involved so that this involvement can be put in its proper context as regards fact management (or case analysis, as it is sometimes called). Further details regarding the procedure adopted by the criminal courts may be found in the *Criminal Litigation and Sentencing* manual and the *Advocacy* manual, as well as specialist practitioner texts such as *Blackstone's Criminal Practice* (published annually).

The popular picture is of the barrister acting as an advocate in the courtroom. However, counsel's role is necessarily much wider than that. This chapter sets out some of the tasks which a barrister instructed in a criminal case may have to perform. You should compare and contrast this chapter with **Chapter 10** (especially **10.3**), which deals with civil cases.

Although counsel may be briefed only for a particular stage in a case, real life does not exist in tidy compartments. For example, counsel may be instructed to apply for bail but, in the course of talking to the client about the bail application, may be asked questions about what plea the defendant should enter or (in cases where there is a choice) which court should try the case. It is therefore vital for the barrister to be able to take an overview of the case as a whole.

Although reference is made to the role of the Crown Prosecution Service (CPS), most of this chapter is written from the perspective of a barrister representing the defendant. This is because barristers in private practice are generally required to have gained several years' experience in the criminal courts as defence advocates before being instructed to prosecute cases.

11.2 Role of the defence barrister

A barrister only represents a defendant if 'briefed' to do so by a solicitor. Solicitors themselves have complete rights of audience in the magistrates' court, and so there is nothing a barrister can do there that a solicitor cannot.

If a barrister is instructed, the brief (generally entitled 'Instructions to Counsel') usually consists of a short introduction to the case written by the instructing solicitor, together with a 'proof of evidence' (i.e. a written statement) from the defendant. At the early stages of a case, the brief sent to the barrister may consist of very little. Indeed, there will be cases where the barrister is the first lawyer the defendant sees in connection with this particular offence. In that case, the brief may consist of only a 'back sheet' (i.e. a sheet of paper containing the name of the defendant, the court in which that defendant is appearing, and the name and address of the solicitors).

When the barrister meets the client, it is necessary to go through the proof of evidence (assuming there is one) with the client. It may be that there are things the client wishes to correct or to add. Where the barrister is taking instructions from the client at court (shortly before the hearing), there may only be a short time available and counsel should give priority to eliciting information which is relevant to the hearing which is about to take place. For example, if the reason for the appearance is to make a bail application, then the information which counsel needs to draw out first from the client should relate to matters which are relevant to bail. Other matters can be dealt with after the more important information has been discovered.

By the time the case is ready for trial, counsel should have a much fuller brief which contains not only a proof of evidence from the client, but also statements from any witnesses whom counsel is to call in support of the defence case. In the case of Crown Court trials, defence counsel will also be in possession of the written statements made by the witnesses whom the prosecution intend to call (as the sending of these statements to the defence is an integral part of the process whereby the case is transferred to the Crown Court). In the case of magistrates' court trials, counsel for the defence should have copies of the witness statements made by the prosecution witnesses. If defence counsel has not received copies of the prosecution witness statements in a magistrates' court case, he or she should ask the CPS to supply such statements.

If the solicitor has not already done so, defence counsel should make sure that the defendant looks through the statements made by the prosecution witnesses and so has a chance to comment on those statements; this may give counsel very useful material upon which to base the cross-examination of those witnesses when the time comes.

In the magistrates' court, where counsel has been instructed on behalf of the defendant, no representative from the solicitor's office will be present. Normally, the brief sent to the barrister will include copies of statements (taken by the instructing solicitor) from each intended defence witness; such statements are important, since the advocate needs to know what the witness is expected to say. If the defendant brings witnesses who have not made statements to the instructing solicitor, counsel will have to take statements from those witnesses.

In the Crown Court, a representative from the instructing solicitor should be present, although this will usually be an 'outdoor clerk' (i.e. a representative who is not legally qualified).

11.3 Legal aid

Publicly funded representation for defendants is available, but legal aid will be granted only if it is in the interests of justice to do so (s 17 of the Legal Aid, Sentencing and Punishment of Offenders 2012). In deciding whether this requirement is satisfied, the following factors are taken into account:

- whether the defendant would, if convicted, be likely to lose their liberty or livelihood or suffer serious damage to their reputation;

- whether the determination of any matter arising in the proceedings may involve consideration of a substantial question of law;
- whether the defendant may be unable to understand the proceedings or to state their own case;
- whether the proceedings may involve the tracing, interviewing, or expert cross-examination of witnesses on behalf of the defendant; and
- whether it is in the interests of another person that the defendant be represented.

As well as satisfying this 'merits' test, the defendant must also satisfy a 'means' test. Where the defendant is in receipt of income support or income-based jobseeker's allowance, the means test is satisfied automatically. In the remaining cases, account is taken of the defendant's income.

11.4   Crown Prosecution Service

In all but very minor cases, the CPS will be involved in the decision whether or not to charge a suspect. In more serious cases, where the police will oppose the grant of bail, the police will charge the suspect but only after having received advice from a Crown Prosecutor on whether there is sufficient evidence to charge the suspect and, if so, with what offence(s). In other cases, the suspect will be released on bail, pending a decision by the CPS whether or not to proceed with the case (and, if the decision is in favour of proceeding with one or more charges, the CPS will issue a written charge and requisition requiring the suspect to appear before a magistrates' court, or else the defendant will return to the police station to be charged there).

In the magistrates' court, the CPS is represented by a Crown Prosecutor or by an 'agent' (i.e. by a solicitor or barrister instructed by the CPS); in the Crown Court, the CPS will usually be represented by a barrister (although increasing numbers of Crown Prosecutors are now conducting Crown Court trials).

In the magistrates' court, the CPS file takes the place of the brief for the prosecutor. In the Crown Court, prosecuting counsel receives a brief which is very similar in form to the brief sent to counsel for the defence. The file or brief, as the case may be, will contain an introduction written by a Crown Prosecutor, copies of written statements made by the witnesses to be called on behalf of the prosecution, and details of the defendant's previous convictions (if any).

In the Crown Court, a representative from the CPS should be available to assist counsel, and the police officer in charge of the case will also be present. In the magistrates' court, the prosecutor will be alone, although the police officer in charge of the case will be present for the trial (but not for any preliminary hearings which precede the trial).

11.5   Stages of a criminal case: a thumbnail sketch

To help you make sense of the rest of this chapter, this section aims to provide a thumbnail sketch of criminal procedure in so far as counsel may be involved.

Where proceedings were commenced by the issue of a 'written charge' and a 'requisition' requiring the suspect to attend court (the procedure established under s 29 of the

Criminal Justice Act 2003), counsel is likely to attend only for the trial itself. This is because the question of bail does not arise (and so remand hearings, where the question of bail is addressed, do not take place).

The other method of commencing proceedings is to arrest and charge the suspect. Under s 24 of the Police and Criminal Evidence Act 1984, a police officer may arrest a suspect for any offence, subject to a test of necessity (for example, to allow the prompt and effective investigation of the offence, or to prevent any prosecution for the offence being hindered by the disappearance of the suspect). A suspect who has been arrested will usually be interviewed at the police station. At the police station, the suspect is entitled to legal advice; that advice will invariably be provided by a solicitor, not by a barrister. If the suspect is to be charged with an offence, either that will happen at the police station (the police having first sought advice from a Crown Prosecutor) or the papers will be sent to the CPS, who will decide whether to charge the suspect and, if so, with what offence (in which case, the CPS will commence proceedings through the issue of a written charge and requisition or else, if the suspect was released on police bail, the charging may take place when they return to the police station, as required by the terms on which bail was granted). A suspect who has been charged at the police station may either be granted bail by the police or else be held in custody until the next sitting of the magistrates' court (when the magistrates can be asked to grant bail to the defendant). If police bail is granted, counsel may attend remand hearings but, assuming the prosecution do not subsequently oppose bail, the grant of bail is a formality and so there is little for counsel to do.

When the CPS are deciding whether a suspect ought to be charged, regard must be had to the strength of the evidence against the suspect and to whether it is in the public interest to continue the prosecution. In complex cases, the CPS may seek the advice of counsel.

If proceedings were commenced by the arrest and charge of the suspect, and police bail was withheld, counsel may be instructed to attend the magistrates' court to make an application for bail on behalf of the defendant. In many cases, however, the first bail application will be made by a solicitor. Where the prosecution wish to oppose the grant of bail, the bail application will be resisted by the CPS representative. If that application for bail is unsuccessful, counsel may be briefed to return to the magistrates' court a week later to make a further bail application.

If bail is withheld by the magistrates after the second application for bail, counsel may be asked to return to the magistrates' court to reapply for bail if there is a material change in circumstances (enabling a further bail application to be made). Where bail has been refused by a magistrates' court, the defendant may appeal to the Crown Court. In the Crown Court, bail will be opposed by a barrister instructed by the CPS or by a Crown Prosecutor.

In addition to the remand hearings in the magistrates' court, if the offence is triable either way (i.e. it can be tried either in the Crown Court or in a magistrates' court), counsel may be instructed to attend the magistrates' court to represent the defendant at the 'mode of trial' hearing: at this hearing, the defendant is asked to indicate whether he intends to plead guilty or not guilty. If the defendant gives no indication or indicates an intention to plead not guilty, the next step is for the decision to be taken whether the case should be heard in the magistrates' court or in the Crown Court; a defendant who indicates a guilty plea is deemed to have entered a guilty plea (and so the court will either pass sentence or commit the defendant to the Crown Court, which has greater sentencing powers). Again, the prosecution will be represented by a Crown Prosecutor or by a solicitor or barrister instructed by the CPS.

In some cases, prosecuting counsel may be asked to advise on evidence and/or on the question of disclosure to the defence of material which the prosecution have but which they do not intend to use at the trial. Defence counsel may be instructed to advise, for example, on the contents of (or even draft) the statement of the defence case which (in the case of Crown Court trials) must be served on the prosecution.

Next, counsel may be instructed to appear at the trial itself. This trial will be in the magistrates' court if the offence is a summary one (i.e. triable only in a magistrates' court) or if the offence is triable either way (i.e. triable in a magistrates' court or in the Crown Court) but both the defendant and the magistrates agreed (at the mode of trial hearing) to summary trial; if the offence is triable only on indictment, or the offence is triable either way and the mode of trial hearing resulted in a decision in favour of trial on indictment, the trial will take place in the Crown Court. In the magistrates' court, the prosecution will be conducted by a Crown Prosecutor or by a solicitor or barrister instructed by the CPS; in the Crown Court, the prosecution will usually (but not invariably) be represented by counsel.

Wherever the defendant is tried, if he or she either pleads guilty or is found guilty, counsel will have to make a plea in mitigation on behalf of the defendant before sentence is passed.

At the conclusion of the case, it may be necessary for defence counsel to advise the defendant on the possibility of appeal against conviction and/or sentence. Where the trial took place in the magistrates' court, that appeal will normally be heard in the Crown Court (although an appeal on a point of law may be made to the High Court, either by way of case stated or by means of an application for judicial review). Where the trial took place in the Crown Court, appeal lies to the Court of Appeal (Criminal Division).

11.6   The stages in greater detail

Having set out an overview of criminal procedure, it is necessary to examine in more detail some of the stages in which a barrister may be involved.

11.6.1   Bail application

In most cases, on the first occasion that a defendant appears before the magistrates' court charged with a particular offence, representation will be provided either by a duty solicitor or by a solicitor from the firm which later instructs counsel. An application for public funding may be made at the time of that hearing.

There will be occasions, however, where the barrister is the first lawyer the defendant meets in connection with this offence. It may be, for example, that the defendant agreed to be interviewed by the police without a lawyer being present and, after being charged with an offence and finding that police bail was withheld, contacted a firm of solicitors they have used before. If there is insufficient time for a solicitor from that firm to see the defendant prior to the first court appearance, counsel may receive instructions by telephone, fax, or email to go to the magistrates' court. In that case, it will be for counsel to take initial instructions from the defendant, to give preliminary advice, and to make a bail application. In other cases, counsel may be making a bail application following an earlier unsuccessful bail application made by the solicitor or by another barrister.

Where bail is withheld, the accused is 'remanded in custody', and will be held in prison until the next court appearance.

The role of defence counsel when attending court to make a bail application involves a number of elements, including preparation, advice, and advocacy.

In particular, counsel will have to:

(a) *Take instructions from the client:* If a proof of evidence from the defendant is included in the brief, it is important to check with the client that it is complete, accurate, and up to date; if there is no proof of evidence, it is up to counsel to elicit all the necessary information from the defendant. In deciding what questions to ask the defendant, counsel should consider the factors set out in the Bail Act 1976 (e.g. risk of absconding, committing offences while on bail, or interfering with witnesses, all of which are assessed in the light of such matters as the nature and seriousness of the present offence, the defendant's previous convictions (if any), the defendant's community ties, and their record of answering bail in the past).

(b) *Advise the client:* If this is the client's first court appearance, they may need reassurance; it may therefore be necessary to explain to the client what will happen in court. It is highly likely that the client will ask counsel to advise on the probable result of the bail application. Furthermore, the client may seek advice about other aspects of the case. Where such advice is given, a short note of the advice given should be endorsed on the brief, signed and dated by counsel (so that the solicitor knows what counsel has said to the client).

(c) *Address the court in favour of bail:* Assuming the prosecution oppose the grant of bail, the prosecutor addresses the court first and explains to the court the grounds upon which the prosecution say that bail should be withheld. Counsel for the defence then replies to those submissions and will try to show that the prosecution objections to the grant of bail have no foundation or that those objections can be overcome by the imposition of conditions on the grant of bail. No witnesses are called (unless a surety comes forward, in which case that person will usually have to give evidence showing their suitability to act as a surety). The submissions to the court should be based on the matters that the court is required to consider under the Bail Act 1976.

(d) *Advise the client on challenging refusal of bail:* If bail is withheld, counsel should advise the defendant (and, later, communicate this advice to the instructing solicitor) on any steps which might be taken to increase the chance of bail being granted (e.g. the provision of a surety) and/or whether an application for bail should be made to the Crown Court.

The role of the prosecutor is rather more limited: simply making a speech opposing the grant of bail. In doing this, the prosecutor will usually have to rely on notes contained in the CPS file; those notes are based on information supplied by the police. The police officer in charge of the case is unlikely to be present at the bail application.

There may occasionally be some scope for negotiation between defence counsel and the prosecutor. It might be that the prosecutor will agree not to oppose the grant of bail if the defendant agrees that the grant of bail should be subject to certain conditions.

If the first bail application is unsuccessful, the defence may make a second application to the magistrates a week later. This is so even if the second application says nothing different from the first application (although the advocate making the application will normally try to find something different to say). Once the magistrates have heard two fully argued bail applications, however, they can only hear a further application if there is a material change in circumstances (i.e. the defence can put forward an argument which has not been put forward already).

Where bail has been refused by the magistrates following a fully argued bail application, it may be appropriate to make a further bail application in the Crown Court. The procedure in the Crown Court is very similar to that in the magistrates' court (i.e. the prosecutor sets out the reasons for opposing the grant of bail and defence counsel then replies to those submissions). However, the defendant will not usually be present and the CPS will usually (but not always) be represented by counsel.

If the offence is triable in the Crown Court, the case may be sent to the Crown Court for trial after the first appearance in the magistrates' court. If the magistrates refuse bail, any further application for bail will therefore have to be made in the Crown Court.

11.6.2   Mode of trial hearing

Where the defendant is accused of an offence which is triable either way (i.e. triable in either a magistrates' court or the Crown Court), counsel may be asked to advise the client on which court should try the case. This advice will almost always be given orally, and will generally be given just before the mode of trial hearing itself (unless it was given at an earlier remand hearing).

At this stage (if not before), the client may well need advice on plea, since the mode of trial hearing in court begins with a 'plea before venue' hearing (at which the defendant is asked to indicate whether he or she intends to plead guilty or not guilty). If the defendant indicates an intention to plead guilty, this is regarded as a guilty plea. At that point, the magistrates will either proceed to the sentencing stage (if necessary, after an adjournment for a pre-sentence report to be prepared by a probation officer) or else commit the defendant to the Crown Court for sentence (the Crown Court having greater sentencing powers than the magistrates' court). If, on the other hand, the defendant either indicates an intention to plead not guilty, or gives no indication as to the intended plea, the magistrates will proceed to determine the question of mode of trial.

At the mode of trial hearing, the magistrates have to decide whether the case is suitable for summary trial. The key question is whether, in the event of the defendant being convicted, their sentencing powers would be adequate to deal with the case. If the magistrates decide that the case is not suitable for summary trial, only trial in the Crown Court is possible. If the magistrates decide that the case is suitable for summary trial (i.e. they 'accept jurisdiction'), the defendant is asked where he or she wishes to be tried. This is because, in the case of an offence which is triable either way, the defendant has the right to choose to be tried on indictment (i.e. at the Crown Court).

During the mode of trial hearing, the prosecution and the defence both have the right to make representations regarding the appropriate mode of trial. If the defendant wishes to elect trial on indictment, there is little point in the defence making any representations, because of the defendant's right to choose Crown Court trial. If, on the other hand, the defendant wants to be tried in the magistrates' court but the prosecution are seeking trial in the Crown Court, counsel for the defendant will first have to try to persuade the magistrates that the case is suitable for summary trial.

In advising the client on whether or not to elect Crown Court trial in the case of an 'either-way' offence, counsel will need to be aware of the various arguments for and against the two types of trial. Jurors tend to be less 'case-hardened' than magistrates, which may explain why the acquittal rate is slightly higher in the Crown Court than in the magistrates' court. Where it is likely that the defence will seek to have some of the prosecution evidence (such as a confession) ruled inadmissible, Crown Court trial is preferable because matters of admissibility are dealt with by the judge in the absence of the jury; this separation of functions is not possible in the magistrates' court, where the justices are triers of both law and fact (although it should be borne in mind that, under the Courts Act 2003, it is possible to ask a bench of magistrates to make a pre-trial ruling to decide any question as to the admissibility of evidence or any other question of law relating to the case; this pre-trial ruling is binding on the trial court and so, if evidence is ruled inadmissible in a pre-trial ruling, that evidence is inadmissible at the trial and the magistrates who try the case will hear nothing about that evidence).

Another factor relevant to the choice between magistrates' court and Crown Court trial is that trial in the magistrates' court is a little less formal (and so maybe a little less daunting for the accused) than jury trial. Trials in the magistrates' court also tend to be considerably shorter than trials in the Crown Court; those trials also tend to be cheaper (which may be an important consideration to the accused where the defence is not publicly funded). The cap on the sentencing powers of the magistrates cannot be said to be an advantage of summary trial as it is effectively negated by the power of the magistrates' court to commit the defendant to the Crown Court for sentence.

11.6.3 Advising the prosecution

Counsel who has been briefed to prosecute in a forthcoming Crown Court trial may be asked by the CPS to advise on the evidence (and sometimes to draft or redraft the indictment) before the trial takes place. This involves examining the witness statements made by the prosecution witnesses in order to see how strong the prosecution case is. Counsel has to consider if the case can be improved (e.g. advising that the police take further statements from existing witnesses, to fill gaps or clarify ambiguities, or advising that further investigations be made).

The advice given must be both realistic and practicable. It must be remembered that the police do not have limitless resources.

Where the trial is to take place in a magistrates' court, these matters will almost invariably be considered by a Crown Prosecutor, not by a barrister in private practice.

11.6.4 Advising the defendant

Counsel for the defence may be asked to advise on evidence prior to a Crown Court trial. This advice will often be given orally, during a conference with the client, rather than in writing; such conferences usually take place in counsel's chambers (or in an interview room in a prison if the defendant has been remanded in custody). Again, any advice must be realistic and practicable. It must also be borne in mind that, where the defendant is legally aided, further enquiries involving considerable expense are unlikely to be covered by public funds.

Prior to a magistrates' court trial, it is very rare for defence counsel to have a conference in chambers or to give written advice. The conference usually takes place in the court building, shortly before the trial is due to begin.

The function of the pre-trial conference (whether held some time before the date fixed for the trial or just before the trial is due to start) may include some or all of the following elements:

(a) *Taking instructions from the client (i.e. gathering information):* By the time of the trial, counsel will be in possession of a proof of evidence from the defendant which sets out the client's version of events. However, it is still useful to get clients to go through their version of events: the solicitor may have missed something, or the defendant may remember something new. Whilst it is unethical, and therefore strictly forbidden, for counsel to 'coach' the defendant (i.e. to suggest evidence which the defendant might give), there is no objection to counsel questioning the client closely on the evidence he or she will be giving. It is helpful for defendants to go through the evidence they will be giving in court in order to prepare for cross-examination by the prosecution.

Where counsel is in possession of the witness statements made by the prosecution witnesses, the defendant should also be asked to comment on what those witnesses say (so that counsel can decide what questions to ask them by way of cross-examination). It may be that the solicitor has already performed this task, so that the defendant's proof of evidence contains comments on the prosecution evidence; even then, it can be helpful to ask the defendant if there is anything he or she wishes to add to those comments.

(b) *Advising the defendant on plea and tactics:* Where the client has not received full advice on plea (from the solicitor, or from counsel on a previous occasion), it may be necessary for counsel to advise the defendant (based on what the client has said about their version of events) on plea. It may be, for example, that the defendant has indicated an intention to plead guilty but then says something which amounts to a defence (e.g. a person accused of theft says that they did not realise that the property belonged to someone else). Whilst counsel ought to advise on the advantages of pleading guilty (such as a reduction in sentence), the client should be left in no doubt that they should only plead guilty if they are guilty.

Where the defendant is going to plead not guilty, it may also be necessary to advise on tactics (for example, what lines of cross-examination to pursue and what evidence to call).

(c) *Taking instructions on matters relevant to sentence:* Counsel should be careful to have all the information needed to make a plea in mitigation. Instructions should therefore be taken on matters which would be relevant to sentence. This is so even where the client is going to plead not guilty, since (in the event of the defendant being convicted) there may not be time for a further conference between the defendant being convicted and the moment counsel has to start making the plea in mitigation.

(d) *Advising on sentence:* Whether the defendant is going to plead guilty or not guilty, it will almost always be necessary to give advice on the sentence which is likely to be imposed in the event of conviction. Counsel will therefore have to be familiar with the relevant guidelines (issued by the Sentencing Council).

Counsel representing a defendant at an early stage of the proceedings may be asked to give advice about later stages of the case. On occasions, for example, counsel may be instructed to attend the magistrates' court to make a bail application, or for the mode of trial hearing, and may be asked for advice then by the defendant. Provided counsel is sufficiently well acquainted with the background to the case, there is no objection to such advice being given (although a short note setting out the advice given should be endorsed on the brief, so that the instructing solicitor, and any barrister involved in the case at a later stage, knows what was said). However, where the advice is given without full knowledge of the prosecution case and the defence response to that case, it should be made clear to the client that the advice is only provisional and may change if new information comes to light.

11.6.5   Pre-trial disclosure

A particularly important aspect of advising on evidence concerns the rules which govern pre-trial disclosure. The rules which apply to the prosecution are different from the rules which apply to the defence. The disclosure rules are contained in the Criminal Procedure and Investigations Act 1996 (CPIA 1996). Further details can be found in the *Criminal Litigation and Sentencing* manual and in *Blackstone's Criminal Practice*. As regards disclosure by the prosecution, a further distinction has to be drawn between material that the prosecution will be using as part of their case and material which they will not be using.

11.6.5.1   Pre-trial disclosure by the prosecution

By the day of the first hearing, the prosecutor must have provided 'initial details' of the prosecution case to the defence. These details must include a summary of the evidence on which the prosecution case will be based and/or a statement setting out facts or other matters on which that case will be based. If the case is to be tried in the Crown Court, copies of the statements made by the witnesses whom the prosecution intend to call at the trial must be supplied to the defence (if this has not already been done). The defence should also receive the prosecution witness statements prior to any trial in the magistrates' court.

Where the prosecution wish to use a witness whose statement has not already been served on the defence, a 'notice of additional evidence' (including a copy of the witness statement) must be served on the defence prior to the trial.

The prosecution are also under a statutory duty to disclose certain material other than the statements of the persons they will be calling as witnesses. Under the CPIA 1996, the prosecutor must disclose to the accused any prosecution material which might reasonably be considered capable of undermining the case for the prosecution against the accused or of assisting the case for the accused. This applies to all trials (whether in the Crown Court, the magistrates' court, or the youth court).

It follows that, by the time of the pre-trial conference (at the latest), counsel for the accused should be aware both of the case to be met and of any material that has come to the attention of the prosecution and which undermines their case or supports the defence case.

11.6.5.2   Pre-trial disclosure by the defence

The Criminal Procedure and Investigations Act 1996 imposes a compulsory duty of disclosure on the defence, but this compulsory duty applies only to trials in the Crown Court. This disclosure takes the form of a 'defence statement'. This has to:

(a) set out the nature of the accused's defence, including any particular defences on which the accused intends to rely;

(b) indicate the matters of fact on which the accused takes issue with the prosecution;

(c) set out, in the case of each such matter, *why* the accused takes issue with the prosecution;

(d) set out particulars of the matters of fact on which the accused intends to rely for the purposes of their defence; and

(e) indicate any point of law (including any point as to the admissibility of evidence or abuse of process) which the accused wishes to take, and any authority on which they intend to rely for that purpose.

Where the accused wishes to rely on an alibi, the defence statement must give full particulars of the alibi and of any witnesses the accused believes may be able to give evidence in support of the alibi. The defence also have to supply the prosecution with details of any witnesses they propose to call to support the defence case.

In the case of summary (i.e. magistrates' court or youth court) trials, the Act enables the defence to make voluntary disclosure of their case.

Following service of the defence statement, the CPS have to review the unused material to see if there is anything which undermines the prosecution case or supports the defence case. If so, it should be disclosed to the defence.

If the defence fail to comply with their compulsory duty of disclosure prior to Crown Court trial, or if the defence case at trial differs from that disclosed to the prosecution (whether the disclosure was compulsory or voluntary), then adverse inferences can be drawn by the jury or magistrates, as the case may be.

The Bar Standards Board has given guidance on the involvement of counsel in the drafting of defence statements. The guidance makes the point that it will normally be more appropriate for instructing solicitors to draft the defence statement, since counsel will generally have had little involvement in the case at this stage. Nonetheless, there is no reason why a barrister should not draft a defence statement. However, counsel must ensure that the defendant:

- understands the importance of the accuracy and adequacy of the defence statement; and

- has had the opportunity of carefully considering the statement drafted by counsel and has approved it.

11.6.6   Preliminary hearings in the Crown Court

The Criminal Procedure and Investigations Act 1996 requires preliminary hearings to take place before all Crown Court trials. The purpose of the preliminary hearing is to ensure that the issues in the case are defined before the start of the trial and reduce the number of cases where the defendant was due to be tried on a 'not guilty' plea but then pleads guilty at the start of the trial (giving rise to what is sometimes called a 'cracked trial'). Where the defendant intends to plead guilty but did not do so at the 'plea before venue' hearing in the magistrates' court, an 'early guilty plea hearing' will be arranged in the Crown Court so that the defendant can enter the guilty plea.

11.6.6.1   Plea and case management hearing

In the case of Crown Court trials other than those which are likely to be complex or lengthy (in which case, a 'preparatory hearing' will be held), a 'plea and case management hearing' (or PCMH) will take place.

At this hearing, the defendant is asked to enter a plea. Assuming the defendant pleads 'not guilty', a date is fixed for the trial.

Where the defendant pleads 'not guilty', prosecuting and defence counsel are expected to inform the court of matters such as: the issues in the case, the number of witnesses to be called, any points of law likely to arise (including questions on the admissibility of evidence), and whether any technical equipment (such as video equipment) is likely to be needed. It follows that it is very important that, by the time of this hearing, the factual and legal issues in the case have been identified. At this hearing, the judge is empowered to make rulings on the admissibility of evidence and on any other questions of law which are relevant to the case. These rulings are binding for the whole of the trial unless there is an application for the ruling to be altered, but such an application can be made only if there has been a material change in circumstances since the ruling was made.

11.6.7 Trial

Defence counsel and the prosecutor may attend court expecting a trial to take place. However, a trial will not take place if either the defendant pleads guilty to the charge(s) or the prosecution accept a plea to a lesser offence. In the Crown Court, any negotiations with the prosecution regarding the acceptance of a plea of guilty to a less serious offence than that charged will usually take place at the PCMH. Where the case is to be heard in the magistrates' court, such negotiations will usually take place just before the trial.

We have already seen that counsel for the defence may have to give advice to the defendant at the conference which takes place immediately before the trial.

During the trial itself, counsel is involved in three main tasks:

(a) *Making speeches:* At the start of the trial, the prosecution will make an opening speech. The purpose of this opening speech is to prepare the jury or magistrates for the evidence they are about to hear. The prosecution case is summarised so that the jury or magistrates can put the evidence they are about to hear in context.

The prosecution and the defence will, in most cases, each make a closing speech. The purpose of the closing speech is to highlight the strengths of one's case and, where possible, to minimise the impact of any weaknesses. The defence, for example, will stress any doubt in the prosecution evidence and any explanation which the defendant has given for apparently incriminating evidence.

As well as these opening and closing speeches, it may be necessary for counsel to address the court on the admissibility of certain evidence or to make (or, if prosecuting, to respond to) a submission that there is no case to answer.

A submission of no case to answer may be made by the defence at the end of the prosecution case. The essence of the submission is that the evidence adduced by the prosecution is so weak that no reasonable tribunal (jury or bench of magistrates, as the case may be) could convict the defendant on the basis of that evidence. The prosecutor is entitled to respond to this submission. If the court accepts that there is no case to answer, the defendant is acquitted; if the court finds that there is a case to answer, the case continues (the next stage being for the defence to adduce their evidence).

(b) *Examination-in-chief:* This means getting the witness to tell the story (answering questions such as 'who?', 'when?', 'where?', 'describe'). Care must be taken not to 'lead' the witness on matters that are in dispute. A leading question is one which contains or suggests the answer; a question which can be answered with a simple 'yes' or 'no' will usually be a leading question. Before going into court, counsel must have decided what he or she hopes to achieve with the particular witness, since the examination-in-chief should only bring out evidence which is relevant to the case. Counsel will always be in possession of a written statement from the witness (which obviously forms the basis of the questions which will be put to the witness). Counsel should be alert to any inadmissible evidence that may be contained in the witness's written statement (e.g. hearsay, or references to previous dealings between the defendant and the police, unless such evidence has been ruled admissible), so that those areas can be avoided in the questioning.

Examination-in-chief can also be used to anticipate questions which might be put to that witness in cross-examination. For instance, in a case involving identification evidence, prosecuting counsel would, in examination-in-chief, ask a witness who claims to have identified the defendant as the perpetrator about the circumstances of that identification (e.g. distance, lighting, obstructions to view, etc.). The answers to these questions might well make it more difficult for counsel for the defence to cross-examine effectively on the matters.

The defendant has been present in court throughout the trial and so has heard the evidence of the prosecution witnesses. The defendant might be asked, in examination-in-chief, to comment on what he has heard (for example, 'You heard Miss Jones say . . . What do you say about that?').

(c) *Cross-examination:* This means probing the story told by the witness. In the Crown Court, counsel for the defence will be in possession of the written statements made by the prosecution witnesses; in the magistrates' court, counsel for the defence will usually have the prosecution witness statements. However, the prosecution never have the written statements made by witnesses for the defence. Obviously, it is easier to prepare a cross-examination if one has advance notice of what the witness is going to say.

Cross-examination essentially focuses on inconsistencies and on the probing of weaknesses:

(i)   inconsistencies between what the witness is saying now and what they have said in their written statement;

(ii) inconsistencies in the evidence which the witness has given to the court (e.g. in the course of the witness's testimony, the colour of the getaway car changes from dark blue to black);

(iii) inconsistencies between what this witness has said and what another witness says;

(iv) inconsistencies between what this witness is saying and the theory which counsel has formed about the case;

(v)   inconsistencies between what the witness is saying and what common sense suggests actually happened (e.g. a witness who says that a car was travelling at 70 mph and that it braked sharply and stopped within a distance of 15 metres cannot be correct);

(vi) exposing weaknesses in the other side's evidence (e.g. establishing that the witness was some distance from the scene of the crime and that there were obstructions to their observation). Is there a basis for suggesting that the witness is mistaken? Does the witness have a motive for misleading the court?

It is important that in cross-examination you 'put your case'. In other words, if a witness called by your opponent might be able to comment on part of your case, that witness should be given the chance to do so. In the case of counsel for the defence, this will include putting to the witness those parts of the witness's evidence which differ from, or are inconsistent with, the defendant's account of what happened.

Many practitioners have in mind their closing speech from the moment they start to prepare the case. In thinking about your closing speech, you are asking yourself how you are going to persuade the jury (or magistrates) to come to the result that you want them to come to. In other words, how will you persuade them to accept your 'theory of the case'? This will determine what evidence you put before the court through the examination-in-chief of your witnesses, and what questions you ask in cross-examination of your opponent's witnesses.

Much of the case analysis process involves consideration of strengths and weaknesses: the strengths and weaknesses of your case, and the strengths and weaknesses of your opponent's case. Your task is to think about ways of emphasising or maximising the strengths of your case and ways of improving, or minimising the effect of, the weaknesses of your case; also, it is to see if you can reduce the effect of the strengths, and increase the impact of the weaknesses, of your opponent's case.

This process can be expressed as a series of questions:

Strengths of your case

- What evidence supports your case?
- How might your opponent try to undermine the evidence that supports your case?
- How might you be able to prevent your opponent from undermining the evidence that supports your case?

Weaknesses of your case

- What evidence weakens your case?
- How might you reduce the impact of the evidence that weakens your case?
- How might your opponent try to prevent you from undermining the evidence that weakens your case?

Strengths of your opponent's case

- What evidence supports your opponent's case?
- How might you try to undermine the evidence that supports your opponent's case?
- How might your opponent try to prevent you from undermining the evidence that supports their case?

Weaknesses of your opponent's case

- What evidence weakens your opponent's case?
- How might you increase the impact of the evidence that weakens your opponent's case?
- How might your opponent try to prevent you from increasing the impact of the evidence that weakens their case?

11.6.8   Plea in mitigation

A plea in mitigation is required if the defendant either pleads guilty or is found guilty. Sentence is usually passed, either immediately or after an adjournment for preparation of a pre-sentence report, by the court which convicted the defendant. However, if the defendant is convicted in the magistrates' court of an offence which is triable either way, the magistrates may (if they decide that their sentencing powers are insufficient to deal with the case) commit the defendant to the Crown Court to be sentenced (the Crown Court having greater sentencing powers); in that case, a plea in mitigation will have to be delivered in the Crown Court. It should be borne in mind that, where sentence is being passed in a magistrates' court following an adjournment, the magistrates who pass sentence will probably not be the same ones that convicted the defendant.

If sentence is passed immediately after the defendant has been convicted following trial (i.e. the defendant pleaded not guilty but was convicted), the prosecutor will simply tell the court about any previous convictions recorded against the defendant. If the defendant pleads guilty, or is being sentenced at a hearing which takes place after the trial at which the defendant was convicted, the prosecutor will also have to explain to the court precisely what the defendant did.

The next step is for defence counsel to make a plea in mitigation on behalf of the defendant. The essence of a plea in mitigation is to draw the court's attention to any mitigating factors relating to the offence itself and to emphasise any personal mitigating circumstances relating to the offender.

The plea in mitigation will be based on information gathered from the client (in the proof of evidence, and in things said by the client prior to the hearing) and, in many cases, on information contained in a pre-sentence report prepared by a probation officer. A list of the client's previous convictions (if any) should be in the brief; if not, the list can be obtained from the prosecutor. Counsel should check that the defendant agrees that the list of previous convictions is correct (and should seek information from the client about the circumstances of those convictions, since they may be relevant to the sentence to be passed in the present case) and that the defendant is content with the comments made by the probation officer in the pre-sentence report. Counsel should be prepared to probe the client for details of mitigating factors relating to the offence itself or to the client's personal circumstances.

Before advising the client on likely sentence or presenting a plea in mitigation, counsel must be familiar with the approach taken by the courts to sentencing for the particular offence(s) of which the defendant has been convicted. For example, if the 'starting point' is a custodial sentence, counsel should indicate awareness of this before trying to persuade the court to impose a lesser sentence. A useful source of guidance may be found on the website of the Sentencing Council (<http://sentencingcouncil.judiciary.gov.uk/guidelines/guidelines-to-download.htm>) and in publications such as *Blackstone's Criminal Practice*.

11.6.9   Appeals

11.6.9.1   Appeals from the magistrates' court

Most appeals against conviction and/or sentence from the magistrates' court are heard by the Crown Court. An appeal against conviction takes the form of a complete rehearing of the case. The prosecution will be represented by counsel instructed by the CPS or by a Crown Prosecutor. Counsel for the defence may or may not have represented the defendant in the magistrates' court.

Permission to appeal is not required. Because the appeal takes the form of a rehearing, the Crown Court is not concerned with what happened in the magistrates' court; one corollary of this is that a witness who was not called in the magistrates' court can be called in the Crown Court and a witness who was called in the magistrates' court need not be called in the Crown Court. This means that both sides may reconsider any tactical decisions (regarding which witnesses to call) which were taken prior to the trial in the magistrates' court.

Similarly, the hearing by the Crown Court of an appeal against the sentence imposed by a magistrates' court takes the same form as the original sentencing hearing in the magistrates' court, with the prosecutor summarising the facts followed by a plea in mitigation by the defence advocate.

When advising the defendant whether or not to appeal to the Crown Court, counsel should warn the defendant that the Crown Court has the power to increase the sentence imposed by the magistrates' court, up to the maximum which the magistrates could have imposed; this is so even if it is only the conviction (and not the sentence) which is the subject of the defendant's appeal.

Alternatively, in a case which involves a point of law or jurisdiction, the defendant may appeal instead to the High Court. This can be done in two ways. The first is to ask the magistrates to 'state a case' for the opinion of the High Court (known as 'appeal by way of case stated'); the magistrates duly summarise their findings of fact and their rulings on the law, and the High Court considers whether the magistrates reached the correct conclusion. The second way is to apply for judicial review of the decision of the magistrates' court; this method is particularly appropriate where the magistrates exceeded their powers in some way or behaved unfairly. The prosecution can also appeal to the High Court by way of case stated, or seek judicial review, on a point of law or jurisdiction and thereby challenge an acquittal by a magistrates' court.

11.6.9.2 Appeals from the Crown Court

Appeals from the Crown Court against conviction and/or sentence go to the Court of Appeal (Criminal Division).

Sometimes the appellant is represented by the same barrister who appeared in the Crown Court, sometimes a different barrister is chosen. In any event, counsel for the appellant has to examine the notes which were taken during the trial by counsel for the defence to see if any errors occurred during the course of the trial. Particular attention has to be paid to any rulings made by the judge during the course of the trial (e.g. rulings on the admissibility of particular evidence) and to the judge's summing-up of the case to the jury. As far as the latter is concerned, counsel should consider whether the judge stated the law correctly and whether the judge summarised the case for the prosecution, and the case for the defendant, accurately and fairly. Similarly, the comments made by the judge when passing sentence should be scrutinised with care, to ensure that the correct sentencing principles were applied.

If errors were made in the course of the trial and/or in the summing-up, or when sentence was passed, grounds of appeal have to be drafted; these grounds must identify the errors that were made and must refer to any relevant case law. This is an important document, since it forms the basis of the decision by a Court of Appeal judge whether or not to give leave to appeal.

Once an application for leave to appeal against conviction has been lodged, a transcript of the summing-up and any other rulings made by the trial judge will be sent to the barrister who drafted the grounds of appeal; counsel then has the chance to 'perfect' the grounds of appeal (i.e. to relate those grounds to the transcript).

The hearing of the appeal itself takes the form of argument by counsel for the appellant and counsel for the respondent; no evidence is heard except in exceptional cases (e.g. where the conviction is said to be unsafe in the light of evidence that has emerged after the trial).

Under Part 9 of the Criminal Justice Act 2003, the prosecution also have a limited right of appeal to the Court of Appeal against 'terminating rulings' by Crown Court judges made either at a pre-trial hearing or at any time during the trial itself. A terminating ruling is one which has the effect of terminating the trial and includes both rulings that are terminating in themselves and also those that are so fatal to the prosecution case that the prosecution proposes to treat them as terminating and, in the absence of the right of appeal, would offer no, or no further, evidence against the defendant. The prosecution cannot, however, appeal against an acquittal by the jury.

The fact management process

12.1 Introduction to the fact management process

At the heart of the practitioner's work are facts: an incident has occurred or must be prevented from occurring, a person injured, property damaged or likely to be damaged, and loss threatened or sustained. From the first moment of receiving a brief until the last stage of trial, it is the facts of a case that will be the basis of the practitioner's work. 'Facts' are the basis of any evidence given, any speeches made, and any questions asked. It is the barrister's ability to manage the facts, to understand their implications, and to use them as the basis of argument, that will be crucial to the success of a case.

The majority of cases involve disputes of facts, not, despite the emphasis in academic training, disputes about questions of law. The ability of barristers to carry out the task of managing facts has in the past been developed by experience and, until the development of the vocational course for the Bar, very little attempt had been made to consciously define and develop this skill. Very few texts then sought to unravel the fact management process in order to teach others how to carry it out on a step-by-step basis. More recently the importance of high-level skills and a project management approach to engaging with facts has been acknowledged. It is now generally recognised that the ability to prepare a set of papers effectively depends on:

- the need to have a clear picture of what you are preparing for;
- being able to identify what is relevant to your task;
- identifying what the issues are;
- recognising what can and cannot be proved;
- evaluating the strength of the case accurately; and
- putting together, from the information available, the most compelling argument on your client's behalf.

It is even more challenging to manage the facts you do not have. It is rarely possible to completely recreate how an accident happened, different witnesses remember different things, some events are seen by no one and leave no evidence, and evidence of some facts may be so difficult or expensive to collect that it is not realistically available. These potential problems make it vital to deal with facts, and gaps in facts, in a detailed and systematic way.

The working approach advocated in this chapter, the CAP approach (Context, Analysis, Preparation), applies intellectual skills in a practical and structured process to case preparation. The CAP method of preparing a case demonstrates, on a step-by-step basis, every stage in the process—from initial understanding of the legal and factual context, to detailed analysis of issues, evidence, and gaps in information, and finally the construction of persuasive and pertinent arguments to present to a tribunal, a client, or, in negotiation, an opponent.

The chapter also illustrates some of the techniques which can be used to aid analysis and the presentation of a case. Thorough case preparation can be achieved by many different working methods. A variation of CAP that you may encounter in your training, particularly as regards preparation for an opinion or drafting is LEGO (Law, Evaluation, Gaps, Opinion). Find an approach that works for you, and you will find your skills develop and change with time and experience as you get different insights into analysis.

While some may think of this as an objective science, the process involves more than applying a logical method of analysis and presentation. Resourceful barristers also use lateral thinking to identify alternative interpretations of the facts, and to address gaps in information as part of advocacy. One's own perception of how witnesses see and describe events and their effectiveness as witnesses will influence a decision about whether they should be called at trial or how to question them. Finally, the ability to use different methods to communicate information in a clear and persuasive way calls for creativity and thought about how to present the facts in the best light. These qualities are part of the practical aspects of fact management which cannot be separated from the more objective tasks of collecting facts.

You will find that your own ability to analyse and evaluate factual situations, and to use the results to communicate persuasively, will develop best through conscious application of a process and reflection on how effective the results were. You will have regular opportunities to do this in the practical training exercises on which you will work while studying the Bar Professional Training Programme. If you are able to take the opportunity of giving advice through pro bono schemes, or to undertake representation through organisations such as the Free Representation Unit, you will develop further and faster. You will also find yourself developing your abilities further when you move into practice or any other legally related career.

12.2 Starting from scratch: defining basic terms

12.2.1 'Agreed' facts

Every problem will contain 'facts': who the parties are, the history of the situation, what transpired on certain dates, etc. '*Agreed facts*' are those facts which are conceded by your opponent and are not therefore issues in the case. In criminal cases, they may sometimes be set out in a 'formal admission' (see Chapter 1 of the *Evidence* manual). More often, practitioners simply tell the court, 'it is not in dispute that . . . '. In civil cases, the statements of case will disclose what is agreed between parties. Put simply, if a fact is 'admitted', that fact is not in issue and no evidence has to be adduced to prove it.

It is important to note down what facts are agreed between the parties. It helps to narrow down the issues of a case and will be likely to shorten the length of a trial. It may also assist in a negotiation to be able to start from some common ground between the parties.

12.2.2 Facts and evidence

When a 'fact' has been agreed, or can be proved by a witness or document, that fact is then considered to be 'evidence' in the case, and can be taken into account in determining the strengths and weaknesses of the case. The distinction is important: some facts are incapable of proof and (if not agreed) should not be relied upon as part of the case.

12.2.3   Disputed facts and facts in issue

If a fact is in dispute between the parties, that is, the opponent does not 'agree' it, it is deemed to be a *'disputed fact'* in the case. In a criminal case, if the defendant does not plead guilty, then subject to any admission the defendant may make, it is for the prosecution to prove all facts relevant to establishing the guilt of the defendant. In civil cases, you can determine what the 'disputed facts' are by looking primarily at the court papers, although documents and correspondence may bring up other facts that are not agreed. The statements of case (particulars of claim and defence) will show which facts are 'denied' or simply 'not admitted'. If a fact is 'not admitted', the party seeking to prove the fact will have to adduce evidence. By stating 'no admissions are made as to . . .', the other party is saying, 'I will not adduce evidence to contradict this fact but I reserve the right to cross-examine your witnesses to test their evidence on this point'. If a fact is 'denied', the party relying on that fact will have to adduce evidence to prove it and the opponent is likely to be able to bring evidence to contradict it.

It is easy to confuse *'disputed facts'* and *'facts in issue'*. First, bear in mind that it is common for a case to contain many disputed facts. Of these, there will be some that are crucial in the sense that they support points that must be proved in law in order for the case to be successful. It is these facts, i.e. the facts which are not agreed by the opponent and which must be proved in law, that become the 'facts in issue'. For example, D is accused of assaulting the owner of a public house after D and his friend asked to play a game of pool. D's story is that he arrived at the bar 15 minutes after his friend on the evening in question; the prosecution say that he arrived some time before his friend. The time and sequence of arrival are 'disputed facts' between the parties in the sense that there is no agreement as to who arrived first and at what times they arrived. But bringing evidence of the truth of one version or the other is not relevant to proving the elements of the criminal offence of assault and will not affect a successful outcome. Therefore it is not a 'fact in issue'.

The facts in issue will be determined by what legal elements of the charge (in a criminal case) or legal elements of the cause of action (in a civil case) apply. For example, in a contract case where C is suing D for breach of contract and resulting loss, the parties might agree that a contract was made, and the terms of that agreement. However, D disputes that a breach occurred and naturally disputes causing losses. As breach and causation are two of the prima facie requirements for a successful action in contract (and the facts on these two matters are disputed), these become the 'facts in issue' in the case. C will only win the case by producing evidence on these issues to prove that his version of the facts was correct, and that he is therefore entitled to judgment in his favour.

It is important to bear in mind that 'facts in issue' (sometimes called 'factual issues') can be a general heading containing several sub-issues. For example, in a criminal case, the identity of the defendant might be in issue. One element of the identification evidence concerns the colour of his hair. One witness says that he had fair hair, another that he had brown hair. The colour of the hair is therefore a fact in issue. Its proof will affect whether the prosecution have proved their case in that identification of the defendant as the offender is an element of the offence. It will assist you in analysis to identify all the factual issues to divide the case into broad factual issues first, and then look at the facts which are in dispute within each of those main issues. This is covered in more detail later on in the chapter.

12.2.4   Legal issues

These are the questions of law which will have to be answered in the case:

- What are the potential causes of actions or offences?
- What are the potential defences?

- What are the potential legal outcomes or remedies?
- What procedural and evidential questions arise?

In tort and contract cases, there are established frameworks to work from, e.g. elements that the claimant must prove in order to establish a case. In criminal cases, the prosecution must prove the elements of an offence, and in some cases, the absence of a defence. Of the legal issues that apply in a case, only some will need to be formally proved since often there will be no dispute between the parties on some of the issues. Later on in this chapter, we look at establishing legal frameworks and defining the issues to be resolved.

12.2.5   The 'theory' of the case

After the barrister has identified a framework of the legal and factual issues in a case, and done the necessary legal research, a picture should start to emerge. For each case, it is necessary for you to consider a 'theory' of the case, that is, your explanation of how the events of the case are likely to have happened. The 'theory' of the case will influence the nature of the evidence that will be required for a successful resolution and will also be the base for the advocacy in the case.

In a straightforward case, the theory may be fairly clear, and based solidly on legal and factual certainties. But often the law may not be clear, all the facts may not be available, or there may be gaps in the evidence. In those cases, you will need to develop arguments which link the facts and evidence that are available into a persuasive explanation of your client's version of events.

Developing a 'theory' is covered in more detail later in this chapter.

12.3   The CAP approach

Having identified the intellectual elements of fact management skills in **12.1**, barristers may use a number of practical techniques to produce a well-prepared case. Regardless of the task which a barrister might be asked to undertake—to advise on the merits, appear in court, or advise in conference—it is crucial to absorb and analyse the facts of the case. Without a uniform approach and structure to this process, thoughts and theories can become confused. Weak opinions and statements of case most often result from a failure to engage with systematic analysis. Adopting a logical yet flexible framework will not only minimise the chances of missing important pieces of information, but will maximise productivity in terms of your time and effort.

The CAP approach is a step-by-step method of preparing and analysing a case. All barristers develop their own practical styles of working, with or without attaching formal names or titles to their working methods. In order to study the necessary stages, the CAP approach sets out the three main stages involved in efficient preparation:

- Context;
- Analysis; and
- Presentation.

Each stage contains tasks and questions which must be answered before moving on to the next stage. The time necessary for each step depends on the complexity of the case and the specific task you are instructed to do. The advantage of taking an overview of the preparation process is that it enables the student to see how the process develops, from the first reading of the facts, through to the analysis of evidence needed in order to present a successful case. As you gain experience, it is hoped that the CAP framework will allow you to determine selectively what is required by means of thorough preparation for any given case.

It should be remembered that the CAP approach is only one method of achieving a well-prepared case as discussed in **12.1**. Even while following the CAP approach, the tasks within each stage can be done by using any number of techniques, e.g. lists, charts, mind-maps, graphs. As examples, a set of pro forma charts that can be used as part of the CAP approach is included at **12.8**. While their use is by no means prescriptive, they may be helpful in clarifying the various steps involved in thorough case preparation.

12.3.1 The three stages of CAP

Stage 1: The context of the case

(a) Understand the stage of the proceedings: your role and instructions, and the objectives.

(b) Understand the problem: e.g. the history of the situation, nature, and cause of the problem.

(c) Collect the 'facts'.

(d) Identify the agreed facts and facts in dispute—i.e. those facts which are disputed between the parties—e.g. by use of a chart to set out the facts, queries, and each party's version.

(e) Identify the legal framework: in a criminal case, this would be the elements of the offence, possible defences, sentence, jurisdiction, and procedure. In a civil case, this would be the elements required to establish a cause of action or a defence, and to justify or undermine a remedy sought.

Stage 2: Analysis of issues and evidence

(a) Analyse the issues:

  (i) identify the factual issues: i.e. those disputed facts which are not agreed by the opponent and which must be proved in law for a successful outcome;

  (ii) identify the legal issues by applying the facts to the legal framework;

  (iii) identify a potential 'theory' of the case; and

  (iv) identify the gaps and ambiguities in the facts.

(b) Analyse the evidence:

  (i) analyse the strengths and weaknesses of your case and that of your opponent; and

  (ii) establish 'proof'—turning facts into 'evidence'.

Stage 3: The presentation of the case or argument

(a) Revisit the chosen theory and select a theme.

(b) Consider how to support the legal framework.

(c) Consider how to carry out your instructions.

(d) Consider the intended audience—e.g. who will be reading your work or listening to you—and the best method of conveying information.

(e) Ensure that this process enables you to carry out your client's instructions.

12.4 Stage 1: context

12.4.1 Introduction

When you receive a set of papers, they will contain varied information. The first task is a simple one of comprehension. Specialist terminology might be used in a report (for example, to describe a part of a machine used in factory production) and you may need to consult a glossary or trade manual for a full understanding of the term. This occurs frequently with medical terms used in expert reports, e.g. diagnosis of a condition, and practitioners must understand the meaning of the term and its application in the particular context.

Increasingly, information is presented in numerical form and you will need to be able to analyse bank statements, sets of accounts, and possibly graphs or statistics. It is likely that you will be expected to prove and carry out calculations in relation to any figures you have been given. Indeed, in planning for a negotiation or considering a proposed settlement package you would be expected to make accurate calculations without the need to call for an accountant, except in fairly complex cases. (See **Chapter 14** on dealing with figures.) Understanding a variety of information is only part of the task. It is also important that you develop an ability to present that information to others using various modes, and for a variety of purposes (see **Chapter 16**).

12.4.2 Understanding the stage of the proceedings, your instructions, role, and the objectives

Just as the facts in a case must be viewed in the context of all the surrounding information, they can be, and are, interpreted differently according to the standpoint of the interpreter. Before beginning a factual analysis, it is important to understand the stage that the case has reached, what you have been instructed to do and why, and what your client is hoping to achieve.

Your view of the past and present situation will be influenced by whether you are representing the claimant or defendant, prosecution or defence, employer or employee, a consumer or a manufacturer. As you read the papers, it is important to approach them in an objective frame of mind. In some cases, proceedings may have already begun before you become involved in the case. In other cases, the 'present' situation is one where there is a threat of future harmful events and the 'future' solution will be some type of preventative action. However, in being objective, remember you are not the judge. Some facts of the case will be seen differently by each side, because a fact is seen from a different viewpoint.

12.4.2.1 The stage of the proceedings

Fact management skills cannot be divorced from civil and criminal procedure and require a thorough knowledge of the legal process. Ascertaining what stage of the process a case has reached is a crucial starting point and it is wise to make a written note of when proceedings were issued, served, previous court orders made, etc., prior to embarking on further analysis of the case.

Your approach will differ according to your instructions and the development of the case to date. For example, it is common for barristers to be instructed to write an advice on evidence. This is the particular 'task' which is requested, but it can occur at different stages in the life of a case. In a civil case, advice is often requested when a solicitor is preparing for trial and wishes to know if there are any gaps in the evidence or whether to call for further evidence. It is also common for such an advice before disclosure of documents occurs or after an initial wave of disclosure has been completed, or both. Advice may be requested prior to any proceedings being issued, to ascertain whether there are sufficient grounds to support a claim, and if so, the appropriate parties to be sued. In this case, you will be advising only on the evidence available at that particular time. Advice on evidence may be requested at any time before the trial, and analysis must be carried out in the clear context of the stage the case has reached.

Understanding the procedural and factual history, and current and future procedural options, will assist you to appreciate the task requested, define successfully your objectives for the task, and to resolve the problem.

12.4.2.2 Your instructions, role, and objectives

It is perhaps stating the obvious to point out the necessity of understanding the parameters of your instructions to ensure that the advice sought is in fact given, and the requested performance completed to the letter. However, the fact is that, in the process of digesting a multitude of facts, documents, events, and statements, particularly in a complex case, it is easy to lose sight of the specific task that has been requested.

Is your role to be the sole counsel who will see the case from beginning to end? Or are you one of several counsel who will represent the client on one of a variety of ancillary matters? As a junior barrister, it is common to find that you are briefed to appear on a bail application in a criminal case, or an interim hearing in a lengthy and complex civil case. The task involves one small part in the process, and it may be difficult or even impossible in the time available to understand fully the 'past' of the case. While spending hours reading through files in preparation for a hearing is laudable, two points should be remembered.

Firstly, unless you recognise where in the litigation process you (and the court hearing) are, you will be reading the papers without focus. A legally qualified schedule sponge, soaking up facts without a reference point, achieves nothing. Time would be better spent analysing the arguments that may be made, both for and against, at the hearing.

Secondly, you will often find that these arguments (particularly in protracted cases) will already have been considered as part of the general strategy for the case. The senior barrister with overall responsibility may have specific thoughts about the hearing for which you have been instructed. In these cases, it would be unwise to decide that the brief is yours to handle independently: the hearing may not achieve its real purpose (either long-term or short-term). The danger lies in highlighting the wrong areas, or giving away points unnecessarily because your involvement prevented you from seeing their long-term significance. In short, determine your role properly in the context of the size of the case and the stage it has reached. Consultation with the instructing solicitors and the senior barrister (if there is one) is advised.

In answering 'why are you instructed to do this task?' you will need to identify your objectives, which you should realise by now may differ from those of the client. Superficially, your objective may be to win the case or succeed at a particular hearing. Of the several aims that you might have, the most obvious is not necessarily the only one or even of primary importance. In carrying out your task, be it written work or attending hearings, there may be latent as well as manifest reasons for your working methods. For example, when a barrister in court asks his or her own witness, 'what is your name and address?' the manifest purpose is to put on record who the witness is and his or her residence. The latent purpose is usually to settle the witness in the witness box by asking easy and comfortable questions. There may be other latent purposes, for example, to show the judge or jury that the witness comes from a deprived part of the city (if this is part of your theory or theme of the case).

One further point about objectives borrows a page from advocacy skills. Be sure that, in clarifying your objectives and expectations, you have considered your audience. It is common for barristers to speak in front of magistrates, judges, juries, administrative or employment tribunals. Thought should be given to the expectations and agenda of your specific audience, and what methods of persuasion will produce the most successful results.

12.4.3 Understanding the problem

To understand the context of a case, it is essential to understand fully the history of the parties (civil), or background information about the client (criminal), and how the situation arose. For every client and fact situation, there is a past, present, and future. Once you see how and why the problem arose, it will assist you in identifying how to deal with the present problem, and possible solutions for the future. In the civil context, parties might have enjoyed a good business relationship in the past which one or both parties wish to continue in the future. In a criminal case, the defendant's financial situation leading up to the alleged offence may provide an insight into the circumstances.

12.4.3.1   Looking at the cause of a problem

A crucial part of understanding a problem is appreciating the cause. Why has it occurred? What circumstances led to the problem? If an effective solution is to be found, what circumstances must be avoided to prevent recurrence? For example, your client has asked that a court order be obtained allowing him to have contact with his children on a Sunday, rather than the present arrangement on a Saturday. You will need first to investigate why this issue has arisen between the parties. More specifically you would wish to know:

- whether Saturday contact had been agreed or was the subject of a court order;
- whether the agreement or order had worked well, and the history of any difficulties;
- what the nature of any problems had been;
- whether changing the day is considered by the client and/or child carer to make arrangements easier or more difficult;
- how the children have responded;
- whether the children wish to maintain contact;
- why your client wants to see the children on Sundays, e.g. to go to church, because of a work schedule, etc.;
- whether the children want to change to Sunday—any conflict with their activities or school projects;
- if the proposal has been refused, the possible reasons; and
- whether there are any other difficulties between the parties which may be masked by this dispute.

Once this information has been digested, you will then be in a position to understand the problem fully and consider appropriate ways of solving it which will meet the client's objectives.

The process of 'understanding' a problem is achieved by a combination of using your individual sense of perception and intellect. Just as the results of computer output are only as accurate as the data which has been put in, the range and accuracy of facts fed into the human mind will affect the conclusions made from them. You will find that developing an approach or structure for posing generic questions (who did what to whom, when, where, and with what result?) will focus your mind on collecting the crucial facts and appreciating how and why a problem has arisen, thus paving the way to reaching a solution that is appropriate on the facts and desired by the client.

12.4.3.2   The client's objectives

One may wonder why, in a study of fact analysis, the client's objectives, or even those of the barrister, are a part of the process. Simply put, understanding the client's objectives impacts the way the problem-solving process is managed and influences the way facts can be interpreted. In professional terms, your client's objectives are often a part of the instructions you must follow. As you read the papers, a mental picture emerges of the appropriate ways to resolve the problem. The client's objectives may or may not be reflected in the papers. Alternatively, you may find after a conference that the client holds different or additional objectives that will require a rethink on the best method of resolving or presenting the case.

The barrister's day-to-day contact with the legal system and the constant approach to problems solely from a legal standpoint can easily allow his or her own objectives to influence the understanding of the problem and the client's objectives. For example, you might decide that the best course of action would be to negotiate a settlement or seek arbitration to avoid a court hearing. However, your client may want a public investigation (or a day in court) and/or be opposed to settlement where no commercial benefit can be seen in settling the case, for example where the client is a supplier of faulty goods but has already received full payment. Your task is to identify your client's values and interests, to know the extent to which your own objectives may affect a proposed resolution, and base your factual analysis on the strengths and weaknesses of the case.

It should be remembered that clients may have non-legal as well as legal objectives; these may or may not be articulated. Some stated objectives may eclipse the true interests that the client has but, for whatever reason, have not been verbalised. Rather than taking statements at face value, strive for more thorough questioning which may reveal additional reasons for their objectives and which may improve the strength of their position.

It is not too soon, even at this stage of reading the papers, to bear in mind possible resolutions to the problem. In civil cases, while some disputes will ultimately go to trial for final resolution, this may not be in the client's best interest. Various forms of alternative dispute resolution (ADR), such as arbitration and mediation, are becoming more popular as costs escalate and the delays in bringing an action to trial increase, and are actively encouraged by the Civil Procedure Rules. Arbitration is common in construction cases and is increasingly used in commercial and civil cases. Mediation, the process whereby a mediator attempts to bring the parties together into an agreed resolution, is often preferable to a contested trial in family and child cases and neighbour disputes. The Civil Procedure Rules now effectively require reasonable engagement with alternative dispute resolution at all stages in a civil case. Further, there are other remedies that might be suggested by the facts, including use of internal employee complaint procedures, or filing formal complaints with an agency such as the Commission for Racial Equality, or with the local authority. In criminal cases, the client's circumstances may indicate that the best solution would be long-term medical treatment and you might wish to raise with the solicitor the possibility of investigating this option on behalf of the client.

12.4.4   Collecting the facts

The next stage is to collect all the relevant facts in the case. In practice, this work is divided between the barrister and the solicitor. The degree of factual information included in the instructions to counsel will vary according to the type of case (civil or criminal), the size of the case, the stage in the proceedings, and the task which you are asked to do. In the early stages, you may have only a proof of evidence from the client, and possibly a few witness statements. In civil cases, this may be sufficient to provide an advice on the merits, although it would be insufficient for providing, e.g. an advice on evidence and quantum. Where you are briefed to appear at an interim hearing and have been sent copies of the drafts and relevant witness statements, there may be no need to acquire further information, unless the facts require clarification. In defending a criminal case, the defendant is likely to be best placed to provide more information about witnesses, particularly about potential alibi evidence. Prosecuting counsel often request additional information from, for example, police who were at the scene or otherwise involved in the matter.

In some cases, your written instructions to counsel may be minimal. You may need to ask what has taken place in previous conferences between the client and solicitors. If so, you will want to ensure that you understand exactly what was said or done, as different interpretations can easily arise when discussions are relayed second-hand. If the need for information or clarification can best be met by requesting a conference with the client, this is appropriate, but you will want to bear in mind that conferences increase the costs in a case and should only be requested when the information cannot be obtained by other, less expensive means.

Once you have understood the contents of your brief, and held a conference (if necessary), you can begin to clarify in your own mind precisely what is said to have occurred. It is crucial to develop a critical and questioning approach to all information which you receive. Remember that the information that is missing is as important in the context of the situation as what has been said or written. It is not sufficient merely to identify the gaps in the information or inconsistencies in the facts. You must attempt to fill the gaps by acquiring more information and ask, 'why might these inconsistencies exist?'

It is also important to remember that fact finding is an ongoing process. New facts will become available at different stages in a case, for instance, on disclosure of documents. As new facts emerge you must keep an open mind; your view of the case might need to be reconsidered, and your original conclusions reassessed and possibly modified. You may never possess all the facts in a case. Also, be practical about costs—do not ask for information simply because you do not know something. Weigh up how important to the case it is to have the information, and whether the cost of getting it is likely to be proportionate to the matter in issue.

12.4.4.1   Methods of collecting facts

Rather than start with a group of assorted facts, which at this stage may not bear a great degree of logical order, it is more helpful to approach collection with a structure or framework of main questions to be answered. The facts that are currently available can then be filled in, and the areas where more information is needed, or ambiguities exist, be highlighted. Regardless of what task is requested, e.g. to advise, draft, or appear as an advocate, you will find that most practitioners undertake several routine steps in preparing a case. These preparatory steps are important because they assist in understanding the events and problem generally, and the schedules and charts produced as a result (if the information they contain is agreed) are often given to the court in hearings and at trial to assist the court's understanding of the case. This point is important—you need to understand a case not just for your own purposes, but so you can explain it clearly to a judge or other forum. As there is always that possibility, strive for accuracy, clarity, and neatness as you prepare them. There are several methods which can be used, though the purpose of all of them is the same: to ensure that every aspect of the problem is explored thoroughly and from every angle. As you gain experience you will no doubt devise your personal methods of asking the important questions who, what, where, when, why, and how?

12.4.4.2   Construct a chronology and *dramatis personae*

Listing the people involved and the events in the order in which they occurred clarifies what happened, assists understanding, and can be invaluable as the basis of an opening speech. Increasingly, an agreed chronology is handed up to the judge at the start of both civil and criminal trials, which provides a structure for the presentation of the case. Particularly in an interim application, something as simple as a chronology can help a judge to understand events quickly, so the judge has more time to focus on your arguments.

12.4.4.3   Draw a plan of the *locus in quo*

The *locus in quo* simply means the place where the events occurred. It can be represented by maps, floor plans, or other types of drawing. The first plan which you prepare should be entirely uncontroversial: either delete any points which are in dispute or, if they are included, ensure that they are clearly identified as in dispute. The rationale for this is that, where a plan is produced that makes assumptions about facts which have yet to be proved, the plan tends to become fixed in the mind as the true factual scenario and might prevent you from keeping an open mind to consider other possible explanations. An 'undisputed' plan can also be useful in a client conference, where asking the client to explain his or her version of events will test the credibility of the client's evidence.

You also need to devise ways to represent in the plan the areas about which you do not yet have enough information to present the data accurately. For example, in the plan of a bank robbery, you are told that a witness was on the opposite side of the road, but at this stage of the case you do not know precisely where. Guessing the position and marking it on the plan is inaccurate and could lead to subconsciously assuming its truth without obtaining further factual information. Mark it in a way that shows there is doubt, or delete it until further facts are known. Until the location is certain, it is impossible to assess the witness's line of view, obstructions, etc.

It may also be helpful to draw a series of plans. Following the first which is uncontroversial, additional plans might then show various alternative explanations of what may have occurred. The point is not only whether you want a plan—the point is whether a plan helps to put a case clearly to others.

12.4.4.4   Organise by sorting

This method, based on the six basic questions who, when, where, what, why, and how, will assist you to categorise main areas. In **Table 12.1**, column 1 contains main categories of question; column 2 lists possible answers (or possibilities which might lead to answers). You will note that the suggestions in column 2 are appropriate to different factual situations.

Table 12.1   **Sorting method**

Column 1	Column 2
1. Who did what to whom?	Names, addresses of parties, witnesses.
2. With whom does the problem occur?	Friend, employer, supplier.
3. When does the problem occur?	Date, time, season.
4. Where does it occur?	Work, home, public place.
5. In what situation?	Drunkenness, anger, lack of funds, lack of supplies, etc.
6. Is there a pattern?	When contact is refused, when maintenance is unpaid, when supplies are scarce.
7. What triggers it?	Smell, noise, rain?
8. What results from the problem?	. . .

12.4.4.5   Flowcharts

Some practitioners prefer to use general-style, blank flowcharts which provide an overview of the case as well as prompt heads of information which will be needed. The chart shown in **Figure 12.1** is an overview of a civil case. It could be used in its present form in fairly straightforward cases. More complex cases will require a more extensive system of collection and organisation of the facts.

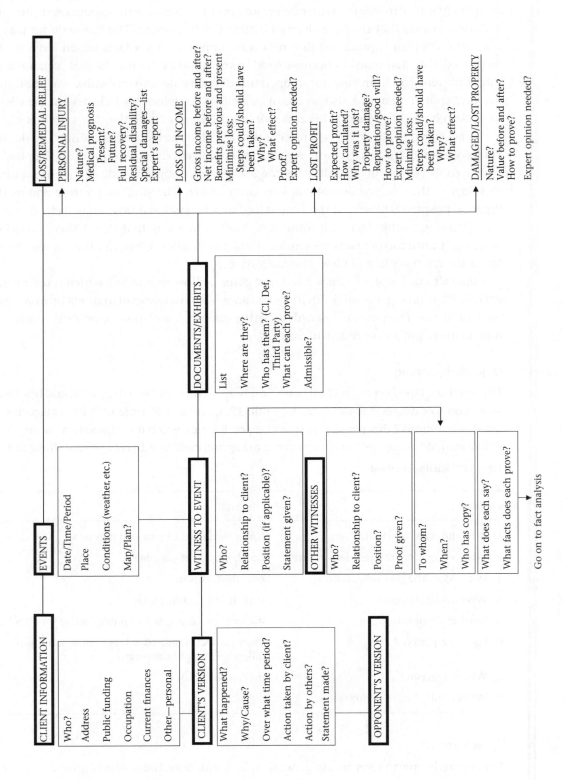

Figure 12.1 Overview of a civil case

12.4.4.6   Checklists

Finally, you may prefer to develop checklists of the information which you will need when you prepare your cases. With experience, you will be able to amend and update your lists to home in on the crucial information, cover new legal developments, and avoid spending time and effort on sorting through information which is not relevant to the issues at hand. Of course, there may be times when papers are received at the last minute and there is not sufficient time to prepare copious checklists. However, if you have developed this structure as part of your working approach, your mind should automatically take you through the generally relevant areas, using the little time which you have to best advantage.

EXAMPLE

An example of the questions that would be included in a checklist in a civil action based on the flowchart illustrated in **Figure 12.1** is as follows:

Personal:

1.   Who is your client?
2.   Where does he or she live?
3.   Occupation?
4.   Other personal details?

Event:

5.   When and where did the event happen?
6.   How does your client say it happened?
7.   What did your client do or say at the time?
8.   Who heard or saw what your client said or did?
9.   Who witnessed it? What do the witnesses say happened?
10.   Can they give evidence?
12.   What points could each prove? Are they consistent with the client's story?

Exhibits:

12.   What exhibits are there?
13.   Where are they? Who has them?
14.   What can each prove?
15.   Who will produce them in court?

Loss or damage:

16.   Type of loss suffered?
17.   If Personal Injury, nature of injury?
18.   Medical prognosis?
19.   Will there be full recovery?
20.   If no, to what extent is disability permanent?
21.   What experts have given or should give evidence?
22.   What other losses are there, e.g. lost income, lost profit, lost or damaged property, pain and suffering, etc.?

If income lost:

23.   What is/was client's gross and net income?
24.   What payments were/are being received from State?
25.   What steps could/should have been done to minimise loss?
26.   Why should they have been taken?

If profit lost:

27.   What profit should have been made?
28.   How calculated?
29.   Why was it lost?
30.   What steps could/should have been taken to minimise loss?
31.   Why should they have been taken?

If property lost or damaged:

32. What was its value before and after the event?
33. What is its value now?
34. Can it be repaired? If so, what is the cost?
35. What could/should have been done to minimise loss?
36. If so, why should they have been taken?

Insurance:

37. Does client have insurance? With whom?
38. Does the policy cover this loss?
39. Has a claim been made? If so, when?
40. Does the other party have insurance?
41. Does that insurance cover this loss if liability can be proved?
42. Has a claim been made?

12.4.5   Identify agreed facts and disputed facts

Once the basic facts have been digested, you will begin to identify the facts which are agreed between the parties and those which are disputed. It is necessary to crystallise these issues and ascertain, for each disputed fact, both your client's version and that of your opponent. This is an important preliminary analysis which should be recorded in a practical form which can be used later in the fact management process. The way in which this information is presented is a matter of style, although its usefulness may be increased if it is neat and can be used, for example, in discussing the case with the solicitor. A suggested format can be found in **Table 12.8** at the end of this chapter.

EXAMPLE

Assume that in a civil case, the defendants are the tenants of the first and second floors of a property. The claimant is the tenant of the ground floor and uses the space to run the Topspin Snooker Hall. A flood occurred from a water pipe outside the building at about the first-floor level, causing damage to the claimant's property. The claimant alleges that the defendants were responsible for the water pipe and their negligence caused the damage. The facts might be recorded as in **Table 12.2**.

Table 12.2   **Record of facts**

A/D	Claimant	Page/ref	Defendant	Page/ref
A	At the time, C was tenant of ground floor, and D were tenants of the 1st and 2nd floors of 83–87 Leeds Road	XX		
A	The pipe located in the 1st floor outside the building burst	XX		
D	Time: it burst between 26 and 31 December 2011	XX	Pipe was repaired within a few hours of bursting on finding it on the 30th	XX
D	D responsible for repairing and maintaining the pipe	XX	Under lease with M. Pike, D *not responsible* for repair or maintenance	XX
D	Pipe was not properly insulated	XX	Properly insulated	XX

There may be many disputed facts in a case and, though it may be a tedious job, it is important that all of them are recorded. From this information, you will be able to determine which of these disputed facts will actually be 'facts in issue' in the case, i.e. facts which are not agreed and which must be proved in law in order to win the case. This will be covered in more detail in Stage 2 of the CAP approach in **12.5**.

12.4.6   Identify the legal framework

Having started with facts, you will need to identify a possible legal framework to which the facts will ultimately be applied. This applies equally whether you are determining the best legal basis for bringing a case, or the best defence. At this stage, the aim is to identify all the legal possibilities which might lead to a resolution of the problem. Later in the analysis process, the framework will be developed and any necessary legal research done.

The process of identifying the legal possibilities may be difficult, particularly where the area of law is an unfamiliar one or several potential legal frameworks are suggested. To start, you will need to list all the possible legally relevant factors which are present. You cannot afford at this point to make snap judgements about the best legal framework or settle for a quickly identified clever answer which might have weaknesses or be less appropriate than another legal basis for bringing or defending the case.

12.4.6.1   List the potential legally relevant factors

Having taken a preliminary view of the facts, it may be tempting to place them into familiar pigeonholes, e.g. contract, misrepresentation, mistake, theft, etc. While this might assist in providing initial focus, it can be restrictive; the best legal solution may not always come from a textbook framework.

First, list all the factors of the case which may possibly have a legal ramification. The index of *Halsbury's Laws of England* or *Halsbury's Statutes* can be a source for ideas. The general categories in **Table 12.3** have legal relevance in most cases.

Table 12.3   **Relevant factors**

Categories	Legally relevant factors
People and parties	e.g. minor, spouse, joint owner, limited company, professional
Places	e.g. occupier's liability, Factories Act, waterways, party resident in France, leased premises
Objects/items	e.g. animals, children's toy, car window, machine part, stereo (consumer)
Documents	e.g. contract, will, bill of lading, deed
Acts	e.g. negligence, intentional, reckless
Omissions	e.g. failure to act or deliver or mitigate
Words	e.g. inducement, fraud, misrepresentation
Dates	e.g. limitation

In making this list, you should include everything that underlies or surrounds the facts, as well as actual words that appear in the papers. For example, in a case that concerns a jam jar, even though there is no Jam Jars Act, you will still need to enter 'jam jar' on the list. There are laws relating to the manufacture of jam jars, filling jars either in a factory or at home (if the contents are for sale to the public), labelling them (including EC regulations), not dealing with jars negligently to cause injury to another, etc. The more comprehensive your list of potential factors, the more pieces are available for choosing a framework.

The completed list of factors can then be organised and grouped together into 'legal frameworks'. The following headings might be used as general categories for grouping factors in a civil case:

- parties;
- cause(s) of action;
- defence(s); and
- remedy sought.

Some factors on the list in **Table 12.3** may apply to more than one heading. For example, under 'Acts' you may have: 'piano owned by client wrongfully taken away from his home'. This factor suggests a possible cause of action (tort of conversion) and also the relief sought (return of piano).

Some potentially relevant factors may not fit easily within one of the headings listed earlier but should not be ignored. Retain them in a general category at the end. They might prove useful, for example by revealing a gap in the case you are preparing.

EXAMPLE

An example of how factors might be grouped in chart form is shown in **Table 12.4**. In this case example, the claimants have suffered loss and damage as a result of their neighbour burning industrial waste from a machine-shop business operated on the property. Column 1 lists the facts which carry a legal implication. Column 2 contains general issue headings. The space in column 3 is for legal frameworks suggested by the facts—in this case, nuisance and a possible breach of statutory obligation. Use the same procedure in criminal cases to explore bases for the offences which might be charged, and potential defences. While many methods can achieve this analysis, the benefit of the tabular form is the visual analysis on a single page.

Table 12.4 Grouping legal factors
Example of grouping legal factors towards developing a full legal framework. In this example, the clients (Mr and Mrs C) are suffering from the burning of industrial waste by a neighbour (D1) who lives on adjoining property and runs a small business. D1 leases the property from a freehold landlord (D2).

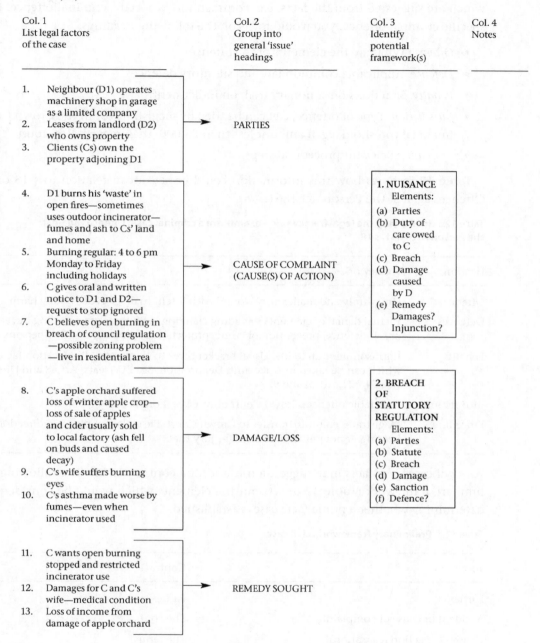

Col. 1
List legal factors
of the case

Col. 2
Group into
general 'issue'
headings

Col. 3
Identify
potential
framework(s)

Col. 4
Notes

1. Neighbour (D1) operates machinery shop in garage as a limited company
2. Leases from landlord (D2) who owns property
3. Clients (Cs) own the property adjoining D1

PARTIES

4. D1 burns his 'waste' in open fires—sometimes uses outdoor incinerator—fumes and ash to Cs' land and home
5. Burning regular: 4 to 6 pm Monday to Friday including holidays
6. C gives oral and written notice to D1 and D2—request to stop ignored
7. C believes open burning in breach of council regulation —possible zoning problem —live in residential area

CAUSE OF COMPLAINT
(CAUSE(S) OF ACTION)

1. NUISANCE
Elements:
(a) Parties
(b) Duty of care owed to C
(c) Breach
(d) Damage caused by D
(e) Remedy Damages? Injunction?

8. C's apple orchard suffered loss of winter apple crop—loss of sale of apples and cider usually sold to local factory (ash fell on buds and caused decay)
9. C's wife suffers burning eyes
10. C's asthma made worse by fumes—even when incinerator used

DAMAGE/LOSS

2. BREACH OF STATUTORY REGULATION
Elements:
(a) Parties
(b) Statute
(c) Breach
(d) Damage
(e) Sanction
(f) Defence?

11. C wants open burning stopped and restricted incinerator use
12. Damages for C and C's wife—medical condition
13. Loss of income from damage of apple orchard

REMEDY SOUGHT

12.4.6.2 Basic legal frameworks

While it would be unwise to conclude at this stage that a particular framework is the only applicable one, it is often a helpful starting point to consider established frameworks which are suggested from the facts, e.g. contract, tort, a specific criminal offence. For a specific criminal offence, you would focus on the following headings:

- *Offence:* What are the elements of the offence?
- *Defence:* Applicable common law and statutory defences.
- *Penalty:* Sanctions on summary trial, on indictment.
- *Jurisdiction:* Type of offence, e.g. can be tried by magistrates or in the Crown Court; financial threshold e.g. if amount less than £5,000, then magistrates' court.
- *Procedure:* Relevant procedural steps.

Table 12.5 shows how this information could be set out in relation to s 18 of the Offences against the Person Act 1861.

Table 12.5 **Identifying the legal framework—example in a criminal case: Offences against the Person Act 1861, s 18**

Heading	Framework
Offence	Unlawfully and maliciously wound with intent to do grievous bodily harm.
Defences	Factual denial of elements including claiming lawfulness of wounding by reason of self-defence, prevention of crime, protection of property or other persons.
Penalty	Imprisonment up to life. Usual bracket three to eight years. Provocation factor which can be taken into account. Deportation. See EU Treaty, Art 48 and Directive 64/221, Arts 3 and 9.
Jurisdiction	Indictable offence. Crown Court only. Class 4 offence.
Procedure	Magistrates commit/transfer to Crown Court. Plea taken at plea and directions hearing. If not guilty, date fixed for jury trial.

For civil cases, the facts may suggest a tort and/or a contract claim. The following preliminary framework (**Table 12.6**) sets out the elements which would be considered in determining whether a prima facie case is established.

Table 12.6 **Preliminary framework: civil case**

Tort	Contract
Parties	Parties
Accident or cause of complaint	The contract
Cause(s) of action (causation)	The terms
Damage or loss	Performance
Remedy sought	Breach
	Damage and causation
	Remedy sought

Even where an established framework fits the facts well, you should in any event investigate other legal bases to ensure that your chosen framework not only applies to the facts but offers the best opportunity to achieve the client's objectives. In civil cases, it may be wise to plead alternative causes of action, join causes of action, or bring in additional parties for the most effective legal solution.

12.4.6.3   Identify areas for legal research

Additional research may be necessary to determine whether the framework is the most appropriate, for example, to determine whether the specific act complained of is covered by statute or constitutes criminal activity. By stepping back and taking a critical view of the framework, it should be possible to see all the strengths and weaknesses within it and to take decisions where there are options.

If additional research is undertaken, notes of it should be recorded for later use, possibly at trial. At a minimum, the following should be recorded:

- *sources:* including the relevant page or paragraph numbers of textbooks, and full citations of case law;
- *short summary of the relevant legal point;* and
- *your view of the answer to the question:* indicating how the point found in research will support a specific fact or issue in the case.

See **Chapters 5** and **7**.

12.4.6.4   How to choose the best legal framework

Surrounded by a myriad of legal possibilities, it is sometimes difficult to know what particular legal framework should be chosen and why. Having an understanding of alternative ways of assessing the case, as well as using your professional judgement in filling gaps, will help you to make the best decision.

12.4.6.5   Which framework makes the best use of the legal and factual strengths? The 'best-fit' approach

If the framework does not provide a single obvious answer, it should nevertheless take you some distance down the road. At a minimum, it should define where there are legal and factual certainties and, if options exist, what the options appear to be. One way to proceed is simply to make an objective valuation of all the legal requirements and relevant facts. The solution that 'best fits' the framework—the one which makes the best use of the legal and factual strengths of the case while placing least reliance on its weaknesses—would be the preferred one. This approach is not suggesting that superficial analysis will do so long as it gives a roughly right answer, but that, on critical analysis of the law and facts, a particular framework would make the best use of the elements in the case.

Even in the 'best-fit' method, the elements which do not sit well with the rest of the framework should not be ignored. They may have some use in reviewing the case at a later stage, or in looking for options for a settlement.

12.5   Stage 2: analysis of issues and evidence

12.5.1   Introduction

Thus far, the potential legally relevant factors have been identified and loosely grouped to suggest a possible legal framework or 'legal basis' to the problem. More than one framework might be suggested. The best legal argument has no point in a court if it is not soundly based on the facts. Equally, the facts of the case need the best legal argument to achieve the best result. Although an analysis of a case should start with consideration of the facts, as the case progresses the roles of law and fact are equally important and the two are closely interrelated. More than that, they are interactive; one moves with the other as more legal or factual input is provided for a case.

12.5.2   Analyse the issues: identify the 'factual issues' and analyse the legal issues by applying the facts to the legal framework

By this stage, you will have identified a possible legal framework and noted what facts are agreed and disputed. From the elements or legal requirements of this framework, you must then determine the 'factual issues' (also called 'facts in issue') of the case. The factual issues will be those disputed facts which, according to the legal framework chosen, must be proved in law for the case to be successful. Where statements of case have already been served, these will specify what issues have to be proved. For example, in a contract case where the claimant (landlord) is suing the defendant (tenant) for failure under the lease to maintain a gas boiler which exploded causing damage to the claimant's property, the analysis might look like **Table 12.7**.

Table 12.7   **Analysis of the issues**

Framework	Facts of case	Disputed/agreed
Parties	Landlord: Mr X; Tenant: Ms Y	Agreed
Contract	By lease dated . . .	Agreed
Terms	Tenant had obligation to maintain	Agreed
Performance	Tenant in occupation, rent paid	Agreed
Breach	On XYZ date, boiler not in order	Denied
Causation	Caused explosion	Agree: explosion
		Deny: causation
Loss	Damaged property	Loss not mitigated

From this analysis, you will see that the legal and factual issues will be breach, causation, and loss. (The loss is a factual issue as the defendant's case is that the claimant's loss is due to his failure to mitigate.) Each of these factual issues must be formally proved by evidence. Thus, each issue must be fully analysed to determine which facts can be proved and by what means. This information should be recorded for clarity and used later in the case.

The aim is to identify, for each factual issue, the name of the witness who can prove the fact; whether oral or documentary evidence is available; on which party the burden of proof lies; and, in a civil case, whether it is specifically raised in the court documents. There are various methods of recording this information and, provided the relevant analysis is done, the choice is left to the practitioner. One chart which can be used for this purpose appears in **Table 12.9** at the end of this chapter.

In finding the factual support for a framework, remember that every disputed fact will need to be proved. As the evidence is gathered, you will need to update the chart or list of all facts for which evidence is still required. Some of the possible frameworks identified early on may prove unworkable. While you can normally expect to have enough factual information for a preliminary determination, it is rare to have all the relevant facts before starting work on a case. As more information comes to light, your view on the most appropriate framework may change.

One final word on the interrelation of law and fact: it is vital to select relevant law with a sound knowledge of the facts and then also to consider the facts in the light of the law to ensure coherence. Although law and fact become interrelated, never be deceived into thinking the law has become more important—the evidence, or the proven facts, will always be just as important as the law.

12.5.3   Identify a potential 'theory' of the case

The theory of the case is a convincing and logical account of why and how the events in the case are likely to have happened. It is based on:

- the principles of law that are likely to be used at trial, i.e. the legal solution or framework;

- what has to be proved and/or disproved at trial for the case to succeed; and

- consideration of which facts are capable of being proved and the inferences which can be made from them.

Formulating a theory, though based on the available facts and evidence, sometimes requires a degree of guesswork to fill in the gaps. In a sense, it puts cement between the bricks of the framework to fill in any factual or legal gaps in order to make a cohesive and persuasive story. It is your theory of the case, which you hope to convince the fact-finder is the true version of events.

The dangers of developing an imaginative theory that is not well founded on the facts cannot be overestimated. The more gaps that are filled by guesswork, rather than proven facts, the weaker the case. It follows that the more that the theory is grounded on persuasive evidence rather than supposition, the higher the likelihood that it will be accepted. Remember that you will ultimately need to prove all the main elements of your case or you will lose. A theory can only help you to identify further evidence you need, and, as part of a persuasive argument, to fill gaps in the evidence you have.

In the context of fact management, developing a theory is an important stage in considering the legal and factual basis for the client's version of events and the chance of successfully obtaining a good resolution. Putting forward a theory is also a basis for persuasive advocacy, used in arguing interim applications and submissions at trial. This is covered more fully in the *Advocacy* manual.

The 'theory' should be an objective analysis of the events, rather than merely the best theory for the client. The opponent will also put forward a theory, and seek to disprove your account, thus it is wise to consider how the other parties may view your theory. Critically analyse the legal and factual weaknesses of the potential theory. Ensure that it is coherent and as capable of proof as possible.

In considering the theory, bear in mind:

(a) The need for the *best* explanation for the client's position from all the possible alternatives. Although alternative theories are possible, it should be remembered that a single explanation is inherently more compelling.

(b) Early in a case, it is desirable to develop provisional theories. The 'theory' may need to be altered as more evidence comes to light with regard to the opponent's defence, disclosure, information received in a criminal case, etc.

(c) Although the theory must be logical, the ultimate form that it takes may be influenced by the 'theme' of the case, which goes beyond logic and may show that your client should be successful on, for example, moral grounds. A theme should be a memorable phrase such as 'victim of fear' or 'scapegoat' which helps the finder of fact to recognise your theory of the case.

12.5.3.1   Ways to develop the 'theory'

If you are fortunate enough to have a substantial amount of factual information, and sources of proof, it may be possible to identify the best legal framework and develop a theory fairly easily. However, where the factual information is scarce, you will have to construct either partially or wholly a theory of the case, alongside the consideration of the best legal framework. Thus, the phrase 'developing a theory' is sometimes referred to as using theory to identify the most appropriate legal framework, or, as is used here, to fit together how and why the events or problem occurred.

Identifying alternative theories can be difficult, particularly where the area of law is unfamiliar to you. The more experienced you are with an area of law, the easier it becomes to appreciate the range of different theories which may apply. If you are in uncharted waters, there are guidelines to assist you in developing a perspective on the situation.

Firstly, the problem at hand may be analogous to another situation with which you are familiar. In civil cases, consider the basic rights and obligations of the parties; the same legal principles may apply. In criminal cases, consider how analogous conduct is treated by the law and whether defences in those situations may be applicable to the case at hand. Secondly, consider whether the conduct or acts are of a nature that may be covered by statute. Research in one of the legislation sources may suggest other legal solutions and alternative theories for the case. Finally, bear in mind that there is no need to re-invent the wheel. You may find that merely asking whether someone in your chambers or firm has experience in the area enables them to point you in the right direction. It will very likely save time, may prevent you from going down the wrong path, and may also give you a different perspective on the case.

12.5.3.2   Logical and lateral thinking

Many of you have played the game where one word is given and the object is to think of all the different words that can be formed from this one word. There are many variations but the challenge remains the same: to brainstorm, or to use another phrase, to use logical thinking to come up with all plausible answers. In this context, you are presented with a proposition that X happened or did not happen. The challenge is to think logically about all the evidence that exists to support that conclusion, even if purely circumstantial. Your analysis must be based on proved—or provable—facts as far as possible. Beware of emotion, intention, and knowledge elements which are particularly difficult to prove. Remember, too, the weakness of logical thinking: the danger of assuming that, because a theory is logical, it is actually true.

Lateral thinking asks, not how events are most likely to have happened, but what are all the possible ways in which they *could* have happened, logical or otherwise. It looks for explanation from different, and often unexpected, angles to a problem. An example of reaching a solution by lateral thinking follows:

EXAMPLE

Problem

John states that, when he came home, he went into the living room of his house and saw immediately that Victoria was lying naked on the floor, and that she was dead. There was broken glass on the floor and a small pool of water. The window was open, but John could not remember if he had forgotten to close it before he went out.

Logical assumptions and focus for questioning

It is natural to assume and concentrate on the following:

- Victoria has been murdered or has died from natural causes such as a heart attack.
- Why was Victoria naked?
- Broken glass—if the window had been closed, an intruder could have broken a window or door for entry.

Logical thinkers would pursue more about Victoria, e.g. how she died and why, and about John, e.g. how long he had been gone, whether Victoria was very familiar to him, etc. Stimulate lateral thinking by putting the problem in the centre of a diagram as in **Figure 12.2**. Follow the 'dos and don'ts' around the path and think of new lines of questioning.

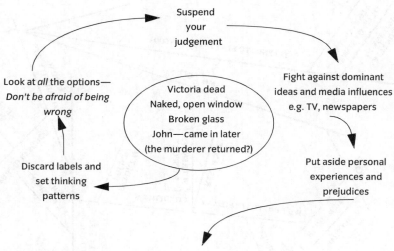

Figure 12.2   Lateral thinking

New lines should include where Victoria lived; whether she was usually clothed and in what type of clothes; who lived with John, including any animals; what objects in the room were made of glass, e.g. vases, ornaments, drinking glasses.

The answer

Victoria is in fact a fish and has died naturally after John's cat knocked the bowl over and ran out through the window!

This, of course, is an extreme example, but does illustrate the trap of simple faith based on assumptions that something is true because it outwardly appears so.

Information rarely arrives in a sequential manner. A piece of information coming in early does not signify that it is particularly important, nor should it prejudice the importance of the other facts arriving later or from unexpected sources.

12.5.3.3   Mind-mapping

Another technique for developing a theory of a case is mind-mapping. When you receive information, your mind processes it in key concepts, interlinking thoughts with other ideas. Each word is received in the context of the words surrounding it, integrating the ideas and concepts to communicate certain meanings. Mind-mapping is a physical picture of the process that is occurring in the mind. Although it can take some time to become proficient at drawing them, the rewards are many as they visually present the structure of the case and indicate where the weaknesses lie.

To start a mind-map, place the main theme or event in the centre. The branches coming out from the centre outline the main characters and events, with descriptive detail forming smaller branches. The more important elements are placed near the centre; the less important ones nearer the edge. There is an example in **Figure 12.3**, which suggests how you might use this technique in preparing a bail application for a client, showing how to link the sort of facts that might arise in a logical way.

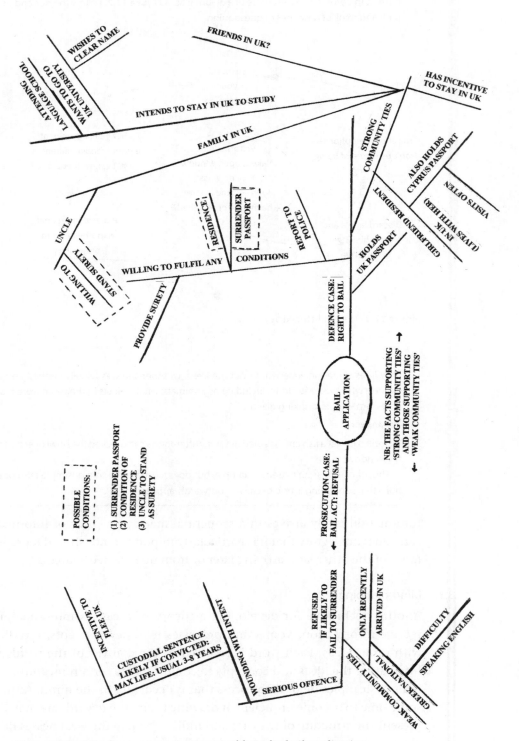

Figure 12.3 Mind-map or concept map of facts for bail application

12.5.4   Identify the gaps or ambiguities in the facts

The advantage of adopting a methodical approach to analysis and recording is that it tends to highlight any gaps or ambiguities in the fact scenario. Sometimes these are fairly obvious, as where some invoices in a regular pattern of trading are missing which are relevant to the disputed fact. More commonly, these are spotted by putting yourself at the scene—try to picture the story and ask yourself what pieces are missing or unclear. For example, in a fact scenario about a bank robbery, there may be a witness to the robbery. Before the picture can be completed you will need to know where the witness was standing, the direction he or she was facing, any obstructions to a clear view such as cars, signs, weather conditions, personal visual disabilities, etc.

In some cases, the client is able to supply missing information and the most cost-effective way of obtaining this may be by requesting a conference. In civil cases, it may be necessary to serve a request for further information on your opponent. Information may be needed from a third party and you will need to ask your instructing solicitor to take a proof of evidence if the identity of the witness is known, or seek further witnesses who can provide evidence on a particular issue.

12.5.5   Analyse the evidence: the importance of analysing the strengths and weaknesses

The question which most clients ask their barristers is 'Will I win my case?' The answer will depend on the strength of the evidence, i.e. on what facts can be proved. Before you are in a position to answer the client's questions, you will need to assess:

- what facts must and can be proved by whom;
- from the facts which can be proved (the evidence), the admissible evidence in support of each proposition which must be proved;
- the degree of conflicting or contradictory evidence; and
- whether the evidence is sufficient to satisfy the standard of proof required.

In a civil case, it will be clear from the claim and defence which facts are in issue and therefore must be proved. By identifying which side carries the burden of proof on each issue and assessing the witness statements and documentary evidence which support your case, as well as the contradictory evidence, you will then be in a position to comment on the likelihood of successfully establishing your client's case. While this information can be collated in a number of ways, you may wish to try using the chart in **Table 12.10**. This gives an overview to ascertain easily all the elements of a case. The importance of this assessment process, often called 'assessing the strengths and weaknesses' of the case, cannot be overestimated. It is not only the key result of the fact analysis process but is also essential before you can competently:

- give sound advice on the likelihood of success at trial;
- negotiate effectively on your client's behalf;
- advise on whether to make or accept a Part 36 offer;
- advise on whether further evidence is necessary, and if so, the nature of that evidence; and
- plan the presentation of the case at the trial.

In a criminal case, the prosecution must prove the commission of the offence beyond reasonable doubt. Whether you are briefed for the prosecution or the defence, an analysis will still be required to assess whether the facts, or inferences drawn therefrom, can be established to the required standard of proof for each and every element of the offence. As in civil cases, this evidence must be balanced against the opposing evidence which may weaken the prosecution case.

12.5.6 From facts to evidence: establishing 'proof'

By this stage, you should have identified, from the information which you have, the facts which are agreed and disputed, their source, i.e. who or what will (may) be able to prove the proposition, and, where available from the claim or defence and disclosure, the facts which your opponent will be putting forward. Facts become evidence when they are proved. There are various methods of 'proving' a fact: by direct evidence, inferences, and generalisations. Regardless of which form the evidence takes, each required element of the case must be proved.

It is at this point that careful thought will have to be given as to whether, by reason of the rules of evidence, any facts will be (or are likely to be) excluded at trial.

12.5.7 Direct facts versus inferences

Direct evidence is evidence which proves the truth or falsity of a fact, and does not need an inference for proof. Evidence by inference, sometimes called circumstantial evidence, allows proof by virtue of the inference of another fact. The inferred fact may be a required element in the case or, as is more common, may prove a secondary fact, which can in turn allow proof of the required element to be inferred. The chain of facts which can be inferred before finally proving the required element is not limited, that is to say, a court is unlikely to reject evidence simply because several inferred facts were needed to prove an element. However, where the inferred facts are so remote from proving the element that an extensive chain is needed, there is more risk that little probative weight will be given to the evidence.

The importance of the distinction between direct evidence and evidence proved by inference is significant, but not because one is necessarily more persuasive than the other. A group of inferences—or for television viewers of courtroom drama, the circumstantial evidence—may carry more probative weight than a single fact of direct evidence. The distinction is necessary to recognise where proof can only be through one or more inferences.

It is not uncommon to find in some cases that the legal elements of the action or offence have been proved primarily, if not wholly, by inference (or circumstantial) evidence. In these cases, the strength of the inferences and credibility of witnesses become crucial as each offers a piece of the overall picture. Witnesses on both sides will have conflicting evidence of what was seen or what happened. Therefore, how credible, accurate, and persuasive a witness is perceived to be will directly influence the weight which the inferred evidence will have.

12.5.8 Using generalisations to link inferred facts to required elements

Inferences are based on premises assumed to be true. The truth is assumed possibly because it is based on widely accepted knowledge or science. But where this support is lacking it is also possible to rely on a generalisation. Generalisations are based on general life experiences which permit a conclusion that something is more likely to be true. As explained by D. A. Binder and P. Bergman, *Fact Investigation: From Hypothesis to Proof*

(West Publishing Co., 1984, at p. 85), the generalisation becomes the premise which enables one to link the specific evidence (inference) to the final elements which are required to be proved:

A generalisation is, then, a premise which rests on the general behaviour of people or objects. How does one formulate generalisations? Usually, one adopts conventional wisdom about how people and objects function in everyday life. All of us, through our own personal experiences . . . through knowledge gained from books, movies, newspapers, and television, have accumulated vast storehouses of commonly held notions about how people and objects generally behave in our society.

EXAMPLE

To illustrate a case example of how inferences and generalisations operate, take the criminal case of Cassie Charnel who has been charged under the Theft Act 1968, s 1, with stealing a bottle of whisky from Super Stores plc. To establish the case, the prosecution must prove several elements which make up this specific offence. These are:

- Cassie took a bottle of whisky;
- the whisky belonged to Super Stores plc;
- she did so dishonestly; and
- at the time, she intended to deprive Super Stores plc permanently of the whisky.

Suppose the Super Stores plc detective has made a statement to the police and that part of it reads as follows:

'I saw the defendant take a bottle of whisky from the spirits display. She did not put it in the store's wire basket which she was carrying but instead she put it in an inside pocket in the coat which she was wearing. She went to a checkout and paid for the goods in the basket but made no attempt to pay for the bottle of whisky. She then left the store. I followed her and stopped her in the street outside.'

Concentrating on proving the elements of the offence, the crucial facts contained in the detective's statement are that she took the whisky from the display at Super Stores plc, put it in her coat instead of her basket, failed to pay for the whisky at the checkout, and left the store with the whisky. However, there is no direct evidence of this. Rather, they are inferences from the detective's statement to this effect.

The move from the detective's statement to the inference that what he stated was in fact true involves several generalisations:

- in the absence of a motive to lie or opportunity for erroneous observation, a person's account of what he or she has seen is likely to be true;
- the detective had no known motive to lie; and
- he had no known opportunity for erroneous observation.

In analysing the evidential support for your case, you will need to consider each fact, whether its proof is by direct evidence or inferences, and what evidence or inference exists to challenge or weaken the proposition. This should highlight where the proof is weak and requires further evidence to strengthen the proposition. It is important in carrying out the analysis that facts do not take on a theoretical superiority, if in reality they cannot be proved to exist, or for evidential purposes they would clearly be inadmissible. Tabulation can be helpful in the analysis and is illustrated in **Table 12.11**.

12.5.9   Wigmore analysis charts

Another method of analysing evidence is by drawing a chart based on a scheme originally proposed by Wigmore (see J. H. Wigmore, 'The Problem of Proof', *University of Illinois Law Review*, 1913, vol. 8, p. 77). The aim of this method is to identify the chain of proof, including inferences which strengthen or weaken the main proposition to be proved. While it can be a time-intensive exercise, many people find it beneficial to produce a visual analysis in this way.

12.6   Stage 3: the presentation of the case or argument

12.6.1   Introduction

The last stage in the CAP approach is to prepare the presentation of the case in light of the task which you have been instructed to do. Presentation is a generic term which in practice means:

- making a final decision on the theory and theme of the case;
- determining how you will support the legal framework;
- considering your task and its intended audience; and
- preparing the results of your analysis for that task.

12.6.2   Revisiting theories: selecting a theme

After the fact analysis process is completed, you will need to consider the theory chosen earlier and be prepared to amend it as required up until the end of the trial. Having chosen the theory, you will need to select a theme (or themes) to fit the theory of the case. The theme may be defined as the part of the 'story' presented in court which is used because of its persuasive effect.

In an essay entitled 'Lawyers' Stories' (originally presented at the Seminar on Narrative in Culture, University of Warwick, in 1987) in *Rethinking Evidence, Exploratory Essays*, 2nd edn (Cambridge University Press, 2006), Professor William Twining defines theme in the following way:

Sometimes it is used to refer to the overall characterization of the situation or story or some element of it that appeals to a popular stereotype. For example: 'This is an example of a grasping landlord exploiting a helpless tenant'; or 'this is a case of property developers needlessly desecrating the countryside'. Another, more precise usage . . . refers to any element that is sufficiently important to deserve emphasis by repetition. An English barrister (Patrick Bennett QC) gives a vivid account of what he calls 'the mantra', as follows: 'In almost all cases there will be a key factor which has played a dominant role in the case from your point of view. It may be stupidity, fear, greed, jealousy, selfishness. Pick your word, inject it into your opening. Put it on a separate piece of paper. Repetition will have a lasting effect. If you have hit the right note and have repeated it often enough, it will echo in the jury's mind when they retire. It will be the voice of the 13th juror. Try to hit the note as soon as possible in opening.'

The theme will be used in opening and closing speeches, and will underpin the questions put to the witnesses. The 'story' should include the items of evidence which support it and exclude any matters that undermine its persuasiveness. Good themes are often very simple. They extend logic and have been defined as the soul or moral justifications of the case, put forward in such a way as to maximise the appeal to the judge or jury.

The theory and the theme must be consistent with each other. The experienced advocate can make the two so consistent that they are virtually indistinguishable. This is done because the better the theme fits with the theory, the greater the moral force of the theory and likelihood of persuading the tribunal of fact to find in your favour. Take, for example, a contested careless driving case in the magistrates' court: a pedestrian steps out onto a zebra crossing, causing the motorist to brake hard and skid. The only substantial dispute on the facts is whether the pedestrian looked to the right before stepping onto the crossing. The defence theme may well be that there is a limit to the care and foresight to be expected of the ordinary competent motorist, especially when faced with a jaywalker. If at the trial it emerged that the pedestrian was late for an appointment, another defence theme might be 'more haste, less speed', and so on.

12.6.3 Supporting your legal framework and reasoning

Whether the law on which your case is based derives from established legal principles or is unsettled, e.g. because previous precedents conflict, a firm basis of legal sources will be required, including any legal research that is necessary to support the chosen legal solution. You may have referred to key statutes or cases in your advice or opinion. You will generally be required to submit a written 'skeleton argument' prior to the hearing. These outlines of the case and the arguments will require legal support for your key propositions. You will be expected to provide your opponents and the court with a list of authorities (e.g. statutes, cases, reports) on which you will rely. Legal research is covered elsewhere in this manual, but a few considerations are included here for thought.

Statute law

If a statutory section is relevant to the legal argument, consider its real role in the case:
- Does the entire section apply to the case, or merely a part?
- Is its effect clear or is its interpretation open to challenge? If so, how could it be challenged?
- What are the relevant principles of statutory interpretation?
- Are there cases interpreting the words of the statute?

Case law

If a case supports your argument, you will want to defend its precedent value; if it does not, you will want to find points on which to challenge or distinguish it, e.g. on the facts, or the application of the principle involved. A case is rarely directly on point and you should consider its real value in constructing the legal arguments supporting the framework. For example:

- On what facts was the decision made?
- What precisely was the *ratio* as opposed to *obiter dicta*?
- Did all the judges agree? (Which judge gave the principal judgment; what is his or her standing?)
- What was the level of the court making the decision?
- When was the case decided?
- And, finally, of most importance—has the case been subsequently reviewed or overturned?

There is rarely a single case on a particular point. It is more common to find a variety or line of cases. The whole line of cases should be reviewed, not simply to make coherence of the decisions, but also to consider what pattern of thinking can be seen through them and how this will fit your purpose.

If appropriate, note the procedural basis on which the decision was made. In some cases, it is not open to the judges to review the facts and their decision is limited to whether the lower decision was properly reached.

Textbooks

While some of the leading textbooks can be quoted in court, and, indeed, judges have been known to adopt passages within their judgments, the support for the legal framework in a case should be based on original sources, rather than textbook comment.

12.6.4 Decide how to deal with gaps in facts

You will rarely have all the facts you need—it is not cost-effective for a solicitor to gather fully comprehensive information before approaching a barrister. It is for the barrister to take a provisional view on the basis of what is available and to give clear guidance to the solicitor on what further information should be collected. This is dealt with in the Opinion Writing part of this manual, and in the *Evidence* manual as regards collection of evidence. In terms of overall fact management there are some general principles:

- Only ask for further factual information that is important with regard to the cause of action and the remedies your analysis has identified—do not build costs unnecessarily or disproportionately to what is in dispute. Note that proportionality is a test for being able to recover costs if you win, and that the client will have to pay for the evidence with no recovery if the case is lost. For a case started after April 2013 you may need to work within an agreed or approved budget.

- Be specific about the facts you still need to know—give the solicitor specific questions.

- Be realistic about what factual information is available and what is not—try to suggest where solicitors should seek the information you request.

- Be realistic about what information will be provided—a person who is employed by a potential defendant may well not be prepared to provide information critical of their employer.

12.6.5 Consider your task and the intended audience

Whether there are any preliminary matters which must be dealt with before you are able to carry out your instructions will depend on the nature of the task requested, the present stage in the proceedings, and the result of your analysis of the case.

In a sense, this is a chicken-and-egg situation, for it is only after you have completed an analysis of the case that it can be determined whether, on the basis of the papers, witness statements, etc. that have been sent by the solicitor, the instructions can be carried out. In some cases, no further information will be needed, save for clarification of confusing points arising in the papers. An example is where you are asked for advice on the merits based on existing facts (which can be proved).

Sometimes, it may be difficult to know what further information to request from the solicitor. You should consider the stage of proceedings as this will influence the degree of detail and range of relevant documents which may be required. Where you are briefed to appear at an interim hearing, you will, of course, require support for the arguments to be used at the hearing, and the relevant court documents. However, it would be unreasonable to ask the solicitor to produce documents which are not relevant to the present hearing. An exception might be where the document or evidence to prove a proposition would eventually be needed in any event and preparation for trial is inevitable. Then, it may be prudent to discuss the matter with the solicitor. The point is that requests for further information should only be made where necessary to enable you to carry out your instructions.

Where you have been asked to provide an advice on evidence, it may also be difficult in some cases to know precisely what to advise, particularly if the area of law is an unfamiliar one. By this time, however, the legal framework and factual issues will have been identified and usually a 'theory' of the case developed. These will provide you with a focus to concentrate on what evidence will be needed to bring out the strengths of the case or highlight the weaknesses in the opponent's case. You will also want to consider the nature of the evidence, whether it is consistent in itself and with your client's story, and where more detailed facts may be needed to fill gaps. For example, the history of parties and disputes are often found in more than one medium, e.g. letters, memos, reports, and faxed communications. Many disputes develop over months or years and the client's position will be strengthened if there is supporting evidence over the entire relevant period rather than patchy samples. Even at the stage of preparing for trial, it may be necessary to embark on further disclosure, where, for example, it comes to light that important evidence is in the custody of a third party and previously unseen.

Finally, it may be necessary for counsel to have a site view or product sample in order to appreciate fully the circumstances or how an injury was alleged to have occurred. This is often the case in complex or technical matters, such as engineering, manufacturing, or property damage cases. Additional briefing may also be needed in cases involving complicated experts' reports and counsel must prepare the examination of expert witnesses for the hearing.

The manner of 'presenting' your analysis and the case also depends on the intended audience. When you are asked to write an advice or opinion, the audience will likely be limited to your client, the solicitors, and possibly other counsel who might become involved in the case. The knowledge that your written work will not be seen by your opponent (in most cases) allows more flexibility in how you present it. On appearances in court, however, your 'audience' will be the judge whom you are trying to persuade and, unless it is an application without notice, the opponents and their counsel.

Careful thought must be given, not only to the content of presentation, but the best methods of relaying facts and evidence in light of the audience. In studies of how people receive information, it has been shown that the majority of human beings are 'visual', meaning that material shown to them using a visual medium, as opposed to, e.g. an aural medium, has the highest degree of impact and influence. A smaller number of people react more favourably to 'hearing' the information. Therefore, consider whether it might be appropriate to use charts, graphs, or other visual aids in presenting the case.

12.6.6   Preparing the results of your analysis

Your final task will to be make sure that you have everything you need to help you carry out your instructions in a form which will support your presentation. It may be useful to present some of the work you have done in preparation to your opponent or to the court itself. Agreed chronologies, summaries of facts, schedules, or plans of the *locus in quo* are frequently handed up before a case begins, can be very compelling, and certainly make you appear well prepared and efficient. It is now usual for civil courts to require that lists of issues, skeleton arguments, and lists of the authorities which will be relied on should be submitted before a case begins. The Civil Procedure Rules governing civil cases provide for skeleton arguments to be used in most cases.

If you are instructed to hold a conference or to negotiate it will help you to have some notes with you so that nothing relevant is forgotten. If you are appearing at court, notes about the points you wish to make on each issue will be helpful. Chapter 5 of the **Advocacy** manual contains suggestions of the kind of notes you might find useful to prepare for your own use.

Everyone adopts a method of organising information to suit his or her own needs. Many barristers use blue notebooks for all their work done on preparing a case, from notes of conferences with clients, to preparations for trial. One particular form of organising information for trial, described as a 'trial book', is explained in detail in T. Anderson, D. Schum, and W. Twining's *Analysis of Evidence*, 2nd edn (Cambridge University Press, 2005), Chapter 5.

12.7   The client's choice: acting on instructions

At the beginning of the CAP approach, you became familiar with the client's objectives and what they hoped to achieve. These should not be forgotten as you proceed with your fact analysis and assess the strength of the case. You may be asked for an advice on the merits, or another task which will result in the client needing to take an immediate decision. Your task may alternatively be part of the overall case management. Apart from your client's overall objectives, other criteria such as costs, time efficiency, the desire to avoid stress or risk, the impact on family or business, and the desire to be exonerated may be factors which determine what decision is made. You will need to bear this in mind and ensure that you present the possible solutions to your client in such a way that all the consequences of a particular course of action are highlighted, thus aiding your client to make an informed decision about the next steps. Remember that the case is ultimately the client's and not yours—if there are options it may be appropriate to put those to the client rather than give your own answer.

12.8   Suggested charts

We have seen that the CAP approach identifies the stages necessary for efficient case preparation and that there are varying techniques which can be used to achieve those tasks. The following four charts (**Tables 12.8, 12.9, 12.10,** and **12.11**) can also be used to aid understanding and analysis. The titles refer to the stages in the CAP process.

Table 12.8 **Stage 1: Context of the case: identifying agreed and disputed facts**

(Note: This form may be used for either civil or criminal cases. 'Ref/page' refers to the source of the statement, e.g. witness statement of J. Bloggs, page 6, para 2.)

	A = AGREED			
	D = DISPUTED			
[A]	CLAIMANT'S VERSION	REF/	DEFENDANT'S VERSION	REF/	QUERIES/
	OR	PAGE		PAGE	NOTES
[D]	PROSECUTION VERSION				

Table 12.9 **Stage 2: Analysis of issues and evidence: identifying issues and relating evidence to issues**

(Note: This form can be used in criminal cases by changing the reference to the claim and defence.)

Ref	Issue	Para of particulars of claim	Para of defence	Para of reply	Burden of proof	Name of witness	Available oral evidence	Available documentary evidence	Notes/comments, e.g. procedure, evidence, gaps

Table 12.10 **Stage 2: Analysis of issues and evidence: analysing the strengths and weaknesses**

(Note: This form can also be used as the basis for examining and cross-examining witnesses.)

Issue	(a) Evidence in support of C's version	Witness	Page	(b) Evidence which contradicts/ undermines C's version	Witness	Page	(c) Evidence which contradicts/ undermines (b)	Witness	Page

Table 12.11 **Stage 2: Analysis of issues and evidence: analysing the evidence proving the case**

ISSUE/ELEMENT:

FACTS IN SUPPORT	WITNESS	INFERENCE IN SUPPORT	CHALLENGE/ WEAKNESS	NOTES

Presentation for the practitioner: the CAP approach in action

13.1 Applying the CAP approach

Once the various stages of the CAP approach have been identified and understood, they should be applied routinely to the preparation of every case until you have developed your own effective methods of preparation. Obviously, the context of every set of instructions will highlight particular aspects and not every stage may be required to be considered for every piece of work. A barrister's task always starts with 'Instructions to Counsel'.

13.2 Instructions to counsel

Each set of instructions would include a back sheet which contains the number allocated to the case, the parties' names, the solicitor's details, and the date. You will see examples of these in the sets of papers you use on the BPTC or on any brief received by a barrister in practice. After the instructions have been carried out, the back sheet should be returned endorsed to the instructing solicitors, together with the completed work (if any). Counsel may be instructed on more than one occasion in respect of different stages of a particular case. Each subsequent set of papers in the same case, in addition to any new documents, would also contain all the papers previously before counsel, together with a copy of any opinion or case statement previously settled by counsel. The contents of any set of instructions are set out in the instructions to counsel prepared by the instructing solicitors. These should always be checked to ensure that nothing has been inadvertently omitted. These instructions will indicate which of a variety of tasks counsel is being instructed to undertake. It may involve advice to a client, either in the context of meeting the client in conference or the writing of an opinion. It may involve the drafting of documents, for example, in civil matters, the particulars of claim, a defence, or a witness statement. Drafting in the criminal field may in-volve drafting an indictment for prosecuting authorities or drafting grounds of appeal (including the associated explanation of the grounds). It may involve representation of the client, either by advocacy in the courts or tribunals, or assistance and representation in mediation or other ADR activities; or by direct negotiation—seeking to come to a settlement. Instructions to counsel should always be checked to ensure that nothing has been inadvertently omitted.

The majority of barristers keep the notes they prepare in blue books so that a complete record of a case from beginning to end is maintained. It is often the case that no further active steps need to be taken on a case. A civil case may settle. A criminal prosecution may be withdrawn. However, a case on which counsel has done work may require further action at a later stage. If counsel is subsequently instructed, the previous notes can be referred to and built upon, thus saving valuable preparation time.

13.3   Practising the skill

All skills require practice. On the BPTC you will encounter a series of briefs which are designed to help you to develop the skills you will use in practice and to learn the adjectival law (the law of procedure and evidence) which you will use in preparing your work and conducting your advice and representation. Each exercise provides you with an opportunity which you can use to practise your own skills in applying the CAP approach until they become second nature and you find that you automatically consider each stage as you get to grips with each new set of papers. Once this level of expertise has been reached, you will no longer need to articulate the stage-by-stage process, but can concentrate on whether you have acquired the ability to carry out your preparation effectively. This can best be achieved by self-consciously reflecting on your preparation of each case presented to you on the course.

13.4   Criteria by which you may assess your own performance

When you have completed your preparation of any set of papers, you may find it useful to review the list of criteria below to consider which fact management skills you have demonstrated by your preparation and which still require improvement. As these skills are required in all the work you undertake, your performance of other skills will be affected by the level of your fact management skills.

Effective preparation entails the ability to:

- understand data presented in a variety of ways;
- identify gaps, ambiguities, and contradictions in information;
- identify and prioritise the objectives of the client in terms both of practical outcomes and of legal remedies;
- place the information in context;
- identify and prioritise the factual issues;
- identify and prioritise the legal issues raised by the facts;
- select possible solutions to the client's problem;
- recognise the interaction between law and fact;
- assess the strengths and weaknesses of a case;
- organise information in a variety of ways:
    — to aid understanding;
    — to prove propositions of law; and
    — to assist at trial;
- distinguish between relevant and irrelevant facts;
- distinguish between fact and inference;

- construct an argument from the facts to support the client's case:
  — by developing a theory of the case; and
  — by selecting a theme to fit that theory;
- evaluate the issues in response to new information and in the light of tactical considerations.

13.5 Preparation: the common foundation to all your work

You will recall that three stages of preparation are recommended. The first two: identifying the context and undertaking analysis, which require both effective legal research and fact management, are common to all the tasks you undertake as a barrister. The third stage, presentation, will differ, depending on the nature of your instructions and the task you have been instructed to undertake. This manual provides you with guidance as to legal research and fact management and then proceeds to introduce you to how to apply the results of those processes to the task of opinion writing. Other manuals will provide you with similar support for the other skills you will need to develop. While *Opinion Writing* involves written advice, the *Conference Skills* manual helps you in providing oral advice to a client. The *Drafting* manual addresses the different types of document you will be required to draft. The *Advocacy* manual will assist with your representation of the client before the courts and tribunals. While this may initially appear to be a purely oral skill, expressing yourself in writing is important as you will often be expected to draft a skeleton argument to support your oral advocacy. Written advocacy is becoming a much more important aspect of client representation.

Remember also that the same basic approach applies to cases which you settle, either through direct negotiation or through one of the ADR procedures. Once again you will need to rethink how you present the results of your legal and factual analysis and to prepare flexibly so that you can apply your preparation to different tasks and to different stages of running a case. You may, for example, be fully prepared to represent a client in court when you are approached by your opponent with a view to settling the matter. Barristers have a reputation for responding quickly and effectively to changing situations and new information. Their ability to do this is founded on sound case preparation.

14

Dealing with figures

14.1 Introduction

Dealing with figures is part of dealing with the facts of a case. This chapter introduces the role of figures in the work of the barrister, and the contexts in which work with figures may be required.

Some people are quite confident in dealing with numbers, others are rather less confident; but in professional terms, no barrister can tell a client or solicitor, 'I never was much good at arithmetic!' A client will want to know exactly what will be recovered under each head of damages, and many tax and accounts issues may need to be dealt with by the barrister in a case where the fees of an accountant cannot be justified in terms of costs.

The importance of being able to deal with figures fluently has grown massively over recent years, especially in civil cases. This has been reinforced with the changes following the Jackson Review of Costs, with a much greater emphasis on costs budgets and proportionality. Schedules of costs and arguments about costs orders are now a part of most interim applications, and the test of proportionality requires a reasonably reliable assessment of the sum in dispute throughout a case. The need to make reasonable use of ADR to avoid costs sanctions also puts a focus on the figures in a case.

14.2 Importance of numeracy

It is a common misconception that law is about words, not figures. Law might be seen as based on written statutes and precedents, with practice being about statements of case and using words in advocacy.

Unfortunately, any suggestion that a barrister can get by without a facility with numbers is not true in practice. Although a contract textbook may have few figures in it, it will include substantial coverage of the legal principles for dealing with figures in awarding damages for a breach of contract. At the end of the day, it is the figures that count—the client will care less about a Court of Appeal precedent than about the figure for a head of damage, bearing in mind mitigation and interest, or whatever else is relevant. The client may need you to assist with quite a bit of arithmetic so that he or she can weigh up the potential financial benefits, and the risks, of bringing a case.

There are many circumstances in which a barrister will have to progress a case without the help of an accountant. In reading and understanding a brief, and in understanding witness statements and expert reports, a barrister may well need to deal with quite complex accounts—not just so as to understand them, but also to be able to see if there is anything unusual, making calculations to check points.

In the simplest terms, as a barrister, you must as a minimum be able to tell the client in detail, using figures, what he or she might hope to get in damages; you need to be able to deal with figures given to you; you need to be able to identify what further figures you need; and you need to be able to talk intelligently about figures to a solicitor or an accountant. Building the ability to do this is part of developing the practical approach of a real barrister in practice.

14.3 Relevance of figures in a barrister's practice

14.3.1 Areas requiring numerical skill

14.3.1.1 Accounts

It is very important to be familiar with the basic terminology of accounting, the elements of a set of accounts, and the principles and interpretation of a set of accounts. You don't need to be able to draw up a set of accounts (unless you are doing your own accounts as a barrister), but you need enough knowledge to be able to read and understand a set of accounts that may come with a brief in almost any sort of case, including tort, contract, family, and crime. A set of accounts can be a useful source of information on many things beyond basic income and expenditure. What is the business worth? How profitable was it at the time the premises were damaged? What parts of the business does a man own, and to what extent might a business fund part of a divorce settlement?

14.3.1.2 Tax law

It is also important to know the basic principles of income and capital taxation. Many earnings, business profits, and assets are subject to tax, and the difference between figures before and after tax may be substantial. In assessing damages, you will need to decide which figures should be taken as more accurately representing the loss. Damages often include a figure for loss of earnings—but should the figure before or after tax be taken? In a divorce settlement, what effect will tax have on the former husband and the former wife?

14.3.1.3 Damages

Principles for assessing damages in the major types of contract and tort actions are outlined in the **Remedies** manual. You should know the principles for assessing damages in the core subject areas. Once you have drawn up a list of heads of damage from the facts of the case, you will have to find a way of providing a figure for each one. This can sometimes be quite complex or even theoretical; for example, to decide what profit a business might have made if its premises had not been damaged you may have to base a calculation on what the business made during a similar period, or on the profits of a similar company.

14.3.1.4 Percentages

Deciding on the level of contributory negligence is a matter of fact, but also of looking at facts through arithmetical concepts. The lawyer needs to decide which facts make which party liable, and then turn that into a percentage for contributory negligence.

14.3.1.5 Interest

In a contract case, a figure that is claimed might carry interest under the contract itself. In many types of case, the court may award interest on damages to compensate for the fact that the claimant has been kept out of money. There are a variety of rules on what rates of interest the court may award in what circumstances, and different rates may apply to different heads of loss.

14.3.1.6   Costs

Even if a client wins, the client may not recover from the other side all costs. Costs will be taxed to ensure that sums spent on litigation are reasonable, once the judge has considered relevant costs budgets and whether the costs are proportionate. If the client does not win, the client is likely to bear his or her own costs, and the costs for the other side. The client needs to know likely costs as part of making a sensible and informed decision whether to sue, and as part of deciding how to conduct the case. Part 36 offers provide the possibility of protecting the client's position as regards costs, and the level of an offer needs to be carefully calculated.

14.3.2   Typical practical issues involving numbers

Dealing with figures requires an agile mind. Figures may reveal interesting aspects of a case. A few practical points to watch out for are summarised here:

(a) *What numerical issues are there in a case?* Never be happy with just the obvious possibility of damages, or dealing simply with the figures you are given. Are there other arithmetical or financial issues?

(b) *What financial needs are there?* You will only get damages if you identify and quantify a loss. If your client has been injured, identify everything he or she had before but no longer has, and find a way to put a figure on what that might be worth.

(c) *What financial resources are there?* If your client is seeking maintenance, you need to know in detail what your client needs, and also how much the other side may have to meet your claim. If you are suing for damages, you may need to consider what a potential defendant might be able to pay.

(d) *Where has the money gone to?* A question you may well wish to ask if your client's money, or property, has passed into the hands of someone else and you wish to reclaim it.

(e) *What is the relevance of an individual figure?* It may be necessary to identify and characterise a particular figure to be able to deal with it properly. Is it capital or income? Does it include tax? Does it include VAT?

(f) *Is a particular figure reliable?* Don't accept any figure without question. A figure may not be accurate. How good is the source of the figure? Has it been reached taking all relevant matters into account? Be suspicious if a figure looks too big or too small—and remember that accounts can hide as well as reveal things.

(g) *What does a figure really mean?* Don't be mesmerised by big figures or long lists of figures. Find out what each of the figures means and which figures are most important.

(h) *Be specific about figures.* Even if the figures given to you are vague, this is no excuse for you to be vague. If you need more factual information on figures then seek it.

(i) *Deal with figures comprehensively.* Make sure you have dealt with every aspect of the figures as fully as every aspect of the case. Deal with all relevant aspects of the figure, the interest, and the tax.

(j) *Be realistic and practical.* It is no use settling for a figure for maintenance for a client if you are not sure it will really cover the client's needs. It is no good offering a figure to settle a claim if you are not sure that your client can raise it.

14.3.3 Types of practice

Numeracy is going to be important to a barrister in any area of practice, from the solely civil to the wholly criminal, albeit in slightly different ways. To provide some examples:

(a) *Commercial practice.* The relevance of figures is obvious in dealing with companies or partnerships, especially as regards a detailed knowledge of accountancy and tax. You are also likely to need to know about commercial finance.

(b) *Chancery practice.* To deal with breach of trust, or for the administration of an estate, you are likely to need to have a thorough knowledge of relevant tax provisions and how to read a set of accounts.

(c) *General common law practice.* This has many elements, but to give some basic examples:

    (i) *Tort.* An accident case may turn on facts, but the assessment of damages can be very complex in cases of severe injury or fatal accident.

    (ii) *Employment law.* Many questions relating to pay may arise, and in some cases there will be a need to deal with statistics.

    (iii) *Family law practice.* Both income and capital provision may require complex calculations. There is not simply the question of how much to pay, but also of how much is really available, how much a person needs to live on, the tax consequences, and so on.

    (iv) *Criminal practice.* The importance of numeracy here ranges from the complex fraud trial to the small-scale fiddling of the books. Complete understanding is essential for clear presentation to the judge and the jury. There are also other possibilities, from being able to deal with tracing the monetary proceeds from the sale of illegal drugs to finding out what fine a defendant may be able to afford.

14.3.4 Working with an accountant

When dealing with a case that has a substantial financial factor it is possible that assistance will be available from an accountant. An accountant may be called in as an expert witness in a case, in which case you may have a role in retaining and briefing the expert witness. You might advise the client to employ an accountant to assist in dealing with particular aspects of a case, and you will be able to get a written report or see the accountant in conference. If the client employs an accountant you may direct questions to the client's accountant through the client.

An accountant can be of great assistance, but this is not an answer in itself. You will still have to talk to the accountant, to know what to ask about, to know exactly what questions to ask to get the answers you need, to be able to understand the answers, and to be able to present relevant information from the answers in court. If an accountant is to be involved in a case, you need to prepare thoroughly, and keep in mind the potential costs of employing the accountant.

In the vast majority of cases, there will be no accountant to help, for the very simple reason that having an accountant costs money and the client either may not be able to afford this, or the financial issues may not be substantial or vital enough to justify the expense of an accountant.

Whenever there is no accountant you will have to deal with all the figures and financial issues personally, finding the figures, analysing them, and coming to conclusions that can be communicated to the client and be presented in court. You will personally have to deal with any relevant accounts and tax issues.

14.3.5   Personal relevance

There is a personal relevance for the barrister in practice having a reasonable arithmetical ability and knowledge of the principles of accounting and taxation. The point is simply that, as a self-employed person, each barrister will be responsible for drawing up a set of accounts each year and will be personally liable for paying his or her own tax.

The reaction of those starting to train for the Bar tends to be that this point is in fact not very important—you employ an accountant to do your accounts and you get a good accountant so that you pay as little tax as possible, so why does a barrister need to be personally concerned? Such a reaction again shows a lack of practical appreciation of how things really work. Even if you are going to have an accountant to draw up your annual accounts, you need to keep all the records on which those accounts are to be based. Indeed, with self-assessment there is a legal duty to keep such records. You need to know what is taxable and should be entered and what is not. It is also in your interests to know what is tax-deductible so that you know what to keep receipts for. Tax rules mean that there is sometimes a choice between doing things in a tax-effective or a non-tax-effective way, and it is in your interests to know which is which. In addition to income tax, the barrister with sufficient income will be liable for VAT, with the need to make quarterly returns. It is easy to obtain software to assist.

With the increasing use of alternative business structures, the situation is becoming ever more complex. There are circumstances in which working through an alternative business structure may be more tax-effective than working as a self-employed person in chambers. You may need advice on this.

14.4   Risk assessment

Although there is respect for legal principle as being strong and long lasting, in fact much litigation involves significant risk assessment. Once you have investigated facts and legal principle, you generally find some points in your favour and some against you—it is necessary to weigh up the actual chance of success by balancing these. Some lawyers hedge their bets and say something like 'there is a good case', but that is very vague. Is that a 60 per cent chance of success? An 80 per cent chance? If the client is to risk money in paying his or her own costs, and potentially also the other side's costs, then the client needs the best assessment of the percentage chance of success that you can give. The client needs to be able to weigh up the likely costs against the chance of success to make an informed decision. Again the situation is becoming ever more complex. With the growing use of damages-based agreements and third-party funding it is ever more important to be able to assess the chances of success in order to take an informed view as to whether a case is worth funding.

This may be difficult until you have enough evidence but it is important to be as accurate as you can be. At an early stage in a case, you need to give a rough figure for the chance of success to enable your client to decide whether to pay to get more evidence. As the case develops and you have more evidence, you need to re-evaluate and refine the figure for the chance of success.

14.5   Stages in a claim when you may need to deal with figures

14.5.1   In a conference

When planning for or carrying out a conference, dealing with relevant facts must include all the relevant figures. The lawyer should identify the figures that will be required to pursue the case and ask the client about them. Any figures that the client provides should be noted. Often the client will not be able to provide the figures personally, in which case you will have to consider with the solicitor how the figure might be obtained. You will also need to collect evidence for each figure.

14.5.2   In preparing a case

Fact management principles cover figures as well as facts. In dealing with the facts of a case, the barrister will need to identify:

- all the areas of the case for which figures will be needed;
- precisely what figures will be needed;
- what figures are already known;
- what figures need to be ascertained;
- how each figure will be ascertained; and
- how each figure can be used and proved.

14.5.3   In writing an opinion

A good solicitor will send you most of the figures that you need, but even a good solicitor is unlikely to send all the figures you need in the initial brief. At that stage, the main issue is whether there is a case and the strength of the case. But figures will still need to be dealt with—even at an early stage, the client will want to know not only whether he or she might win but also, at least in general terms, what damages might be awarded. At an early stage you might be asked to write an opinion on a case on the basis of which a third-party funder will decide whether to back the case, for which key objectives will be to assess the likely damages and chances of success on limited information.

In analysing a brief, you must consider in what areas figures are relevant. In writing the opinion, you should deal with figures as far as possible. The figures that are provided in the brief should be dealt with and other areas where figures are relevant should be dealt with in outline. You also need to decide on a suitable way to present the figures in the opinion, whether as part of the text or in a tabulated form.

In writing an initial opinion, it is easy to underestimate the numerical and arithmetical side of a case simply because detailed figures may well not be available. Figures must never be underestimated—the barrister is not there to accept what is provided, it is for the barrister to indicate what information is needed for the case to progress. Areas where more detailed figures are required should be clearly identified in an opinion. Also, remember to deal with the figures comprehensively in writing.

If you advise your client that he or she can expect £40,000 in damages, it is verging on the negligent not to advise that the money will be liable to 40 per cent tax, if that is the case. If you are advising a potential funder about a case you will need to get the figures sufficiently right to avoid an action for professional negligence.

14.5.4   In drafting

A draft is a summary of the facts that are the foundation of a case. You should always consider carefully how far figures are facts that need to be included. Detailed figures or facts relevant to the calculation of damages may need to be included in the body of a draft or added as a schedule. You may need to cover a number of areas, including all heads of damage resulting from an accident, personal injury, or financial loss. You may also need to include facts and figures relevant to interest. A summary of damages and interest may also need to be included in the prayer. Examples are provided in the *Drafting* manual.

An affidavit or witness statement in a case may require figures to be included in great detail. A draft order will of course need to have any relevant figures specifically included. If the figures are complex they should be presented in a schedule.

14.5.5   In advocacy

When presenting a case to a judge or jury, it goes without saying that it is vital for the barrister to have total command of any figures in the case, be they sums of money, measurements, or anything else. Only if the barrister has personally gathered all the relevant figures and mastered them will he or she have any chance of explaining them clearly, let alone convincing someone of their relevance. Even someone who is confident in dealing with figures in writing may find it more challenging to deal with them orally.

There are various ways in which a barrister may have to deal with figures in the course of presenting a case in court. First and most simply, figures may need to be dealt with in opening and closing speeches. Second, figures will need to be dealt with in offering evidence, whether through documents or witnesses. Clearly, the barrister must be capable of examining or cross-examining a witness on figures. At every stage, you need to be able to present any numerical information in a way which really communicates your meaning to the jury and the judge. Even if you understand the figures, helping someone else to understand them can be very difficult.

If you have complex figures, you may need to plan very carefully how to present them in court. Paper may well be enough, but clear presentation can help comprehension. Flip charts and overhead projectors may be useful. Computers and video display units are increasingly used if appropriate.

At an interim hearing, you will normally need to provide a summary of the costs to date, and to present coherent arguments about what costs order should be made in respect of the hearing. In a case where a costs budget is relevant you may have to present arguments in relation to a budget being approved or updated. Your solicitors will be more familiar with the overall costs position than you are—ask for any information you need before the hearing.

14.5.6   In settling a case

Before attempting to settle a case, you must have all the relevant figures to evaluate the case and identify the most and the least that the client might expect to win or pay. Sometimes a settlement is seen as a quick and easy way of avoiding a legal claim, but of course no settlement should be contemplated until one has a full grasp of all the relevant figures. It would be potentially negligent to agree a final settlement without a full understanding of the facts of a case. Full calculations should form the background to any ADR process, especially negotiation or mediation, where relative informality does not make full arithmetic any less important.

With the growing emphasis on proportionality of costs and reasonable use of ADR it is increasingly important to consider ADR options on the basis of likely damages and actual and potential costs regularly throughout a case.

14.6   Collecting evidence of figures

Figures need to be ascertained just like other matters of fact, and admissible evidence will need to be found to prove each figure just as much as any other fact in the case. Having identified an area where figures are relevant, you need to sort out precisely what evidence you need and exactly where it may be obtained. Some figures the client will be able to provide, but you will still need to find evidence to support the figure in most cases. For others, it is for the barrister to indicate to the solicitor what figures are required and for the solicitor to endeavour to find the amount and the proof.

The sources of evidence of figures are wide ranging, from a full set of accounts, to cash books, invoices, and receipts. There may also be less direct ways of proving figures. Even if the client has not kept bank statements, it is possible to get copies. Every figure needs to be proved but, at the end of the day, it is especially important to be able to prove the larger figures that are most important to the damages.

You also need to be aware of the procedural ways of getting evidence of figures that your client does not have. An obvious possibility is disclosure, but there are many others that are covered in the civil litigation and evidence parts of the course.

You need to be aware of the problems that can arise in presenting such evidence. If you need to take an accountant through his or her evidence, you will have to be familiar with all the appropriate terminology. You need to be able to present evidence in a form in which it can be understood. Most important of all, you will sooner or later need to be able to cross-examine on the figures presented by the other side, which requires a most thorough understanding.

Having stressed the importance of figures, it is equally important for the barrister to be able to deal with the lack of figures—you will come across cases where you need certain figures to advise in detail and they are simply not obtainable. You can only do your best. Try to think of all the sources from which figures might be obtained. If there are no sources, or if the figures are in any event theoretical, you will have to do your best to argue what the figure should be, from common sense, analogy, or some other source. There can, for example, be a problem in arguing for loss of future profit in a breach of contract case. If there is a claim for future loss of profits, students tend to think that the claim is weak if it is difficult to assess what the potential profits might have been. This is of course a problem, but it is by no means fatal. The fact that a figure is difficult to assess simply means that you need to set about constructing a good argument for how it might be assessed. Refer to profits over recent years, or profits of similar businesses, to construct an argument.

14.7   Statistics and graphs

14.7.1   When may the use of statistics be helpful to you?

Statistical methods and statistical terms are used in reporting the mass data of social and economic trends, business conditions, opinion polls, and the census. You should get used to reading statistics and utilise them whenever you seek to prove by inference that in your submission a state of affairs exists. Such information is particularly useful when seeking to establish racial or sexual discrimination; risk factors in such areas as sentencing, parole release from mental hospital, danger from chemicals and other environmental pollutants; risk factors in giving informed consent to medical treatment; future profit forecasts; blood test evidence; genetic fingerprinting evidence; etc.

14.7.2   The language of statistics: averages

There are three different kinds of average: the mean, the median, and the mode.

The mean is the arithmetic average arrived at by totalling the number of each of whatever it is you want to average and then dividing that by the total number in the sample. For example, you want to know the average (mean) number of cigarettes that Bar students who smoke smoked on a particular Monday. If 400 of you smoke, and the total smoked by all 400 on the Monday in question was 8,120, the mean would be 8,120/400 = 20.3.

The median, using the same example, is the number of cigarettes which half the smokers smoke more than, and half smoke less than. In this example, the figure could be less than the mean, and might be about 19.

The mode, again using the same example, is the number of cigarettes which the largest number of people in the sample smoke, so that if the greatest number of people in the group actually smoked 16 cigarettes on Monday, then 16 is the modal number.

If presenting an average to the court, always know what kind of average you are using; and if you are confronted with statistical information by your opponent, always ask what kind of average is being used.

14.7.3   The reliability of statistical information

The major difficulty with all statistics is that they may be biased or based on too small a sample to give anything like a reasonable or believable result. Statistical data is generally developed from information collected in questionnaires. It is important to know: how many were sent out, how the respondents were selected, how many were returned, who did not return them, and whether the respondents were likely to respond truthfully to the questions posed or whether there may have been a desire to give a pleasing answer. To be valid, the sample must be representative and randomly selected.

14.7.4   Sources of statistics

Government websites can provide very useful statistical information, see for example the Office for National Statistics at <http://www.statistics.gov.uk>. The internet can of course provide many more sources of statistical and arithmetical information, but you may need an expert witness to be able to use relevant evidence in court.

Communication and information technology use in case preparation and presentation

15.1 Introduction

Most barristers in independent practice use communication and information technology (C&IT) to prepare and present their cases in court. Solicitors may require written opinions prior to the case going to court, judges frequently demand skeleton arguments when legal arguments are presented to them, and it is often necessary or preferable to carry out legal research when at home, at court, or on the move, rather than in chambers.

Communication by email is essential and solicitors frequently send instructions or seek advice this way. Briefs or other documents are often sent as attachments to emails by solicitors, and it will sometimes be necessary to scan documents back to them.

Although barristers are members of chambers, there tends not to be a uniform use of technology, even between members of the same set. Some well-organised sets have IT committees, but in most sets of chambers barristers develop their C&IT use in an ad hoc way, depending on the needs of their practice and their own financial resources. A barrister will have to devote time to learning new skills throughout his or her practice, as technology changes and new developments occur.

As prospective pupils, now is the time to ensure that your use of C&IT is up to date and that you are proficient in the most important and essential skills. You will be extremely busy during pupillage and will not have time to learn new C&IT skills then. Those pupils who are able to use C&IT well will have a distinct advantage.

15.2 Modern practice

Practice varies from barrister to barrister and from chambers to chambers. The way a barrister works depends largely on the type of work he or she does and the type of solicitor or agency who sends the work.

15.2.1 Receiving the brief

The traditional form of contact from the solicitor was by sending hard-copy briefs by post or DX (Document Exchange, which is a kind of postal method frequently used between members of the legal profession), by faxing documents, and by telephone.

Increasingly, however, solicitors send briefs by email, often as large attachments to emails. This method of instructing counsel is likely to increase, particularly with the desire of certain agencies (e.g. CPS) to become 'paperless'.

15.2.2   Preparing the brief

In every case, on receipt of the papers it will be necessary to read them and liaise with the solicitor or agency involved. This is increasingly also done by email as well as by phone. It goes without saying that emails should be checked regularly and responded to promptly once received. Instructing solicitors will not react well to unanswered emails and may not instruct you again if you do not communicate effectively.

Equally, solicitors will receive advices, statements of case, requests for further information, and other correspondence from counsel direct by email. Often both solicitor and counsel will send scanned pdf documents to each other instead of original ones. It is wise to send a signed hard copy or pdf of any final advice or statement of case, in addition to any emailed copy.

15.2.3   Contact with the court

Experience of C&IT use with the courts is variable. Much will depend on the willingness and/or ability of the judge or his clerk to liaise directly with counsel by email. Contact with judges, when made, is usually concerned with the service of skeleton arguments, draft orders, or corrections to judgments. Where it is necessary to sign grounds of appeal, such documents should be sent as hard-copy documents.

Clerks are increasingly liaising with the list offices of courts by email, particularly in relation to long-term case management and date fixing. Daily contact is still maintained by phone, but the increasing preference of the courts is to send any requests about listing in writing by email.

15.3   Essential skills

It is essential that every prospective pupil is able to use C&IT. Proficient word processing and document formatting are now necessary tools of the barrister's trade. Email and online legal research are also essential and will make practice at the Bar more efficient and up to date. The ability to scan documents into pdf format is also increasingly important.

15.3.1   Word

It is absolutely essential that every prospective pupil is able to use Word (whether Microsoft or its Apple counterpart) and is able to type and format documents quickly and in the correct form. Opinions, skeleton arguments, statements of case, and other documents are written daily by barristers in practice and it is often necessary to draft them quickly. Every prospective pupil must be proficient at typing and word processing to ensure an efficient use of time. Touch-typing is a distinct advantage.

15.3.2   Excel

Many cases benefit from data being set out clearly in spreadsheet format, e.g. chronologies, financial ancillary relief schedules, damages schedules, and other data-handling documents. Excel software is by far the best software for producing such spreadsheets in this context. Proficiency in advance of pupillage will enable any pupil to be able to deal with such working documents competently and efficiently and in a way which is immediately useful to their pupil supervisor.

15.3.3   Outlook

Email is now an important part of contact between many of the parties in litigation. When sending email at a professional level, it is preferable to use Outlook (or an equivalent) rather than a typical web-based email, such as Yahoo! or Hotmail. In fact they should not be used at all for sensitive and/or confidential data. CJSM is the secure email which government agencies such as the CPS will use to send emails and documents.

15.3.4   Online legal research

An ability to conduct thorough, precise, and efficient legal research is one of the most important skills any barrister can have. It is the basis for the understanding and presentation of any case, whether written or oral. Increasingly, barristers work not only in chambers, but also at home, and whilst on the way to court or at court. They require access to up-to-date law at all times. Online legal research tools are therefore increasingly important to them.

The skill in using such tools requires practice and a thorough understanding of the way the particular service functions. Any such service is only as good as the person using it and the search term chosen by that person. **Chapters 2** to **9** of this manual will assist you as a starting point in developing these skills. However, such a skill can only ever improve with training and frequent use.

Useful and frequently used services include *Westlaw*, *LexisNexis Butterworths*, *Lawtel*, *Casetrack*, *Justis*, *Jordans*, *BAILII*, and *CrimeLine*.

The extent of use of online subscription services, however, is hampered by two practical considerations. Firstly, the courts' Wi-Fi networks can be variable and sometimes only work in certain areas within a particular building and not in the courtroom itself, and so access to the internet at court or whilst travelling to and from court requires an individual barrister to set up an internet link, usually via a mobile phone. Secondly, subscription to many of these online services can be expensive for an individual barrister or set of chambers. There are many providers and some are more affordable than others. Of course, the quality of service offered may be reflected in this difference.

15.3.5   Use of CD-ROMs

Many texts are now also available on CD-ROM. This makes it easier for a barrister to transport what is effectively a library of material on his or her computer, making access at court or at home much easier. Some CD-ROMs are more user-friendly than others. Again, it is practice and frequent usage that makes these tools easier and more efficient to use.

Some useful and frequently used CD-ROMs include *Archbold*, *Blackstone's Criminal and Civil Practice*, *The White Book*, *Kemp & Kemp*, *The Planning Encyclopaedia*, *Crime Desktop*, and *Family Law Practitioner* etc.

15.3.6 Navigation of the Web

When preparing a case, it may often be necessary to expand your general area of knowledge. Such knowledge broadens your understanding of the factual background of a case and gives you a wider insight into the problem you are dealing with. You may need to research a geographical location, an industrial process, a medical term, or other topic. Make use of the Web. Do not assume that you know everything. You should be interested in the factual background of the case you are preparing. A broader knowledge will not only be useful to your own understanding, but will also reassure your solicitor and lay client.

Many government agencies have useful websites. These often contain policy documents or notes for guidance which will assist you in your research and analysis of a problem.

There are also websites which help you navigate rules of etiquette and conduct, the court structure and hierarchy, barristers' names and chambers, and the logistical arrangements which are integral to practice at the Bar.

Some useful websites

<http://www.barstandardsboard.org.uk/>
<http://www.justice.gov.uk/>
<http://www.courtserve.net/>
<http://www.judiciary.gov.uk/>
<http://www.legislation.gov.uk/>
<http://www.cps.gov.uk/>
<http://www.sentencing-guidelines.gov.uk/>
<http://new.eur-lex.europa.eu/>
<http://www.curia.europa.eu/>
<http://www.criminalbar.com/>
<http://www.piba.org.uk/>
<http://www.flba.co.uk/>
<http://www.combar.com/>
<http://www.propertybar.org.uk>
<http://www.landregistryservices.com/>
<http://www.environment-agency.gov.uk/>
<http://www.hse.gov.uk/>
<http://www.tradingstandards.gov.uk/>
<http://www.companieshouse.gov.uk/>
<http://www.corporateaccountability.org/>
<http://www.fsa.gov.uk/>
<http://www.graysinn.info/>
<http://www.innertemple.org.uk/>
<http://www.lincolnsinn.org.uk/>
<http://www.middletemple.org.uk/>
<http://www.timeanddate.com/>
<http://www.nationalrail.co.uk>
<http://ico.org.uk/>

15.4 Data protection and security

Every organisation that processes personal information must notify the Information Commissioner's Office (ICO), unless they are exempt. Failure to notify is a criminal offence. It follows that every barrister must now register with the Information Commissioner. Guidance is offered by the ICO on data retention and other responsibilities in connection with the processing and storing of data. It goes without saying that opinions and other legal documents contain confidential and privileged personal material and need protecting. Password protection and computer and email security should be observed at all times when storing and handling such material (see <http://ico.org.uk>.

Part III

Opinion Writing

16 Words and the barrister   243
17 Qualities of good writing   246
18 Plain English   253
19 Opinion writing   269
20 The use of law in an opinion   293
21 Getting started   302
22 Advice on evidence in a civil case   314
23 Advice on evidence in a criminal case   329
24 Checklist for opinion writing skills   347

Words and the barrister

16.1 Introduction

It is inevitable that anyone embarking on training for the Bar already has considerable skill in the use of the written word. Doubtless part of the reason you have chosen this profession is because you feel you already have such skill, or have the potential to develop it and are willing to work hard to do so. Nevertheless barristers do use words in particular ways that you will not have come across before and for purposes which are new to you. It therefore makes sense to spend some time examining the ways in which a barrister uses words, and the standards expected in the profession, before going on to introducing the skill of opinion writing itself.

16.2 Tools of the trade

For the barrister, arguably more than for any other profession, words are the dominant tool of the trade. A barrister can do nothing of consequence without using words. Surgeons, architects, surveyors, accountants, soldiers, and police officers can all carry out their professional functions to a greater or lesser extent without the use of words. But virtually everything a barrister does involves speaking or writing. A barrister's performance will be judged almost exclusively on how well he or she speaks or writes.

16.3 Speaking and writing

Speaking and writing are two ways of communicating. Communication is the only purpose of either activity. Whenever we speak or write, either in everyday life, or professionally, we are trying to communicate some inner content: thought, idea, feeling, information, or message. That inner content is largely expressed in words. The better we express ourselves, the better we choose our words, the better we put them together, the more effectively we communicate.

16.4   Communication

A barrister must communicate well; so a barrister must use words well. To explain something to your client, you must put it in such a way as to be sure your client understands. To make a point to a judge or jury effectively, not only must they understand it, you must express it in the most telling way. To get what you want from a witness, you must frame the question in exactly the right way. All this involves skill in the choice of words, the order in which they are put, and the structure of sentences, paragraphs, and speeches. In the ideal world, a barrister's every word would be chosen, and every sentence composed, with great care.

16.5   The spoken word and the written word

There is no difference in essence between spoken word skills and written word skills: only the context changes. You may use different words in writing than you would orally, and your sentence structure may change, but you should still choose your words with care, putting them into the best order and composing the whole piece of writing or speech with a view to achieving perfection. The need to communicate effectively, to be clear in what you say, to be precise in what you mean is unchanged. In drafting, particularly, there is a need for precision and unambiguity in what you write that exceeds what is required in any other context.

16.6   Standards

A barrister is a specialist lawyer. No matter what kind of practice you have, you will be presumed a specialist in advocacy, in the provision of written advice, and in drafting. All these skills are dependent on your word skills. A barrister is supposed to be an *expert* in the use of words and the use of language. You must not just speak and write well—by the standards of everyday life you must speak and write *exceptionally* well. You will be offering your services and charging a fee for which you undertake to speak and write better than those paying you could have spoken or written.

It follows that the standards of clarity, precision, grammar, punctuation, and stylistic elegance that you need to set yourself throughout your professional career are almost certainly higher than the standards you have regarded as satisfactory up until now. And you need to set your standards even higher when you are writing than when you are speaking. In speech, the advocate is largely extemporising, having to compose sentences and thoughts even while speaking. Errors and stumbles can and do creep in. You don't always manage to think of just the right word. You don't always express something as accurately as you would like. But when you are writing, you have the opportunity to revise, correct, and improve. There can be no excuse for errors and inaccuracies.

You should make up your mind that you will strive to reach these very high standards. With practice, you can attain them.

16.7   Good writing

But what makes good writing? What sort of writing is expected of the barrister? In the next two chapters we shall examine the qualities of good writing, and the importance of plain language.

17

Qualities of good writing

17.1 The qualities

To write a chapter on the qualities of good writing takes some courage. There is a danger of being controversial, hypocritical, and idealistic. Controversial because good writing is impossible to define, and so there will always be different views as to what constitutes good writing. Hypocritical, because one can only too often find in one's own writing the very faults one is criticising in other people's. Idealistic, because it is very rare to find a piece of writing with all the qualities described in this chapter in full measure. Nevertheless, some guidance as to what constitutes good writing is desirable, so that you can take steps towards improving your writing.

Rather than attempting to define good writing it seems simpler to describe some of its qualities. It goes without saying that the qualities described are those required of barristers, but doubtless many of these qualities are desirable in other contexts too.

17.2 Making choices

Everything that appears in the final version of what you are writing should be there because you intend it to be. Nothing should have crept in by accident, or thoughtlessness; nothing should have been left out by oversight. What you end up with should be exactly what you want. Every word you have used should be there because you have chosen to use that word as opposed to any other. The words should appear in the order you have decided upon. The sentences and paragraphs should be composed as you have designed them. The whole piece of writing should be structured in the way that you have decided works best.

In other words, you have choices. You can only write well by making choices. Those choices may be conscious, where you have weighed up two alternative words or phrases and chosen one rather than the other; or they may be subconscious, where a word or phrase has come into your mind and you have put it down because it is clearly right. But where a word or phrase comes to you intuitively, you still have a choice: whether to keep it, or to discard it and search for something better. Never, if you can avoid it, simply write down the first thing that comes into your head without examining it critically and *deciding* that it is just right.

When we speak, we frequently say things we do not mean to say, or we do not say them in the best possible way, or we forget to say things. This is the natural result of extemporising. A barrister must of course learn to minimise 'accidents' when speaking, but you will never eliminate them entirely. When writing, however, you have an opportunity you do not have when speaking: to go back over what you have written and improve it. Do not waste this opportunity. At every stage you have a choice: to leave what you have written or to improve upon it. Make that choice.

17.3 The English language

The English language is both your resource and your vehicle. Good writing involves drawing upon it and using it well. You should understand the language and the way it works, you should understand its vocabulary, so that you can make the language work for you rather than find it to be a hindrance or an obstacle that gets in the way of what you are trying to say.

Plain language is important: it has the qualities listed here. Try to write in plain English wherever possible. This means avoiding inappropriate jargon, archaic words and phrases, unnecessary verbiage, pedantic superfluities, and antiquated sentence structures. 'Legalese' gives lawyers a bad name, creates barriers between you and your client, and can narrow rather than broaden your thinking.

Nevertheless you are a lawyer and what you are writing may serve a specialised legal purpose rather than a general one. Plain English involves using the simplest and clearest language possible in the circumstances, bearing in mind who you are writing to. It is not the same thing as writing simplistically. A lawyer cannot sacrifice precision by oversimplification, or clarity for the sake of shorter words. It is more important that what you are writing should fulfil its function than that it should make sense to someone who has no need to understand it.

There are times, therefore, when technical terms are preferable to lay terms; when uncommon words carry precisely the meaning you want while commonplace ones do not; when a long complex sentence gives the right emphasis while a short simple one distorts it. The rule is to use everyday language wherever possible but not at all costs.

17.4 Clarity

Good writing has total clarity. The meaning springs instantly from the words, which do not need to be pondered, reread, or analysed. If you ever feel that a sentence you are writing is not expressing the idea behind it clearly, stop, and start writing it again.

The whole purpose of much of what a barrister writes is to clarify what would otherwise be unclear. An opinion may try to explain a complex situation so that it can be understood. A statement of case tries to define issues and bring them into the open. It follows that there is a great need for clarity in what a barrister writes. If it cannot be understood by those reading it, or if it is open to different interpretations, not only is it poorly written, but it has failed to serve the very purpose for which it was written.

Clarity of expression can never be achieved without clarity of thought behind it. In other words if you are not clear in your mind about what you think or what you want to say, you haven't the slightest chance of being any clearer in writing. So a barrister never, except in cases of extreme urgency, writes anything without long and careful thought first. Everything you set out to write must be planned and thought through.

Thereafter clarity will best be achieved through a logical structure, correct spelling, grammar, and punctuation, precision, conciseness, completeness, and style, which are dealt with in the following paragraphs.

17.5 A logical structure

Clarity depends not only on the choice of words and word order, but also on the structure of what is being written. The whole piece of writing needs to be composed in a clear and coherent manner. This will almost always mean that the structure should be logical.

Whatever it is you are trying to say can be broken down into smaller pieces of content. You cannot make a point without explaining the point you are making and justifying it in some way. You cannot express an opinion without giving reasons for that opinion. So in most pieces of professional writing there will be a reasoning process that you need to set out. That process needs to be logical. The reasons you give must actually lead to the conclusion you express. If they do not, then what you write will lack clarity; it may even appear unsound.

The reasoning process is likely to be a series of small links in a logical chain. Each link must be placed in the right order, and be connected correctly to the other links. This involves logical thought, logical explanation, and a logical structure to what you are writing. A piece of writing that has this structure is easy to read, clear, and compelling in its persuasiveness. A piece of writing that does not is likely to be muddled, confusing, and unprofessional.

Once again, clarity of thought is crucial to achieving this aim. You need not only to have clear thoughts, but to organise them logically as well.

17.6 Spelling

Good writing should be free from spelling errors. Spelling errors make you look unprofessional. Unfortunately they are very common. A barrister should take all reasonable steps towards eliminating them. The first step is to accept that spelling matters. So many people in ordinary life think it is unimportant.

In the modern age a great many spelling errors occur not because the writer cannot spell, but because he or she is clumsy on the keyboard, makes typographical errors, and then fails to correct them. If you care as much as you should about spelling, you will be constantly alert to this danger. A computerised spell-checker can pick up a great many of them, but never all, because all it can do is recognise whether a word exists in its dictionary or not. It cannot distinguish between commonly confused words, both of which exist. It is therefore your responsibility, not your computer's, to make sure your spelling is correct.

Of particular importance in the professional world is to spell names correctly, especially that of your client. Always study the spelling of any name you are given and make sure you reproduce it precisely. People called Emmet with one 't' get very annoyed indeed when they are addressed as Emmett with two 't's, especially if they know the writer has the correct spelling in front of them.

17.7 Grammar

A barrister's writing should be free from grammatical error. The rules of grammar dictate word forms, word order, and sentence structure. If a verb is in the wrong tense, an adverb in the wrong place, or a sentence improperly composed, the only possible result is obscurity of meaning. You cannot write clearly if your writing is not grammatical.

Grammar is particularly important where you are using long sentences. If the structure of a sentence is not abundantly clear at first reading, almost certainly it suffers from being too long. Any grammatical inconsistency is therefore likely to destroy the value of the long sentence.

Good grammar is the grammar of clear usage, rather than the grammar of pedants. Beware of absolute rules of grammar, such as 'Never split an infinitive', 'Never put a comma before "and"'. In the end the best grammar is the grammar that makes the meaning clearest.

17.8 Punctuation

Good writing must be properly punctuated. This is often essential for clarity in all forms of writing. It can be crucial to the meaning of a legal document. Take care to use full stops, commas, semicolons, and colons properly and in the right places. The sense of a sentence can be destroyed by a comma in the wrong place or the lack of a comma where one is needed. The structure of a sentence can become immediately unclear when a comma is used instead of a semicolon. A full stop in the wrong place can spoil the connection between two linked thoughts and result in a sentence with no main verb. Do not open a bracket and then fail to close it. Do not start a subordinate clause with a dash and end it with a comma. None of these common errors belongs to good writing.

Barristers need to take particular care over punctuation when drafting. Drafting can occasionally involve complex grammatical structures, long sentences, and numbered subclauses. The wrong punctuation can easily destroy the whole relationship between various parts of the sentence, or detach a subclause from the main clause to which it belongs. The choice of punctuation marks is just as much a part of drafting as the choice of words.

17.9 Precision

Barristers need to write with precision. Everything you write should ideally say exactly what you want to say, neither more nor less. This is an essential part of clarity and is inevitably something you have always attempted to achieve whenever you have written anything. But there are degrees of precision. Whenever we communicate either orally or in writing, we always manage to say more or less what we mean, otherwise we would fail to communicate altogether. We trust that our listener or reader will interpret what we say or write in the way we intend. We are usually inclined to be rather more precise when we write than when we speak, because we have the opportunity to be (see **17.2**). But even then, we frequently express our thoughts and feelings in a vague or generalised way. Only occasionally do we attempt to write with exactitude.

As a lawyer you will need to write with a greater degree of precision than you would probably use in everyday life. This is true generally, particularly true of opinions and advices, and quite fundamental in drafting. In statements of case there can be no room for anything less than absolute precision. The words you use must be chosen for their precise meaning; the sentences you write must be composed to convey a precise sense. Lack of precision will at best result in a degree of confusion; at worst it may mean you are in effect telling lies.

The more precise what you are writing needs to be, the more carefully you will need to compose it. This takes time and thought. You need to ponder the words and phrases you are using. With experience you will learn to avoid the worst traps and become adept at spotting ambiguities. But it involves setting yourself standards of accuracy beyond those you would regard as sufficient for everyday communication.

17.10 Non-ambiguity

This is a special kind of precision which is of particular importance. Very often in everyday life we use words which mean precisely what we intend them to but which are capable of bearing another meaning if looked at from a different viewpoint or in a different context. We frequently do not notice this alternative meaning because both we and the person we are communicating with share the same fixed viewpoint. Even if we are aware of the possible ambiguity we frequently do not worry about it because we are sure that what we say or write can only be received in the context we intend.

But when you are writing in a legal context you must be aware of all the different viewpoints from which your words might be seen and ensure that what you write is genuinely unambiguous. You should reckon that if what you write could reasonably bear another meaning than that which you intend, someone somewhere will probably try to read it in that way. A quick glance through the law reports will show how many cases arise through an ambiguity in somebody's written words, an ambiguity that obviously never occurred to the person who wrote them. Learn to be aware of and avoid all possible ambiguities. Again, this is particularly important in drafting, but generally true of all a barrister's writing.

17.11 Conciseness

Good writing is concise. This does not mean it should be abbreviated, or even short; rather that it should be succinct and to the point. Try to avoid repetition, waffle, long-windedness, or digression. Leave out what is unnecessary or that which obstructs your flow or meaning without adding anything. A good piece of writing should never be a word longer than it needs to be.

But beware of trying to be too concise. If what you are writing merely becomes a summary of what you mean to say, it will not do. Clarity is more important than brevity. Ideas are sometimes more accurately expressed in 20 words than ten. Arguably even style should be given a higher priority than excessive conciseness. Make sure that your writing, as well as being concise, is also always complete.

17.12 Completeness

This is the quality which must be balanced with conciseness. When you write you must express your ideas completely. If what you write has only partially expressed what you are trying to say, or has only set out half the story, or does not explain your full reasoning step by step, then it is incomplete. If incomplete, it is also almost certainly imprecise, ambiguous, and unclear.

Just where you draw the line between completeness and conciseness is a matter of fine judgement. You will not always draw the line in the same place. Sometimes you will know that what you are writing will serve its purpose better if you err on the side of conciseness; on other occasions you will realise that it is essential to get everything down in full even if that means you are not as concise as you might have been. But always be aware of the balance that has to be achieved in a good piece of writing.

17.13 Style

Style may not be high on everyone's list of priorities, but it is not to be ignored. Good writing has good style. Style is very hard to define, since it is a matter of artistic impression, but good style is nevertheless something we recognise and appreciate when reading a piece of writing. It is certainly an important quality in anything we describe as 'well written'.

Good style is elegant. Elegance cannot be allowed to become the prime objective of a lawyer's writing: something that seems to have been written chiefly to impress the reader with its beauty and composition rather than for practical business purposes will look out of place in a legal context. If it is in conflict with precision, non-ambiguity, or completeness, then clarity demands that elegance should to some degree be sacrificed. But it is usually possible, if enough care is taken, to achieve elegance as well as each of the other qualities of good writing.

No one can tell you how to write elegantly. You will decide what feels and looks elegant for yourself. But good style involves a creative rather than a pedestrian or awkward use of language. Avoid clumsy phrases, tortuous constructions, and jarring words. Maintain variety: do not use the same words or structure of sentence over and over again. Use a wide vocabulary: do not be repetitive in your choice of words, unless for effect. But do not use obscure words merely to show off.

Elegance is also very much a matter of flow and rhythm. Elegant writing usually sounds good when read aloud, as well as carrying the reader easily along the printed page.

17.14 Appearance

Appearance is also important. What you write should look clear and neat on the page. That makes it easier to read. So do not pack the type too densely, nor space it too widely. Do not use a type-size that is too small or too large. Allow reasonable margins. Give your headings and subheadings appropriate weight, neither too heavy nor too light. Do not use enormous numbers of footnotes.

Be consistent in your formatting. This applies, for example, to subheadings (font, type-size, weight); the spacing and indentation of paragraphs, subparagraphs, and bullets; and the use of bold and italic type and capitals. If there are more than two pages, number them.

17.15 The reader

You should always have the reader in mind when you write. Just as you only speak to communicate with a particular person or people, so when you write you should always be aware of the person you are writing for. A letter is addressed to a particular individual and must be written in a way that will communicate easily with him or her. Do not use legal terminology if you are writing to a non-lawyer. Do not write to a solicitor as if he or she were a lay client. Do not make jokes that will not seem amusing to the person concerned.

An opinion may be addressed to a solicitor, but frequently a lay client will wish to read it and it should be comprehensible to him or her. Statements of case need to be understood only by other lawyers, but they must make sense to a lawyer who has no other knowledge of the case. Always be aware of the characteristics and background of the likely reader of what you write and gear it to that reader.

17.16   **Reading over**

Usually, anything you write will come back to you in printed form, either from a typist or your computer. Never be satisfied with what you have written until you have read over and checked the printed version. If you care as you should about the quality of your writing, you will care enough to wish to correct typographical errors and to give yourself one final opportunity to improve in any small way you can on what you have written.

Plain English

18.1 Introduction

We have already mentioned plain English in **Chapter 17**. In one sense 'plain English' simply means English that is clear and well-written. But it has come to acquire a slightly narrower meaning, as the alternative to obscure legalistic jargon, or 'legalese'. This chapter looks at the differences between plain English and legalese, and how you can go about learning to write in plain English as a lawyer.

It goes without saying that plain English is just as important to oral communication as it is to written communication, so do not be misled into using it only when you are writing. Use plain English whenever it is appropriate to do so, in advocacy, in conference, in negotiation, in opinion writing and in drafting, just as you probably use it in everyday life. It is however when you are writing rather than speaking that you are most likely to slip into legalese.

18.2 What is plain English?

Plain English involves the use of 'plain and straightforward language which conveys its meaning as clearly and simply as possible without unnecessary pretension or embellishment' (Richard Wydick, *Plain English for Lawyers*).

Expanding on this, let us say that plain English is language that enables the reader to read fluently with understanding. So the reader:

- Never needs to go back to the beginning of the sentence and reread it to understand it.
- Never needs to stop and examine the sentence in order to comprehend its structure.
- Can always see how the next sentence follows on from the one before.
- Finds no words that they do not understand.
- Grasps what you have said on one reading.

In other words the reader understands at the same speed as they read.

18.3 Why use plain English?

The Law Reform Commission of Victoria put it this way:

The language of the law has long been a source of concern to the community. It has been the subject of continuous literary criticism and satire. Critics have highlighted its technical terms, its convolutions and its prolixity. These faults have been noted by judges and by practising and academic lawyers as well. Calls have regularly been made for the use of a more simple and straightforward style. Some improvements have been made in response to those calls. But legal language remains largely unintelligible to most members of the community. It even causes problems for members of the legal profession. In some cases, the obscurity may arise from the complexity of the law and of its subject-matter. In other cases, however, it is due to the complexity of the language in which the law is expressed. Some lawyers do not take sufficient care to communicate clearly with their audience. Letters, private legal documents, and legislation itself are still drafted in a style which poses unnecessary barriers to understanding. (*Legal Language*, para 14.)

Many legal documents are unnecessarily lengthy, overwritten, self-conscious and repetitious. They consist of lengthy sentences and involved sentence construction. They are poorly structured and poorly designed. They suffer from elaborate and often unnecessary cross-referencing. They use confusing tautologies . . . They retain archaic phrases . . . They use supposedly technical terms and foreign words and phrases. They are unintelligible to the ordinary reader and barely intelligible to many lawyers. (*Legal Language*, para 17.)

The kind of legal writing being described presents a barrier to effective communication. The advantage of plain English is that it readily conveys its message to its audience. It saves time and effort. Research has shown that lawyers confronted by a piece of legislation drafted in two ways, first in old-fashioned legalese, and second in plain English, will find the answer to a given question significantly faster in the plain English version. Non-lawyers will often fail to find the answer at all in the legalese version, or will get it wrong.

18.4   What does legalese look like?

Legalese is never too hard to spot. Here are some of the worst examples. They are included to illustrate just how hard it can be to get away from legalese. If you try to think how you could rewrite them you will see how difficult a task that might be unless you started completely from scratch.

18.4.1   First example—a statute

This is s 2 of the Slave Trade Act 1824 (still in force):

. . . It shall not be lawful . . . for any persons to deal or trade in, purchase, sell, barter, or transfer, or to contract for the dealing or trading in, purchase, sale, barter, or transfer of slaves, or persons intended to be dealt with as slaves; or to carry away, or remove, or to contract for the carrying away or removing of slaves or other persons, as or in order to their being dealt with as slaves; or to import or bring, or to contract for the importing or bringing into any place whatsoever slaves or other persons, as or in order to their being dealt with as slaves; or to ship, tranship, embark, receive, detain, or confine on board, or to contract for the shipping, transhipping, embarking, receiving, detaining, or confining on board of any ship, vessel, or boat, slaves or other persons, for the purpose of their being carried away or removed, as or in order to their being dealt with as slaves, or to ship, tranship, embark, receive, detain, or confine on board, or to contract for the shipping, transhipping, embarking, receiving, detaining, or confining on board of any ship, vessel, or boat, slaves or other persons, for the purpose of their being imported or brought into any place whatsoever as or in order to their being dealt with as slaves; or to fit out, man, navigate, equip, despatch, use, employ, let, or take to freight or on hire, or to contract for the fitting out, manning, navigating, equipping, despatching, using, employing, letting, or taking to freight or on hire, any ship, vessel, or boat, in order to accomplish any of the objects, or the contracts in relation to the objects, which objects and contracts have herein-before been declared unlawful; or to lend or advance, or become security for the loan or advance, or to contract for the lending or advancing, or becoming security for the loan or advance of money, goods, or effects employed or to be employed in accomplishing any of the objects, or the contracts in relation to the objects, which objects and contracts have herein-before been declared unlawful; or to become guarantee or security, or to contract for the becoming guarantee or security, for agents employed or to be employed in accomplishing any of the objects, or the contracts in relation to the objects, which objects and contracts have herein-before been declared unlawful; or in any other manner to engage or to contract to engage directly or indirectly therein as a partner, agent, or otherwise; or to ship, tranship, lade, receive, or put on board, or to contract, for the shipping, transhipping, lading, receiving, or putting on board of any ship, vessel, or boat, money, goods, or effects to be employed in accomplishing any of the objects, or the contracts in relation to the objects, which objects and contracts have herein-before been declared unlawful; or to take the charge or command, or to navigate or enter and embark on board, or to contract for the taking the charge or command, or for the navigating or entering and embarking on board of any ship, vessel, or boat, as captain, master, mate, petty officer, surgeon, supercargo, seaman, marine, or servant, or in any other capacity, knowing that such ship, vessel, or boat is actually employed, or is in the same voyage, or upon the same occasion, in respect of which they shall so take the charge or command, or navigate or enter and embark, or contract so to do as aforesaid, intended to be employed in accomplishing any of the objects, or the contracts in relation to the objects, which objects and contracts have herein-before been declared unlawful; or to insure or to contract for the insuring of any slaves, or any property, or other subject matter, engaged or employed or intended to be engaged or employed in accomplishing any of the objects, or the contracts in relation to the objects, which objects and contracts have herein-before been declared unlawful.

This is perhaps a slightly unfair example: no modern statute would have a single section as long as this. The very length of it is daunting. It consists of a single sentence of 668 words. These days you would want to take a completely different approach, breaking it down into a considerable number of subsections and using definitions to get away from the long lists of verbs and nouns.

18.4.2 Second example—a lease

The following subclause was in a lease which was the subject of the action in *Inglewood Investment Co Ltd v Forestry Commission* [1989] 1 All ER 1:

> Subject to the provisions of the Ground Game Act 1880 the Ground Game (Amendment) Act 1906 and the Forestry Act 1919 all game woodcocks snipe and other wild fowl hares rabbits and fish with the exclusive right (but subject as aforesaid) for the Appointers and all persons authorised by them at all times of preserving the same (except rabbits) and of hunting shooting fishing coursing and sporting over and on the appointed hereditaments and premises *Provided always* that as regards rabbits the Commission shall have an equal right with the Appointers to kill the same and the Appointers shall not keep or permit to be kept any rabbit warren in or in the immediate vicinity of the appointed lands.

Can you understand it? What does it mean? It consists of over 100 words. It was one of a list of reservations in a schedule, which is why there is no main verb. The plaintiffs (the successors in title to the appointers) were contending that under this clause they had exclusive rights to shoot deer on the land. The court held however that they did not, because 'game' meant only those animals listed, and 'preserving...hunting shooting fishing coursing and sporting' also covered only the game listed.

The difficulty is that the clause is trying to say too many things all at once. If rewriting it, you would try to say one thing at a time, breaking it down into several sentences; maybe also into several subclauses. It is unlikely that a rewrite would be any shorter than the original. In situations like this the plain English version, though clearer, is often longer.

18.4.3 Third example—a contract term

Here is a term from a real contract drafted in recent years by a junior lawyer at a very well-known firm of solicitors.

> To indemnify and keep safe and harmless the Transferee against any damage howsoever caused directly or indirectly by the Transferor, its servants, employees, agents or any other persons authorised by it to the Railway or structure crash barriers or other protective barriers all measures against any damage by breach of any of the terms of this Transfer or otherwise and in case such damage is caused to the Transferee, its servants agents, visitors or invitees to make good the same upon an indemnity basis to the Transferee and to take all reasonable steps from the date hereof to keep safe and harmless the Railway, and structure from time to time.

It is almost incomprehensible isn't it? And it is not even grammatical. How on earth did this clause ever come to be drafted as it was? The answer is almost certainly that it was first drafted a very long time ago, maybe even a century or more. It has been lifted and amended into many different contracts since then, the drafter always reckoning that it is quicker and easier to borrow an established clause from another contract than it is to draft something new from scratch. After a few amendments, it falls into the hands of someone who doesn't actually understand it properly, and cannot grasp its grammatical structure, but who tries to amend it anyway. So it ends up looking as it appears above.

It's unlikely that anyone could redraft this in plain English until they understand what it is actually trying to say. You would need further instructions.

18.4.4 Fourth example—a court order

Before *Practice Direction* [1994] 1 WLR 1233; [1994] 4 All ER 52, a freezing injunction might have looked a bit like this:

> UPON hearing Counsel for the Plaintiffs ex parte AND UPON reading the affidavit of MILES KING, sworn herein on 11th June 1994 AND UPON the Plaintiffs by their Counsel undertaking:
>
> (1) To abide by any order this Court may make as to damages, in case this Court shall be hereafter of opinion that the Defendant should have sustained any loss and damage by reason of this order for which the Plaintiffs ought to pay.
>
> (2) To indemnify any person (other than the Defendant, his servants or agents) to whom notice of this Order is given against any costs, expenses, fees or liabilities reasonably incurred by him in seeking to comply with this Order.
>
> (3) To serve upon the Defendant as soon as practicably possible the Writ in this action, this Order and the affidavits specified above.
>
> (4) To notify the Defendant as soon as practically possible of the terms of this Order.
>
> (5) To notify and inform any third parties affected by this Order of their right to apply to this Court for this Order to be varied or discharged insofar as this Order affects the said third parties.
>
> IT IS ORDERED THAT:
>
> (1) The Defendant, whether by himself, his servants or agents or otherwise, be restrained until trial or further order from removing any of his assets out of the jurisdiction, or disposing of or charging or otherwise dealing with any of his assets within the jurisdiction so as to deplete the same below £44,809.
>
> (2) Without prejudice to the foregoing, the defendant be restrained until further order from drawing from, charging or otherwise dealing with the account standing in his name at the Threadneedle Street branch of Barclays Bank at Threadneedle Street, London EC4, except to the extent that any credit balance on it exceeds £44,809.

(3) Provided nothing in this Order shall prevent the Defendant from expending:

    (i)   up to £300 per week on living expenses;

    (ii)   reasonable sums in respect of the legal expenses of this action;

    (iii) such sums as shall have been previously approved in writing by the Plaintiffs.

(4) Liberty to apply on 24 hours' notice to the other party.

(5) Costs reserved.

Would an ordinary lay person have much chance of understanding this? Would he or she know what was the effect of not complying with the order? Or what steps now needed to be taken? Probably not, without the help of a solicitor. Look now at the Annex to PD 25A under the Civil Procedure Rules 1998, which sets out the current standard form for a freezing injunction.

You will notice that the meaning and effect of the order is set out in plain English, such that a lay person who takes the trouble to read it would understand his or her position. But, not surprisingly, this takes much longer than the old-fashioned order.

18.4.5   A final example—a letter

The following letter is taken from *Yes, Prime Minister* by Jonathan Lynn and Antony Jay:

Dear Prime Minister,   *Cabinet Office*

I must express in the strongest possible terms my profound opposition to the newly instituted practice which imposes severe and intolerable restrictions on the ingress and egress of senior members of the hierarchy and will, in all probability, should the current deplorable innovation be perpetuated, precipitate a progressive constriction of the channels of communication, culminating in a condition of organisational atrophy and administrative paralysis which will render effectively impossible the coherent and coordinated discharge of the functions of government within Her Majesty's United Kingdom of Great Britain and Northern Ireland.

Your obedient and humble servant, Humphrey Appleby

Reproduced with kind permission of BBC Enterprises Ltd, London.

This is of course a fictional spoof, and has been included mainly for fun, but it contains the style of language we are trying to avoid. The situation behind the letter is that the Prime Minister has locked a door which was previously unlocked and which allowed Humphrey Appleby immediate access from his offices to the Prime Minister's. Try re-writing the letter in plain English. 'Please unlock the door' is tempting, and it is plain English; but it will not do, because it gives no reasons for the demand and because it does not have the tone of a formal protest which is what the writer clearly intends. It is not particularly difficult to do, but you will probably lose the flavour of the original. This is because the original, for all its pomposity, is actually very fluently and elegantly written, and full of character.

18.5   Why do lawyers write legalese?

18.5.1   Why did legalese originate?

There can be no clear answer to this question—it has been around for centuries. It is arguable that to some extent it was created by lawyers showing off their drafting skills: they were writing for each other rather than for the benefit of clients or ordinary citizens.

It has even been suggested that sometimes lawyers wrote legalese precisely to ensure that clients and lay people *couldn't* understand it. Then they would always need a lawyer's help to understand, apply, or enforce their rights and obligations. It might be justified on the ground that clients would respect lawyers more if they wrote legalese, because it made them look more professional. Believe it or not, this attitude still persists in some quarters today. Lawyers who resist plain English have been known to argue that clients trust them more when they write legalese.

However, on a more positive note, legalese could be justified on the ground that it possesses three qualities much prized by lawyers and clients: it is very precise, it is very concise, and it carries the tone of formality which is sometimes necessary in legal writing. And this may be true when it is 'good' legalese. But as we see later in this chapter it is perfectly possible to be precise and (when appropriate) formal in plain English if you take enough trouble over it; and conciseness is only a virtue if what you write does not become so dense that it is impenetrable.

And why did old legalese have so little punctuation? There is a simple explanation. Before the days of photocopiers, when a document needed to be copied, it had to be copied out by hand (or, from the late nineteenth century, by typewriter). Lawyers employed clerks to do this for them. It was only too easy for the clerk to make a small error in copying, particularly when it came to punctuation. So lawyers attempted to draft documents in such a way that they would retain their meaning regardless of how they were punctuated; and the easiest way to achieve this was to put in no punctuation at all.

18.5.2   Why is legalese still perpetuated?

Lawyers don't talk legalese in everyday life, but as soon as they start writing to each other, or to clients, they slip into it.

This is largely because of habit, convention, and immersion. It is very easy to fall into the rut of writing like this because such language is all around you, in precedents, forms, contracts, statutes, and the writing of your fellow lawyers. You pick it up without thinking about it. When you start to write something in a formal context the words just come into your head because you have heard them so often. You have stopped thinking about what you want to say and just allowed familiar words to suggest themselves to you. So you are really using other people's words, not your own.

And your bad habits may be reinforced by tutors, pupil masters, or employers, who expect to see legalese rather than plain English, because they too have become immersed in it. You will be praised for writing like that, and any attempt to write plain English will lead to your drafts being 'corrected' into legalese.

As a result, the worse you write, the more like a lawyer you will start to feel. You will not notice that you have become more formal, less clear, even pompous in your writing. So if this has happened to you, you need to do something about it. It is hoped that the rest of this chapter will inspire you to do so and show you how.

18.6   What is being done to promote plain English?

The legal establishment, in particular the judges and the parliamentary counsel, are becoming increasingly aware of the need to write in plain English and to insist that others do so as well (where they have the power to enforce this). More and more court orders, standard forms, statutes, and regulations are being drafted in plain English. Reform is, however, a long process because old habits die hard, and there is resistance in some quarters.

A major revolution was brought about by the Civil Procedure Rules 1998 which came into force on 26 April 1999. These are all drafted in plain English and are specifically designed to enable a lay person to deal with a civil action in person. The ethos behind these rules has resulted in many more documents being drafted in plain English over the last decade, particularly statements of case.

But 15 years later, by the standards of 2014, even the CPR are now looking somewhat dated in their style. They would be written in even plainer English these days. And look at recently drafted statutes. One can see a difference between the style of drafting now and that of even five years ago. It is fair to say that the legal establishment is now firmly behind plain English, and lawyers are no longer the worst offenders. You will find a great many more examples of obscure incomprehensible language these days in the world of business (where it is known as 'business speak') and in universities (where it is known as 'Academish').

See also regulation 7 of the Unfair Terms in Consumer Contracts Regulations 1999:

7. *Written contracts*

   (1) A seller or supplier shall ensure that any written term of a contract is expressed in plain, intelligible language.

   (2) If there is doubt about the meaning of a written term, the interpretation which is most favourable to the consumer shall prevail . . .

This regulation has had a very significant effect on the drafting of consumer contracts.

18.7   Learning to write plain English

Is there a cure for legalese writers? Yes there is, and it's actually quite simple once you have made up your mind only ever to write plain English. It only takes a few days to put yourself on the right path.

The first step is to understand what plain English is. There is more on this in **18.8** and **18.9**.

The next step is to start examining your own writing and recognising when you have strayed from the plain English path. You can do this as you write. If you find something that is not plain and clear, ask yourself whether you wrote it because you chose to, or because it more or less wrote itself. If it contains some obscure or dense word or phrase, ask yourself where this came from.

Then you can start translating what you have written into plain English. The more you do it, the more enjoyable it will become. You will start to discover the beauty and elegance of simplicity. Don't however think that plain English is simplistic—it isn't. You will find that it is still possible to be precise and concise in plain English; it may just take a bit of wrestling to start with. The biggest danger, certainly when drafting, is to sacrifice precision for the sake of simplicity. You must take great care to avoid this. Often what looks simple is only simple because it is more general and imprecise than what you started with.

You may need to make several drafts. Most lawyers, even when they are trying to write in plain English, do not write as plainly as they could in their first draft. The more you write, the more you can see how it could be made simpler and clearer. The more you simplify and clarify your words, the more precise and clear the thought behind them becomes, which in turn leads to even plainer language. It can take longer to write good plain English than it does to write legalese, at least when you first start.

And finally, very importantly, learn to *laugh*. Don't be ashamed or defensive when you catch yourself writing legalese. In fact *we all do it*! We just need to recognise when we are doing it, and laugh at the awfulness of what we have just written. If it helps, share the joke with someone else.

18.8   Basic rules of plain English

It is not possible in this manual to cover all the rules of plain English, or all the good and bad words and phrases that exist. There are other books that go into this more fully. They are listed in **18.11**.

However, some very basic rules can be identified and they are these:

18.8.1   Your objective

Your aim in writing plain English is to write concisely and clearly so that the reader can understand easily what you are saying, as they read it. See again **18.2**.

What is plain English and the extent to which you need to write in plain English does therefore depend on who your reader is. If your reader is another lawyer then you may use legal terminology and words that draw fine distinctions because your reader will understand them and appreciate them. If your reader is a lay person it may be unwise to use legal jargon and unnecessary to draw fine distinctions: you will not help, but may cloud his or her understanding by using such words. Where you are writing for a mixed readership, as for example when you are writing an opinion, you will need to strike a balance. You want your opinion to be accessible to your lay client, while at the same time to be professional and precise for your instructing solicitor.

18.8.2   Use short sentences

Everyone has their own idea of how short a short sentence is, and what is short for lawyers may be long for journalists. We suggest you regard a sentence of 25 words and under as short. Try to write for the most part in short sentences. You can usually achieve this if you do not try to express more than a single thought in each sentence. But do not go out of your way to avoid longer sentences when they are appropriate. Good and elegant writing usually requires that sentences should vary in length rather than all have about the same number of words. Variety maintains the reader's interest.

18.8.3   Use correct grammar and punctuation

Although it may sometimes be more concise, or more like everyday speech, to use bad grammar, in written English grammatical errors can only mean a lack of clarity. For most people correct grammar is instinctive, and mistakes only occur when we do not conceive a sentence as a whole. Always read through whole sentences, trying to phrase them as you would if speaking them aloud, and any grammatical errors will probably leap out at you.

Punctuation is also important. It is essential to plain English that you should take care over punctuation, since it is part of the structure and clarity of your sentences. You can often spot the need for punctuation marks, or the need to remove them, if you speak or think your sentence through aloud.

18.8.4 Use everyday English

We have already seen that there is a place for legal terminology and a time to avoid it. Jargon, and other technical terms, should be dispensed with wherever possible. There are many occasions when there are perfectly clear and straightforward alternatives to jargon words. Only occasionally is the technical term the only suitable word.

Legalese at its worst goes beyond simply using legal terminology and uses totally obscure or archaic words and phrases that nobody uses in everyday English. There really can be no excuse for these in ordinary writing.

It is also important to resist all the other absurd jargons that creep into written and spoken English from time to time, and are known variously as 'computerspeak', 'Haigspeak', 'Socialese', etc. Such language only makes what you are writing sound obscure and pompous. A student once complained in a letter that there was 'a comprehension dissonance' between his tutor and himself. He wanted to know why his written work had been marked down for lack of clarity!

18.8.5 Use simple structures

Avoid putting an idea in a complicated or roundabout way when it can be put in a simpler one. Almost everything you write at a first attempt can in fact be put more simply and in fewer words. Avoid in particular compound structures which use three or four words to express a single concept, double negatives, and the passive rather than the active voice.

Of course this cannot be an absolute rule. The compound structure or the double negative may occasionally carry a shade of meaning or precision which the alternative does not. The passive voice may give the sentence the correct subject. For example, 'The defendant was sued by the claimant' tells the reader that you are writing about the defendant. The alternative 'The claimant sued the defendant' introduces a sentence about the claimant.

Avoid word-wasting idioms and phrases like 'In the light of the fact that' (since), 'In the event that' (if), or 'In the region of' (about). Also make sure you get rid of redundant words, as in 'null and void', 'totally and utterly'.

Avoid nouns standing in for verbs, for example 'the lorry was in collision with the car', when one could simply say 'the lorry collided with the car'.

18.8.6 Use the first and second person

Wherever appropriate it is always clearer to talk in terms of 'I' and 'You' rather than in the third person or in a wholly impersonal way. There are certain formalities in opinion writing and drafting that must be observed and do not allow for the use of 'I' and 'You', but these apart, never be impersonal when you can be personal. It is clearer, shorter, and more honest.

18.8.7 Arrange words with care

A great deal of poor English can be improved simply by changing the arrangement of words and phrases. If you put clauses in a better order, the meaning of a sentence often becomes much clearer. If you reduce the gap between a subject and the verb or the verb and its object you can often make a sentence much easier to understand. Always try to arrange your material so that the reader is assisted through it, and it is easy to absorb. If the reader ever has to stop, go back and reread, then you have not written plain English.

18.8.8   Use a good layout

Although sometimes what a lawyer writes will be in conventional paragraphs, on most occasions a barrister writes in numbered paragraphs, clauses, and subclauses. If these are well marked, they will be easier to read. If a contract term consists of 200 words for example, it will be more easily understood if broken up and subdivided than if it appears as a solid block of text. Even conventional paragraphs are often easier to read if they are numbered and subtitled; and it goes without saying that several shorter paragraphs are usually easier to read than a few very long ones.

18.8.9   When you are stuck

When you know you are writing a bad sentence or paragraph, but can't find a way to put it into clear English, try this:

- Look up from your desk.
- Imagine the person you are writing to.
- Speak to that imaginary person as if on the phone, or face to face.
- Then write it the way you spoke it.

This simple technique usually works very well.

18.9   Bad words and phrases

Table 18.1 shows some examples of the sort of bad words and phrases that legalese writers use, and their plain English equivalents:

Table 18.1   **Bad words and phrases and plain English equivalents**

Legalese	Plain English
'[The] above'	'This'
'Accordingly'	'So'
	'Therefore'
'Advise' e.g.:	To advise is to give advice, not information.
'Please advise me'	'Please tell me'
	'Please let me know'
'Please be advised that'	Redundant— delete
'And/or'	This phrase does have its uses, but sometimes you should simply choose 'and' or 'or'.
'Be of assistance'	'Help'
'By reason of'	'Because of'
'Confirm' e.g.:	To confirm means to reinforce something already stated, or to make express what was only implicit. If what follows is something new, do not use this word.
'I confirm that'	Delete.
'Please confirm'	'Please let me know'; 'Please tell me'.
'Please confirm receipt'	'Please acknowledge receipt'

'Documentation'	'Documents'
	'Documentation' is an abstract noun referring to the creation, accumulation, collation or provision of documents.
'Forthcoming'	'Next'
'For the reason that'	'Because'
'Forward'	To forward is to 'send on'. Often used where to 'send', 'enclose', or 'attach' is more plain and correct.
'Furnish me with'	'Send me'
	'Let me have'
'Further to'	'Following'
	'After'
	'With reference to'
	'Please refer to'
	'As we discussed'
	Or find another way round it.
'[A] further'	'Another'
'Had it not been for'	'But for'
'Have a willingness to'	'Be willing to'
'Have the ability to'	'Be able to'
'I am mindful that'	'I understand that'
	'I realise that'
'In consequence of'	'As a result of'
'In the absence of'	'Without'
'In the event that'	'If'
'In the light of the fact that'	'Since'
'I should be grateful if you would'	'Please'
'Make payment for'	'Pay for'
'Omitted to'	'Did not'
'On a regular basis'	'Regularly'
'Please find enclosed document A'	'I enclose document A'
	'Document A is enclosed'
'Prior to'	'Before'
'Proceed to'	Usually redundant—delete
'Provide a response'	'Reply'
'Provide me with'	'Send me'
	'Let me have'
'Pursuant to'	'Under'
	'In accordance with'
	'Duly'
'Reiterate'	'Repeat'. To 'iterate' is to repeat. To 'reiterate' is to say something for a third or subsequent time.
'Save that'	'Except that'
'Scenario'	'Situation'
'Subsequent to'	'After'
'Supply me with'	'Send me'

'Thereafter'	'Then'
	'After that time'
	Next
'Thereby'	'By that…'
'To date'	'Yet'
	'So far'
'To the effect that'	'That'
'I am in receipt of'	'I have received'
'I am of the understanding that'	'I understand that'
'Whereby'	'By which'
'Would'	Often redundant, e.g:
	'I would advise that'—'I advise that'
	'I would bring to your attention'—'Please note'
	'I would remind you that'—'May I remind you that'

18.10 Some exercises

Here are some exercises to enable you to practise translating legalese into plain English. Unlike the examples in **18.4** these are not too difficult, but illustrate certain techniques. Suggested answers and commentary are given in **18.12**.

18.10.1 Exercise 1

Rewrite the following contract clause in plain language.

> It shall be a breach of the terms of this agreement for any member to fail to post a notice in a prominent place that is in no way obscured from public view listing that member's retail prices for all items offered for sale, saving only that those items offered at a special sale price for a period not exceeding seven days need not be listed on the said notice.

18.10.2 Exercise 2

Rewrite the following by-law in plain English.

> It shall be and is hereby declared to be unlawful for any person to expel, discharge, or expectorate any mucus, spittle, saliva or other such substance from the mouth of the said person in or on or onto any public pavement, street, road or highway, or in or on or onto any railway train, bus, taxicab or other public conveyance, or in or on or onto any other public place of whatsoever kind or description, and any person who does so expel, discharge or expectorate any such substance as defined above in any place herein delineated shall be guilty of an offence.

18.10.3 Exercise 3

Rewrite the following contract term in plain English.

> In consideration of the performance by the contractor of all the covenants and conditions contained herein and contained in the plans and specifications annexed hereto, the owners agree to pay to the said contractors an amount equal to the cost of all materials furnished by the contractors, and the cost of all labour furnished by the contractors, to include the cost of tax and insurance directly connected to such labour, together with the amounts payable to subcontractors

properly employed by the said contractors in completion of their obligations herein set out. In addition to the amount hereinbefore specified, the owners agree to pay to the contractors a sum equal to 10% of the value of the construction on completion, the total amount payable to fall due only on satisfactory completion of the said construction. It is specifically agreed by the parties hereto that notwithstanding the term the owners shall not be required under the terms of this agreement to pay to the contractors an amount in excess of the sum of Five Hundred Thousand Pounds.

18.10.4 Exercise 4

Try rewriting section 286(2) of the Taxation of Chargeable Gains Act 1992 in plain English.

> A person is connected with an individual if that person is the individual's spouse or civil partner, or is a relative, or the spouse or civil partner of a relative, of the individual or of the individual's spouse or civil partner.

18.11 Further reading

Asprey, Michèle M., *Plain Language for Lawyers*, 4th edn (Federation Press, 2010).
Cutts, Martin, *Oxford Guide to Plain English*, 4th edn (Oxford University Press, 2013).
Gowers, Sir Ernest, *The Complete Plain Words*, 3rd rev edn, Sidney Greenbaum and Janet Whitcut (eds) (Penguin, 1987).
Swan, Michael, *Practical English Usage*, 3rd edn (Oxford University Press, 2005).
Trask, R. L., *Mind the Gaffe—The Penguin Guide to Common Errors in English* (Penguin Books, 2001).
Truss, Lynne, *Eats, Shoots & Leaves—The Zero Tolerance Approach to Punctuation* (Profile Books, 2003).
Wydick, Richard, *Plain English for Lawyers*, 5th edn (Carolina Academic Press, 2005).

18.12 Suggested answers to exercises in 18.10

18.12.1 Exercise 1

Points to consider:

- It is redundant to say 'it shall be a breach of the terms of this agreement'. That goes without saying if you say to someone that they must do something.
- Using 'shall' in this way is not modern English.
- You want to get rid of the double negative: to tell someone that they must not fail to do something is a convoluted way of telling them what they must do.
- 'In a prominent place that is in no way obscured from public view' can be simplified. The requirement is that the notice must be clearly visible to the public.
- The repetition 'that member's' is awkward. 'Their' will do fine.
- 'Retail prices for all items offered for sale' says more than it needs to. Items that are not offered for sale don't have a retail price attached, so just 'retail prices' will do.

- 'Saving only' is archaic language. Modern English would use 'except'.
- 'A special price' does the same job as 'A special sale price'.
- 'A period not exceeding' is a cumbersome way of saying 'no more than'.
- 'The said notice'—the word 'said' is archaic and quite unnecessary.

So your translation might look like this:

> Every member must display to the public a clearly visible notice listing all their retail prices, except for those items offered at a special price for no more than seven days.

18.12.2 Exercise 2

Points to consider:

- It is fairly obvious that this by-law is intended to prohibit spitting in public. But the word 'spitting' does not appear. This is odd and unhelpful. The word should be used, even if it needs to be defined.
- It may be tempting just to reduce this to 'No spitting', but that won't do. It would be sufficient if this was just a notice asking people not to spit, but it is a law which creates a criminal offence, so greater certainty is required.
- A single sentence is far too long. It needs to be broken down into several sentences, probably several clauses.
- It is unnecessary to say both that spitting is unlawful and that someone who spits is guilty of an offence. If you create the offence, the unlawfulness can be taken for granted. Anyway 'shall be and is hereby declared to be' is plainly repetitive and the words 'shall' and 'hereby' need to go.
- Do you need all three of 'expel, discharge or expectorate'? No. 'Discharge' would cover the other two.
- Do you need all three of 'mucus, spittle or saliva'? You can't make the translation narrower than the original, so you do need mucus and one of spittle or saliva, though not both. Do you need 'or other such substance'? Arguably not, as it is difficult to think of any other substance of the same kind as mucus or saliva, but it may be safer to keep it just in case the original drafter is thinking of a substance you haven't thought of.
- Could you simply get rid of 'mucus, spittle, saliva or other such substance' altogether and replace it with 'any substance'? No. That would make the revised version much broader than the original. It would forbid a person even to exhale breath!
- Do you need 'from the mouth of the said person'? You can get rid of 'of the said person', but not 'from the mouth'. As it stands it is not an offence to sneeze; but removing 'from the mouth' would make it so.
- Where must a person not spit? In essence, in any public place (you can certainly get rid of 'of whatsoever kind or description'). Does 'public place' need to be defined so as to include all the examples given? Arguably not, except possibly so as to include public conveyances, which might otherwise be held not to be 'places'. So include them to avoid doubt; but 'conveyance' is a rather old-fashioned word. Is there a better alternative?
- Do you need 'in or on or onto' a public place? Probably yes. Spitting 'onto' a public place would include someone spitting out of their window onto the street. This is clearly an offence under the original, and must remain so in your redraft. What

about 'on'? You might get away without that, but just one possibility occurs: if someone spits on the top deck of an open-top bus are they in the bus or only on it? Again, for safety's sake, it's probably best to retain 'on'.

- The best approach to drafting a plain version of this by-law is to start with the basic proposition, and make it an offence to spit in public; then go on to define spitting, and what constitutes a public place.

So your translation might look like this:

(1) A person who spits in a public place is guilty of an offence.
(2) A person spits if they discharge any mucus, saliva, or other such substance from their mouth.
(3) A person spits in a public place if they spit in, on, or onto such a place.
(4) A public place includes any public vehicle.

18.12.3 Exercise 3

Points to consider:

- The key to this one is structure. Although you have an excessively long block of text, there are really only four elements to it: (a) what the payment is in consideration for; (b) what the owners agree to do (pay the contractor); (c) when they must pay; and (d) much the longest part, how the sum to be paid is to be calculated.

- With a little simplification, especially of what the payment is in consideration for, the first three elements can be incorporated into a longish, but still fairly straightforward sentence. You can then break down the various sums to be paid into a list. This will make it possible to get rid of the constantly repeated 'together with'.

- The last sentence is a proviso that can actually be covered in only a few extra words, without repetition, if you put it in the right place.

- It should by now go without saying that you will remove all the archaic words: 'said', 'herein', 'hereto', 'furnished', 'hereinbefore', 'notwisthstanding'.

So your translation might look like this:

In consideration of the performance by the contractors of all their obligations under this contract, the owners agree to pay to the contractors, when the construction has been completed satisfactorily, the following amounts, up to a maximum sum of £500,000:

(a) 10% of the value of the construction upon completion; and
(b) the following expenses incurred by the contractors in the performance of their obligations under the contract:

(i)   the cost of all materials supplied by them;
(ii) the cost of all labour supplied by them;
(iii) the cost of tax and insurance directly connected to that labour;
(iv) the amounts payable to subcontractors properly employed by them.

18.12.4 Exercise 4

Points to consider:

This section (which is still in force) is a wonderful example of a piece of legalese so dense that it takes long and careful study to unravel its meaning. No one in the world will grasp it on one reading. So your aim must be to open it out and make it more immediately accessible to a reader.

The term 'relative' is defined elsewhere in the Act and it includes a large number of possible relationships. If you include all the possible relationships that could make a person connected with an individual, you will end up with getting on for a hundred. So listing all the possible relationships might seem a good idea at first but it won't help. You need to stick with 'spouse or civil partner' and 'relative'.

If you just treat 'spouse or civil partner' and 'relative' as single concepts, you can work out that there are five ways a person can be connected with an individual. If you just list them, you are well on your way to achieving a plain English version.

Another useful technique is to label person as 'P' and individual as 'I'. This shortens the draft and actually makes it easier to read.

So your translation might look like this:

A person (P) is connected with an individual (I) if:

(a) P is I's spouse or civil partner,
(b) P is a relative of I,
(c) P is a relative of I's spouse or civil partner,
(d) P is the spouse or civil partner of a relative of I, or
(e) P is the spouse or civil partner of a relative of I's spouse or civil partner.

Or even (longer but arguably clearer):

(d) I has a relative and P is that relative's spouse or civil partner, or
(e) I's spouse or civil partner has a relative and P is that relative's spouse or civil partner.

Opinion writing

19.1 Why learn to write opinions?

Opinion writing is something that all barristers do. It is a common misconception that a barrister's work consists solely of appearances in court, advocacy, or advising clients orally, in a face-to-face situation. In fact a considerable part of most barristers' work, for some the most part, is done in chambers and in writing.

Barristers usually think of their work as falling into two categories: court work and chambers work. For court work, they are using their interpersonal and expressive skills: their skill at advocacy, their communication skills, their ability to think and speak at the same time, their skill at questioning, and occasionally their negotiating skills. For chambers work they are using their writing and thinking skills: their ability to manage factual information, to carry out legal research, to draft, to advise. Before the introduction of the Bar Vocational Course, surprisingly few barristers used to identify opinion writing as a skill in itself.

But they were wrong not to do so. In reality neither a barrister's work nor a barrister's skills can be divided so neatly into those two categories. Giving advice to a client in conference, that is, in a face-to-face situation, may happen either at court or in chambers. A negotiation may be conducted anywhere, even by telephone. A barrister is just as likely to have to write an opinion on a train returning from court or at the kitchen table as at his or her desk. Communication skills form an important part of opinion writing; thinking skills, fact management skills, even drafting skills are an important part of advocacy. In learning opinion writing, you are actually learning skills, aptitudes, and a way of thinking that prepare you for all aspects of a barrister's work.

19.2 What is opinion writing?

19.2.1 Paperwork

As well as (rather mistakenly) dividing his or her work into court work or chambers work, a barrister will usually identify (more accurately) a specific category of chambers work: 'paperwork'. All barristers have paperwork to do. Some have more of it than others, depending on the nature of their practice, but none will ever get away from it entirely. 'Paperwork' is a relatively self-contained aspect of a barrister's work; it consists of two things: opinion writing and drafting.

19.2.2   Instructions

Paperwork arises in response to a written set of instructions. 'Instructions' come from solicitors, called your instructing solicitors, and look like a brief, tied up with red ribbon, but rather than containing instructions to appear before some tribunal (a brief) they contain instructions to advise in writing, draft documents, or both. If you are instructed to draft a statement of case, or other documents, you do so. If you are asked to advise in writing, what you write and send back is called an 'opinion'. An opinion is therefore your written response to instructions to advise.

These instructions are likely to be your first contact with the case or dispute. The instructing solicitors have sent the papers to you because the time has arisen when they can no longer advise the client or handle the client's case without reference to counsel. It may be that they want a second opinion; it may be that the case is in an area in which you can give specialist advice; it may be that the case is bound to result in court proceedings and they consider it best therefore to bring in counsel at the earliest possible moment; it may be that a statement of case needs to be drafted: it does not make sense to ask you to draft without also advising; it may be that a favourable counsel's opinion is required in order for the client to be granted public funding. However, there are many other situations, and later stages, at which counsel's opinion may be sought.

19.2.3   Contents of instructions

Included in the instructions will be (a) a document from your instructing solicitor, setting out what you are asked to do, the background to the case, possibly a description and analysis of the issues, maybe even the solicitor's own answer to the problem; (b) all other relevant documents, plans, photographs, etc. These are likely to include copies of any claim form which has been issued, statements of case which have been served, documents which have been drafted; copies of any contract, conveyance, lease, will, or other instrument out of which the dispute arises; copies of all correspondence which has passed between the parties and their solicitors and/or insurers; statements of any witnesses, including your client(s) or representatives of your client company; expert reports, medical reports, etc.

The instructions, when analysed, consist broadly of a question, or, more likely, a series of questions. These questions are asked by your instructing solicitor, on behalf of the client. Your opinion is your answer to these questions. An answer must always tell the questioner what he wants to know (not necessarily what he wants to hear!). Since your questioner is the solicitor, the answer is basically addressed to him or her. But since the solicitor is only asking the questions so as to be able to advise the client, the answer must also concern the client specifically and the advice given must be advice to the client, not just to your instructing solicitor.

Probably the most common questions asked in instructions are: 'Does the client have a good case? If so what remedies are available? How much would be recovered in damages?' or 'Is there a good defence to this action? If not, how can liability be minimised? How much is the client likely to have to pay in damages?' Your opinion answers these questions, gives advice, and is returned to your instructing solicitors with the instructions.

19.2.4   Advisory character of opinions

Once again: an opinion is your response to instructions to *advise*. It follows that it must contain advice. In learning to write opinions, you are more than anything else learning to *advise*. Advising is not just an activity, something you do. You do not advise someone simply by telling them what to do. You do not advise someone by writing a lengthy essay and putting 'That is my advice' at the end of it. Nor is it just a way of saying things: you do not give advice simply by starting every third sentence with the words 'I advise that'. Advising is inextricably linked to the mental attitude with which you approach opinion writing, the thinking process that precedes the actual writing of the opinion, and the writing process itself. We need therefore to look at these three aspects of opinion writing: the mental attitude, the thinking process, and the writing process.

19.3 The right mental attitude: the practical approach

The mental attitude required to write a good opinion, or give good advice, is that of a practitioner as opposed to an academic. The approach required is a practical as opposed to an academic approach. Practical rather than academic thought is needed.

19.3.1 Abandoning an academic attitude

Whatever course in law you followed at the academic stage, and however practical it appeared to be, it is inevitable that your approach has been largely academic so far. This is because at the end of the course you were going to be examined not on what you did, but on what you knew. Practitioners are not much concerned with what they know, but with what they do. So long as your concern has been knowledge of the law, seeking to understand the law, considering what the law is or should be, rather than solving problems, advising people, deciding what to do next, your approach has been fundamentally academic.

The most academic academics tend to have a theoretical approach to the law, studying it for its own sake. If confronted with a legal problem they will regard the research and the analysis of the law as an end in itself and may even regard the reaching of conclusions or the answering of the problem as something of an irrelevance. To the academic, the problem is more important than its answer.

The practitioner abhors a problem with no answer. He or she will always seek to reach a conclusion, to provide the best possible answer to the problem. The practitioner will regard the law as relevant only insofar as it helps to find an answer. His or her mind will be focused on the client rather than the law. However academic or practical your approach has been hitherto, it must now become more practical.

None of this has actually defined the right mental attitude or the practical approach. Even if a definition is possible, it is probably not desirable. The practical approach is something to be developed and acquired, and defining it does not necessarily help. But it is possible to give some guidance on how you can develop the right mental attitude. Here are four fundamental principles to remember at all times:

- You are dealing with a real situation.
- The facts are more fundamental than the law.
- The law is a means to an end.
- Answer the question.

19.3.2 You are dealing with a real situation

It goes without saying that every case in practice involves a real situation. You must deal with every case in training as if it were a real situation too, even though it may not be easy: some of the problems can be slightly artificial, deliberately simplified; events may seem somewhat contrived. But you should treat the case as real.

In a real situation there is a real client with a real problem who wants your advice. Imagine, if it helps, that a client, Mr Smith, is sitting opposite you. What would you say to him? How could you help him? This focuses the mind on what Mr Smith actually wants, or the reason he is seeking your advice.

Mr Smith has not come to see you so that you can show off your knowledge. He has a problem and wants help in finding the right answer. He does not specifically want to know what the law says, but rather how he stands in relation to the law. He wants to know what his legal position is and what he ought to do about it. That's the problem. It's *his* problem. And it's a real problem.

But where does the reality of the problem lie? It does not lie in the questions of law that the problem raises, or even in the questions of fact which you will have to answer. It lies in the facts themselves. It is not because of the law that the problem exists, but because of the facts. The facts are the reality. So the second principle is:

19.3.3   The facts are more fundamental than the law

Because they come first. It follows that in dealing with a case, in advising a client, in writing an opinion, your starting point will always be the facts. This may seem obvious and you may protest that you have always taken the facts as your starting point. But have you?

During the academic stage, when confronted with a problem, what thoughts first ran through your mind? Quite possibly, thoughts like 'Is this a tort case or a contract case?' or 'What's the point of law in this case?'—legal questions, rather than factual questions.

The first thoughts that run through a practitioner's mind in reading instructions are questions like 'What's happened?', 'What's the situation?', 'What's the problem?', 'What does my client want?', 'What should be done?', and 'What advice can I give?' Such questions address the facts, not the law. The facts are fundamental because they give rise to the problem and to any questions of law that may be answered in order to achieve a solution to the problem.

So if the facts are more important than the law, where does the law fit in? The answer lies in the third principle:

19.3.4   The law is a means to an end

And frequently a very important means, but not an end in itself. The law is what you consult, and use where appropriate, to help you produce a solution to the problem. The law provides a framework which enables you to shed light on the facts, organise the facts, analyse the facts, and interpret the facts, and within which you are able to form an opinion on the facts and answer questions of fact.

The golden rule is: use the law to help you form an opinion on the facts, not the facts as an excuse to form an opinion on the law. This becomes clear when you look at what your client is actually asking. For example, the claimant company in *Photo Production Ltd v Securicor Transport Ltd* [1980] AC 827 would not have asked its legal advisers, and did not want to know the answer to, the question 'In what circumstances can a party in fundamental breach of contract rely on an exclusion clause?' The question it would have asked, and wanted an answer to, was 'Can Securicor, in the events which have happened, rely on this exclusion clause?' or even, quite simply, 'Is Securicor liable to pay this company the cost of rebuilding its factory?' So an answer expressed in the form of, 'In my opinion the decision of the House of Lords in *Suisse Atlantique* was correct' is quite meaningless. What your client wants is an answer expressed in the form: 'In my opinion Securicor can rely on its exclusion clause and the claimant will fail to recover damages'. In other words, since the question arises out of the facts of the case and not the law, the answer must address the facts and not just the law.

The lawyer who, when consulted by a client, investigates the law and answers only the questions of law, is like a doctor who, when consulted by a patient, investigates the symptoms, informs her what she is suffering from, and packs her off without prescribing treatment. The law must also be used to help your client attain his or her objectives. This leads into the fourth principle:

19.3.5   Answer the question

Your instructions are a series of questions, all of which need to be identified and answered. Not only must you answer all the questions, you must answer the actual questions asked and not those which have not been asked, as illustrated earlier. You will not tend to answer the right questions if your mental attitude is wrong, and if you don't answer the right questions you will not be advising your client properly.

This is not as easy or as obvious as it sounds. It is very rare that you will be able to say yes or no, win or lose. But what the practitioner cannot do is say, 'I can give no answer'. There may be no *definite* answer, but there *must* always be *an* answer. Just how you do this is described later in the chapter (see **19.4.6** and **19.7.1**). But as far as the mental attitude goes, the essential principle is that you should always be seeking to answer every question as clearly and as completely as you can, and this means not only questions where the answer is clear, but also those where it is unclear; not only questions of law, but questions of fact as well. Dealing with questions of fact is likely to be something you have not yet been asked to do, or have avoided doing, at the academic stage. A barrister, in writing an opinion, has to deal with questions of fact. All of them. As clearly and completely as it is possible to do. There may be no definite answer to them, but they must still be dealt with.

19.4   The thinking process: preparing to write an opinion

If you can appreciate and adopt the four principles of the practical approach, then you will be in the right frame of mind, an advising frame of mind, to start the first stage of writing an opinion, which is the thinking process.

The thinking process can be divided into seven stages, but you should note that these seven stages are not separate such that stage 2 only begins when stage 1 is complete, and so on. Rather they overlap, and your thoughts will be going on to later stages even while you are completing the early stages. They are set out here in the logical order in which they first come in to your thinking process. The first step, obviously, is:

19.4.1   Stage 1: read and digest your instructions

Surprisingly, this does not necessarily mean, at this stage, reading every word of them. In practice they could be hundreds of pages thick, and it will not be productive to plough through them page by page only to discover that half of them are irrelevant. What you are trying to do in reading your instructions is to find out exactly what your instructions are, what is required of you, what the case is about, what are the basic facts, and what your client actually wants to know.

In fact you will find that your instructions frequently set out quite expressly what you are asked to do. In reading your instructions, you will begin with that, but will start gathering the facts from whatever documents seem appropriate, referring back and forth through your instructions all the time. You will frequently find, for example, that if there are statements of case enclosed, that is the best place to start, because they will encapsulate the story; then you may find that your client's witness statement is the best thing to read next, followed by your solicitor's comments on it, but always referring to items of correspondence whenever they are mentioned. There is no best rule: you will quickly develop skill at assimilating your instructions fast. While you are doing this, you will in fact also have started stages 2 and 3: you are likely to discover the answer to the primary question fairly early on, and you will be absorbing and organising the facts even as you read. Stage 2 is:

19.4.2 Stage 2: answer the primary question: what does my client actually want to know?

This is very important. You must have a clear idea of what your client wants to know if you are to address your mind to the right issues and give proper advice. Your objective is, after all, to tell your client what he or she wants to know.

As we have seen, your client does not really want to know the law. He or she does not even primarily want to know the answer to questions like 'Has there been a breach of contract?' or 'Was the driver of the other car negligent?', though these are questions you will certainly have to address your mind to and give an answer to. Your client, at the end of the day, is interested in the *result* as it affects him or her and examples of questions he or she is seeking an answer to in reality are shown in **Table 19.1**.

Table 19.1 **Your client's questions in reality**

Not	*But*
Will the claimant establish liability?	Will I have to pay damages to the claimant? If so, how much?
Will my claim under the Fatal Accidents Act succeed?	Can I get compensation for the death of my husband? Will it be enough to maintain my standard of living?
Is the restraint of trade clause valid?	Can I take my new job or can't I?
Is the gift in clause 3 of the will valid?	How much do I give to Mary and how much to John?

Until you have accurately identified what your client wants to know, you have no basis on which you can tackle stage 3, which is:

19.4.3 Stage 3: absorb and organise the facts

This is a process of fact management, a skill which is central to any lawyer's work and which you must acquire. It requires a clear, logical, and incisive mind.

The facts must be absorbed: everything that is important or relevant in the case must be at your fingertips. You must make sure you have a comprehensive grasp and understanding of all the material facts. This cannot be done simply by absorbing or memorising facts: they must also be organised or marshalled. There are many different ways of doing this: note making, schedules, time plans, charts, diagrams, etc. are all useful, both on paper and in your head.

As you organise the facts, you will discover that a great many facts included in your instructions—a lot of the information provided—will in the end turn out not to be relevant to the questions you have to answer or to the issues in the case. Such irrelevant material can be discarded from your thoughts. There will also, inevitably, be gaps in your instructions, facts that are not included, information or documents not provided. You will need to identify these and formulate the right questions to ask to elicit precisely the further information you require.

Your instructing solicitor may well have expressed a view on what are the material facts. That view may well have affected his or her decision as to what information to provide. Your instructing solicitor may also have identified the issues which he or she thought were important in the case. If this has been done well, you will find your solicitor's work very helpful when you are organising the facts and identifying the issues for yourself. But do not regard your instructing solicitor's view as definitive. You may well take a different view of the case, and regard different facts and issues as important. You may even see different issues arising altogether. It is important to keep an open mind and not to assume that you have to agree with your instructing solicitor's view of the case.

The process of organising the facts must inevitably be coloured by, and therefore takes place to a considerable extent in parallel with, the next stage, which is:

19.4.4 Stage 4: construct a legal framework

At this point the law comes into your thinking. Eventually, you are going to apply the law at two stages and for two different purposes. The one you might think of first, to help you answer the question, or even to provide the answer to the question, comes later. At this stage you apply the law to help you to organise the facts and to discover the questions which need to be answered, to identify the issues of fact and law involved in the case, and to put them into a proper order.

What you are in fact doing is constructing a framework for the case and for your opinion in the case. This framework consists of a sequence of issues, each issue basically encapsulating a single question. The issue arises, and the question needs to be posed, because, from your knowledge of the law or your research, you have identified it as an essential ingredient in the chain of questions of law and fact all of which have to be answered to determine the answer to the question your client is asking. Two examples of well-established frameworks may help to illustrate the point:

- In a personal injury action, based on negligence:
  - Did D owe C a duty of care?
  - Was D in breach of that duty (i.e. was he or she negligent)?
  - What are C's injuries and losses?
  - Were they caused by D's negligence?
  - Was C contributorily negligent?
  - Was the damage reasonably foreseeable?
  - Did C mitigate?
  - What is the quantum of damage?
- In a claim for damages for breach of contract:
  - Was there a contract?
  - What were its terms?
  - Has D acted in breach of the contract?

- What loss has C suffered?
- Was that loss caused by D's breach?
- Was that loss caused by D's breach?
- Did C mitigate?
- What is the amount of the loss?

Every case has such a framework, either a standard one, like these examples, or a standard one adapted to exclude issues that do not arise or include other issues that do arise, or a framework specially constructed for the unique facts of the case.

Such a framework can only be constructed by an application of the law. You may know the law, or you may have to research it. If research is required, this may be a lengthy process, involving reading many cases, textbooks, and statutes. Inevitably, when you are doing that research you will not only have in your mind the sequence of issues you are trying to construct, but also the search for an answer to them. However, identifying the issues logically comes first.

It is very important when looking up or researching the law to do so with the facts of the case that you have absorbed and organised clearly in your mind. You should never conduct legal research without knowing what question you are seeking the answer to, otherwise it will be without purpose or direction. In constructing your framework, you will have in mind such questions as 'What must be established before the claimant can succeed in this case?' or 'In what circumstances will I advise the executor to give the money to John, and in what circumstances to Mary?' Research without such questions in your mind is likely to be lengthy, disorganised, academic, and fruitless.

Identifying your sequence of issues and constructing your framework will also help you in the process of organising facts. It will tell you which facts are relevant and what is the relative importance of various pieces of information. It will show you how the facts fit together, and what depends on what.

As well as identifying the specific issues upon which your client's case depends, you must also identify all the questions upon which an answer is required. Some of these questions will have been specifically posed in your instructions. But other questions are only implied. Some examples of the sort of implicit questions you might find are:

- Do I have a good case?
- What are the chances of success?
- How strong is the evidence?
- Is it worth proceeding in this matter?
- Is any further evidence required?
- What is the procedure?

And one question which you should regard as implicit in every set of instructions:

- What is the next step?

Every implied question must be identified and given a place in your sequence of issues to be answered.

A place will very probably also have to be found in your framework for issues relating to the case for the other side. You cannot consider your client's case without considering the likely opposing case. Possible defences that might be raised give rise to additional issues. The likely evidence that the other side will produce will give rise to evidential issues. These evidential issues belong in your structure just as much as legal or factual issues.

By the time you have organised the facts and produced your legal framework, you should have arrived at stage 5, which is:

19.4.5   Stage 5: look at the case as a whole

Before you can go further, it is important that you should be able to see the case as a whole, see how everything hangs together, where each question leads. You will see the starting point in your line of reasoning, the direction it will take, and the destination you will arrive at. All the issues involved in the case, and all the material facts, interrelate. The case is a unity which you understand and can find your way around. It has shape and structure. This structure will, incidentally, almost certainly provide the skeleton plan for your written opinion.

It is at this point, also, that you should clearly see what gaps there are in the information and evidence available to you. You must identify these gaps and make a request for any additional material required to be provided, bearing in mind what it is realistic to expect your solicitor to provide. You must also be ready to answer the issues you have raised in alternative ways, depending on how any additional evidence or facts turn out.

You may have started on the next stage already, even while you were organising the facts and constructing your framework, but you can only really deal with it when you have seen the case as a whole.

19.4.6   Stage 6: answer all the questions

Every question in your sequence of issues must now be answered. Every question has an answer. The answer may not yet be clear, it may have to be determined by a court, but nevertheless you can give your answer. You do this by forming an opinion.

A few of the issues that need to be dealt with will have a clear answer, yes or no, A or B. Such an answer can only be given where the facts and law are so clear that there can be no real doubt, or where there is only one answer in law. If, for example, you are dealing with a case involving a collision between two motor vehicles on a public highway, you can state categorically that the defendant driver owed a duty of care to the claimant; that is not a matter for your opinion. Where you have a written contract between two parties, neither of whom has challenged its validity, you can state that that is the contract; to express the 'opinion' that it is 'probably valid' would be ridiculous.

But it is unlikely that you will be able to answer many of the issues in this way: certainly not major issues around which the dispute turns, unless your research into the law provides a definite answer. If the overall answer, or the answer on a central issue were so clear, it is unlikely that your instructing solicitors would have sought your opinion at all. Most of the issues you will not be able to answer in a definite way. There can be no conclusion of certainty on a question of fact. Rather, you will have to reach a conclusion of uncertainty, where you exercise your judgement to form an *opinion*.

You may have to exercise your judgement to form an opinion on questions of law or fact, questions of mixed law and fact, or all three. Your research into the law may have provided a clear legal answer to any question of law, but more likely you will have to form an opinion on the law itself, or its applicability to the facts of the case. Hence the necessity only to carry out your legal research knowing what question you are trying to answer. The judgement you use in forming an opinion on the law is your lawyer's judgement, using your skill at legal understanding and interpretation.

But more importantly you will use your judgement to form opinions on questions of fact as well. There can be no certain answers to questions like 'Was the driver negligent?', 'Did the claimant behave reasonably?', 'Is this piece of evidence convincing?'

or 'Is this version of events credible?' No statute or reported case can ever answer such questions. And yet you must answer them. You must reach your own conclusion insofar as the law and facts allow, even though your conclusion is a conclusion of uncertainty. You exercise your judgement to form an opinion. The judgement you use in answering such questions is not just a lawyer's judgement, but your judgement as an experienced practitioner, as a man or woman of the world, as a decision-maker. One of the qualities that is most respected in good barristers is their ability, when exercising their judgement, almost always to be right. It is a quality you should cultivate.

It is important to emphasise at this point that you are exercising your judgement, not giving judgement. You are not the final judge of the case, deciding who should win and lose, resolving questions of fact with findings of fact which cannot thereafter be challenged. In exercising your judgement you are weighing up all the information you have before you, and forming an opinion about what would be the likely decision of a judge on *that information* alone. You are exercising your judgement for the purpose of giving advice, not for the purpose of determining the case. You cannot see yourself as the final judge; and you must remember that there is a case for the other side that must in the end go into the balance as well.

It follows that you cannot answer all the questions asked simply by looking at your instructions and the facts as presented to you and exercising your judgement on them. You will need also to use your powers of inference or even your imagination to examine the likely case for the other side. The mere fact that your client appears to have a good case does not mean your client will succeed. The other side doubtless think they have a good case as well. In the end a court is likely to have to resolve disputes of fact; there will be a conflict of evidence. There can only be a clear case when the facts are virtually certain or agreed between the parties. A good *answer* to a claimant's or the prosecution case does not mean the *defence* will succeed. Your client may turn out to be an unreliable or an incredible witness. It is important therefore to look at what the other side may say in court and take this into account in exercising your judgement.

Your instructing solicitor may have expressed a view as to what the answer to one or more questions is. While you should have due regard for his or her opinion, you must not adopt it instead of your own. You may disagree.

So you must answer all the questions in your sequence of issues, exercising your judgement where necessary, deciding what your opinion is, what you think. This is all part of advising your client. Having answered all the questions in your sequence of issues, you will have found your answer also to the central question of what it is your client actually wants to know, and you can come on to the final stage, which is:

19.4.7   Stage 7: consider your advice

In other words, you do not just form an opinion on your client's case or problem, you also advise your client what he or she should or could do. If your client has a problem, he or she does not only want to be told the solution, he or she wants to be shown how to go about obtaining that solution. What your client needs is good practical advice, so you should consider also the practical steps that you advise your client to take. This will be a very important part of the written opinion.

19.4.8   The seven stages

These seven stages of the thinking process are not, to a practising barrister, conscious stages which he or she goes through mechanically. But they are all logically present in the thinking process and every competent barrister goes through them subconsciously, bringing them in in the order set out earlier, even if he or she has never actually thought about them! They are all necessary in order to be prepared for the actual writing of the opinion.

19.5 The writing process: the opinion itself

You have now been through the thinking process: everything is clear in your mind. You know what your answers are, what advice you are going to give. You have to: you cannot possibly write an opinion until you know what your opinion is. But simply knowing your opinion, knowing the answer, does not mean the writing process is a mere formality. You have to know how to express yourself in an opinion, how to transfer the thinking process on to paper. What you do *not* do is simply write out the thinking process itself. Rather, you set out the *fruits* of the thinking process. We need to look a little more closely at what an opinion is and what it is for.

19.5.1 The purpose of the opinion

We have already seen what your opinion is in essence: it is your response to instructions. Your response has, however, three different aspects, all of which we have touched on, but which we can now state more clearly ((a), (b) and (c)), and an objective ((d)):

(a) *Your opinion is your answer* to a series of questions asked of you by your instructing solicitor on behalf of your client. Therefore every question must be identified and answered. We have already seen the necessity of this, and discussed how you identify issues and answer them as part of the thinking process. We shall shortly consider how you actually express your answers in writing.

(b) *Your opinion is a kind of interim judgement* on your client's present position as you see it. You must be objective, as a judge would be. Although, at the end of the day, if the case is to proceed, it will be your duty to do the best you can for your client, to fight the case on his or her behalf, to show his or her case in the best possible light, and to win the case so far as the law and facts allow, you have not reached this stage yet. At this point you are not trying to fight a case, win it, or show it in the best possible light: that would be to mislead your client. You may consider *how* the case may be fought and won, and assess the chances, but nevertheless you must judge the strength or weakness of your client's case coolly and accurately. We have already considered the importance of exercising judgement. This is always an objective process. The only subjective element is that you are judging the case put to you by one side only, rather than the case put to you by both sides, as a judge would at trial. But, again remember, you are *not* the judge. You are not *deciding* the case.

(c) *Your opinion is a piece of advice* to your client regarding his or her position and what he or she should do. This *is* subjective: you are obviously trying to help your client as opposed to anyone else and to solve that client's particular problem. Advising is not just a matter of advising someone what to do, but is closely bound up with the whole process of answering questions and exercising judgement.

(d) *Your objective in writing the opinion* is to lead your client to the clearest possible understanding of his or her position, so that he or she can decide, on your advice, what to do about it. So your opinion should be clear, complete, unambiguous, easy to read, easy to follow, and an accurate representation of what you actually think. It should be definitive, rather than discursive, but it must be a *reasoned* opinion. An opinion is incomplete if no reasons are given. It must also look to the future and indicate the way forward.

19.5.2 Some things that an opinion is not

(a) An opinion is not an *argument*. Arguments seek to persuade somebody of something and there is no element of persuasion in an opinion. You are not arguing your client's case, presenting it to a court, or trying to prove anything. You may well *rehearse* the arguments for and against your client's case: but that is part of the reasoning for your opinion, which is your view on those arguments.

(b) An opinion is not an *essay*. An essay discusses, explores, considers; it is discursive rather than definitive. An essay, typically, sets out the thinking process, rather than the fruits of the thinking process. Your opinion should never resemble an essay.

(c) An opinion is not a *submission*. When making a submission, you are putting forward an argument, or a theory for someone else's judgement. In an opinion you are exercising your own judgement, giving your own advice. Your opinion should *never* contain the words 'It is submitted that' or 'I submit that'. Such words betray a fundamental misunderstanding of the whole concept of opinion writing. If you find yourself writing them, delete them and write what you really mean, which is 'It is my opinion that' or 'I think that'.

(d) An opinion is not an *instruction*. Although your opinion is definitive, and you are giving judgement, in layman's terms 'laying down the law', you cannot go too far. You can tell your client what his or her position is and advise your client what to do; you can tell him or her how to go about things and give instructions about the conduct of a case. But you cannot *tell* your client to bring a claim or abandon one; *tell* him or her whether to enter into a contract or not; or *tell* him or her to plead guilty or not guilty. Decisions such as these are your client's to make (except in very rare circumstances): your task is not to make the decision for your client, but to give him or her all the information and advice needed in order to make the right decision.

19.5.3 For whom is the opinion written?

One thing you will find quite hard to sort out in the early stages of learning to write opinions is whether you are really writing for the instructing solicitor or for the lay client. The strict answer is that you are writing for the instructing solicitor. He or she has sent you the instructions and posed the questions; it is to him or her that you are replying. A more complete answer is that you are writing for both the solicitor and the lay client, but in different ways and to a different extent in different cases. You should ask yourself 'Who is going to act on this advice?' If it is the solicitor, then you are writing primarily, or occasionally exclusively, for his or her benefit. But if it is the lay client, you must make sure that your opinion is written in such a way as to be intelligible and helpful to them.

However, writing for the lay client does *not* mean that you should avoid legal terminology or explain legal principles in layman's terms. To the extent that you are giving legal advice, you are writing as one professional lawyer to another, and you should assume that your instructing solicitor has the same knowledge of general principles as you do. Just take care to avoid unnecessary obscurity and jargon. It is where you are giving practical advice which will affect your lay client that you should make sure the lay client can understand the advice you are giving, and the reasons for it.

There is a balance to be struck, which is not easy to explain, but which comes quite naturally once you have read a few opinions and had some practice.

19.6   How the opinion should be set out

We can at last come on to the questions of how you actually set out the opinion and express yourself in it.

The first thing to be clear about is that there is absolutely no correct or incorrect way to write an opinion. You may do it however you wish. Every barrister has to a greater or lesser extent their own individual style. However you write your opinion, there will always be a barrister who will say, 'I don't like your style, I wouldn't write it like that'. During your training you will probably hear contradictory views forcefully expressed.

Nevertheless, there are undoubtedly such things as good opinions and bad opinions. We have already examined quite thoroughly the qualities that a good opinion should have and the functions it should serve, and you cannot give it those qualities or fulfil those functions simply by writing it any old way that happens to take your fancy. In the interests of clarity, it *must* have a clear structure; in the interests of completeness, it must have full reasoning; in the interests of readability it must follow a clear line. In the end, you will discover your own style and write your own opinions as you wish, but it is good to have a starting point.

The following structure is therefore a suggested starting point. It is safe, mildly conventional, and unadventurous; but if followed it should lead to a good rather than a bad opinion.

19.6.1   Skeleton plan

Before you start writing your opinion, you must have a skeleton plan. This plan will have evolved during the process of thinking and analysing the issues. Without such a plan (which may be on paper or in your head) your opinion is bound to be disorganised, rambling, and poorly structured. Having prepared that skeleton plan, try as hard as you can to stick to it. Do not wander off at a tangent, or allow yourself to drift into discussing an issue you had decided to take at a later stage, unless it is clear to you that this is an improvement on your original plan.

A good skeleton plan should actually save you time. You should find it is quicker to write the opinion after you have constructed your skeleton than it would have been without it. It is important therefore to draw up your skeleton in a helpful way. Your skeleton will not save you time if it is just the barest of bare bones: a few words, maybe a few paragraph headings. You need more flesh on the bones. It should tell you not just what you are going to write *about*, but what you will actually *say*. So it should give you a clear indication of the issues you will deal with, in what order, and roughly how much space you will devote to each. It will list the points you want to raise in relation to each issue. It will tell you what your conclusion on each issue is going to be. It may even tell you exactly how many paragraphs your opinion will contain, and what will go into each paragraph.

On the other hand, you will also not save yourself time if your skeleton is too full, amounting to the entire opinion in note form, or even containing some half-written paragraphs. This will lead to much duplication of your efforts.

19.6.2 Back sheet and heading

Your opinion has a back sheet on which should be printed the title of the case as it appears in your instructions. This may be a full court heading (as in statements of case) or it may just be the name of the client. Use whatever your instructing solicitors have used. Underneath appears, in capitals, in tram lines, 'OPINION' or 'ADVICE' as the case may be. Thus:

<u>Mary Smith v International Pancakes Ltd</u>

<u>OPINION</u>

The same heading, or an abbreviation of it, will usually appear also on the inside, immediately above your first paragraph.

Your opinion may be called 'Opinion' or 'Advice'. There is not a hard-and-fast distinction. Traditionally, it is an opinion when you are advising on law, questions of fact, liability, merits, quantum of damages, etc.; and an advice where the emphasis is on evidence or procedure or the practical steps to be taken. Try to differentiate, but do not worry too much if you cannot. As a rough guide, call it an opinion in civil matters (except for an advice on evidence) and an advice in criminal matters. But many barristers will disagree with this.

After the heading, there follows the body of the opinion, written in numbered paragraphs. You write in the first person, i.e. you refer to yourself as 'I', not as 'counsel'. But you refer to your client and your instructing solicitor in the third person, 'he, she, it or they', rather than in the second person, 'you'.

19.6.3 The opening paragraph(s)

The opening paragraph(s) should contain a brief statement of what the case is all about, and your objectives. In other words, you identify the fundamental facts, the key issues, and what you are asked to advise about.

Sometimes you will be told that the opening paragraph(s) should contain all the material facts. There are good reasons why this may be useful in some instances, but generally speaking the facts are well known to the client and the instructing solicitor and little purpose is served by setting them all out. What you should certainly not do is simply copy out your instructions at great length or regurgitate all the facts unselectively and uncritically. The introduction to the opinion should be concise. As a guide, include those facts which:

- Identify the parties and set the scene
- Need to be known for someone to read and understand your opinion
- Form the basis for your opinion
- Have wide relevance to many or all of the issues.

Matters of detail, and facts which are of minor importance, or which are relevant only to specific issues, are much better brought in later as and when they arise.

Identifying the issues and stating what you are asked to advise about should not take long. Do not go into great detail. Remember you are just trying to explain what the case is all about. This will usually come after you have set out the main facts, but there are occasions on which you will find it is more convenient to state the overall question(s) and purpose of the advice first, because you can set the scene more clearly that way.

19.6.4   Overall conclusions

Next, you should state your main conclusions and give your overall opinion on the case. Some barristers actually put their conclusions at the end of the opinion, but you are encouraged to put them at the beginning while learning the skill. It is helpful to both the solicitor and client and an aid to clarity. If the overall conclusion is already stated one can read the subsequent reasoning knowing where it is leading. It is also a very good discipline to make yourself state the opinion at the outset, as it ensures that you cannot start writing without having decided what your opinion is.

But do not fall into the trap of trying to explain your conclusions in any detail at this point. You have plenty of time to give your reasons later, and you do not want to duplicate yourself. You can usually state your overall conclusions in only two or three lines. More than that and they will actually lose impact and clarity.

If the conclusions are not stated at the beginning, they must be clearly stated at the end of the opinion. Wherever they are set out they should be unmissable, because your instructing solicitor will almost certainly want to look at your conclusions first before reading the opinion in full.

19.6.5   Subsequent paragraphs: your reasons

19.6.5.1   Setting out your reasons

Use however many paragraphs you need. This is where you set out the reasoning that has led you to your overall conclusions. You do this by taking each issue in its logical order, saying what you think on that issue and why; that is, stating your opinion and reasons, and giving advice.

The logical order should be clear once you have applied the correct legal framework and put the problem into shape (as part of the thinking process). So, for example, if your overall conclusion is that in your opinion Mary Smith has a very good chance of establishing that International Pancakes Ltd is liable to her for her injuries and that she is likely to recover damages in the region of £25,000, your reasoning might go like this:

1   International Pancakes owed her a duty of care, because . . . [identify the specific facts and why they gave rise to a duty, applying the appropriate law].

2   The company was in breach of duty, i.e. negligent, because . . . [identify the acts and omissions that constitute negligence and if necessary explain why].

3   There is some difficulty about causation, but in my view this can be overcome because . . . [give reasons].

4   Most of the loss and damage suffered by Mary Smith is recoverable but one or two small items were not reasonably foreseeable, because . . . [give reasons].

5   The heads of damage are . . . [set out] and in my opinion they will be quantified as follows . . . [give your quantification and reasoning on each head].

This is a very simple example. Many of the above issues may well subdivide, in which case you might state your overall opinion on the issue of negligence before going on to deal with each sub-issue in turn, indicating the reasoning that has led you to the opinion that International Pancakes was negligent.

On any issue where your opinion is required, you should state it. Do not leave it to be deduced or inferred; do not hint at it or obscure it. Ten pages of waffle with the words 'That is my opinion' at the end will not do. Use phrases such as 'I think that', 'It is my opinion that', 'I have come to the conclusion that'. And whenever you express an opinion, you must always give your reasons for it. This applies not just to your overall conclusion, but to each separate issue as well. For the reasons explained earlier, it is a good idea to state the opinion first and give the reasons for it second.

Giving reasons is not always something which comes easily. It may be relatively straightforward to give reasons for an opinion on the law, because the reasons will then be reasons of law. But when you express an opinion on a question of fact, you cannot use the law as your reason. It is nonsense, for example, to say 'The defendant was negligent because he owed the claimant a duty of care' or 'Clause 6 is unreasonable because the Unfair Contract Terms Act 1977 applies'. Your reasons for an opinion on a question of fact can only come from the facts themselves. For example, 'The defendant was negligent because he had read the instruction manual which stated quite clearly that the machine should never be switched on without the safety guard in place and nevertheless he did so'; or 'Clause 6 is unreasonable because in effect it makes the claimant responsible for checking the quality of the defendant's workmanship, which she would have neither the skill nor the knowledge to do'.

Another common fault is the reasoning which simply repeats the conclusion. It is meaningless to write an opinion which states, expressly, or in effect, 'The defendant was negligent because he failed to take reasonable care for the claimant's safety' (i.e. he was negligent because he was negligent); or 'Clause 6 is unreasonable because it fails to satisfy the test in section 11 of the Unfair Contract Terms Act 1977' (i.e. it's unreasonable because it's unreasonable). Make sure you avoid such circular statements.

Giving reasons actually constitutes the bulk of your opinion. It can be a lengthy process, especially if the issues are complex or there is a lot of law involved. It is important therefore that your reasoning should be easy to follow. It must follow a clear line; the reader should always know where that line has come from, where it is going to, and what stage along the line he or she has reached. This is why it is impossible to write a good opinion without having prepared a skeleton plan first, and why you should stick to it.

It is to help you stick to your plan that it is suggested you write in numbered paragraphs. It is a useful discipline and recommended, at least while you are learning to write a good opinion. Other helpful aids are subheadings: put a title to each section of your opinion, as some judges do to their judgments in the law reports. Subheadings tell the reader at once what issue you are dealing with at each stage, and help you to stick to it. Also useful are short linking sentences explaining the structure of your opinion, for example, 'So for the reasons stated I think that clause 2 was a valid term of the contract and I shall now consider whether the defendants were in breach of it'.

19.6.5.2   Avoid irrelevance

The worst enemy of clear reasoning, apart from muddled thinking, is irrelevance. Your opinion must of course be complete, so everything relevant must be included; but it should also be as concise as possible, and so it should contain nothing irrelevant. It should be fairly easy to identify what is relevant and irrelevant if you ask yourself three questions:

- Is it part of my opinion in this case?
- Is it a necessary step along my line of reasoning?
- Is it part of the advice I am giving to this client?

If the answer to any of these questions is yes, then it is obviously relevant. You may get more than one yes, but if you get no three times, then it is almost certainly irrelevant.

Irrelevance is likely to creep in if you fall into the trap of setting out your thinking process or all your research into the law rather than the fruits of your thinking process or legal research. Other common examples of irrelevance are:

(a) Simply setting out the facts of the case or copying out your instructions without comment. You may well need to examine and analyse the facts with great care and in some detail, but only as part of the reasoning process.

(b) Giving an elementary law lecture, e.g. 'A person owes another a duty of care if there is a sufficient relationship of proximity between them and it is reasonably foreseeable . . . etc.' This makes you sound like a first-year undergraduate, not a professional lawyer.

(c) General exposition of the law in a particular area, quite irrespective of whether it actually touches on the facts of the case you are dealing with.

(d) Detailing all the case law you have researched. You may well have read a lot of cases, and having read them, come to a conclusion on the facts of this case. But it is most unlikely that every single case you have read forms part of your reasoning. You do not need to mention every case just because you read it. A general examination of case law is part of the thinking process, not part of your opinion. Do not describe your research in writing. State the conclusion you have come to and set out your reasons.

(e) Following blind alleys of reasoning. Do not take an issue, discuss it for several paragraphs and come to the conclusion at the end of it that it is irrelevant or makes no difference to your opinion. Such a discovery should have been made before you started writing, so you can simply state, 'Such and such is irrelevant because . . .'.

(f) Seeking to distinguish cases that are so wholly different that nobody would ever have thought of relying on them in the first place; similarly, discussing statutory provisions which obviously do not apply.

(g) Wasting time on hypothetical cases: 'If the facts were not as they are but something else', followed by several paragraphs of irrelevant discussion, concluding 'but that is not the case here so I do not need to concern myself with this possibility'.

(h) Advising your client of what he or she already knows.

Overall: keep your reasoning clear, sharp, and to the point.

19.6.6 'Rules' of structure

19.6.6.1 Liability and quantum

One 'rule' of structure that should never be broken is that liability is dealt with first, then quantum. Do not mix the two together, or jump between them unless you have a very good reason to do so.

So, for example, if you are considering the liability of two potential defendants arising out of the same facts, the correct order of issues is usually:

(1) Liability of D1

(2) Liability of D2

(3) Quantum against D1

(4) Quantum against D2

and NOT, as students frequently attempt, (1), (3), (2), (4). Only do it this way round if D1 and D2 are potentially liable for completely different damage.

19.6.6.2 Separate parties

If you are considering the liability of two defendants, take each of them in turn, and consider possible causes of action against each of them separately. The correct order of issues, for example, might be:

(1) Liability of D1 for breach of statutory duty

(2) Liability of D1 in negligence

(3) Liability of D2 for breach of statutory duty

(4) Liability of D2 in negligence.

It might possibly, but rarely, be more appropriate to take the issues in the order (1), (3), (2), (4). But in no circumstances should you merge (1) and (2) or (1) and (3) into a single issue.

19.6.7 Subsidiary points

Having stated your overall conclusions, set out your reasoning, and given advice, the main part of the opinion is complete. However, there may well be some subsidiary points to deal with and your next paragraph or paragraphs will deal with these. There are quite possibly some specific questions put to you in your instructions, which, while not being part of the overall opinion, must nevertheless be answered. There are also likely to be some implied questions to be dealt with. Every implied question must be identified and given a clear and complete answer, just as express questions must be. Some may be answered as part of your overall opinion, but others will be answered when you are dealing with subsidiary points. Remember that one question is always implicit and must be dealt with: What is the next step?

A major matter which may well need to be dealt with at this stage is evidence. Sometimes you will be asked specifically to advise on evidence, in which case you will either write a separate 'advice on evidence' or deal with it fully in your opinion. Even if you are not asked specifically to advise on evidence, it would, however, be odd to make no mention of it in your opinion. You cannot consider your opinion on the strength of a case, or your advice to your client on what you think he or she should do, without reference to evidence. It is in the end on the evidence that a case is won or lost. So you should be addressing your mind to what can be proved and cannot be proved on the evidence you have, and to what further evidence is required. Anything important must be mentioned in your opinion. It is no good advising your client that he or she has a good case if, say, a piece of machinery was not properly serviced, if in fact you do not have any evidence to show that it was not properly serviced. Indicate what evidence is missing, and from where it might be obtained.

Points of procedure may need to be dealt with. You may, for example, want to advise that a request for further information should be made, or that an application should be made to the court. You may want to advise for or against making a Part 36 offer, or accepting a Part 36 payment. You may want to advise that an attempt should or should not be made to settle the action. All these are examples of matters that should properly be dealt with in your opinion.

Also important is reference to any issue involving costs. In your client's mind there will always be an overriding question: 'How much is all this going to cost me?' You should make sure you are aware of your client's financial position, eligibility for public funding, etc. You should *never* advise that any step should be taken which might have implications in terms of costs, without advising your client what those implications are.

19.6.8   Further advice

It may well be that having dealt with all the issues, having answered all the questions and advised your client, there will still be other helpful advice you can give, in which case give it. Only give it if it is relevant and helpful. To decide whether it is helpful, remember your overall objective: to lead your client to the clearest possible understanding of his or her position, so that the client can decide, on your advice, what to do about it. Any advice which fulfils this objective, whether by clarifying the position or advising on the steps to be taken, is likely to be helpful.

19.6.9   Next steps

An essential part of your opinion will usually be to indicate what steps the instructing solicitor or lay client should take next. If your opinion simply leaves this question hanging in the air, so that after reading it the solicitor has to contact you and ask what happens next, it is an incomplete piece of advice. Always leave the ball in the client's court. It may be that the next step is simply for the client to decide whether or not to act on your advice, but at least make sure that they are in a position to make that decision and that they understand that that is the next step.

Sometimes advice on next steps needs to be quite detailed. If, for example, there are several steps that need to be taken in a particular order, set them out in order and number them. If any step needs to be taken by a particular date (for example issue of proceedings before the expiry of the limitation period) state clearly by when that step should be taken.

Advice on next steps should come at, or very near, the end of your opinion.

19.6.10   The conclusion

Your final paragraph should round your opinion off in some way. This is actually more a point of style than of content. Barristers like to think that a good opinion is not just a functional piece of writing, but a work of good literature as well. In the same way as no good literature just suddenly stops, but rather rounds itself off neatly or tellingly, so should an opinion. It needs an end as well as a beginning and a middle. You can do this in any way you like, according to your literary abilities. You may well decide to finish with your statement of what the solicitor and/or client should do next.

But if you can think of nothing better, a common solution is to finish with a summary of advice. This may be unnecessary if you have already stated your conclusions at the outset, but it does at least solve the stylistic difficulty. However, a summary of advice is essential if you have not stated your overall opinion at the outset of the opinion, because it is important that your client and instructing solicitor should be able to extract your advice easily. Your advice should always be plain to see, not buried. It may also be a good idea if, for example, you have a corporate client and it is likely that your opinion will be summarised for a board or committee rather than presented in its entirety. In such a case it is wise that the summary should be yours rather than anyone else's.

If you do include a summary of advice, make sure that it is entirely consistent with any overall advice given at the outset or advice given in the main body of the opinion. Conclusions that are slightly contradictory, especially as to the strength of a case, are highly dangerous, and are quite a common error in students' opinions.

If you have also produced some other piece of writing, usually a statement of case, note this in your final paragraph as well.

19.6.11   Counsel's signature

At the bottom of the opinion, counsel's name and signature appear, with date, and usually chambers address.

19.6.12   Variations in practice

Please remember that this description of the structure and content of an opinion is only given as a starting point. You will probably not find a single barrister who agrees with every word of it. Do not expect every opinion you see to follow it precisely. Different opinions serve different purposes and their structure and layout will vary as the content varies.

There remain a few points of content, style, and professional conduct to be dealt with.

19.7   Points of content

19.7.1   Answering questions that have no definite answer

The importance of answering questions is something we keep coming back to, and we have seen how most questions do not have a definite answer, a conclusion of certainty, but can only be answered by a conclusion of uncertainty, where you exercise your judgement to form an opinion. We must now look at the difficulty of expressing an opinion when you cannot be certain. The answer you give has got to be clear and complete. It is quite possible to give such an answer, and be helpful, without being definite. You must reach *conclusions*, i.e. you must be conclusive, but you do not need to be definite in your answer. It is understood by all concerned that the barrister's opinion is only an opinion: infallibility is not expected. The rule is to be as definite as you can be but no more than you can be. It is a difficult balance to strike. The most common complaint of pupil masters is that their pupils tend to be too definite: to say 'The case will succeed' when they should say 'The prospects are good'. On the other hand, another common failing of beginners is not to be definite enough: to say 'The claimant may or may not succeed in his claim, depending on how things turn out'. Sometimes this vagueness is couched in definite terms: the opinion which, on close analysis, in effect states, 'In my opinion the claimant will succeed in this claim if the judge finds in his favour'!

You have to strike the right balance between certainty and uncertainty. If the question is 'Will the claimant succeed in his action?', do not answer 'yes' when you mean 'probably'; 'probably' when you mean 'possibly'; 'possibly' when you mean 'unlikely'; 'good chance' when you mean 'fair chance', 'reasonable chance' when you mean 'remote chance'; 'some chance' when you mean 'no'; or 'no' when you mean 'slight chance'. What you do is find a form of words which seems to you exactly to express your feeling about the strength of the case. For example:

I do not think that Mrs Jones has any good prospects of establishing liability in this case, but there is enough evidence before me to justify sending a letter of claim to the other side to see what response it provokes.

There are numerous obstacles to be overcome in establishing liability in this case, but on balance I think they can be overcome and once they are, Mrs Jones's prospects of success are good.

Take care, also, when expressing your opinion on a subsidiary question of fact. For example, 'In my opinion the driver of the car was negligent' sounds very definite. In this case it would probably not be understood as being quite so definite, because what you really mean is 'In my opinion a court would find him to have been negligent'; but take care. Phrases like 'In my opinion he was negligent' can appear in opinions, but they can mislead others and even you into treating as definite a question of fact which has yet to be decided. It is much better to say 'I think a court would find him liable'. Beware also of saying 'I would award the claimant damages of £50,000', when all you mean is that £50,000 is your estimate of a likely award by a court.

But, of course, a conclusion of uncertainty must not only be expressed, it must also be reasoned. This may be a lengthy process: probably the less certain you are able to be, the more reasoning you will need to justify your conclusion. To give your reasons for a conclusion of uncertainty, and to give advice in so doing, you will probably need to go through the following points. You will need to set out fairly fully the client's position as you see it, not just the legal position but the factual position, the position the client finds himself or herself in in the light of the law; you will need to consider the pros and cons, weigh up the evidence, assess the chances (not necessarily numerically); you should certainly make clear the circumstances in which your client would succeed and the circumstances in which he or she would not. You may well need to explain your view of what the other side's case is likely to be and the strength of it. All in all you identify and explain everything that has gone into the balance as you have weighed up your opinion, and let your client know exactly where he or she stands.

19.7.2   Citing cases and other authorities

Cases are mentioned, discussed, applied, and distinguished in your opinion, just as they are in a judge's judgment. But whereas judges are obliged to deal with the arguments they have listened to and so need to discuss most of the cases they have been asked to read, in your opinion you should only cite a case where it is relevant to your opinion, reasoning, or advice. Do not try to get in as many cases as you can. Do not mention every case you have read. Apply the relevancy test. Not every opinion needs to have cases in it. In practice a great many opinions are written that mention no case law at all. If no case is relevant, put none in.

Cases may be properly cited where they are authority for a point of law, where they form part of your reasoning, or where they have helped you to reach your conclusion. They should not be cited just to show you know them. You should not, for example, put '*(Donoghue v Stevenson)*' every time you write the word 'negligence'. When you cite a case, cite it in the proper manner. If you simply put a case name at the end of a sentence, you are citing it as authority for what you have just said. Make sure you do not cite a case like this as if it were authority on a question of fact, e.g. 'In my opinion the defendants were in fundamental breach of contract *(Photo Production Ltd v Securicor Transport Ltd)*'. If the case is simply being cited as the source of a proposition, or as an illustration or as part of your reasoning, this should be made clear. Cases that form part of your reasoning, either because they have led you to your conclusion, or because they need to be distinguished in order to justify your conclusion, can and should be cited for this purpose: use them in such a way that their relevance is clear. Otherwise do not cite them at all.

It will usually be sufficient simply to mention the name of the case in an appropriate and relevant way. It will only occasionally be relevant to set out the facts and *ratio* of a reported case, in which case try to make it part of your reasoning, rather than simply setting it out descriptively, like a chunk from a textbook. Never copy out headnotes of cases in your opinion.

Wherever you cite a case, or refer to a textbook, give the full reference, so that your instructing solicitor can look it up, and for your own future use.

19.7.3   Dealing with lack of information

You will never receive a set of instructions that contains every single point of information you could possibly want. There will always be some gaps. What you cannot do is use lack of information as an excuse for not advising. You must *never* say, 'I cannot advise on this point because I have not been told whether . . .' and then go no further.

You must always advise as fully as you can on the information you have. Even if there is something absolutely central to your opinion missing, you can still follow this rule. Sometimes the less information you have, the longer your opinion needs to be, because you will have to advise in such a way as to cover several eventualities. If your opinion depends on whether the claimant did or did not know that he had a flat tyre, you must say what your opinion would be if he did know and what it would be if he did not.

Where there are gaps in your instructions, it is essential that you should identify them and point them out to your instructing solicitors in your opinion. If there is information you need, you ask for it. In practice, if you could obtain it by telephoning your instructing solicitor, you should do so. Otherwise ask for it in your opinion. But do not ask for further information just for the sake of it. Always make it clear what you want that information for and how it will affect your opinion. If it will not make any difference to your opinion, do not ask for it.

If you have asked for a large number of points of information or evidence during your opinion, it may well be helpful to your instructing solicitors to pull them all together in the form of a list towards the end of your opinion.

19.7.4   Length

The question of the right length for an opinion is a tricky one. Some barristers write at greater length than others. Excessive length and excessive brevity are both common faults in students' opinions.

The aim must be to write an opinion that is just the right length in all the circumstances. A balance must be struck between completeness and conciseness, both as a matter of content and as a matter of style. But in fact the right length for an opinion is more an issue of content. Differences simply of *style* do not affect the length of an opinion all that much.

An opinion that is too short is usually too short because of inadequate analysis of the issues, inadequate thought, or inadequate reasoning. In other words it is superficial. Only rarely is excessive brevity the result of over-enthusiastic pruning. More usually an opinion which is too short fails to say all that needs to be said and does so because the writer has failed to identify what needs to be said.

An opinion that is too long is usually too long because of an over-academic approach by a writer who has failed to distinguish between an opinion and an essay. The essence of an opinion is that it sets out the fruits of the research and thinking process, not that process itself. You should not bring in to the opinion every avenue of thought and reasoning that you have pursued. You should set out the conclusions you have reached at the end of the day and the advice you accordingly wish to give. If the case is complex, you do not 'do it justice' by writing a complex opinion, but rather by penetrating to the core of the matter, stripping it down to its bare essentials, unravelling all the complexities and encapsulating the result in a clear and concise opinion.

For this reason, if for no other, opinion writing is a skill in a way that essay writing is not.

19.8   Style

It goes without saying that your opinion should be written in clear, stylistic, fluent English. This will, however, inevitably be of your own individual style. Some barristers tend to write in short, punchy sentences; others prefer immaculately constructed, mellifluous sentences of 100 words or more. Either will be fine, if the opinion has all the qualities of a good opinion. Short, punchy sentences must not result in inaccuracy, or incomplete reasoning; long sentences must still be grammatical and easy to read. Your opinion should be complete, but not a word longer than necessary. If you have the ability to be concise, brief, and snappy without any sacrifice of content, this is ideal.

Within the opinion, use plain English: stick to ordinary, everyday language, and avoid archaisms and pomposities like 'the said motor vehicle', 'the matters aforementioned', 'hereinafter referred to as the relevant date'. Phrases like this are derived from statements of case, and even there they are out of date. They have no place in an opinion, where there is no need for excessive formality or pedantic accuracy. The one and only formality which remains conventional and which you should adopt is to refer to your instructing solicitors as 'Instructing Solicitors', usually with capital initials, and in the third person rather than the second person throughout. But do not refer to yourself in the third person: write 'I advise that', not 'counsel advises that'.

Be polite, both to your client and to your instructing solicitor. Address your client as you would address him or her face to face: 'Mr Jones', not 'Jones' or 'Jack'; it is preferable to call him or her by name rather than to refer to him as 'the claimant'. Do not suggest that your client may be lying. Do not pass moral judgements upon him or her. Do not start an argument with your instructing solicitors, or accuse them of incompetence. Treat them with respect, as fellow professional lawyers.

Finally remember what has already been said: there is no one right way to write an opinion. Strive for perfection, but do not expect you will ever achieve it, or that there can ever be such a thing in reality. No two barristers will agree about the perfect opinion.

19.9   **Professional conduct**

19.9.1   **Code of conduct**

You should be aware of the following provisions of the Code of Conduct of the Bar of England and Wales (now in Part 2 of the *Bar Standards Board Handbook*).

Core Duties:
CD2—
You must act in the best interests of each client.
CD3—
You must act with honesty and integrity.
CD7—
You must provide a competent standard of work and service to each client.

Rules:
rC9—
Your duty to act with honesty and integrity under CD3 includes the following requirements:

1 —you must not knowingly or recklessly mislead or attempt to mislead anyone.

2 —you must not draft any statement of case, witness statement, affidavit or other document containing:

    a —any statement of fact or contention which is not supported by your client or by your instructions.

    b —any contention which you do not consider to be properly arguable.

    c —any allegation of fraud, unless you have clear instructions to allege fraud and you have reasonably credible material which establishes an arguable case of fraud.

    d —(in the case of a witness statement or affidavit) any statement of fact other than the evidence which you reasonably believe the witness would give if the witness were giving evidence orally.

3 —you must not encourage a witness to give evidence which is misleading or untruthful.

rC15—

Your duty to act in the best interests of each client (CD2), to provide a competent standard of work and service to each client (CD7) and to keep the affairs of each client confidential (CD6) includes the following obligations:

1 —you must promote fearlessly and by all proper and lawful means the client's best interests.

4 —you must not permit your professional client, employer or any other person to limit your discretion as to how the interests of the client can best be served.

rC18—

Your duty to provide a competent standard of work and service to each client (CD7) includes a duty to inform your *professional client*, or your client if instructed by a *client*, as far as reasonably possible in sufficient time to enable appropriate steps to be taken to protect the *client's* interests, if:

1 —it becomes apparent to you that you will not be able to carry out the instructions within the time requested, or within a reasonable time after receipt of *instructions*.

Guidance

gC38—

CD7 requires not only that you provide a competent standard of work but also a competent standard of service to your *client*. Rule C15 is not exhaustive of what you must do to ensure your compliance with CD2 and CD7. By way of example, a competent standard of work and of service also includes:

1 —treating each client with courtesy and consideration; and

2 —seeking to advise your client, in terms they can understand; and

3 —taking all reasonable steps to avoid incurring unnecessary expense; and

4 —reading your instructions promptly. This may be important if there is a time limit or limitation period. If you fail to read your instructions promptly, it is possible that you will not be aware of the time limit until it is too late.

19.10 Further reading

This chapter is designed to be read in conjunction with the additional chapter *An illustration of the opinion writing process*, available on the OUP Online Resource Centre. The web address appears on the back cover of this manual. You are strongly advised to go there, download it, and read it.

Blake, Susan, *A Practical Approach to Effective Litigation*, 7th edn (Oxford University Press, 2009).

The use of law in an opinion

20.1 Introduction

The purpose of this chapter is to explore further the part played by law in an opinion.

It is in the use of law that the difference between writing an essay and writing an opinion becomes clearest. In essay writing the main object is to write about the law. In opinion writing, however, the main object is to advise a client about their chances of success and what should be done next. In opinion writing, the law is simply a means to an end; it is never an end in itself. The law is merely part of the reasoning process.

Whilst it is impracticable to draw up a list of hard-and-fast rules, this chapter is intended to provide some guidance on how law should be used in opinion writing.

20.1.1 Do not give a law lecture

Even though an opinion may require legal research and will have to contain advice given within a legal framework, the opinion must not give abstract advice. It must be firmly anchored in the facts of the case with which you are dealing. It follows that the law must be related carefully to the facts of the case.

The opinion must be written in a way which is practical, not academic. Neither your instructing solicitor nor your lay client will want to read a legal treatise. They will want advice which is specific to the instructions with which you are dealing. It is therefore important that you do not try to give a law lecture in your opinion. If you find yourself setting out the law in the sort of detail to be found in textbooks and articles, you are almost certainly writing an essay, not an opinion.

For example, if you are advising on damages in a case involving breach of contract, the following text would need considerable pruning:

The object of the award of damages in a case of breach of contract is to put the claimant in the position, so far as money can do so, he or she would have been in had the contract been properly performed. It was held in Hadley v Baxendale *(1854) 9 Exch 341 (followed in* Victoria Laundry v Newman *[1949] 2 KB 528) that loss would be recoverable only if it was within the contemplation of the parties at the time they entered into the contract. This will be the case in either of two circumstances:*

> *(1) the damage is such as may fairly and reasonably be regarded as arising naturally, ie in the ordinary course of things, from the breach; or*
> *(2) the defendant was aware that this particular type of loss would flow from the breach of the contract because of special knowledge which he had at the time of making the contract (usually derived from something the claimant has said to the defendant).*

For example, if A contracts with B that A will repair a piece of machinery belonging to B but A fails to repair the machinery properly and B thereby loses an exceptionally lucrative contract, A would only be liable for the resulting loss of profit, insofar as it exceeds the loss of profit which could be expected to arise in any event, if he knew of its existence.

In tort, on the other hand, the test of remoteness (see The Wagon Mound [1961] AC 388 and The Wagon Mound (No 2) [1967] 1 AC 617) is whether the type of loss sustained by the claimant was a reasonably foreseeable consequence of the tort committed by the defendant. If the type of loss is a reasonably foreseeable consequence, it does not matter that the degree of loss is much greater than expected (Smith v Leech Brain [1962] 2 QB 405).

The law in this example is set out in far too much detail (especially in light of the fact that the principles would already be well known to your instructing solicitor). Moreover, the paragraph about tortious damages is of course irrelevant to a case where the only possible liability is contractual. It would have been much better to write something like this:

The first loss which the company sustained was the loss of profit on its contract with Widgets Ltd. The repairer had visited the company's premises on three occasions before the contract was finalised and must have seen that the company had only one moulding machine. It must therefore have been within the contemplation of the repairer that if this machine were to be out of action for longer than anticipated, the company would be unable to manufacture goods produced by that machine. The consequent loss of profit must therefore have been within the repairer's contemplation, and so is recoverable under the well-known principles set out in Hadley v Baxendale *(1854) 9 Exch 341.*

This advice is of course clearly based on the relevant legal principles but focuses on the facts of the case in which advice is sought.

One way of making sure that you are not writing a law lecture is to ensure each principle of law you refer to is related to the facts of the case in which you are advising, so that each statement of law is followed immediately by a reference to the facts.

20.2   Dealing with the well-known principle of law

There is no need to set out basic principles of law with which your instructing solicitor will be familiar.

EXAMPLE

Suppose that you are writing an opinion in respect of a claim arising from a road accident. To write, '*Following the neighbour principle established in* Donoghue v Stephenson [1932] AC 562, *one road user owes a duty of care to another road user*' is unnecessary. It is obvious that one road user owes a duty of care to another, and so the point does not have to be made expressly. The appropriate starting point would be to say that, '*The defendant was [or, as the case may be, was not] in breach of the duty of care owed to the claimant because . . .*'

In the example in the previous section, the reference to *Hadley v Baxendale* stands as shorthand for the principles that case establishes. The solicitor will be familiar with those principles and so there is no need to set them out.

20.3   Only cite authorities on points of law

Do not make a statement of fact and then cite a case to support it.

Suppose that you are writing an opinion in respect of a claim arising out of the alleged negligence of a doctor. It would be wrong to include a sentence which reads, *'In my view, the court will find that Dr Finlay was in breach of the duty of care he owed Mrs McPherson: see* Bolam v Friern Hospital Management *[1957] 1 WLR 582'.*

The relevance of the *Bolam* test is that it establishes that a doctor is to be judged according to the standard of what a reasonable doctor would do. It follows that this authority should be dealt with like this: *'In* Bolam v Friern Hospital Management *[1957] 1 WLR 582 it was held that a doctor is to be judged according to the standard of what a reasonable doctor would do. In the present case, Dr Finlay failed to do what a reasonable doctor would have done in the circumstances in that . . . '*

20.4 How to cite cases

Where it is necessary to cite a case, you should always give a citation for that case, for example *Caparo v Dickman* [1990] 2 AC 605. For cases decided since January 2001, the 'neutral' citation should precede the reference to a particular set of law reports, e.g. *Transfield Shipping Inc v Mercator Shipping Inc* [2008] UKHL 48; [2009] 1 AC 61.

The rest of this section is concerned with deciding which case(s) to cite in the opinion.

20.4.1 Dealing with a minor point

Where you wish to refer to a point of law with which your instructing solicitor may well be familiar but where you also wish to show that there is support for the proposition of law you have just set out, it is usually sufficient to set out the proposition of law and then cite the authority for that proposition. In this instance, you are summarising the overall effect of the earlier decision, not relying on a specific dictum. Here, it is sufficient to set out the proposition of law and then give the name of the case, together with its citation.

An accountant is only liable for negligently prepared accounts if reliance by the claimant on those accounts was reasonably foreseeable (Caparo v Dickman [1990] 2 AC 605).

20.4.2 Dealing with a more important source

Where the source plays a more important role in your reasoning process, you generally need to deal more carefully with that source. You should set out the basis of the decision you are relying on, and then apply the law you have stated to the facts upon which you are asked to advise.

You are asked to advise someone who was prosecuted by the police because the police had been given incorrect information by an informant who bore a grudge against your client. One of the possible causes of action you consider is a claim for malicious prosecution. Your legal research reveals a case called *Martin v Watson* [1996] AC 74, decided in the House of Lords.

That part of your advice might read as follows:

In Martin v Watson *[1996] AC 74 it was held by the House of Lords that, for the purposes of a claim for malicious prosecution, the person who supplied the information on which the police acted may be regarded as the prosecutor. However, this will only be so where the prosecution is brought by the police as a result of information received from the informant, the informant agrees to give evidence against the accused, and the informant is the only person who could give evidence against the accused (there being no other witnesses).*

In the present case, the evidence of the informant was supported by that of another witness. Thus, the prosecution in this case did not result exclusively from information supplied by the informant; there was other evidence upon which the police were able to base their judgement to arrest the accused. It follows that the informant in the present case cannot be regarded as the prosecutor, and so a claim for malicious prosecution against her would be bound to fail.

20.4.3 Set out the facts of the case and then paraphrase or quote part of a judgment

In many instances, it is sufficient to refer to the overall effect of the case without referring to a specific dictum. If a case is central to your reasoning, however, it may well be appropriate to quote from the judgment(s). In many instances, the words you are relying on will only make sense if the context of those words is made clear and so some of the background to the case may have to be set out. When setting out the words you rely on you should (unless the precise wording is crucial) paraphrase rather than quote from your source if you can shorten the text by so doing.

EXAMPLE

Imagine that you are researching the law on unfair dismissal in a case where the employee was suspected of misconduct. You discover that a leading case is *British Home Stores Ltd v Burchell* [1980] ICR 303, and you find that the relevant part of the judgment of Arnold J is at p 304. His Lordship said this:

> What the tribunal have to decide every time is . . . whether the employer who discharged the employee on the ground of the misconduct in question (usually, though not necessarily, dishonest conduct) entertained a reasonable suspicion amounting to a belief in the guilt of the employee of that misconduct at that time . . . First of all, there must be established by the employer the fact of that belief; that the employer did believe it. Secondly, that the employer had in his mind reasonable grounds upon which to sustain that belief. And thirdly, we think, that the employer, at the stage at which he formed that belief on those grounds, at any rate at the final stage at which he formed that belief on those grounds, had carried out as much investigation into the matter as was reasonable in all the circumstances of the case. It is the employer who manages to discharge the onus of demonstrating those three matters, we think, who must not be examined further. It is not relevant . . . that the tribunal would themselves have shared that view in those circumstances . . .

Even with some editing this is quite a long dictum, and so it would be better to paraphrase it. This might be done thus. In *British Home Stores Ltd v Burchell* [1980] ICR 303, the employee was dismissed for alleged theft. Arnold J (at p 304) said that an employer who wishes to dismiss an employee for misconduct must establish a genuine belief that the employee had committed the misconduct, that there were reasonable grounds for that belief, and that the belief was based on such investigation as was reasonable in all the circumstances. His Lordship went on to emphasise that the tribunal should not ask itself whether it would have come to the same conclusion as the employer.

20.5   Show the relevance of the case

Whichever of the methods suggested in **20.4** you decide to adopt for a particular case, it is essential that you make it clear *why* you have chosen to cite a particular case. In other words, you must set out the principle of law you have derived from that case.

This is good discipline. If you are unable to show why you have cited the case, then either that case is irrelevant or else you have not properly understood the effect of that case. In either situation, it has no part to play in the chain of reasoning which leads to the conclusion(s) you have reached.

20.6   Which case(s) to cite

If there are several cases which appear relevant, you do not need to cite them all. Certain general principles may be applied:

(a) Cite the case which is the most authoritative: if a House of Lords or Supreme Court decision is on point, you should cite that in preference to a later decision of the Court of Appeal which merely applies the law stated in the House of Lords or Supreme Court case.

(b) Where a later case interprets, or seeks to resolve an ambiguity in, an earlier case, you will need to cite both if the later interpretation is relevant to the case in which you are advising.

(c) You should generally cite only the case which lays down the general principle; do not cite cases which merely apply that general principle without adding to it in any way. For example, when dealing with the requirement of confidentiality which is implied into contracts of employment, it is usually enough to cite the leading case, *Faccenda Chicken v Fowler* [1987] Ch 117.

However, there will be instances where one case sets out a general principle and a later case then applies that principle to a set of facts which are very similar to those of the case in which you are advising. For instance, *Caparo v Dickman* [1990] 2 AC 605 sets out the general principle that liability for economic loss due to negligent advice is usually confined to cases where the advice has been given for a specific purpose, of which the giver of the advice was aware. In *Spring v Guardian Assurance plc* [1995] 2 AC 296 the House of Lords had to consider whether a person who supplies a character reference to a prospective employer owes a duty of care to the job applicant to ensure the accuracy of the reference. If you were to be instructed in a case involving an inaccurate employment reference, or something analogous to such a reference, it would be appropriate to cite *Spring*, rather than *Caparo*.

(d) Do not cite earlier cases if a later case sets out authoritatively the principles to be applied. So, where one Supreme Court or House of Lords case restates a principle set out in an earlier decision of the Supreme Court (or House of Lords), you need only refer to the later decision.

(e) In some instances, the law which is relevant to the opinion you are writing will be based on a series of cases. This will be so where an area of law is being developed by the courts, so that each of a series of cases adds something new to the case which preceded it. Sometimes, it is appropriate to refer to the cases all together; sometimes you should deal briefly with each case, showing what each case adds to the principles established by the earlier cases. But remember that you must always focus on the principles that are relevant to the specific case in which you are advising.

(f) You must avoid giving a history lesson, for example by referring to a source which no longer represents the law. An example of this fault would be to write:

In Hollington v Hewthorn *[1943] 1 KB 587 it was held that evidence of a conviction in a criminal court could not be tendered in evidence in a civil case based on the same facts. The effect of this decision was reversed by the Civil Evidence Act 1968, s 11, which states that evidence of a conviction is admissible in civil proceedings if it is relevant to an issue in those proceedings.*

The effect of *Hollington v Hewthorn* is irrelevant (since it was reversed by the statute) and should therefore be omitted: you should set out the law as it is, not as it was.

It would have been much better to write:

Civil Evidence Act 1968, s 11, states that evidence of a conviction is admissible in civil proceedings if it is relevant to an issue in those proceedings.

(g) It follows from these general guidelines that some of the law which you find in the course of your legal research should be omitted from your opinion. The following summary should help to remind you of some of the pitfalls:

   (i) Do not cite several cases which all say the same thing.

   (ii) Do not go off at a tangent (ask yourself whether you are writing things which are really relevant to your instructions).

   (iii) Remember that *all* the law you cite must be relevant to the case in which you are advising. It will often be the case that you spend a considerable length of time finding some law, only to decide that it is not sufficiently relevant to merit use in the opinion you eventually write.

20.7   Using statutory materials

Much of what has been said about the use of case law applies equally to statutes. In particular:

(a) Only cite a statutory source if it is an integral part of the reasoning which supports your conclusions.

(b) Only cite the statutory source which is in force at the time when the facts of the case in which you are advising took place.

(c) If you can paraphrase the statutory wording, so as to make it shorter or clearer, then you should do so.

EXAMPLE

The Theft Act 1968, s 6 says that:

A person appropriating property belonging to another without meaning the other permanently to lose the thing itself is nevertheless to be regarded as having the intention of permanently depriving the other of it if his intention is to treat the thing as his own to dispose of regardless of the other's rights; and a borrowing or lending of it may amount to so treating it if, but only if, the borrowing or lending is for a period and in circumstances making it equivalent to an outright taking or disposal.

It would be better to paraphrase this fairly long and convoluted provision:

> *Theft Act, s 6, provides that a person can appropriate property even if he does not intend the owner to lose the property permanently. This will be the case where the appropriator treats the property as his own, regardless of the other person's rights. If a person borrows property belonging to someone else, the borrower can still intend to deprive the owner of the property permanently if the borrowing in fact amounts to an outright taking.*

If you decide to paraphrase rather than to quote from a statute, you must of course ensure that your paraphrase is accurate.

Statutes should be referred to by their short titles: for example, the Coroners and Justice Act 2009. Statutory instruments should be cited with both their title and number: for example, the Credit Rating Agencies Regulations 2010 (SI 2010/906).

Where a statute (or statutory instrument) has been amended, you should only cite it in its amended form (assuming that the amendment was in force at the relevant time). For example, it would be appropriate to write: 'The Children and Young Persons Act 1933, s 49(5) (as amended) provides that . . .'.

20.8 Which sources to cite

Usually, you should cite only *primary* sources (that is statutes, statutory instruments, and cases). However, the citation of textbooks and articles is acceptable in some instances. For example, where there is no authority on a point, academic opinion may be a useful guide to the answer; similarly if there are conflicting decisions and the conflict cannot be resolved by applying the doctrine of precedent (for example, where the only relevant decisions are conflicting decisions of the High Court) academic opinion may well be of assistance.

20.9 Apply the law to the facts

A common fault is to cite a case but not show how the case supports the proposition for which it is cited. If a source (such as a case) is worth citing, the relevance of that source should be made apparent. You should show how any source you have cited helps you to reach your conclusion.

There is a technique which you can apply to make sure that you are doing this. After you have made a statement of law, apply it to the facts. This is a good way of ensuring that you are not writing an essay.

EXAMPLE

In Alcock v Chief Constable of South Yorkshire [1992] 1 AC 310 the House of Lords held that one of the preconditions to a claim for nervous shock by a bystander who suffers psychiatric illness as the result of injuries negligently caused to someone else is that the bystander should witness the accident or its immediate aftermath. In the present case, Mrs Jones did not see the injuries sustained by her son until she saw him in hospital some six hours after the accident. In my view, this was not sufficiently close in time to the accident to satisfy this requirement.

20.10   Producing sound conclusions

If you are writing an essay, there is often no need for that essay to set out a firm conclusion; it is enough for there to have been a wide-ranging discussion of the law. In an opinion, of course, the same does not hold true. Conclusions must be expressed; otherwise your instructing solicitor and your lay client will not have been advised what to do next (and so the fundamental purpose of the opinion will not have been achieved).

If the result of your legal research is that there is clearly a right answer to a particular question, that answer must be stated and the reason why it is the right answer must be made apparent. If, on the other hand, the result of your legal research is that there is no single right answer, as where there is no statutory provision or case law directly on point, the possible answers should be set out and the opinion should suggest which answer is most likely to be right and must give reasons for that view.

For an opinion to be of an acceptable standard, the conclusions it contains must be sound and must be supported by sound reasoning. In this context, the word 'sound' may be taken to mean 'the right answer or, if there is no single right answer, an answer which may properly be argued with a reasonable prospect of success'.

When you are writing an opinion, you must remember that you are no longer writing an essay for a law tutor but you are learning to write an opinion for a real client with a real problem. This means that your advice must be realistic. For example, it is not appropriate to advise a client that they have a strong case if the weight of authority goes against your client's case but you think that the Supreme Court may ultimately support it. So it would in the vast majority of cases be wrong to say that your client has a good case on the basis that a previous decision of the Court of Appeal is incorrect. It follows that you should not base your opinion on a dissenting judgment in the Court of Appeal, even if you think that the dissenting judgment would ultimately be approved by the Supreme Court; similarly, dissenting speeches in the Supreme Court (or House of Lords) should not form the basis of your conclusion.

20.11   Summary

The *Practice Direction (Citation of Authorities)* [2001] 1 WLR 1001 contains directions on the citation of cases in civil courts (a similar approach is taken in the Court of Appeal (Criminal Division): see *R v Erskine* [2009] EWCA Crim 1425; [2010] 1 WLR 183; see also the Criminal Practice Directions XII (paragraphs D.2 and D.3)). Although these directions are aimed at advocates in court, they serve as useful guidance on the use of case law in opinions. The Practice Direction states that, where a case is cited, courts will pay particular attention to any indication given by the court delivering the judgment that it was seen by that court as only applying decided law to the facts of the particular case, or otherwise as not extending or adding to the existing law. Advocates who seek to cite such a judgment will be required to justify their decision to cite the case. Similarly the opinion writer ought not to cite cases which do not add anything substantive.

The Practice Direction goes on to say that advocates will be required to state, in respect of each authority that they wish to cite, the proposition of law that the authority demonstrates, and the parts of the judgment that support that proposition. Similarly, it is important for the opinion writer to be able to identify the specific principle to be derived from the case. Furthermore, the Practice Direction says that if the advocate seeks to cite more than one authority in support of a given proposition, he or she must state the reason for taking that course; likewise, the opinion writer should not cite two cases where one will do. The Practice Direction also requires the advocate to demonstrate the relevance of the authority or authorities to the argument being put forward, and that citation of the authority is necessary for a proper presentation of that argument. The same principle applies equally to opinion writing: if you cannot show the relevance of the authority to the point you are making, the authority is redundant.

21

Getting started

The preceding chapters should have equipped you with the theory that you need in order to be able to write an opinion. In this chapter, we put some of the advice to use in the context of a fairly straightforward problem.

The focus of this chapter is on the analytical process which precedes the writing of an opinion. It is worth emphasising at the outset that, although it is vital to be thorough and painstaking in your analysis, a lot of your analysis will not be included in the opinion that you ultimately write.

21.1 The problem

A brief received by a barrister is likely to contain:

(a) Instructions to Counsel, usually summarising the key issues in the case and seeking counsel's advice (sometimes asking for advice on specific points, sometimes seeking general advice, sometimes both);

(b) a number of enclosures, such as:

    (i) a 'proof of evidence' (or witness statement) from the lay client;

    (ii) proofs of evidence (or witness statements) from potential witnesses;

    (iii) other documentary evidence, such as contracts, correspondence, maps/plans.

Note that a proof of evidence only becomes a witness statement once it complies with the requirements of the CPR on witness statements (for example, including a declaration of truth by the maker of the statement): CPR r 22.1. Once the evidence of a witness has been put into the form of a witness statement it will (at the appropriate stage in the timetable of proceedings and assuming that the evidence is to be used as part of the client's case in court) be disclosed to the other side and will stand as the evidence-in-chief of that witness at the trial.

In this chapter we will assume that the problem can be summarised very briefly as follows (and in the form very similar to the summary of facts which usually appears at the start of an opinion):

Mr and Mrs Roberts own a large house. The top floor comprises a self-contained flat, which they let to tenants. At the beginning of March 2014, Mrs Roberts engaged Mr Cork, a painter and decorator, to redecorate the flat. It was agreed that the work would be done during the last week of March and that Mr Cork would be paid £6,500. The flat was due to be let to a Mrs Heller for 6 months from 1 April 2014 at a rent of £1,500 p.w. Mr Cork carried out the work at the agreed time but the standard of workmanship was very poor. Indeed it appears that the work was so bad that Mrs Heller refused to move into the flat and went to live somewhere else. Mr and Mrs Roberts had to get the flat redecorated (at a cost of £3,750) and had to find a new tenant. They had to instruct an agent to find a new tenant. Eventually, a new tenant was found; he moved into the flat on 1 September 2014.

Counsel is asked to advise Mr and Mrs Roberts whether Mr Cork is liable to them, and if so what damages they can expect to recover.

21.2 The analysis

In this part of the chapter, we work through the analytical process which has to be carried out in order to decide what your opinion will say.

It is vital that you go through the analysis step-by-step. That is not to say, however, that all the matters you consider during the analysis stage have to appear in the final opinion. But your advice is likely to be incomplete and/or unsound if you have not adopted a very systematic approach to the analysis. For example, it can be very tempting to get straight to the question of whether there has been a breach of duty—but if you do this you may miss out important matters that have to be examined to see whether there was a duty in the first place, and to whom that duty was owed. If you adopt a systematic, step-by-step, approach, you can be sure that your analysis will be complete, and that important matters have not been left out.

The structure of the analysis naturally varies a little depending on the nature of the cause of action. In a **contract** case, you should use this structure for the purposes of analysis:

- Was there a contract between the parties?
- What are the terms of the contract insofar as they are relevant (dealing first with express terms and then with implied terms)?
- Has the defendant breached any of those terms (if so, which)?
- What loss or damage has the claimant suffered?
- Each head of damage should then be considered separately:
  - Was that damage caused by the breach of contract?
  - Was that damage within the contemplation of the parties at the time when the contract was made?
  - Has the claimant acted reasonably to mitigate the loss?

In a **tort** case, you should use this structure for the purposes of analysis:

- Did the defendant owe the claimant a duty of care?
- Was the defendant in breach of that duty (if so, how)?
- Was the claimant contributorily negligent?
- What injury, loss, or damage has the claimant suffered?

- Each head of damage should be considered separately:

  - Was it reasonably foreseeable?
  - Has the claimant acted reasonably to mitigate the loss?
  - What is the amount of the loss (i.e. the quantum)?

You therefore need to decide whether the present case is a contract case or a tort case, or a case where both causes of action have to be considered.

At each stage, it is necessary to consider how the facts of the case in which you are advising relate to the legal principles that apply. It is also necessary to consider which matters are likely to be in dispute between the parties. If you are advising in a case after the defence has been filed, you will be able to tell from the defence what matters are/ are not in dispute. If you are advising before proceedings have been issued, there is likely to have been correspondence with the intended defendant in which he or she responds to the points made on behalf of the intended claimant, and so you will be able to work out (at least to some extent) where the areas of dispute are. Where matters are (or are likely to be) in dispute, it is important that the case analysis process includes consideration of what evidence might assist the claimant to prove the disputed matters (or evidence which might be called to rebut evidence adduced on those matters by the defendant).

With that in mind, let us now start to analyse the case against Mr Cork.

21.2.1   What is the cause of action?

It is pretty obvious that this is a breach of contract claim.

21.2.2   Was there a contract?

It is highly unlikely that there will be any dispute over the existence of the contract. Mr Cork has done the work, so it is almost inconceivable that he would assert that there was no contract.

21.2.3   Parties: does it matter that it was only Mrs Roberts who had dealings with Mr Cork?

Our instructions state that 'Mrs Roberts engaged Mr Cork', suggesting that the contract was between Mrs Roberts and Mr Cork. However, we are also told that 'Mr and Mrs Roberts own' the house where the work was done (in other words that the house is owned jointly by Mr and Mrs Roberts).

Two legal principles are relevant here: first, there is privity of contract. A person who is not a party to a contract cannot (subject to the provisions of the Contracts (Rights of Third Parties) Act 1999) sue on that contract. Secondly, loss should be claimed by whoever has suffered that loss. It is easy to get bogged down in this sort of issue. Suggesting that Mr Roberts could sue in tort, and Mrs Roberts in contract, overcomplicates things and is unnecessary. It is much simpler to argue that Mrs Roberts entered into the contract not only on her own behalf but also on behalf of her husband (that is, acting both for herself and as his agent). It is very unlikely that the other side would bother taking any issue on this point, or that a County Court judge would not readily accept your argument on it. Taking this straightforward and practical approach means that the opinion in this case will not have to deal at length with the question of parties.

21.2.4   Terms: which terms of the contract are relevant?

The most important terms of the contract are those which we will allege to have been breached. We therefore need to identify which terms may have been breached. In considering the terms of the contract, one should consider express terms first and then go on to consider implied terms.

21.2.4.1   Express terms

There may be express terms that are relevant to the quality of the work done by Mr Cork. For example, the contract might specify the materials to be used. Can you think of any other express terms about the quality of the work that might have been expressly agreed between the parties?

It is unclear whether the contract was oral or in writing. Counsel should ask whether the contract was in writing (or, if oral, whether there is any documentary evidence of the terms of the agreement). It is important that any written agreement should be checked (for example, there may be an exclusion clause in the contract). Who should check the contract or documentary evidence? In cases where a substantial amount of money is at stake, it would be appropriate for counsel to look at the documents. However, in a case where less money is at stake, the added cost of seeking further advice from counsel would not be proportionate; in a case such as this, it would therefore be appropriate for the solicitors to check the documents themselves.

The solicitors should, of course, have included any written contract (or written evidence) in the brief if they had it (assuming the lay client to be in possession of the paperwork—bear in mind that people have an annoying tendency to lose important bits of paper!). Unless your brief makes it clear that the contract was oral, and that there was no written evidence of its terms, you should ask your instructing solicitor to check with the lay client to see if there is any relevant paperwork.

In the present case, it may be that the contract was an oral one and that there is no relevant paperwork. In that case, Mrs Roberts will have to be asked for her precise recollection about exactly what was said between her and Mr Cork.

21.2.4.2   Implied terms

The present case is about poor workmanship, so (assuming there are no relevant express terms) we need to find a term that relates to the quality of the workmanship. Some types of contract contain specific terms, for example because of statutorily implied terms. We are concerned here with a contract for the supply of services. Such contracts are governed by the Supply of Goods and Services Act 1982 ('the 1982 Act').

Section 13 of the 1982 Act provides that 'in a contract for the supply of a service where the supplier is acting in the course of a business, there is an implied term that the supplier will carry out the service with reasonable care and skill'.

In other words, provided that the work was done in the course of a business, it should be done to a reasonably competent standard. It is highly unlikely that Mr Cork will dispute that he entered into the contract in the course of a business. But can you think of ways in which you might, if necessary, satisfy the court that Mr Cork was acting in the course of a business when he entered the contract?

Where you are relying on a statutory provision, it is important that you read the provision carefully and check to see if there are any statutory exceptions to the provision you are relying on and whether there is any case law interpreting the provision or defining its ambit.

Section 16(1) of the 1982 Act provides that 'where a right, duty or liability would arise under a contract for the supply of a service by virtue of this Part of this Act, it may . . . be negatived or varied by express agreement. . .'.

Where the agreement expressly states that the obligation to provide the services is to be judged subjectively by the supplying party, this express provision for a subjective standard in the agreement itself overrides the s 13 implied term which would otherwise be implied: *Eagle Star Life Assurance Co Ltd v Griggs* [1998] 1 Lloyd's Rep 256. So it is very important to ascertain whether there is anything in the contract (or, if the contract was wholly oral, whether anything was said) that might override the effect of s 13.

All of this underlines the importance of checking whether the contract made any specific provision for the quality of the work, and of reading the relevant statutory provisions.

21.2.4.3   Is Mr Cork likely to dispute the existence of an implied term of reasonable care and skill?

Unless he argues that something was said which would have the effect of removing or modifying the statutorily implied term, it is unlikely that Mr Cork could deny the existence of the implied term. It seems unlikely that he will seek to argue that he was not acting in the course of a business.

On the basis that it is unlikely that Mr Cork will deny the existence of the implied term, the opinion is not going to have to set out the basis for implying the term in great detail. Merely stating the term and its statutory basis will suffice.

21.2.5   Breach: have any relevant terms been breached?

This is where the case becomes a little more controversial. It is possible that Mr Cork will admit that his work was sub-standard. However, it is perhaps more likely that he will deny this.

It follows that one of the main issues that the opinion will have to deal with is the question whether or not Mr and Mrs Roberts can *prove* that Mr Cork acted in breach of contract.

21.2.6   How can Mr and Mrs Roberts prove the breach?

As we have already seen, the standard of workmanship to be expected of Mr Cork under s 13 of the 1982 Act is that of a reasonably competent painter and decorator. Since Mr Cork may well dispute the allegation that his workmanship fell below the appropriate standard, Mr and Mrs Roberts will need evidence to establish, on the balance of probabilities, that the work fell below that standard.

So the opinion will have to point out the need for proof and to identify possible sources of appropriate evidence. In particular, an opinion should consider whether there is a need for expert evidence (in other words, opinion evidence from someone with special knowledge of the subject matter of the claim). In deciding what evidence is needed, and especially whether expert evidence is needed, regard must be had to the value of the claim. It must always be borne in mind that expenditure must be proportionate to the amount being claimed, since this is one of the requirements of the Civil Procedure Rules, and is expressly included in the Overriding Objective set out in Part 1 of the Rules.

In some cases, it may well be that expert evidence is in fact unnecessary. It may be that the court can draw the necessary inferences from the factual information that is put before it, without the need for opinion evidence from an expert. In the present case, it is likely that the physical evidence of the poor workmanship will have been obliterated by the remedial work done by the second painter, so there may be little that an expert could do in any event.

21.2.7 Evidence

In this section we therefore look at some of the evidence which may help Mr and Mrs Roberts to prove their case.

The lay client is usually a very important source of evidence. In most cases, when counsel is asked to write an opinion, the solicitors will include a statement from the client (usually called a 'proof of evidence') in the brief. Even so, it will often be necessary to ask the client to provide more detailed information on specific points. In the present exercise, the opinion will have to identify all the matters which Mr and Mrs Roberts should deal with in their proofs of evidence. For example, they should be asked to describe in as much detail as possible what was wrong with the work done by Mr Cork.

There might also be supporting evidence—so they should, for example, be asked if they took any photographs of Mr Cork's work. This would be useful evidence to supplement the oral evidence of either or both of them.

The second decorator is likely to be a very important source of evidence. He is in a good position to identify what is to be expected from a reasonably competent painter/decorator and to enumerate the ways in which Mr Cork's work fell short of that standard. However, it is important to distinguish between two types of evidence so far as this potential witness is concerned. First, there is his purely factual evidence as to what he saw when he first attended the newly decorated flat. Secondly, there is evidence as to the standard reasonably to be expected of a painter/decorator, and as to whether or not the work of Mr Cork fell below that standard. As regards the second, care is needed as this sort of evidence is likely to stray into the giving of opinion evidence.

A witness can only give opinion evidence if he or she is an 'expert' (and so within the ambit of Part 35 of the CPR and the Practice Direction related thereto). Under r 35.1, expert evidence must be 'restricted to that which is reasonably required to resolve the proceedings'. The value of the present claim is such that the parties would almost certainly be expected to try to agree on a jointly instructed expert (if expert evidence is required at all). It is highly doubtful that the decorator would have the necessary independence to be regarded as an expert. Given the relatively low value of this claim, the opinion can deal with this fairly briefly. Opinion evidence may even be unnecessary, in that it is possible for the court to infer from the factual evidence given by the second decorator whether or not Mr Cork's work was of an appropriate standard.

It may be that Mrs Heller might be able to give evidence about the decorative state of the flat, assuming that she can be located and that she is willing to cooperate (both are matters which cannot be taken for granted). She might be unwilling to cooperate for a number of reasons, not least because she might suffer a degree of inconvenience if she agrees to help Mr and Mrs Roberts (e.g. having to provide a statement to your instructing solicitor and later to attend court would be quite time-consuming). People are often reluctant to get involved in other people's disputes, and so you should never assume that a witness will be willing to cooperate.

21.2.8 Losses: what were the results of the breach of contract?

Mr and Mrs Roberts can claim for each of their losses provided that the loss in question:

- was caused by the breach of contract (i.e. it resulted from the breach);
- was in the contemplation of the parties at the time the contract was made (i.e. it is not too remote); and

- is not something that could reasonably have been avoided (i.e. the claimants have mitigated their loss).

These principles are well known and so do not need to be set out at length in an opinion. However, in our analysis of the case, each of these principles has to be applied to each of the losses sustained by Mr and Mrs Roberts.

The first stage is to list the losses sustained by the claimants. In the present case, the list comprises:

- the cost of redecoration;
- loss of rent; and
- the cost of finding a new tenant.

At the analysis stage, each item of loss has to be considered separately. When it comes to writing the opinion, however, it may be appropriate to deal with some losses together.

21.2.9 Redecoration

21.2.9.1 Causation

The need to redecorate (and remember that Mr and Mrs Roberts will have to prove that redecoration was appropriate) clearly flows from the poor workmanship of Mr Cork.

21.2.9.2 Remoteness

This is loss that is almost certain to be regarded by the court as having been within the contemplation of the parties at the time of the contract because it is loss which flows naturally from the breach (i.e. it falls under the first limb of *Hadley v Baxendale* (1854) 9 Exch 341).

21.2.9.3 Mitigation

If the work done by Mr Cork was sub-standard, there remains the question of what was the appropriate remedial action. For example, was complete redecoration of the flat a reasonable response to the condition in which Mr Cork left the flat? Or could the problems reasonably have been remedied by something less drastic?

In an opinion it is important to suggest solutions, as well as identifying problems. So there should be advice on how to decide whether the Roberts mitigated their loss appropriately. This will have to include advice on likely sources of evidence on the question of mitigation.

The second decorator would be well placed to give evidence on this (though it has to be borne in mind that he may have had a vested interest in that he may have earned more money by doing a total redecoration).

Can you think of other evidence that might be available on this issue?

21.2.10 Lost rent

21.2.10.1 Causation

The loss of the tenant probably flows from the poor decorative state of the flat, although the case could be strengthened on this point. Again, the opinion should indicate how. For example, by evidence from Mrs Heller—if her evidence is available—that she rejected the flat because of its decorative state.

What if Mrs Heller's evidence is not available? Mr and Mrs Roberts will have to explain to the court why they were unable to let the flat to Mrs Heller.

21.2.10.2   Remoteness

Whether this loss is too remote depends on the state of knowledge of the parties at the time when they entered into the contract. This loss is unlikely to fall under the first limb of *Hadley v Baxendale*. However, it may fall under the second limb, namely such loss as may reasonably be supposed to have been in the contemplation of both parties, since this is dependent upon the actual knowledge of the parties.

Again, the opinion must give practical advice. How might Mr Cork have known that the flat was to be let for profit? In answering this sort of question, you should consider who might have told him and what he might have observed for himself.

A key question, of course, is whether he was told by Mrs Roberts about the intended use of the flat. If not, was there anything else that might have led him to realise that the flat was to be let for profit? The proof of evidence supplied by Mrs Roberts will have to set out what information she gave Mr Cork about the intended use of the flat.

Think about whether there might have been any other way that Mr Cork could have realised that the flat was going to be let.

21.2.10.3   Mitigation

Finally, there is the question of the amount of the claim. Did Mr and Mrs Roberts act reasonably in trying to keep their losses down? It is always necessary to apply general questions such as this to the facts of the case. So, the question can be reworded by asking whether it took Mr and Mrs Roberts an unreasonably long time to find a new tenant. Did they act as reasonable claimants would act in such a situation by appointing an agent? Did they supervise the agent appropriately? Should they have appointed more than one agent?

Consider ways in which these questions might be resolved.

21.2.11   The agent's fees

This head of loss must stand or fall with the claim for lost rent, and so it can be dealt with more briefly in your analysis of the case and, of course, in the opinion itself.

21.2.11.1   Causation

If the loss of rent was caused by the breach of contract, it must follow that the costs of trying to find a new tenant will also be recoverable.

21.2.11.2   Remoteness

If the loss of rent was within the contemplation of the parties at the relevant time, the costs of trying to find a replacement tenant must also have been within their contemplation.

21.2.11.3   Mitigation

It seems reasonable to use an agent to try to find a replacement tenant. It is therefore almost certain that the fees (unless excessive) will be recoverable (assuming the loss of rent is recoverable). If Mr Cork were to argue that the agent's fees were unreasonable, what evidence could Mr and Mrs Roberts adduce to rebut this?

21.2.12   Can Mr and Mrs Roberts recover the contract price?

Mr and Mrs Roberts may well wonder whether they can get their money back, as well as receiving compensation for their losses. They might be thinking to themselves, 'He did a dreadful job—why on earth should we pay him a penny for it?'

The usual aim of damages for breach of contract is to put the parties in the (financial) position they would have been in had the contract been performed correctly. This is sometimes known as 'expectation loss' (although this is a term which should not be used in an opinion, as it is too academic and potentially misleading to a lay client).

We have to apply that general test to the facts of the particular case. If the contract in the present case had been performed correctly, what would the financial position have been? Mr and Mrs Roberts would not have incurred the expense of redecoration and would not have lost their prospective tenant, but they *would* have had to pay Mr Cork the money they had agreed to pay him.

Another way of thinking of it is to use the benefit/burden analysis of contractual relationships. Each side undertakes a burden in order to receive a benefit. So, the customer undertakes the burden of paying the price and receives the benefit of the work being done; the decorator undertakes the burden of doing the work in return for the benefit of the contract price. So, the payment of the contract price (the 'burden' from the point of view of Mr and Mrs Roberts) confers on them the right to have their flat decorated to an appropriate standard (the 'benefit'). They cannot receive the benefit without paying the burden.

We are not told whether Mr Cork was in fact paid for the work he did. You should think about whether this would prevent Mr and Mrs Roberts from suing him at all, or whether he would simply be able to counterclaim for the contract price (which would then be set off against the damages he has to pay to Mr and Mrs Roberts).

It would be legitimate not to mention the question of the recoverability of the contract price in the opinion, unless you have been asked specifically to advise on it. As you have identified the losses that are recoverable, the reader can assume that any losses not specifically mentioned in the instructions to counsel are not recoverable if you have not advised that they are recoverable.

21.2.13 The conclusion

Every opinion must give advice, since that is what the client is paying for. Sometimes it will be possible to give a fairly certain prediction about the outcome of the case (based on the evidence as it currently stands). In other cases, counsel has to ask for more information or evidence in order to be able to give more definite advice as to the likely outcome. The present case falls into the latter category.

It is important to advise on the prospects of success for each issue and for each head of loss or damage. For example, there may be two causes of action but one is stronger than the other; there may be several heads of loss but the prospects of recovering damages for some are better than the prospects of recovering damages for others.

Mr and Mrs Roberts appear to have a good claim against Mr Cork, but only if there is evidence that his workmanship fell below the appropriate standard; whether or not some of the losses are recoverable depends on the state of Mr Cork's knowledge and the reasonableness of what Mr and Mrs Roberts did after the breach of contract by Mr Cork. The conclusion of the opinion in this case will therefore have to reflect the need for further evidence before firm advice can be given.

21.2.14 Next steps

An opinion should also give advice on the 'next steps' to be carried out. In a case such as the present, the next steps to be taken involve the acquisition of the evidence that is needed in order to enable more definite advice to be given. In other cases there may be specific procedural steps to be taken, such as seeking permission to amend a statement of case or to join an additional party to the claim.

The next steps must take full account of the procedural context of the case. We must consider, even at this early stage, which track the case will be allocated to. That allocation will necessarily affect the steps which have to be taken to pursue the claim and the volume of evidence that it is legitimate to gather, remembering always that the costs spent pursuing—or defending—a claim should be proportionate to the amount of money involved in the claim. Expenditure which is not proportionate would not be recoverable from Mr Cork even if Mr and Mrs Roberts were to win the case against him. It follows from this that you should attempt to estimate how much the claimants are likely to recover.

How much do you think Mr and Mrs Roberts are likely to recover? To which track do you think their claim will be allocated? What restrictions does this impose on the expenditure which can be incurred in bringing the claim?

You can find further details of track allocation, and the consequences thereof, in the *Civil Litigation* manual and in *Blackstone's Civil Practice*.

One step that should be considered is the availability of some form of alternative dispute resolution. For example, if the intended defendant is a member of a trade association or professional body (a fact that will usually be apparent from their headed notepaper or invoices), it may well be that the body offers an arbitration scheme. Care should be taken before agreeing to participate in such a scheme as appeals from the decision of the arbitrator may be very limited and use of the scheme may preclude subsequent litigation. The extent of the scheme should be examined carefully—does it, for example, cover all the losses that your client has suffered and could potentially claim in court proceedings?

21.3 Writing the opinion

It is important to adopt a structured approach to the task of case analysis prior to the writing of the opinion; you should adopt a similarly structured approach when writing the opinion itself.

The structure in the present case will be along these lines:

- What is the cause of action?
- How will breach of contract be proved?
  - Give specific advice on the evidence that is needed to prove that Mr Cork's work was sufficiently far below the acceptable standard to amount to a breach of contract (which will involve thinking about how the standard itself will be proved).

- Identify the losses suffered by the claimants.
  - Is there any reason why some or all of the losses may not be recoverable?
  - What evidence is needed to prove those losses?
  - What evidence is needed to resolve the question of recoverability of losses?

By convention, most opinions begin with a summary of the facts of the case. This is not an invitation to regurgitate the entire story contained in the brief. Rather, it requires you to explain *concisely* the really important facts of the problem. The ability to set out the salient facts is an important aspect of case analysis, as it shows your ability to identify the most crucial facts of the case. You should not attempt to include every fact which you intend to discuss at some point in the opinion. Rather, the summary should be a brief description of the key facts so that the reader can understand the nature of the case about to be considered in detail in the body of the opinion.

Another convention is that the opinion should summarise what counsel has been asked to do. This paragraph (which usually appears after the paragraph summarising the facts) often begins, 'I am asked to advise . . . '. Again, this is important. If your instructing solicitor has asked you to advise on specific matters, you must ensure that you do so. Noting any specific requests for advice in an introductory paragraph in the opinion helps to ensure that you do not neglect to deal with these specific matters.

Some barristers also have a further paragraph at the start of the opinion setting out their conclusions (which should normally include advice about the client's prospects of success in making or defending the claim, or recovering each of the heads of loss, as the case may be). Although not all barristers set out their conclusion at the start of the opinion, it is an extremely good discipline. It is essential that, before you start to write out your opinion, you know exactly what advice you are going to give. Otherwise, the opinion is likely to be rambling and discursive. In essence, you should set out your conclusions and then, in the main body of the opinion, show how you have reached those conclusions (and what further steps need to be taken). If you do not set out your conclusions at the beginning of the opinion, you must set them out at the end. Think about how you would express your conclusions in the case of Mr and Mrs Roberts.

Note that your reasoning will generally be confined to the body of the opinion and will not also appear in the paragraph which summarises your conclusions.

Your opinion will normally contain a section on 'Next Steps', in which you give advice on how to proceed with the case. This is, of course, one of the major differences between academic essay writing and practical opinion writing. In some cases there is very little to say, but usually there is advice that you can usefully give on procedural matters. You may also wish to include advice about how to deal with the problem outside the courts. Sometimes you may wish to comment on matters which may affect the lay client's decisions on how to proceed, such as their present or future relations with the 'other side'. This section conventionally (and logically) comes at the end of the opinion.

There is a further section that may appear at the end of your opinion. Because you are writing a practical document, you will have been considering evidence throughout the body of your opinion. It may be appropriate to add a summary of all the evidence or further information mentioned in the body of the opinion. This can be very helpful to the instructing solicitor, particularly if the opinion is a long one. It goes without saying that if you do add such a section it should match exactly the evidence/further information sought in the body of the opinion (and requests for further evidence/information should not be made for the first time in this section, which serves only as a summary of requests that have been made in the body of the opinion).

Remember that this chapter has focused on the analytical process which must precede the writing of an opinion. Much of the material produced in the analysis can safely be discarded when you come to write the opinion itself.

Make sure that you read through your opinion once you have written it. When you read through your opinion, you should ensure that:

- you proofread it carefully (correcting any errors of spelling, grammar, or punctuation, and rewriting any parts that are not expressed clearly);
- you have covered all the matters that should be covered (including any matters upon which you were specifically asked to advise and any matters on which your advice is sought implicitly);

- your conclusions on the client's prospects of success on each issue are set out clearly and prominently and that those conclusions are consistent with your reasoning;

- you have given advice on what steps should be taken next (e.g. procedural steps or the gathering of further information or evidence).

You should now have a go at writing out an opinion in the case of Mr and Mrs Roberts. This chapter has been written about a brief in the form you might receive it from your instructing solicitors. Note, however, that under the 'Bar Direct' scheme barristers may receive instructions directly from the lay client.

In **Appendix A** (which can be found on the Online Resource Centre) there is a sample opinion in the case of Mr and Mrs Roberts. It should be borne in mind that each barrister has their own personal style of opinion writing, and so you should avoid the temptation to use this sample as any sort of precedent. Rather it is intended to set out the matters that ought to be covered in the advice to those particular clients (remember that every case is different!) and to illustrate one way in which a barrister might express that advice.

22

Advice on evidence in a civil case

22.1 An approach to writing a civil advice on evidence

22.1.1 What is the purpose of a civil advice on evidence?

The purpose of the advice on evidence in a civil case is to tell the solicitor what further things need to be done in order to ensure that the case is in proper order for the trial.

22.1.2 What should an advice on evidence contain?

A good advice on evidence should tell the instructing solicitor, clearly and succinctly, precisely what needs to be done in order to prepare the case for trial. It will provide the solicitor with a plan of campaign, both for dealing with all outstanding preliminary matters and for assembling and presenting the evidence which counsel will tender to the court on the client's behalf at trial.

The contents of an advice on evidence will vary from case to case. There are no rules which govern what must and what must not be said. What is required is a practical advice, suited to the particular case and to the particular solicitor to whom it is addressed.

However, almost every advice on evidence will contain at least the following:

(a) A list of the matters in issue in the claim, stating on whom the burden of proving each issue lies. The purpose of this is to help the solicitor in the preparation of the case, by identifying the relevance of the items of evidence which must be produced. It also serves to identify the matters upon which it is *essential* that evidence is tendered on the client's behalf in order to make out his or her case. Even in apparently simple cases, claims may be lost for want of some certificate or other formal piece of proof.

(b) A list of the things which need to be done to get the case ready for trial. The preparation of this list will usually involve:

   (i) a review of the statements of case that have been served and of the disclosure that has been given;

   (ii) a review of the case management directions that the court has made (including any costs management orders) and of the requirements of the CPR applicable to the case, and a consideration of what has been done so far and what needs to be done in the future, to comply or to compel compliance with those directions and requirements;

   (iii) a consideration of what other steps might be taken (such as requesting further information or specific disclosure, putting written questions to the other side's expert, reviewing and (if necessary) revising any costs budget, making or responding to a Part 36 offer, etc.) or other directions might be sought (for example, to limit the issues to which factual evidence may be directed or to limit the number of witnesses, or in relation to expert evidence, or for a split trial or a trial of preliminary issues, etc.) to advance one's own case or to attack one's opponent's case prior to trial;

(iv) a consideration of what further practical steps (such as making further enquiries, searching for additional documents, taking further witness statements, asking your side's witnesses to comment on what is in the other side's witness statements, commissioning reports by experts, etc.) should be taken to obtain evidence for the trial.

(c) Details of the evidence to be tendered at trial, giving the names of the witnesses who will be required to attend court to give evidence, a list of the documents which need to be included in the trial bundles, etc.

(d) Advice on the things that need to be done in order that evidence may be tendered to the court at the right time and in the proper manner (e.g. exchanging witness statements, serving any necessary notices under the Civil Evidence Act), advice on the expert evidence, advice on the form and content of the trial bundles, etc.

22.1.3   Structure

A barrister's advice on evidence is almost always set out in the following way:

(a) The advice is headed with the names of the parties.

(b) Underneath that, the words 'Advice on Evidence' appear in block capitals between tramlines.

(c) The advice itself is written in short, numbered paragraphs, in clear grammatical English. If the advice deals with a number of different topics, it will often be helpful to divide the advice up by using subheadings.

(d) At the end, the advice is signed by the barrister in the bottom right-hand corner (usually above his or her typed name) and the barrister's chambers address and the date of the advice are stated in the bottom left-hand corner.

22.1.4   How should I set about writing an advice on evidence?

Every barrister has his or her own way of approaching this task, which is one of the most important parts of the work of a junior barrister.

Just as success at trial so much depends upon the care with which the case is got up beforehand, the writing of a successful advice on evidence depends upon careful analysis and preparation. As with all of a barrister's written work, the golden rule is: think before you write. Once the thinking and analysis have been done, the actual writing will be straightforward.

An important part of this analysis is the barrister's ability, using his or her experience and knowledge of the rules of civil procedure and evidence, to run the case through in the mind, from the very first words of the case to the last. The barrister must imagine what is likely to happen at each stage during the trial, anticipate what may go wrong, fill in any blanks, and ensure that everything that needs to be done to be prepared for each point in the trial is noted and put in hand.

22.1.5   When should the barrister be asked to write an advice on evidence?

In cases of any substance, counsel may well have been involved from a very early stage. Under the Civil Procedure Rules 1998, parties are expected to carry out thorough investigations and, where possible, to attempt to resolve their disputes by negotiation before starting proceedings. Starting proceedings should usually be a step of last resort, and proceedings should not normally be started when a settlement is still actively being explored: see the Practice Direction—Pre-Action Conduct, para 8.1, and the various Pre-Action Protocols[1] made under that Practice Direction.

The structure of the Civil Procedure Rules therefore assumes that each party will know its case from the outset, and so will be able to assist the court in its active management of the claim at each stage. Counsel may therefore be asked to advise on matters of procedure and evidence at any point. In particular, counsel's advice may be sought before the action is started, at the directions questionnaire stage (CPR, r 26.3), at the case management conference stage on the multi-track (CPR, rr 29.3 and 29.4), and at the stage of listing (CPR, rr 28.4 and 28.5 (fast track), and 29.6–29.8 (multi-track)).

In cases allocated to the fast track or the multi-track, the ideal time for counsel to be asked to write a formal advice on evidence will usually be after disclosure but before the service of witness statements. However, the appropriate time will vary from case to case.

In reality, the point at which counsel is asked to advise on evidence is entirely in the hands of the instructing solicitor; and it is a part of a barrister's practical skill to be able to tailor the advice given accordingly. For example, if counsel is asked to advise only days before the date fixed for trial to begin, there is little point in advising lengthy further investigations unless (which is unlikely) it is practical to obtain an adjournment of the trial date.

22.1.6   A step-by-step approach

In order to ensure that they do not leave out any important matters, many barristers adopt a step-by-step approach to writing their advices on evidence. By following the same scheme as a checklist on each occasion they can ensure that they have considered all of the relevant points.

One such step-by-step approach goes like this:

22.1.6.1   Step 1: read the brief

(a) *Ensure that you have been sent the materials that you need to write your advice.* The first step in writing any advice is to read your instructions; and the first stage in reading your instructions is to look at the list of contents with which your instructions will usually begin and to check that you have, in fact, got all the enclosures which the solicitor says have been sent down to you.

The second stage is to ensure that the solicitor has sent down to you all of the things that you need in order to be able to write your advice. You should normally expect to have been sent:

(i)   copies of all statements of case and requests (and responses to requests) for further information (including those in any additional claims brought under CPR, Part 20) that have been served;

---

1   These presently cover the following areas: Personal Injuries; Clinical Disputes; Construction and Engineering; Defamation; Dilapidations; Professional Negligence; Judicial Review; Disease and Illness; Housing Disrepair; Possession Claims Based on Rent Arrears; Possession Claims Based on Mortgage Arrears etc.; Low Value Personal Injury Claims in Road Traffic Accidents; and Low Value Personal Injury (Employers' Liability and Public Liability) Claims.

(ii)   copies of all completed directions questionnaires and pre-trial checklists that have been filed, together with copies of any accompanying case summaries, and the latest costs budgets;

(iii)   copies of all interim orders giving case management or costs management directions that have been made;

(iv)   copies of all other interim orders that have been made, and of any witness statements used on any interim applications that have been made;

(v)   copies of any pending applications for any interim orders, and of any witness statements served in support of or opposition to such applications;

(vi)   copies of any Part 36 offers that have been made (and of any responses);

(vii)   copies of the lists of documents that have been exchanged and of the documents referred to in those lists;

(viii)   copies of any witness statements that have been exchanged; or, if you are advising prior to the exchange of witness statements, draft witness statements from at least the principal potential witnesses on your side;

(ix)   copies of any experts' reports that have already been obtained or disclosed.

It is often helpful for you also to see the material parts of the correspondence between your instructing solicitor and your client, and of the correspondence between your instructing solicitor and the solicitor on the other side.

If any of these items is missing, you should telephone your solicitors and ask them to send you the missing item. It is important that you read your instructions as soon as possible after you receive them, so that no time is wasted in getting together the materials that you need in order to be able to write your advice.

(b)   *Extract the relevant information from the materials you have been sent.* Before you can start your analysis, you must master the contents of your instructions and ensure that you have an overall 'feel' of the case.

Each barrister must work out his or her own system for 'gutting' a set of papers, flagging important documents, and highlighting relevant passages. If you have not already done so, now may be a good time to make a *chronology* and a list of the *dramatis personae* in the case.

A useful tip is also to make a list, as you read through your papers, of any obvious points, inconsistencies, omissions, etc. that you notice as you go along. By writing these down as you first think of them, you save yourself from forgetting them when it comes to writing your advice.

22.1.6.2   Step 2: examine the statements of case

(a)   *Check your own statements of case.* You should examine your own statements of case in the light of the witness statements and documents that you have been sent, to see whether they actually put forward the case which you will wish to, and be able to, put forward at the trial.

Statements of case are important. Although the court will usually grant permission to amend where any injustice to the other side can be compensated by a suitable award of costs, there are some cases which are won and lost on points arising from problems with the way statements of case are formulated (see e.g. *Furini v Bajwa* [2004] EWCA Civ 412; [2004] 1 WLR 1971), and applications to amend which are left too late are likely to be refused: see e.g. *Swain-Mason v*

Mills & Reeve LLP [2011] EWCA Civ 14, [2011] 1 WLR 2735. In any event, the statements of case are usually the first documents which the judge considers. It is desirable that they should present your case as well and convincingly as possible.

Also, you will use the statements of case in the next step in the preparation of your advice on evidence to find out what the issues in the case are. If some material allegation is missing from your statements of case, it will also be missing from the list of issues.

The purpose of this check is to satisfy yourself that your statements of case are *sufficient in law and accurate in fact.*

(i)   *The law.* If you did not settle the statement of case, you will want to ensure that the view of the law taken by whoever drafted the document is the view which you consider ought to be put forward on your client's behalf at trial.

Even if the statements of case are your own drafts, you should reconsider them at this stage. The law may have changed or been clarified by decisions of the courts, or your own view of the law may have changed since you prepared your drafts.

(ii) *The facts.* You are likely to have more factual information about your case than was available when the statements of case were settled. You will have seen the other side's statement of case. If there have been any interim applications (e.g. for summary judgment) there may be witness statements or other written evidence telling the story from different points of view. Disclosure will have made available the other side's documents. You may have additional written evidence and further documents from your own side. Depending upon the stage in the case at which you are advising, you may even have your own and the other side's witness statements before you, so that you can see what the evidence-in-chief at trial is likely to be.

You should check that your case as set out in your statements of case is (1) the best case that your evidence will support, but (2) is also one that can properly be verified by a statement of truth, and (3) is one that can be established by the evidence that is likely to be available to you at trial.

(Note the provisions of the *BSB Handbook*, especially rC8, rC9, and rC20, concerning your obligations to act with honesty and integrity when drafting statements of case, witness statements, and other documents, and your obligation to exercise your own personal judgement in such matters, notwithstanding the views of your client, professional client, employer, or any other person.)

(iii) *Amendment.* If you want to change the way that your case is put—e.g. because you can tell at this stage that there is likely to be a discrepancy between what is said in your statements of case and the evidence that you are going to call at trial—now is the opportunity to seek to amend.

But remember: any change in the way that you put your case on the facts may undermine the credibility of your evidence, and all amendments have costs consequences, some more serious than others. *Necessary* amendments have to be made, but the possible advantages of merely *desirable* amendments should be weighed against their possible disadvantages. You must use your judgement.

If you consider it is necessary or desirable to seek permission for your statements of case to be amended, then settle draft amendments and make a note to advise your solicitor that these amendments need to be made, and how to go about getting permission. Make a note to warn the solicitor of any serious risks and of the costs consequences involved in the course which you propose.

(b) *Look at the other side's statements of case.* The purpose of this examination is threefold. First of all, to find out what the other side's case is going to be. Secondly, to see whether the other side's case is sufficient in law and accurate in fact, so as to identify any strengths or weaknesses. Thirdly, to see whether the other side's statements of case tell you enough about their version of events.

If the other side's statements of case do not provide sufficient details, or allow them too much latitude at trial, draft a request for any further information to which you consider that you are entitled and make a note to advise your solicitor to administer that request, and how to get the further information in the event that the other side does not supply it voluntarily.

22.1.6.3 Step 3: list the issues

Once you are satisfied that the statements of case are adequate, then use them to prepare a list of issues.

By following each allegation in the particulars of claim through the defence and the reply, and each allegation in a counterclaim through the defence to counterclaim, etc., you should be able to isolate from the statements of case what matters are in issue in the claim.

This gives you a list of the matters to which evidence will have to be directed at trial. By analysing on which side the burden of proof on each of these issues lies, you will be able to tell the issues upon which your side *must* adduce evidence if it is to make out its case.

Many barristers prepare their list of issues in the form of a table. The left-hand column gives a reference number, the next column states the issue, the next columns (one each for particulars of claim, defence, reply, etc.) identify the paragraphs in the statements of case which give rise to that issue, and the column after that states on whom the burden of proof on that issue is placed.

Other columns in the same table can be used later on in preparing to write your advice on evidence to identify the issues upon which particular witnesses are able to give, or might be able to give, useful evidence, to list the documentary evidence available on each issue, etc.

22.1.6.4 Step 4: consider what evidence is available to you on each issue

Your consideration of the evidence should be a two-stage process: (a) What is available? and (b) What should we tender? At each stage, it is often useful to run through the various types of evidence, taking each separately, in order to reach your decision.

There are some things which one need not prove. For example, there are some matters of which the courts will be prepared to take judicial notice. Also, some issues may have had a special direction made under CPR Parts 32 to 34 as to the mode of proof. It is useful to note these issues on your table of issues.

(a) *Oral evidence.* Go through the witness statements (or draft statements) that are with your papers. Mark on your table (perhaps with a tick) the issues upon which each witness can give useful evidence. Where it seems possible from the circumstances that the witness would be able to give useful evidence on an issue, but their statement does not deal with it, mark that (perhaps with a question mark) on your table as well.

When you have completed this exercise, your table will be able to show you how many witnesses can give evidence on each issue. It will show up any issues upon which you have no (or not enough) oral evidence available. It will also highlight the issues on which you should ask your solicitor to take further statements from the witnesses you intend to call, so that you know the outline of *all* of the evidence that they will give at trial.

It is also useful at this stage to mark on the table any special considerations affecting the witnesses, e.g. that it may be difficult to get them to trial (e.g. because they are ill or old, overseas or likely to prove reluctant, etc.). In this way you can identify whether any special steps need to be taken to ensure that their evidence is available to the court if, at the next stage, you decide it would be desirable for their evidence to be tendered.

(b) *Expert evidence.* You should consider on what issues it is necessary or would be helpful for you to be able to tender expert evidence.

One of the objectives of the Civil Procedure Rules 1998 is to limit the use of expert evidence to that which is reasonably required. Where possible, matters requiring expert evidence should be dealt with by a single expert. Expert evidence must, wherever possible, be given by written report. Permission of the court is always required to call an expert or put an expert's report in evidence.

You should therefore always consider first what directions (if any) the court has already given with regard to expert evidence, and what expert evidence has already been obtained and/or disclosed.

If the court has given directions under CPR, r 35.7 for a single joint expert, and that expert has not yet reported, you may need to consider what instructions have been and/or need to be given to that expert on behalf of your side. If that expert has already reported, you may need to consider whether you wish to put further written questions. In either case, you should draft whatever is necessary and make a note to advise your instructing solicitor of the necessary procedure.

If directions in relation to expert evidence have not been given, you should consider what directions would best assist your client. Would a single joint expert be appropriate, or are there good reasons for each party to instruct its own expert?

If your side already has an expert, you need to consider whether that expert has the right expertise. Does your expert understand his or her duty to the court? Does the report comply with the requirements of CPR, r 35.10 and PD 35? Does it deal with the right issues? Is it necessary (or would it be helpful) to obtain further information from the other side under CPR, r 35.9 for your expert to comment on? Do you (as a last resort) need to suggest finding another, more helpful, expert?

If experts' reports have already been disclosed, you also need to consider the contents of the other side's expert's report. Does their report comply with the requirements of CPR, r 35.10 and PD 35? Does it deal with the right issues? Is it necessary (or would it be helpful) to put written questions to the other side's expert under CPR, r 35.6? Would it be helpful to seek a direction directing a discussion (or a further discussion) between experts under CPR, r 35.12?

In any event, you may need to consider whether it might be helpful to seek a direction from the court under PD 35, para 11 that experts from like disciplines should give their evidence concurrently (the procedure known in Australia as 'hot-tubbing'). If so, you may need to ask your expert for his views on this proposal, and to consider and advise on the process for setting the agenda, based upon the areas of disagreement identified in the experts' joint statements under CPR, r 35.12.

(c) *Documentary evidence*. Consider the disclosure given by your client and that of your opponents.

Has your client disclosed all the documents which ought to have been disclosed? If there is a possibility that documents have not been disclosed, make a note to advise your instructing solicitor to ensure that your client gives that further disclosure.

Have the other side given full disclosure of documents? If not, then consider whether you should make an application for specific disclosure. If so, make a note to advise how this should be done. If necessary, draft the application and supporting written evidence.

Consider whether you wish to challenge the authenticity of any document included in the other side's list of documents. If so, make a note to advise your solicitors (i) to give notice under CPR, r 32.19 (if they have not already done so), and (ii) of the evidence, for example from a professional examiner of questioned documents, which will be needed to make or support that challenge. Add this issue to your list of issues.

Finally, consider which of the documents before you are relevant to which issues, so that you know the strength of the documentary evidence available on each of these issues.

(d) *Hearsay evidence*. This category overlaps with the previous category. Consider whether there is hearsay evidence available to you which is relevant to any of the issues, and whether a hearsay notice needs to be served under CPR, Part 33.

22.1.6.5   Step 5: selection of evidence

(a) *Oral evidence*. Decide who should be called to give oral evidence. Do not omit to call any witness whose evidence is the only evidence that you have on an issue on which the burden of proof is on you. However, do not necessarily call all the witnesses available to you on every point; and take into account any orders that have been made under CPR, r 32.1 and/or CPR, r 32.2(3), identifying or limiting the issues to which factual evidence may be directed, or identifying the witnesses who may be called or whose evidence may be read.

Consider whether witness summonses should be served on any of your witnesses. Consider whether any other special step (such as an application for permission for evidence to be given by video conferencing—see Practice Direction 32, Annex 3) needs to be taken to ensure that the evidence of any particular witness is available to the court. This may be particularly important if any of your witnesses is likely to be overseas at the time of the trial. In the last resort, consider applying to move the trial date to allow an important witness (who would otherwise be prevented by urgent surgery or some other unavoidable cause) to attend.

If one of the witnesses whom you wish to call to give oral evidence is elderly or very ill, consider the desirability of ensuring that a signed statement or a deposition is taken from them, so that in the event of their death that statement or deposition can be tendered in evidence.

(b) *Exchange of statements*. Having chosen which witnesses you would wish to call to give oral evidence, check that your side are able to comply with the direction for the exchange of witnesses' statements. The order will have been made either in the directions made at the allocation stage or at the case management conference.

Consider what more needs to be done in order to convert the draft statements which are with your papers into statements which are suitable for exchange (and ensure that they comply with any direction that may have been made under CPR, r 32.2(3)(c) limiting the length or format of witness statements). You may need to settle the witness statements yourself at this stage. Make a note to give the necessary advice to your solicitor.

(Note again the provisions of the *BSB Handbook*, especially rC8 and rC9, concerning your professional obligations when settling witness statements.)

Detailed requirements for witness statements are set out in CPR, PD 32. These include requirements that witness statements must:

   (i)   be expressed in the first person;

   (ii)   give the full name and residential/business address of the maker;

   (iii)   state the occupation of the witness;

   (iv)   state if the witness is a party to the proceedings or has a connection with any party (e.g. is an employee/relative);

   (v)   be divided into consecutively numbered paragraphs;

   (vi)   generally be in chronological sequence;

   (vii)   include a statement of truth;

   (viii)   be signed by the witness;

   (ix)   be dated.

CPR, r 32.5(2) provides that unless the court orders otherwise, exchanged witness statements will stand as the witnesses' evidence-in-chief. Rules 32.5(3) and (4) go on to say that witnesses will only be allowed to amplify their statements or to deal with new matters arising since service of witness statements if there is a 'good reason' for doing so. Consequently, you must ensure your witness statements contain all the evidence which your witnesses can be expected to give and which would be asked of them in examination-in-chief. Further, the statements must accord with the oath/affirmation to tell the truth, the whole truth, and nothing but the truth.

(c) *Expert evidence.* Consider the expert evidence available to you and to the other side, and decide whether expert evidence should be presented to the court and, if so, what evidence should come from your side and how that evidence may most advantageously be deployed. Bear in mind the costs consequences.

Consider how far the expert evidence can be agreed. Consider what directions (if any) have already been given under CPR, Part 35. Decide what further directions (if any) should be applied for. Do you want permission for your expert to give evidence orally? Do you need a direction permitting you to cross-examine the other side's expert? Consider whether (exceptionally) you want to use the other side's expert's report as part of your own evidence, under CPR, r 35.11.

When you have decided these matters, make a note to advise your solicitor accordingly.

(d) *Documentary evidence.* Consider what documentary evidence should be put before the court, and the form in which that documentary evidence should be presented.

Decide what advice you need to give on the preparation of the bundles for use at the trial, and make a note accordingly. It is the responsibility of the solicitors for the claimant to prepare the trial bundles, but the solicitors for the other parties will naturally want to have some input into the matter. In any event, PD 39, para 3.9 requires that the contents of the trial bundles should be agreed where possible, and that the parties should also agree where possible (1) that the documents contained in the bundle are authentic, even if not disclosed under CPR, Part 31, and (2) that those documents may be treated as evidence of the facts stated in them, even if no Civil Evidence Act notice has been served. Where it is not possible to agree the contents of the trial bundles, a summary of the points of disagreement must be included with the bundles filed.

The claimant's solicitors must file the trial bundles between three and seven days before the trial. They must also make sufficient copies (a) to supply for the use of their own team, (b) to supply an identical copy to all other parties to the proceedings, and (c) to bring to court for the use of the witnesses.

Consider what advice you need to give on the contents and ordering of these bundles, bearing in mind para 3.2 of PD 39 (which lists what the trial bundle must include) and any relevant specific directions that have been given. Be selective, particularly in deciding what items of correspondence and other documents need to go into the chronological bundle. Do *not* automatically advise that copies of all disclosed documents should be included.

Consider reminding your solicitor of the practical requirements of PD 39, including the requirements that:

(i)   The trial bundles must be in ring binders or lever arch files, and each volume must be clearly distinguishable by different colours and/or letters.

In larger cases, it is often helpful to use both colour coding and clear labelling, so that (for example) the claim form, statements of case, requests for further information and responses, and interim orders are in red files labelled A1, A2, etc., the affidavits and witness statements used on interim applications are in green files labelled B1, B2, etc., the witness statements and witness summaries to be relied on are in purple files labelled C1, C2, etc., the experts' reports and responses, etc., are in yellow files labelled D1, D2, etc., the correspondence and other documents are arranged chronologically in black files labelled E1, E2, etc., and the core bundle is in a blue file, labelled F.

(ii) If there are numerous bundles, a core bundle must be prepared containing copies only of the essential documents. It is your job to advise which documents are essential. It is usually better if the documents in the core bundle retain the page numbers given to them in the chronological bundle, and are not given new numbers. In that way, each page has only one reference number, not two.

(iii) Every page of every document in the trial bundle must be fully and easily legible. Each page in each bundle must be numbered consecutively.

Make a note to remind your solicitor that the originals of all documents in the trial bundle must be brought to court for the trial.

(e) *Hearsay evidence.* Consider whether any of the evidence which you wish to adduce is hearsay. If so, consider what notices need to be served pursuant to the Civil Evidence Act 1995 and make a note to advise accordingly.

Consider any notices served by the other side, to see whether you should serve a counter notice.

Consider how to deal with any issue raised by any counter notice which has been served by either side.

22.1.6.6 Step 6: final considerations

Bring together in a final note all of the other preparatory matters that you have considered.

Consider how best you can advance your own case or attack your opponent's case. Is there anything more that you need to do to the statements of case, or by way of further information or specific disclosure? Are there any more investigations that need to be made by your instructing solicitor, or an enquiry agent, or accountants, or other experts? Should you apply for security for costs (or additional security)?

Is your case ready for each stage of the proceedings up to and during the trial? Are your witness statements and expert reports ready for exchange? Have all necessary notices been prepared and served? Does your solicitor know what needs to go in the trial bundles? Are your witnesses ready, willing, and able to appear at the trial? Should you serve witness summonses on any of the other side's witnesses?

Would it be in your client's interests, even at this late stage, to revisit the possibility of a negotiated settlement or ADR? If so, how might that best be pursued? Would it be in your client's interest to consider making or increasing a Part 36 offer? Is there an outstanding Part 36 offer from the other side, to which your client needs to respond?

Finally, consider whether your instructions have raised any particular matters for your advice. Are there any specific questions which your solicitor has asked? If so, you should give a specific answer.

22.1.6.7 Step 7: writing

Finally, when all the thinking and analysis have been completed, write your advice. You will already have prepared lists of the things that you will want to say. For example, you will already have notes as to any amendments to the statements of case or further information which needs to be requested or given (from step 2). Your list of issues is already ready (from step 3), as is your list of witnesses to give oral evidence (from step 5), etc.

After setting out the title of the claim and the title of the advice, resist the temptation to begin your advice with a long introduction. The most you are likely to need is one or two prefatory sentences, something like:

> In this claim my client, Mrs Bloggs, seeks damages against her former employers for personal injuries which she suffered in an accident at work. I am asked to advise on evidence.

Then, list the issues (so that you can refer to each issue by number at later stages in the advice) and set out step by step precisely what you advise your solicitor to do, in accordance with the notes that you have made as you have gone through your analysis.

Divide your advice into short numbered paragraphs.

When you get to the end, remember to sign it and to put the date and your chambers address at the bottom.

22.2 Sample advice on evidence

ALPINE SYSTEMS BV v MIDWEST BANK PLC

(1) CHARLES DICKENS AND HENRY JAMES (2) THOMAS HARDY

(3) CHARLES DICKENS

(Third Parties)

ADVICE ON EVIDENCE

1   The claimant in the main proceedings, Alpine Systems BV ('Alpine'), claims SWF 3,365,105.70 and interest said to be due from Midwest Bank plc ('the Bank') under the terms of an agreement which Alpine alleges is contained in a letter dated 5th August 2012 which the Bank wrote on behalf of a customer, Paulton Magna Armaments Limited ('PMA'), to Alpine. In the additional claim which the Bank has brought against the third parties, the Bank claims an indemnity against Alpine's claim from the three guarantors of PMA's indebtedness (the 'Guarantors'). Trial is fixed for 18th May 2015. I am asked by the Bank to advise on evidence. Directions for trial were given by Master Snow at a Case Management Conference on 6th October 2014.

The statements of case

2   I have reconsidered the Bank's Statements of Case in the main proceedings and in the additional claim, in the light of the further documents and information now available. I do not think that any amendments are required.

3   In its answer to the Bank's Request for Further Information under paragraph 3 of the Particulars of Claim, Alpine stated that it could not give further information until after disclosure. Disclosure has now taken place.

4   Similarly, the Guarantors' Further Information under paragraphs 4, 5 (Request 3) and 6 (Request 6) indicates that they cannot give proper information until after they have had access to PMA's records, which were then with the liquidator. Since the liquidation has now been completed, any necessary access could and should by now have taken place.

5   In the circumstances, we should renew our requests for this information. Drafts of the necessary Requests accompany this Advice.

The issues

6   The real issues in this case can be stated very shortly. Did the Bank, by its letter dated 5th August 2012, take on a liability to Alpine to make payment if it received funds? If so, is the Bank entitled to an indemnity for that liability under the Guarantees, bearing in mind (a) the purpose for which those guarantees were taken, and (b) the terms of Mr Dickens' letter of 28th October 2012 and of the Bank's replies dated 1st November and 11th November 2012?

7   However, the issues set out in the statements of case are a little more complex. They are:

(a) *On the Claim:*

Issue	PofC	Def
1. Is Alpine a company incorporated in the Netherlands Antilles?	1	1
2. In August 2012	2	2/3

    (a)   Did PMA owe Alpine SWF 3,365,105.70?

    (b)   Was Alpine pressing for payment of that sum?

    (c)   Was PMA supplying goods to Ruritania and anticipating payment of a substantial sum for those goods later in the year?

    (d)   Did the Bank know any of (a)–(c)?

3. Was any written agreement made between Alpine and the Bank, by the Bank's letter dated 5th August 2012 and Alpine's reply dated 12th August 2012? (Against the background, *inter alia*, of the two similar letters written by the Bank on 7th September 2011, and what happened under those.)	3/4	4/5
4. Did the Bank on behalf of PMA receive sufficient money from Ruritania in October/November 2012 to pay Alpine?	5	6
5. Did PMA subsequently instruct the Bank to pay trade creditors in preference to Alpine? If yes: (a) Was the Bank entitled to act on those instructions? (b) Did the Bank do so?	5	7
6. Was the Bank's authority/duty to make payments to Alpine ended by the winding up of PMA?	5	7

(b) *In the additional claim*

Issue	Gtrs' Def	Gtrs' Rep
1. What was PMA's business?	2	3
2. Did PMA enter into a contract with the Ruritanian Government in November 2010 for the supply of 20,000 medical kits, and need increased overdraft facilities for that? Did the Bank know of this?	3	3
3. Were the guarantees given specifically to obtain (in October 2010, June 2011 and March 2012) increased facilities for that purpose?	3/5	3/5
4. Did the Bank know of this and 'accept . . . the purpose and consideration for which the guarantees were given'?	6	1
5. Did the Bank on behalf of PMA receive sufficient money from Ruritania in October/November 2012 to extinguish its overdraft?	7	6
6. Did the Bank, *inter alia*, by its letters dated 1st November and 11th November 2012, treat the guarantees as having been discharged (except in the event of a wrongful preference claim)?	8/9	7/8
7. As a result of (3) to (6), is the Bank estopped by convention or representation from asserting that its liability to Alpine is covered by the guarantees?	12	9
8. Did PMA request or authorise the Bank to incur personal liability to Alpine? If not, can the Bank in any event recover from PMA or the Guarantors?	13	10

Two issues not set out in the Defence served by the Guarantors, but which might be raised at trial, are:

9. Were the Bank's letters dated 1st November and 11th November 2012 effective as a release of the guarantees?

10. What was the effect of Mr Dickens' letter dated 28th October 2012 which purported to give notice of discontinuance prior to any demand being made?

Oral evidence

8   Master Snow's Order provided for witness statements to be exchanged by 5 December 2014. The preparation of these statements is therefore now urgent. The Bank's principal witness will be Mr Donne. I should be very grateful if Mr Donne could be sent a full set of the relevant printouts of the Bank's records and documents, statements of case (including further information) and witness statements, to refresh his memory of events. Then a full statement should be taken from him, dealing specifically with the contents of each document and with each issue raised in the statements of case.

9   In particular, I am curious to know whether there is any substance whatsoever in the suggestion in the Guarantors' Defence that Mr Donne and the Guarantors, by common consent, treated the guarantees as covering (or assumed that they covered) only the Ruritanian contract indebtedness and no more. His letters dated 1st November and 11th November 2012 give a little support to this allegation. Similarly, I should like to know (a) why, having stated that he had irrevocable instructions to pay Alpine, he did not institute procedures to act on those instructions and did not, in the event, act on them; and (b) what happened to the payments from Indonesia, etc., in respect of which he had previously written similar letters to Alpine. The distinction between Mr Forster's guarantee and the others will also need careful explanation.

10   Apart from Mr Donne, Mr Marvel also seems to have been involved with Mr Dickens' affairs (see, e.g. Mr Donne's email dated 29th June 2011 referring to a telephone conversation between Mr Marvel and Mr Dickens). Relevant Bank record entries have the initials STC and WW. Mr Byron and Mr Shelley seem also to have written relevant letters and emails. I should be grateful if statements could be taken from them (after sight of the documents), and from anyone else that they or Mr Donne can identify as having been involved with PMA/Mr Dickens. We can decide whether or not to serve statements from them when we have had the opportunity to consider what they are able to say.

Documentary evidence

11   *Further disclosure*   The correspondence with the liquidator is not privileged, is at least arguably relevant to the matters in issue in these proceedings, and ought (as my instructions suggest) to be disclosed in a supplemental list. I cannot see any reference to PMA's bank statements in our List of Documents. Those for 2012 onwards (at least) might be relevant to the issues in this claim, are not privileged, and should also be disclosed.

12   *Bundles for trial*   I suggest that the trial bundles should consist of the following: Bundle (A): Statements of case (together with further information); statements of case in the additional proceedings (together with further information); interim orders; summary judgment witness statements and exhibits. Bundle (B): The guarantees; the relevant bank statements. Bundle (C): Correspondence, etc. (including the relevant Bank records), in chronological order. Bundle (D): Witness Statements.

13   I have flagged the pages in sections (8), (9), and (10) in my instructions which I consider should go into Bundle (C) with yellow sticky markers in the top right-hand corners of the pages. Since the Claimant's solicitors will probably be the ones to prepare the bundles, we might tactfully remind them that each page of each bundle must be legible and should be numbered at centre bottom, in accordance with Practice Direction 39. A little nearer the time, it might also be sensible to remind them (again as tactfully as possible) to instruct their advocate to contact me with a view to agreeing a draft trial timetable (which must be filed with the trial bundle (see *The Queen's Bench Guide* para 7.4.1)), a list of issues, and a chronology (see *The Queen's Bench Guide* para 7.11.10).

Notices

14   I do not think that it is necessary for us to serve notices on the Claimant or the Guarantors at this stage. If Mr Donne is available to give oral evidence, a *Civil Evidence Act* notice will be unnecessary. The statements of case contain sufficient admissions to make the service of notices to admit unnecessary.

Security for costs

15   My Instructing Solicitor should check that the amount of our present security for costs is sufficient to cover the anticipated costs of a five-day trial. If it is not, we should ask Alpine (and if necessary apply) for more.

Costs Budget

16   This action was begun in October 2013, after CPR, Pt 3 Section II and PD 3E came into force. However, the papers sent down to me have not included any copy of the agreed or approved costs budgets. My instructing solicitors should, when considering the issue of further security, also review the costs budgets that they have agreed or which have been approved, to ensure that they remain suitable in the light of what has happened since those budgets were set and of the further steps that I have proposed should be taken. If any upward or downward revision is appropriate, my instructing solicitors should (as required by PD 3E, para 2.6) seek to agree those revisions with the other parties or, in default of agreement, apply to have them approved by the Court.

Settlement

17   There is no new material in the papers now before me to make me revise my view that the Bank is likely to be held liable to Alpine but entitled to an indemnity from the Guarantors. Three matters, however, suggest that a reasonable commercial settlement might be in the Bank's best interest.

18   First of all, there is the risk that the Bank may be the subject of critical judicial comment. For example, the judge might comment adversely on Mr Donne's actions in stating that he had irrevocable instructions but then not even protesting when those instructions were revoked and/or ignored. The judge might also criticise the Bank for not honouring its word to Alpine if, as I think is likely, he finds that the Bank is liable to them.

19   Secondly, this is a small claim compared with its complexity, even allowing for interest. The costs are likely to be out of proportion to the amount at stake. Thirdly, there is the inevitable litigation risk that the case will not in the event turn out as we now anticipate.

20   The Bank may be in a good position to 'broke' a without prejudice settlement between the Claimant and the Guarantors. The inevitable discussions about bundles and other preparations for trial may provide a good opportunity to initiate settlement negotiations (or, at least, to suggest that the parties revisit the possibility of some form of ADR). Of course, the ideal settlement from the Bank's point of view would be for the Guarantors to pay off the Claimant and pay the Bank's costs. However, some discount from this ideal position may have to be made to reflect the risks I have outlined and the irrecoverable costs of fighting this case through to trial.

LEWIS ELLIOT

Gray's Inn Walks Chambers
Gray's Inn
London WC1R 5EA

8th November 2014

Advice on evidence in a criminal case

23.1 An approach to writing a criminal advice on evidence

If you are prosecuting, you must (applying the CPS Code for Prosecutors) consider whether there is a realistic prospect of conviction (in other words, whether it is more likely than not that the accused will be convicted). If you are defending, you must ensure that you understand the nature and the strength of the case against the accused, and you must consider how that case can best be met. In either case, the advice on evidence is written in order to assist those instructing counsel in their preparation of the case. It is not seen by the other side; you are therefore able (indeed obliged) to be candid. The advice given must be practical and should demonstrate that you are in command of all the facts and issues.

It is unusual for a written advice to be produced in a magistrates' court case, and so this chapter will focus on Crown Court trials.

The advice should demonstrate that you are thinking ahead to how the trial will be conducted. The jury will know nothing about the case before they come into court. The Crown will have to present the evidence—and the defence will have to meet that case—in a way that the jurors can follow. How are the pieces to be put together in a coherent way? Can anything be made the subject of formal admissions so that the issues are narrowed? Can the case be presented in a way that will make it easier for the jury to understand and to concentrate on what really is in dispute? The more complex the case, the more necessary it is to put it into a digestible form to aid juror comprehension.

The advice given must always be realistic. For example, restrictions on criminal legal aid mean that requests for expenditure of money are scrutinised with great care. The Crown Prosecution Service (CPS) and the police are also restricted by their budgets. This could give rise to difficulties, e.g. an apparently short, simple case may be decisively defended by the evidence of a handwriting expert or by DNA analysis, but the gravity of the offence may not 'justify' such an expense. Rule 1.1(2)(g) of the Criminal Procedure Rules requires that cases should be dealt with in ways which take account of the gravity of the offence alleged, the complexity of what is in issue, the severity of the consequences for the defendant and others affected, and the needs of other cases; in other words, the steps taken in a case must be proportionate.

Rule 1.2(e) also requires that the case should be dealt with 'efficiently and expeditiously'. This requires cases to be disposed of as quickly as possible. This in turn requires the issues in the case to be narrowed as much as possible. Moreover, because of the requirement of Defence Statements, and of the manner in which judges conduct preliminary hearings, the defence cannot keep all their options open. Defence counsel must draw a distinction between those areas where there is no dispute, and those areas where it is proper to insist that the prosecution prove its case. Prosecution counsel, in turn, must decide which aspects of the evidence need to be given in full, and which matters are more formal and can be summarised.

23.1.1   The charge(s)

The advice should first set out the counts which are on the indictment, and point out their relationship to each other. Are they different ways of looking at the same set of facts? Are they alternatives? Are the particulars sufficiently detailed? Is joinder of the counts appropriate, or should they be separated? Prosecution counsel will often find that the CPS has already served an indictment of their own drafting. However, that does not release counsel from the obligation to ensure that it is drafted correctly and to bring any proposed changes to the attention of the CPS for their agreement before applying to amend the indictment. If counsel is asked to draft the indictment, then the analysis of the evidence should include an explanation as to why you have drafted the indictment as you have, and why (if appropriate) you have not followed the charges that were sent for trial.

23.1.2   Summarise the evidence in the light of charges

This should be an analysis, not a mere regurgitation of the facts set out in the brief. The analysis should show how, in their various ways, the witnesses—both by the oral evidence they will give and the exhibits which they will produce—will tell the story and prove the case. You should comment on the various strengths and weaknesses in the evidence and point out any discrepancies. This of course requires extremely careful reading of the entire brief. Have all the documents referred to in the statements been exhibited, and are copies of all the exhibits in your bundle? If something is missing, you must ask for a copy.

23.1.3   Further statements may be necessary

If you are prosecuting, you must look for gaps in your case, and identify who is best suited to fill them: is it an existing witness or a new one? Counsel must indicate what statements are required and should set out the issues that need to be addressed by the witness(es). (This is, of course, *not* an invitation to suggest that the existing witnesses should think better of what they have already said.)

Having noted any discrepancies between witnesses, you must decide what (if anything) can be done. It may be that two people, looking at the same events, have simply remembered events in a different order. Or do the discrepancies reveal a more fundamental flaw in the case?

It is important to recall that the defence are entitled to notice of what a prosecution witness is going to say. Prior to the trial, the defence will have received copies of the witness statements made by all the prosecution witnesses. Any evidence coming to light after the statements have been served on the accused must be sent to the defence with a 'notice of additional evidence'. This means that prosecution counsel cannot use examination-in-chief to bring out, for the first time, significant evidence against the defendant. If the case is to be fleshed out significantly, then a further statement will be required from the witness (and it will have to be served on the defence before the trial).

Prosecuting counsel must also consider the extent to which matters raised by the defendant after arrest should be dealt with. For example, a defendant might, when interviewed, claim to have an alibi (or an alibi might be raised in the defence statement). Counsel should advise that appropriate investigations be made by police to see if it is possible to undermine the alibi; similarly, counsel may advise on whether any defence witnesses whose details have been provided to the prosecution by the defence ought to be interviewed by the police.

Counsel should also consider whether prosecution witnesses should be asked to deal with matters which the defence are likely to raise in cross-examination. Witnesses who are confronted with allegations for the first time when they are in the witness box may not deal with those allegations very well. Where appropriate, they can be asked to make further statements, e.g. 'I have been asked by the officer how I could have recognised the suspect. I have seen him in the pub several times before'.

It follows that prosecution counsel should consider this question: 'If I were defending, what would I consider to be the weak point(s) in the prosecution case?'

The prosecutor must also consider the question of disclosure (under the Criminal Procedure and Investigations Act 1996) of unused material which appears to undermine the prosecution case or support the defence case (considered in more detail later in this chapter). If this is a matter where a Public Interest Immunity application in respect of unused material is appropriate, that issue should also be addressed.

23.1.4 Never expect the defence to admit anything

Even though the defence are under an obligation to provide a Defence Statement, they are not obliged to admit to anything which the Crown cannot prove. The advice written by prosecuting counsel should set out each element of the charge and say how the evidence deals with it, bearing in mind that some things can be proved directly and others only by inference.

When advising the defence, counsel should bear in mind that many of the rules relating to the admissibility of evidence apply equally to the defence. Evidence which would otherwise be inadmissible does not become admissible merely because the defence (not the prosecution) wish to adduce it.

23.1.5 Witnesses are different

In law, the evidence of civilians and of police officers is of equal weight. In practice, there is an important difference in the way they usually give evidence in court. Any witness may, in the witness box, refresh their memory from a document made or verified earlier by that witness, provided that the recollection of the witness is likely to have been significantly better when the earlier document was produced (see s 139 of the Criminal Justice Act 2003). Police officers habitually make notes, within a few hours, in an 'Evidence and Action Book' (AEB). Their witness statements are typed up from that. It is common practice for officers who were at the scene together to make their notes together, so that there is an agreed version of events. Because the officers will almost certainly be entitled to refresh their memory from their original notes when in the witness box, and since the statement is effectively the notebook entry, officers, in examination-in-chief, can be expected to say (more or less verbatim) what is in their statement, and, indeed, will corroborate what the other officers will also say about those events. However, it is essential to check each police statement against the others to see whether there are discrepancies. If so, these should be noted, as with any other discrepancy, and an explanation sought.

Civilians are less likely to have made contemporaneous notes. Their version of events is normally recorded for the first time in a statement which is taken from them by a police officer. If it was taken very shortly after the event, then they may refresh their memory from it in the witness box, and so it is worth checking to see whether a prosecution witness is in that position. More often, though, the statement will have been taken several hours, days, or even weeks later, and the trial may be months after that. The witness is then only entitled to read their statement outside court. Once in the witness box, the witness has to recall things as best as he or she can. The result is that the oral evidence may well differ from the written statement in particular details (e.g. the gist of a conversation will be remembered rather than the exact words). Prosecution counsel must anticipate that there will be a certain amount of leeway and take this into account, especially if certain elements of the offence can only be proved if the evidence comes out in a particular way.

In respect of all witnesses, it should be borne in mind that there may be typographical errors in the statements, and these may also have to be addressed.

23.1.6 Admissibility

Counsel should consider the admissibility of all prosecution evidence against each defendant. This may become more complicated if there is a co-defendant.

Sometimes, the police take very detailed witness statements, which contain conversation and comments which may be inadmissible because they are irrelevant or unfairly prejudicial to the accused. Defence counsel in particular should consider these passages: do you wish them to be excluded? Or are they, for example, a source of cross-examination on consistency? Counsel should point out where editing needs to be done, and every effort should be made to agree this with your opponent. If agreement is not possible, you must seek the judge's ruling.

The Police and Criminal Evidence Act 1984 and the Codes of Practice are the basis on which most admissibility arguments are founded. You must be wholly up to date with these provisions and with the relevant case law. You should not assume that simply because a police officer followed a certain course of action that he or she was correct to do so. Counsel must see whether the rules were in fact adhered to. If there appears to have been a breach, then say so. If you are prosecuting then you must warn the CPS that certain evidence may be excluded. Where admissibility is likely to be an issue, you should set out the arguments for and against exclusion of the evidence in question and advise how likely it is that the judge will exclude that evidence.

It is important to make sure that you have a copy of the recording of the police interview, of the custody record, of any CAD messages (i.e. radio messages to and from the police control room), and of the CRIS entries (i.e. computerised record of reported crimes). If you are defending and you think there is evidence which may be relevant but which has not been disclosed by the prosecution, you should ask for it to be disclosed. This is subject to any prosecution arguments that the material is not disclosable because it does not undermine their case. Even if the prosecution are not obliged to disclose the material, it may nonetheless be disclosed voluntarily, but you should not assume that your opponent will agree to this.

23.1.7 Preliminary hearings

The Criminal Procedure and Investigations Act 1996 requires preliminary hearings to take place before all Crown Court trials. The nature of the hearing differs according to whether or not the trial is likely to be lengthy or complex. However, in both cases, points of law and arguments relating to the admissibility of evidence should be raised at the preliminary hearing.

Where the case is likely to be complex or lengthy, the judge may order a 'preparatory hearing' to take place. The purpose is to identify the issues in the case, to see how the jury can be assisted to understand those issues, to expedite the trial, and to assist the judge's management of the trial (s 29). Under s 31, the judge can make rulings on the admissibility of evidence or other questions of law likely to arise in the trial. An advice on evidence in such a case should therefore address these issues.

In the case of trials other than those which are likely to be complex or lengthy (in other words, the majority of cases), there will be a pre-trial hearing known as a 'Plea and Case Management Hearing' ('PCMH'). At this hearing, the defendant is asked to enter a plea. Where the defendant pleads 'not guilty', prosecuting and defence counsel are expected to inform the court of matters such as: the issues in the case; the number of witnesses to be called; any points of law likely to arise (including questions on the admissibility of evidence); and whether any technical equipment (such as video equipment) is likely to be needed. It follows that it is very important that by the time of this hearing, the factual and legal issues in the case have been identified.

At the PCMH, the judge is empowered to make rulings on the admissibility of evidence and on any other questions of law which are relevant to the case. These rulings are binding for the whole of the trial unless there is an application for the ruling to be altered under s 31(11) on the basis that the interests of justice require the judge to vary or discharge it. This is so whether or not the preliminary hearing and the trial are presided over by the same judge. The advice on evidence should therefore deal with the matters that will have to be considered at the PCMH.

23.1.8 Plans or photos

On reading the brief, it may seem that the jury would be assisted by seeing a plan of the area (or of a particular building) or photographs. You should bear in mind that photographs are not an accurate representation of what things look like, in terms of distances, compared to actually being at the scene. A 'view' (that is, a visit to the scene as part of the trial) is an exceptional procedure and requires a good deal of organisation by the court. If you feel it is essential, then the court should be warned ahead of time and the matter should be canvassed with the judge as early as possible (ideally at the PCMH).

23.1.9 Expert evidence

Expert evidence is governed by Part 33 of the Criminal Procedure Rules. A party wishing to adduce expert evidence must serve it on the court and on each other party to the proceedings. The report must be provided 'as soon as practicable' and, if the other side request it, they must be provided with a copy of the record of any 'examination, measurement, test or experiment' on which the finding or opinion is based.

The first step is to ask your instructing solicitor to obtain a report from the proposed expert. Once the report has been obtained, the second step is to decide whether or not it advances your case. Reports of prosecution witnesses who conduct forensic tests which have an inconclusive result or which may support the defence case in some way have to be served on the defence as unused material.

Always have regard to what expertise your witnesses in fact have. For example, the person who can give evidence of the value of goods is someone who is in that type of business. Police officers can be experts in drugs matters, if they have the appropriate experience in the drugs squad. This applies, for example, to the value of particular drugs and how they are normally packaged and sold.

23.1.10 Further witnesses for the defence

Although the defendant does not have to prove anything, in practice the defence must consider the question of possible defence witnesses. Can someone corroborate the defendant's version of events? Even if a witness can deal with only some of the issues, a patently honest defence witness can persuade a jury that the defendant might well be telling the truth about other matters as well.

23.1.11   Witnesses to attend court

At the PCMH, it should be agreed which witnesses will be called to give evidence at the trial. The court must be informed if these requirements change. The defence can agree to witness statements of prosecution witnesses being read to the jury (rather than the witness attending to give 'live' evidence). This will be the case if there are no questions to be asked by way of cross-examination of that particular witness. You should not ask for the attendance of witnesses unless they are really needed (and so witnesses should not be asked to attend on a 'just in case' basis).

23.1.12   Disclosure

As we have already seen, an important aspect of the case that has to be monitored is disclosure under the Criminal Procedure and Investigations Act 1996. This requires the prosecutor to disclose to the accused any prosecution material which might reasonably be considered capable of undermining the case for the prosecution against the accused or of assisting the case for the accused (see s 3). The prosecution are under a continuing duty of disclosure (under s 7A), and so the question of disclosure must be kept under regular review.

The defence must (in Crown Court cases) or may (in magistrates' court and youth court cases) serve a defence statement. Under s 6A, this has to:

(a) set out the nature of the accused's defence, including any particular defences on which he or she intends to rely;

(b) indicate the matters of fact on which the accused takes issue with the prosecution;

(c) set out, in the case of each such matter, why the accused takes issue with the prosecution;

(d) set out particulars of the matters of fact on which he intends to rely for the purposes of his defence; and

(e) indicate any point of law (including any point as to the admissibility of evidence or abuse of process) which the accused wishes to take, and any authority on which he or she intends to rely for that purpose.

Where the accused wishes to rely on an alibi, the defence statement must give full particulars of the alibi and of any witnesses the accused believes are able to give evidence in support of the alibi. The defence also have to supply the prosecution with details (including name and address) of any witnesses they propose to call.

If the defendant fails to comply with the duties imposed by the Act, adverse inferences may be drawn. This can happen where, for example, the accused fails to give an initial defence statement or does so late (where one is mandatory); at trial, puts forward a defence which was not mentioned in the defence statement, or relies on a matter which was not mentioned in his defence statement when it should have been mentioned, or adduces evidence in support of an alibi without having given particulars of the alibi or of the witnesses to be called in support of the alibi.

Once the defence statement has been served, the prosecution review the unused material in their possession to see if anything which has not been disclosed already ought to be disclosed because it undermines the prosecution case or supports the defence case. If the defence have reasonable cause to believe that the prosecution have not disclosed material which ought to have been disclosed, an application for an order for disclosure may be made under s 8 of the 1996 Act.

These are all matters which have to be considered carefully in any advice on evidence, whether counsel is advising the prosecution or the defence. As well as considering whether there has been full compliance by one's own side, one should also consider whether any point can be taken against the other side on the basis of their non-compliance.

23.1.13   Defence solicitors contacting the prosecution

Defence counsel should ask their instructing solicitors to deal with any matters which involve contacting the prosecution. Some examples are:

(a) Section 9 statements of certain defence witnesses. It may be clear that some matters, e.g. medical evidence, are capable of agreement. Statements by such witnesses should be put in proper s 9 form and served on the prosecution in good time.

(b) Discontinuing proceedings. If defence counsel feels that the prosecution should consider discontinuing the proceedings (e.g. having regard to the defendant's mental or physical condition), instructing solicitors should be asked to invite the CPS to reconsider the matter.

(c) Offering a plea to a lesser charge. It may seem from your instructions that the defendant could properly plead guilty to a lesser charge, whether or not that appears on the indictment. If so, you should advise accordingly and, if the defendant accepts this advice, ask that the offer be put forward to the prosecution.

In addition, the defence are obliged to inform the prosecution whether or not they agree the proposed summary of the interview conducted by the police. Having first listened to the recording of the interview, defence counsel must advise on this, and must then ask the solicitors to send a copy of any proposed amendments of the summary to the prosecution in good time before the hearing, so that prosecuting counsel has an opportunity to consider them. Amendments which are put forward at court may require the CPS to do the editing there and then, with consequent delay to the trial and criticism by the judge. Prosecution counsel should also listen to the recording: the police summary may be inaccurate or inadequate. Both counsel may, during the trial, suggest that the jury listen to the recording itself.

23.1.14   Continuity

Each exhibit in a case must be given a number at the time it is taken into custody. Each witness who deals with it must refer to it by the same number. For example, a police officer should refer to a suspected stolen object as AB/1. If the officer shows it to the real owner, the latter must also refer to it as AB/1. It is not enough for the loser to say, 'I have been shown a television which I recognise as mine'. The same rules apply to drugs cases, where there must be continuity from the moment the exhibit is found to the time it is re-sealed by the forensic scientist after analysis. If there are gaps in continuity, then further statements should be requested.

23.1.15   Summarising

It is often helpful for the advice to conclude with a summary listing all the matters on which action is to be taken. This summary should be complete, as those instructing may well use it as a checklist.

23.2   Sample advice on evidence for prosecution

IN THE CROWN COURT SITTING AT OXTON   T0156/14

THE QUEEN

v

STUART GAINSFORD

ADVICE ON EVIDENCE

1   Stuart Gainsford was sent for trial on a charge of aggravated arson, contrary to s 1(2) of the Criminal Damage Act 1971. It is alleged that, on the evening of 26th November, Mr Gainsford threw a lighted bottle containing petrol through the window of a shop owned by Ms Valerie Downland. The prosecution case is that Mr Gainsford had a grudge against Ms Downland, whose recently opened shop was in direct competition to Mr Gainsford's shop in the same high street. Fortunately, the automatic sprinklers extinguished the fire before it could take hold, though some damage was caused.

2   I am asked to advise on whether the indictment is drafted appropriately and on the evidence in the case, with particular regard to any further steps that need to be taken in order to prepare for the trial.

The indictment

3   I am sorry that I have to advise those instructing that the indictment as presently drafted is incorrect. Where the aggravated form of arson or criminal damage is charged, there should be two counts in the indictment, one alleging intent to endanger life, and the other recklessness as to the endangerment of life (see *R v Hoof* (1980) 72 Cr App 126). This is to enable the court to know, for the purposes of sentencing, on which basis the jury has convicted the accused. It follows that the existing count would have to be split into two separate counts.

4   However, in my view, there is insufficient evidence to justify a charge of arson with intent to endanger life. If, as the evidence tends to suggest, this was a 'grudge' attack, the only person whose life the accused intended to endanger was Valerie Downland. However, the words allegedly shouted by the arsonist—'I wish you were here to burn, you witch'— seem to negative any intent to endanger life. It seems from these words that the arsonist believed that Ms Downland was not in the shop at the time, and so (being unaware that she was in fact working in the office at the back of the shop) cannot have intended to endanger her life. There is no other evidence from which the jury could infer the specific intent to endanger life, and so I take the view that this charge should not be pursued.

5   Nonetheless, I think that there are reasonable prospects of establishing a charge of arson being reckless as to whether life would be endangered. It is not necessary to show that anyone's life was in fact endangered, only that the fire created a risk that life would be endangered (*R v Parker* [1993] Crim LR 856).

6   The danger to life must have been created by the damage that the accused intended to do (in this case, the fire), but it is the damage which the accused intended, or as to which he was reckless, which is relevant, rather than the actual damage which happens to have been caused (see *R v Dudley* [1989] Crim LR 57, where only trivial damage, not likely to endanger life, was actually caused, but the appellant's conviction was upheld since he created a risk of much more serious damage which was capable of endangering life). It is therefore irrelevant that the fire in the present case was extinguished before it could do any serious damage.

7   So far as recklessness is concerned, in accordance with *R v G* [2003] UKHL 50; [2004] 1 AC 1034, it must be shown that the accused was subjectively aware of the risk of endangering the life of another. The more obvious the risk of endangering life, the more likely that the jury will conclude that the accused was indeed aware of that risk unless he gives some plausible explanation of why he would not have appreciated the obvious. Since there was a flat above the shop, there was an obvious risk that someone's life could be endangered; the jury is likely to conclude that the accused was actually aware of the risk and thus liable even under this subjective test.

8   There is an advantage in charging the defendant specifically with endangering the lives of Marian Shipley (the tenant of the flat) and her six-month old baby, since the wife of the accused, Alison Gainsford, would then become a compellable witness for the prosecution under s 80(3) of the Police and Criminal Evidence Act 1984, which makes a spouse compellable if the offence charged 'involves' injury or a threat of injury to a person under the age of 16.

9   An amended indictment accompanies this advice. In addition to a count alleging arson with reckless endangerment of life, the draft also includes a count alleging simple arson. The evidence against the accused in relation to the aggravated offence, even by recklessness, is not unassailable and it would, in my view, be appropriate to give the jury the opportunity to convict the accused of the lesser offence if they are not sure that he is guilty of the more serious offence. Indeed, were the accused to offer a plea to simple arson, I would suggest that serious consideration be given to accepting that offer (though it would be important for a written basis of plea to be drawn up to assist the judge when assessing the seriousness of the offence).

Evidence

10   The main issue in this case is identity. As the evidence currently stands, the prosecution must seek to establish that the accused was the arsonist through a chain of circumstantial evidence:

- (i)   The attack occurred in the High Street at 11.30 p.m. on 26th November.
- (ii)   The accused was seen running down the High Street (Patrick Trowton) at approximately 11.45 p.m.
- (iii)   The accused was seen (again by Mr Trowton) getting into a Ford Mondeo motor car (VH05 YTT).
- (iv)   That vehicle had been hired to the accused by Ready Rental cars for the two days 26th and 27th November (see the statement of Susan Yelford).
- (v)   On 2nd December, a blue rag smelling of petrol and a plastic container with a small amount of petrol in it were found in the boot of that vehicle (see the statements of DS Greene and PC Peters, together with the forensic evidence).
- (vi)   The blue rag found in the vehicle matches the rag found at the scene (DS Greene, PC Peters, and the forensic evidence).
- (vii)   The rag found at the scene was used to light the petrol (DS Greene, PC Peters, and the forensic evidence).

11   There is, however, a significant gap in this chain. The accused returned the car to the rental company on 27th November but the car was not searched by the police until 2nd December. It needs to be shown that the blue rag could not have been left in the car by anyone else who hired it. Further enquiries should be made and a further statement taken from Ms Yelford.

12   The case against the accused may be strengthened considerably by the admissions which he made to his wife (if she is compellable as a prosecution witness) and to Julie Forrester. Moreover, inferences can be drawn (under s 34 of the Criminal Justice and Public Order Act 1994) from his failure to mention his alibi when interviewed under caution by the police.

13   I shall deal with these and other matters as I consider the evidence of individual prosecution witnesses.

Valerie Downland

14   A further statement should be taken from Ms Downland. She should be asked to deal with the following matters:

(a)   The voice shouting 'I wish you were here to burn, you witch': Did she recognise the voice? If not, is she at least able to say whether the voice was male or female? Also, how far away was she from the window—close enough to hear clearly what was said?

(b)   'I noticed a strong smell of petrol': this arguably amounts to opinion evidence. In any event, the forensic evidence of the presence of petrol on the blue rag is sufficient on this point.

(c)   'The only person I can think of who would want to harm me is Stuart Gainsford': the defence are likely to succeed in having this evidence ruled inadmissible, at least unless Ms Downland gives much more detailed and specific evidence of the unpleasantness between Mr Gainsford and herself to which she refers. She should give full details of everything said to her by Mr Gainsford when he complained that her shop was taking away his business.

15   Ms Downland should also be asked to provide details of the cost of repairs to the window and the shop itself, and the value of the damaged stock. This will be of relevance to the seriousness of the offence in the event of Mr Gainsford being convicted.

16   Ms Downland also says in her statement that, 'If the fire had taken hold Marian and the baby would certainly have died'. This speculation is clearly inadmissible. If Marian Shipley and her baby were indeed present in the flat, Ms Shipley should be asked to make a statement to that effect.

17   Ms Downland's second statement gives details of her conversation with Julie Forrester, in which Ms Forrester says that Mr Gainsford admitted fire-bombing the shop. Ms Downland's evidence of these admissions to Ms Forrerster is hearsay and so inadmissible. Ms Forrester should be traced and a statement taken from her, setting out in as much detail as possible what Mr Gainsford said to her.

Patrick Trowton

18   The major difficulty in relation to the evidence of Mr Trowton is his apparent reluctance to give evidence. His second statement, dated 2nd March, simply refers to two anonymous telephone calls saying that he should 'keep quiet or else'. This does not provide an adequate explanation of his reluctance. These matters should be investigated fully by the police. Charges of witness intimidation (under s 51 of the Criminal Justice and Public Order Act 1994) or the common law offence of perverting the course of justice may well be appropriate. If the police are able to establish that it was Mr Gainsford who made the telephone calls (or that he caused them to be made), such a charge could (in accordance with the principles laid down in *R v Barrell and Wilson* (1979) 69 Cr App

R 250) properly be joined in the same indictment as the charges relating to the arson attack, given that the intimidation would not have occurred but for the arson.

19   Much fuller detail of the alleged threats is required, in any event, to support the application which will have to be made under s 116 of the Criminal Justice Act 2003 to allow Mr Trowton's original statement to be read to the jury on the basis that he is not testifying through fear, if he persists in his refusal to testify because of the threats he has received.

20   If Mr Trowton does not testify, the fact that he is not doing so through fear will have to be proven by admissible evidence (see *Neill v North Antrim Magistrates' Court* [1992] 1 WLR 1220 and *R v Waters* (1997) 161 JP 249) in order for his original statement to be admissible. Thus, a police officer will have to give evidence that Mr Trowton is refusing to testify because of fear.

21   In deciding whether to allow Mr Trowton's statement to be read, the court will consider whether its admission would result in any unfairness to the accused (having particular regard to how difficult it will be to challenge the statement if he does not give oral evidence) and whether a special measures direction, under s 19 of the Youth Justice and Criminal Evidence Act 1999 should be made instead. In my view, it is almost certain that, even if the court is satisfied that the reason he is not testifying is fear, it would refuse to admit Mr Trowton's statement under s 116. His evidence relates to identification, and the court would be very reluctant to admit documentary evidence of identification where the evidence forms the principal element of the prosecution case on that issue.

22   If the result of the police investigations does not bear out the allegation that Mr Trowton has been threatened, but suggests instead that he has simply changed his mind about testifying, a witness summons should be sought (at the PCMH) under s 3 of the Criminal Procedure (Attendance of Witnesses) Act 1965, since his evidence is clearly highly relevant and it is in the interests of justice that he attends to testify. He should be warned that if he fails to attend court he will be liable to be arrested.

23   Mr Trowton's statement contains a number of gaps. A further statement should be taken from him dealing with the following matters:

(a)   What were the circumstances in which he made the observation (how far away was he from the man he identified as Mr Gainsford)?

(b)   How far away was the car when he observed its registration number? What was the duration of these observations?

(c)   Were the street lights working?

(d)   Was the man he saw running towards or away from Ms Downland's shop?

24   Assuming Mr Trowton does testify, he will probably be allowed to refresh his memory from the piece of paper on which he wrote the registration number of the car he saw, so long as he did so fairly quickly after the sighting. His further statement should therefore say how long after the sighting he wrote down the registration number. Those instructing should ensure that this piece of paper is available at the trial. It would also be helpful to have a plan showing the layout of the High Street.

25   I note that Mr Gainsford's request for an identification procedure to be carried out was refused by the police on the ground that Mr Trowton is acquainted with him and so such a procedure would serve no useful purpose. I think that the police were correct in coming to this view. In my opinion, it is highly unlikely that the judge would rule that there has been a breach of Code D of PACE.

Susan Yelford

26   Ms Yelford's evidence is based on the car hire form exhibit SY/1, which shows the dates that the car was hired by Mr Gainsford. This document is admissible as it falls within s 117 of the Criminal Justice Act 2003, in that it was created by a person in the course of a business (Ms Yelford), the person who supplied the information (Mr Gainsford) had personal knowledge of the matters dealt with, and Ms Yelford cannot reasonably be expected to have any recollection of the matters dealt with in the statement (having regard to the length of time that has elapsed).

27   Ms Yelford should, however, make a further statement dealing with whether the vehicle in question was hired to anyone else after its return by Mr Gainsford on 27th November, up to the time when it was examined by DS Greene and PC Peters on 2nd December.

Alison Gainsford

28   Mrs Gainsford's evidence would be of great help to the prosecution as she gives evidence of a very damaging admission by her husband, saying that he had 'sorted out that witch once and for all'. The use of the word 'witch' links with what Ms Downland heard the arsonist say and so is highly relevant to the central issue of identity.

29   I note from Mrs Gainsford's statement that she does not wish to testify against her husband. As noted above (at para 8), she will be compellable as a prosecution witness provided that the indictment includes a count alleging the reckless endangerment of the life of Marian Shipley's baby. A witness summons should be sought in respect of Mrs Gainsford at the PCMH.

Forensic evidence

30   The evidence of the Fire Investigation Officer that petrol was the accelerant used to start the fire will be sufficient on this point. In any event, it seems from the defence statement that this matter will not be disputed at trial.

31   The evidence of the forensic scientist shows that the rag found in the car and the rag found at the scene came from the same piece of cloth. I note, however, that there is nothing in Mr Sanderson's statement to confirm that the liquid in the plastic container found in the car was in fact petrol. Mr Sanderson also appears to have swapped the exhibit numbers for the two pieces of cloth (SG/1 and SG/3); he also makes no mention of re-sealing the bag containing the plastic container (SG/4). He should be asked to check his records and to make a further statement dealing with the contents of the plastic container and correcting these discrepancies.

32   There is nothing in the papers to suggest that the plastic container or the remnants of the glass bottle were checked for fingerprints—this should be done. If no evidence assisting the prosecution is found, the defence should be informed as this fact would be disclosable under s 7A of the Criminal Procedure and Investigations Act 1996.

33   The piece of charred blue rag found at the shop (SG/1), the remnants of the glass bottle found in the shop (SG/2), the piece of blue rag found in the car (SG/3), and the plastic container found in the car (SG/4), should also be available at the trial.

Alibi

34   Although Mr Gainsford made no mention of an alibi when interviewed by the police, his defence statement asserts that he was at the Green Baize snooker club at the time of the arson attack. The police should interview the two alibi witnesses named in

the defence statement, Sidney Larkhall and Paul Stevens; the questioning should probe how certain they are of the date and time they were with Mr Gainsford. Enquiries could usefully be made at the club itself. It would also be helpful to know the distance between the club and Ms Downland's shop.

Summary

35   It may assist if I summarise the various items of evidence that ought to be sought:

(a) An additional statement from Valerie Downland dealing with:
   (i)   the voice;
   (ii)   the damage of the shop and its contents;
   (iii) the facts behind the alleged grudge held by the accused (paras 14 and 15).

(b) A statement from Marian Shipley (para 16).

(c) A statement from Julie Forrester (para 17).

(d) Investigation of the threats allegedly made against Mr Trowton (paras 18 to 20).

(e) A further statement from Mr Trowton dealing with circumstances of his identification of the accused (para 23).

(f) The piece of paper produced by Mr Trowton showing the registration number of the vehicle to be made available (para 24).

(g) Street plan for the High Street (para 24).

(h) An additional statement from Susan Yelford dealing with the rental history of the car (para 27).

(i) Confirmation of contents of SG/4 and correction of discrepancies in continuity of forensic evidence by Mr Sanderson (para 31).

(j) Fingerprint analysis of SG/2 and SG/4 (para 32).

(k) Investigation of Mr Gainsford's alibi (para 34).

Conclusion

36   Once the further evidence I have requested is available, I would welcome the opportunity to review the case again, in particular with a view to advising on whether the prosecution have sufficient evidence to proceed with the charge of aggravated arson.

Peter Norvic

City Chambers WC1

23.3   Sample advice for defence

IN THE CROWN COURT SITTING AT OXTON   T0155/13

REGINA

v

JOHN HANSON

and

OTHERS

ADVICE ON EVIDENCE

1   John Hanson is charged with violent disorder contrary to s 2 of the Public Order Act 1986, Causing Grievous Bodily Harm with Intent to Resist Arrest contrary to s 18 of the Offences Against the Person Act 1861, and Attempted Robbery contrary to s 1(1) of the Criminal Attempts Act 1981. On the 17th July Mr Hanson was sent to the Oxton Crown Court to stand trial and his Plea and Case Management Hearing is listed for the 21st August. I am asked to advise John Hanson, on evidence, plea, and possible sentence.

The alleged offences

2   The charges of violent disorder and assault arise from an incident on the Abbey Estate, in which a police officer, PC Kemp, sustained a number of quite serious injuries. The prosecution case is that after the officer had attempted to mediate between Mr Spring and his girlfriend, he was punched by Mr Spring. While he was in the process of arresting Mr Spring, PC Kemp was set upon by a group of young men and was repeatedly kicked by his assailants. John Hanson is alleged to have kicked the officer's radio away from him and kicked him in the face. The crowd dispersed when a number of other officers arrived and arrested several of the participants, including Mr Spring.

3   As far as the charge of attempted robbery is concerned, this arises from an incident at an off-licence in which a man, said to be John Hanson, burst in, pulled his jacket over his face and demanded that the owner open the till and give him money. The would-be robber was frustrated by the entry of the owner's brother, whom he punched before escaping. No weapon was involved. Mr Hanson was arrested while he was in a car about an hour later, apparently on the basis that he and the car answered the description given by the witnesses at the off-licence.

Summary

4.   In summary, Mr Hanson's instructions suggest a plea of not guilty on all counts, with the exception of the driving charge. There are defects and discrepancies in the evidence against him, such that his chances of an acquittal on the violent disorder and assault charges are good. Until more information has been received regarding the attempted robbery, it is difficult to evaluate his chances on that count. There are a number of steps which need to be taken by Instructing Solicitors in the next few days to prepare for trial, and these are set out in paragraph 21.

5.   A draft defence statement has been prepared and is appended hereto. Please note that the defence statement should not be served on the CPS or the court until the CPS have complied with their duties of disclosure. Following service of the unused material schedule the defence statement should be amended to include any unused material sought.

Misjoinder

6   It would be in Mr Hanson's interests for the charge of attempted robbery to be separated from those arising from the attack on PC Kemp. The attempted robbery does not appear to arise from the same facts, nor does it form part of a series of offences of the same or similar character. Therefore, inclusion of the attempted robbery count is impermissible in light of Crim PR, r.14.2(3). I would advise that this point should be taken at the Plea and Case Management Hearing. It is likely that the prosecution will apply either for Count 3 to be deleted or for leave to be granted to prefer two fresh indictments out of time, one containing Counts 1 and 2 and the other containing Count 3. The original

indictment could then be stayed. In my view, the judge would accede to either application but the prosecution are most likely to follow the latter course.

Assault and violent disorder

7   As far as the counts of violent disorder and causing grievous bodily harm are concerned, Mr Hanson's primary defence is that of alibi. There is some doubt about this, in that his recollection of the events of the afternoon is unclear, and there is no statement as yet from Vicky Bryant or any of the others who may have been present in the various public houses in question that afternoon. It follows that those instructing me should as a matter of urgency take statements from these potential alibi witnesses. In doing so, of course, such times as the witnesses can recollect will be crucial, together with any reasons they might have for remembering dates and times. Those instructing me will no doubt be aware of the requirement, by virtue of s 6A of the Criminal Procedure and Investigations Act 1996, to provide the prosecution with details of the alibi and any witnesses to be called in support of the alibi. At present the only alibi witnesses I have included in the defence statement are Anthony Mead and Vicky Bryant. I have been unable to include their dates of birth (one of the required particulars) as this information is not in the papers I have before me. Once the process of taking statements from the potential alibi witnesses has been completed, it will be necessary to update the defence statement.

8   Mr Hanson's possible defence of alibi throws into question the strength of the prosecution's identification evidence. The evidence as to Mr Hanson's presence depends largely on what PC Kemp says about 'Man 2', whom the Prosecution allege to be Mr Hanson, and the consistency between the description of that man and Mr Hanson on arrest. When PC Kemp's description of the man who assaulted him is compared with PC Keith's description of Mr Hanson on arrest and Mr Hanson's description of himself in interview, it is apparent that there are a number of similar features. However, by itself the description is rather bland and could fit a large number of people.

9   The Prosecution's case is strengthened by three other pieces of evidence. First, Nuala Carroll says in her statement, 'I also think I recognised John Hanson in the crowd that had gathered round'. PACE 1984 Code D 3.12 requires that, whenever a witness has purported to identify a suspect and the suspect disputes being the person the witness claims to have seen, then an identification procedure must be held unless it is not practicable or would serve no useful purpose. If Mr Hanson is particularly well known to Ms Carroll then the police decision not to hold an identification procedure may be justifiable. However, there is nothing to suggest that this is the case on the face of the papers and it would appear that the police were under a duty to hold an identification procedure. If so, there is a strong argument for excluding her purported identification under s 78 PACE 1984 at trial.

10   Second, the man in the brown jacket (who is apparently, on the Prosecution's case, Mr Hanson) drove off in a blue Vauxhall Cavalier—the same colour and make of car as the one in which Mr Hanson was a passenger when he was arrested (see PC Keith's statement). However, I note that PC Robinson noted that the first three letters of the registration were 'CLP', whereas the registration of the car Mr Hanson was in began with the letters 'CLY'.

11   Third, PC Kemp recalls that Mr Spring shouted at the group and in particular shouted at 'Man 2' to 'Get him off me . . . or you're out of my house and back on the

fucking street'. It is clear from the custody record that Mr Hanson gave Mr Spring's house as his address. However, Mr Hanson states in his proof of evidence that Anthony Mead was also staying at Spring's house and so Spring could equally have been directing his words to him. Copies of the transcripts of the interviews with the other defendants, and in particular Anthony Mead, should be obtained to see whether they contain any statements supporting Mr Hanson's case.

12   In my view, the identification of Mr Hanson as a participant in the assault is relatively weak. In the light of this, it is very surprising that no prosecution witnesses appear to have been invited to attend an identification procedure in accordance with PACE Code D, and the police failure in this regard can clearly be raised at trial in order to underline the weakness of the evidence of Mr Hanson's presence. Incidentally, it appears from Mr Spring's interview that PC Kemp knew Mr Hanson, and was responsible for his conviction on an earlier offence. The facts surrounding this allegation need to be ascertained from Mr Hanson. If it is true, it means that PC Kemp's failure to mention that he recognised 'Man 2' means that it is very unlikely that it was Mr Hanson.

13   In the interview Mr Spring stated that Mr Hanson was a participant in the violent disorder and assaulted PC Kemp by kicking him in the face, an action which PC Kemp attributed to 'Man 2'. The interview is not evidence against Mr Hanson and an application should be made to exclude the prejudicial parts of it at trial under s 78 PACE 1984.

14   If Mr Spring gives evidence at trial to the same effect as his interview the jury will have to decide which, if either, defendant they believe. Mr Spring may attempt to support his case by seeking to adduce evidence of Mr Hanson's bad character. Under s 101(1)(e) of the Criminal Justice Act 2003, a defendant's bad character may be admitted where it has substantial probative value in relation to an important matter in issue between the defendant and a co-defendant. Mr Spring may argue that Mr Hanson has a propensity to commit offences of violence and that this propensity is of substantial probative value as it makes Spring's account of Hanson's role in the incident more credible. Mr Hanson has previous convictions for offences under s 4 of the Public Order Act 1986, Affray and Actual Bodily Harm which may be capable of establishing such a propensity. If I am provided with the details of his previous convictions, I will be able to give Mr Hanson some further advice about the likely outcome of any application made on behalf of Mr Spring. From Mr Hanson's proof of evidence it appears that he does not propose to give evidence against Mr Spring and, as a result, evidence of Mr Hanson's bad character will not be admissible in relation to the issue of his truthfulness.

15   I note that Mr Spring also has previous convictions. If Mr Spring gives evidence which is consistent with what he says in interview, he will be deemed to have given evidence against Mr Hanson and evidence of Mr Spring's previous convictions will be admissible to the extent that they have substantial probative value in relation to his truthfulness. While not every previous conviction is capable of having substantial probative value on that question there is a reasonable prospect that that the judge would admit Mr Spring's previous convictions for theft, taking a vehicle without consent, and affray for that purpose.

16   The effect of Mr Hanson's interview also needs to be considered. The fact that he refused to answer questions relating to the assault could potentially lead to adverse inferences being drawn under the s 34 of the Criminal Justice and Public Order Act 1994 which could strengthen the case against him. In order to confirm this, it is necessary to know whether he was cautioned prior to or during the interview about the effect of the refusal to

mention matters which he might later wish to make use of in his defence. For this reason, and also to check the accuracy of the transcript generally, I will need to listen to a tape of the interview and would be grateful if those instructing could request a copy from the CPS.

17   As those instructing are aware, under s 101(1)(d) of the Criminal Justice Act 2003, a defendant's character may be admitted as part of the prosecution case where it is relevant to an important matter in issue between the prosecution and the defence. As noted in paragraph 12 above, the court may find that Mr Hanson's previous convictions are evidence of a propensity to commit offences of violence. Such a propensity would most obviously be relevant to the issue of whether Mr Hanson committed the offences of Violent Disorder and Causing Grievous Bodily Harm with Intent. However, the Prosecution may also seek to adduce the evidence in relation to the offence of Attempted Robbery being an offence which involves the use or threat of force. Once I have details of Mr Hanson's previous convictions I will be able to advise more fully. Should evidence of a propensity to commit offences of violence be admitted in relation to any offences, it will also be relevant to the credibility of Mr Hanson's defence in relation to those charges (*R v Campbell* [2007] 2 Cr App R 28).

Attempted robbery

18   As far as the attempted robbery is concerned, there are substantial gaps in the evidence which need to be filled before Mr Hanson can be properly advised. In particular, according to Mr Hanson's proof of evidence, there appears to be an in-store video on which he is alleged to have appeared. A copy of the CCTV footage and Mr Hanson's further instructions on it need to be obtained, so that I can assess its likely evidential weight. Again, there is the failure to hold an identification procedure, which means that, in the absence of an admissible video, the prosecution will find it difficult to prove that it was Mr Hanson who attempted the robbery.

19   In addition, there is the question of the words which Mr Hanson is alleged to have uttered on arrest at the police station: 'I only tried to rob the place'. Its admissibility ought to be challenged, under s 78 of PACE 1984. It is remarkable that the custody record entry for 21:10 hours states that these words were uttered on arrest and yet Mr Hanson had been arrested shortly after 19:30 hours by PC Keith; and was booked in by PS Waller at 19:45 hours. This anomaly needs explanation at the least, and is likely to undermine the admission it contains, even if the judge rules that it is admissible.

Sentence

20   As far as sentence is concerned, if convicted, Mr Hanson faces a custodial sentence on each of the violent disorder, assault and attempted robbery charges. It is likely that the first two would together attract a sentence of two to three years' imprisonment, given that serious injuries were caused to a policeman by kicking him while he was on the ground, and while the assailant was acting as part of a group. In coming to this conclusion, I have taken into account Mr Hanson's substantial record, which includes several offences of violence. As far as the attempted robbery is concerned, there is likely to be a consecutive sentence since the offence was entirely separate. Given the embryonic and disorganised nature of the offence, however, and the fact that no weapon was involved, the sentence may be no more than 18 months, despite the fact that one of the victims was punched. These estimates are based on conviction after trial. A substantial discount of as much as a third would be likely in the event of an early plea of guilty.

Action to be taken

21   It will be apparent from the points made above that there are a number of actions which I advise my Instructing Solicitors to take. In particular, I would ask that:

(a) statements be taken from Vicky Bryant and anyone else who may be able to establish Mr Hanson's presence in the various public houses in question on the afternoon in question;

(b) a copy of the CCTV footage be obtained from the CPS as a matter of urgency. If there are any difficulties in making a copy available, arrangements should be made for it to be viewed at the police station;

(c) an early conference be arranged in order to obtain Mr Hanson's instructions on various of the matters canvassed above, and advise him more fully;

(d) the CPS be asked for the schedule of unused material, a copy of Mr Hanson's tape of interview, summaries of the interviews of the co-accused, copies of the criminal records of the co-accused and any witnesses, the crime report sheets and any relevant radio/telephone messages;

(e) once the schedule of unused material has been served, the defence statement be updated to include any unused material sought;

(f) the defence statement be updated to deal with the additional matters set out in paragraph 5, once these have been clarified;

(g) a map of the estate be agreed;

(h) expert evidence be sought as to the effect of combining Prozac and alcohol in the way in which Mr Hanson did.

22   The case is not yet in a state where the Plea and Case Management Hearing Questionnaire can be completed, but that position should be reached once a conference with Mr Hanson has been held. I would be grateful if those instructing me could arrange a conference as soon as possible.

23   If I can be of any further assistance, please do not hesitate to contact me in Chambers.

MAHENDRA DHONI

2 Atkin Building
London WC1

Checklist for opinion writing skills

24.1 The purpose of this chapter

As you will have discovered by working through this manual, a barrister may be asked to write an opinion or an advice in many different contexts and for many different purposes. But the main types which you have learned about are:

- Opinion on the merits.
- Opinion on liability.
- Advice on quantum.
- Advice on evidence.
- Advice on procedure.
- Advice on practical steps to be taken.
- Advice on specific issues.
- Advice on appeal.

The legal content of the opinion may be within a civil or a criminal case, at any stage from before commencement of proceedings until the hearing of an appeal. You may be asked to advise any party to the proceedings or matter in dispute.

So now would be a good time to go back and remind yourself of what you have learned in terms of the skills of opinion writing. There is nothing new in this chapter, but we bring together in the form of a checklist an overview of all the things you need to do, and all the skills you need to practise, in order to produce a good opinion or advice. Of course not all of the points will be relevant to every type of opinion, but you can easily work out which points are applicable when.

Obviously, this is intended to be helpful if you are preparing for an assessment in opinion writing. But we hope it will have a practical use during the learning process as well, and even after.

24.2 Language and style

Whenever you are writing as a lawyer, it goes without saying that you need to take care of your language, both in terms of using correct English, and in terms of adopting an appropriate style, as well as showing professional skill in the use of language. So take care that you heed the following points.

- *Clarity*. Your draft should be written in clear English. This means that it must be comprehensible, preferably with ease on a first reading. The words you use must make sense, and have their correct meanings. So, for example, do not muddle 'claimant' and 'defendant'; do not write 'negligence' when you mean 'negligent'; do not use the word 'infer' to mean 'imply'. The overall effect should be that your opinion is clear and easy to read, but has a professional and confident tone.

- *Use appropriate language.* Appropriate language is basically plain English, but with just the right degree of formality according to the context. Avoid archaic, pompous, and overly dense language. Remember there is a difference between an opinion and a statement of case, for example: do not use pleading language in your opinion. But do not allow your writing to become too informal or colloquial. Your writing should be fluent, and if possible elegant—avoid note form, and if you use abbreviations make them sensible ones. Be polite both to your instructing solicitor and to your lay client.

- *Use correct terminology.* It is always appropriate to use correct legal terminology when writing in a legal context—do not translate legal terms into modern English just for the sake of it. Refer to yourself in the first person, and to your instructing solicitors and your client in the third person. Make sure you get case names and the names of statutes right. Use the correct words when referring to legal concepts: if they need to be explained in everyday language, do this as well. Don't write 'it is submitted that'. Don't be too judgemental about your client.

- *Grammar, punctuation, and spelling.* You should write without spelling mistakes, grammatical errors, or incorrect punctuation. For example, verbs should be in the correct tense, nouns should have the appropriate article, every sentence should have a main verb, and sentences should be separated by a full stop, not a comma. Spell names correctly. Do not miss out words, or use note form. Your sentences should be properly constructed.

24.3   Content

The content of an opinion is of crucial importance. You cannot write a good opinion if you do not write about the right things. So take note of the following points.

- *Identify the material facts.* The facts of the case are always your starting point in analysis, and so they should be in your opinion. You have a good opportunity in your introductory paragraph(s) to set out the facts you consider to be material. Take care over this. The first few paragraphs often signal very clearly what the quality of the opinion is going to be. If, when introducing the case, you ignore important facts, or get them wrong, it is likely to be because you are not going to address the right facts. If you churn out all the facts uncritically, you are signalling clearly that you have not worked out what is material and what is not.

- *Deal with the material issues.* From your reading of the facts, you must apply the law and so identify what are the real issues in the case. You should then deal with them. Take care that you deal with all the right issues and make sure you do not miss any important issues out, or deal with irrelevant issues. It is the structured way of thinking that you have been taught that will enable you to identify the correct issues. Muddled thinking or an academic approach will quite possibly lead you to deal with the wrong issues.

- *Get the law right.* It is impossible to identify the correct facts and issues if you do not identify and apply the law correctly. And it is your careful analysis of the facts that enables you to identify the relevant law. It is not enough to understand the law, you must apply it—in other words you must deal with the law in a practical, problem-solving way, not an academic way. Your opinion will have almost no merit at all if you go off on a tangent and base your whole advice on the wrong law.

24.4 Conclusions and reasoning

The whole purpose of writing an opinion is to give advice and offer conclusions, which must then be properly reasoned. So always make sure of the following points.

- *Get the answer 'right'*. There is rarely only a single right answer; but there may be any number of wrong answers. An answer is 'right' if it is a justifiable conclusion to reach on the basis of the facts and the law, and is as far as possible in accordance with the client's needs. In other words, it is a conclusion which a competent practising barrister might reach in this case. This overall conclusion must be expressed prominently. You must say what you think, not leave it to be deduced.

- *Make your conclusion clear*. Your overall conclusion must be expressed in unambiguous terms. If it is vague or unclear, this is usually a sign that you are uncertain what conclusion you ought to be expressing and are trying to hedge your bets. This is a serious fault and it stands out a mile. Even worse are contradictory conclusions. It is by no means uncommon for a student to express one conclusion at the beginning of an opinion (e.g. 'quite a strong case') and the opposite conclusion later on (e.g. 'unlikely to succeed'). Such a contradiction is a clear sign that you do not really know what your opinion is.

- *Express your conclusion appropriately*. As explained in **19.7.1**, it is important neither to be too definite nor too indefinite in your conclusion. Both are common faults in students' opinions. As well as expressing a sound conclusion, you need to be careful to get the strength of that conclusion right. It is not sound to advise a client there is a strong case, when the probability of success is only just better than even. It is useless to advise a client that a case may or may not succeed, if you give no indication of the chance of success. Take care over your choice of words when expressing your conclusion.

- *Answer every question*. Remember you must express a conclusion on every issue you have been asked to deal with. If you do not do so, your advice will be incomplete, or even misleading. If you do not even identify the question, this is even worse. Remember that not all questions are asked expressly. For example, instructions to advise 'whether Jane Smith has a claim in respect of her injuries' implicitly asks:

  (a) how strong a claim?

  (b) against whom?

  (c) what would be the cause(s) of action?

  (d) what might be recovered in such a claim?

  (e) should proceedings be commenced?

And maybe other questions too, depending on the context.

Everything that has been said above about reaching a justifiable overall conclusion and expressing it clearly of course applies equally to your conclusion on each subsidiary issue.

- *Give reasons for your conclusions.* It is not enough to reach conclusions, you must give reasons for those conclusions, and your reasoning must be clear. Sound reasoning involves careful and methodical construction of an argument, allowing the reader to see how your analysis of the issues, law, and facts leads step by step to your conclusions. Your reasoning cannot be clear if your analysis is faulty in the first place.

- *Give sound reasoning.* As well as reaching sound conclusions, you must be able to justify those conclusions on the basis of the law and your analysis of the facts and issues. This will, of course, not be possible if your conclusions are unsound, or if your analysis is faulty, or if you simply fail to give reasons at all. But the reasoning you use must itself be sound. As you were reminded earlier, there is not often a definite conclusion that you can reach on any issue. If you express an indefinite conclusion, you must explain why you cannot be certain, and what the answer will eventually depend on. You may need to consider alternatives, and explain the circumstances in which each of those alternatives will be the right conclusion.

24.5 Structure

The structure of your opinion is also of great importance if you are to achieve clarity and accuracy. So note the following points.

- *Formalities and format.* Your opinion should be properly headed, in accordance with your instructions, written in numbered paragraphs and signed (with a pseudonym for assessment purposes) at the end. Use capital letters when naming an Act, use italics (when typing) or underlining (when writing by hand) for case names. Format is also important. If you are word-processing, you are strongly advised to take the time to ensure that the formatting is neat and consistent. Take care over line spacing and indents. Do not use very small or very large type. If you are writing by hand, as you will be in an unseen assessment, use space. Do not write into the margins, leave a space between paragraphs and generally ensure that the finished result looks neat. If you have planned your opinion properly, you should not need to write so fast that your handwriting deteriorates.

- *Division into paragraphs.* If you divide your opinion into carefully identified paragraphs it will help you not to muddle issues together, but to separate them clearly from each other. If you do not keep each issue distinct, you will have an incoherent opinion, which will be very hard to unravel. As a general rule, try to deal with each issue in a separate paragraph. If you are considering separate causes of action, deal with them in separate paragraphs, or sections of your opinion. If you are considering the liability of more than one potential defendant, deal with them separately as well. If there are several items of potential loss to be dealt with, take them separately, in separate paragraphs or subparagraphs, unless they can more conveniently be taken together (for example because the issues are identical).

- *Deal with the issues in a logical order.* This is very important. If you do not, you will do great damage to the clarity of your opinion. You cannot achieve this if you have not also managed to keep separate issues separate. You are strongly advised to have a skeleton plan for your opinion, and then to follow it, so as to ensure that what you write has a coherent structure and enables the reader to follow your reasoning. In most cases the logical order is that which coincides with conventional expectations. So in a case involving breach of contract, the reader would expect to see you deal with the issues in the order—contract, terms, breach, causation, loss. You may occasionally decide to deviate from this, but be careful, and be sure you know why you are doing so. Never deal with quantum before liability.

- *Use subheadings.* Subheadings are very useful, and it is most unlikely that an opinion without any subheadings will be as clear or as easy to read as it could be. But do not use too many—it is clumsy and unhelpful to have a subheading at the top of every paragraph or to label every small sub-issue in this way. Nevertheless, too few, and you are losing clarity. At the very least one would expect to see an opinion divided into 'liability' and 'quantum'. When you do insert a subheading, make sure it is an accurate description of the content of the section that follows. It is misleading and unhelpful to head a section 'causation', for example, if what follows is to do with remoteness of damage.

- *Give each issue its due weight and significance.* You should not spend a lot of your time on peripheral issues at the expense of major ones. The longest sections of your opinion should be those dealing with the most important, or the most complex, issues. Deal with simple or relatively unimportant matters more briefly. One of the most common faults in students' opinions is a poor introduction. When you set out the material facts and issues, you should ensure that you mention concisely anything of real importance, but do not go on at great length. It is not uncommon to see an unedited churning out of every fact, which takes up a page or more (typed) of the opinion. Be critical, analytical, and selective.

- *Set your conclusions out clearly and prominently.* Your conclusions should be quick and easy to find. You are encouraged to put the overall conclusions near the beginning of the opinion, but you do not have to do so. Wherever you put them, by the time the reader comes to the end of your opinion, they should be left with a very clear idea of what your conclusions are, and what advice you have given. Never leave your conclusions buried in the middle of a section or paragraph. Do not expect the reader to have to pull them together from several different places. This may indeed mean that there is an element of repetition in your opinion, but it is well worthwhile. It is also common for students, when setting out their overall conclusions near the beginning of the opinion, to go on at great length, beginning to explain the reasons for those conclusions, and so repeating what is about to follow. There is no need to do this.

- *Overall length.* There is no correct length for an opinion, and what is suitable varies according to the complexity of the case and the style of the writer. But your opinion should not be excessively short (probably because you have failed to identify the issues, or not given them their due weight) or excessively long (probably because you have dealt with irrelevant issues, or given some issues too much weight). For further guidance, see **19.7.4.**

- *Length of paragraphs.* The paragraphing in an opinion should follow the normal rules of good prose. Do not allow your paragraphs to get too long, or too short. Do not be afraid to have paragraphs of varying length. Ideally each paragraph should deal with one and only one segment of your reasoning, and each paragraph should tend to begin with a new issue or step in your reasoning. What is appropriate is what best puts over your opinion and explains the reasons for it. Paragraphs should be numbered.

24.6 Practicality

As well as everything else, your opinion must in all ways be practical, because it serves a practical purpose. To help you in this, follow the guidance below.

- *The client's objectives.* Your opinion must address the needs and objectives of the client. Of course this means that you must answer all the client's questions and deal with the issues raised, but it goes beyond that. It is also to do with thinking practically and realistically. Always be aware of what your client is trying to achieve. Remember that your client is a real person, who will act on your advice. Be aware of what the consequences will be for the client. Identify any risks, and above all be aware of the cost implications of any step you have advised. If you have had to give the client bad news, still think what is the best advice you can give them in the circumstances. Make sure that any advice you give is helpful, sound, and ethical.

- *Lack of information.* There are always gaps in the information you are provided with. The further information you need, because it will affect your conclusion, must be asked for, and put into context. Do not just ask for it, but explain why you need it and what difference it will make. If there are major gaps in your instructions, you must identify them and ask for them to be filled. But do not ask for information that you do not need, or which cannot realistically be obtained. Think practically—if you ask for further information, be aware of who you are asking to do what.

- *Advise on evidence.* Central to being practical is your consideration of the evidence in a case. Even if you are not expressly asked to advise on evidence, your advice can never be practical if you do not think in terms of how a case can be proved. You must show an awareness of the evidence you know you have, because it is mentioned or included in your instructions, and the evidence that must be obtained before the case can succeed. Such evidence must be clearly identified to your instructing solicitor, and wherever possible you should indicate how and where it is to be obtained. It should also be apparent from your advice what purpose the evidence you have asked for will serve, so that the solicitor understands why it needs to be obtained. So clearly relate it to the issue that that evidence will go to prove. If the opinion is basically an advice on evidence, then this is what you will spend almost all of your time writing about.

- *Practical steps and procedure.* The first point here is to be aware of the stage at which you are advising. If the case involves the possibility of court proceedings, think whether you need to give any relevant advice on procedure. For example, is the pre-action protocol being complied with? Should proceedings be commenced now or later? What steps should be taken before proceedings are commenced? If proceedings have already been commenced, then you are in the middle of a timetable, and there will most certainly be some procedural advice that needs to be given, if only to remind instructing solicitors of the next step required. But in any event, there is always some practical step that needs to be taken, even if it is not a procedural step under the CPR. Having received your advice, who needs to do what next? This should be made clear in every opinion.

INDEX

A

abstracting and indexing services 65
academic approach 271
accountants 229–30
accounts 227
Acts 15–16, 34–40
  ambiguities, *Hansard* reference 83–9
  amendments 35
  annotated statutes 35
  chapter numbers 35
  citation 35
  commencement 35
  consolidated 35, 86–7
  finding 34–5
  in force 35, 37
  passage of bill *see* **parliamentary
    procedure**
  provision inserted by later Act 87
  repealed 35, 37
  researching 38
  short title 35
  title not known 35
  updating 35, 37
  year unknown 35
admissibility of evidence 332
advice
  next steps 310–11, 312
  see also individual types e.g. **criminal
    advice on evidence**
advisory character (of
  opinion) 270–1
alibi evidence 180–1
All England Law Reports 44, 48, 51,
  67
ambiguities
  in facts 211
  Hansard reference 83–9
analytical process
  breach of contract 306
  cause of action 304
  evidence 307, 312
  existence of contract 304
  losses 307–8
  next steps advice 310–11, 312
  parties 304
  proof 306
  structure 303–4
  terms of contract
    breach 306
    express 305
    implied 305–6

annotated statutes 35
appeals
  case stated 186
  civil cases 142, 169
  from Crown Court 186
  from magistrates' court 185–6
  judicial review 186
applications by barristers
  to court 157–8
  injunctions 151
  interim payments 157
  orders to assist evidence
    collection 151
  procedure 151–2
  security for costs 157
  summary judgment 157
archaic language 348
argument
  no place in opinion 280
assessment of performance 123,
  224–5
Atkin's Court Forms 33
authorities *see* **citation of authorities**

B

bail
  appeal against refusal 174
  application 174, 175–7
  Crown Court application 177
  duties of counsel 176
  magistrates' courts 174
  police 174
  second application 174, 176–7
barristers
  advising 146
  advocacy 146
  agency relationship with client 148
  applications *see* **applications by
    barristers**
  briefing *see* **instruction and briefing
    of counsel**
  defence in criminal case 171–2
  drafting 146
  fee, civil cases 165
  as legal experts 5
  opinion on merit or
    quantum 148–50
bibliographic services 66
Bills *see* **Acts; parliamentary
  procedure**

brief *see* **instruction and briefing of
  counsel**
British and Irish Legal Information
  Institute (BAILII) 47, 48
*Butterworth's Human Rights
  Cases* 62

C

CAP (context, analysis and
  presentation) approach 4,
  190–222
advising on evidence 159–61
analysis of issues and evidence 190,
  191, 205–13
  establishing proof 212, 222
  factual and legal issues 206, 207,
    220
  gaps or ambiguities in facts 211
  inferences 212
  inferred facts 212
  required elements 212–13
  strengths and weaknesses 211–12,
    221
  theory of case 207–10
  Wigmore analysis charts 213
applications to court 158
context of case 190, 191–205
  collection of facts 195–200
  instructions, role and
    objectives 192–3
  legal framework
    identification 201–5
  stage of proceedings 192
  understanding problem 193–5
    cause 194
    client objectives 194–5
exchange of witness
  statements 161–2
expert reports 163
instructions to counsel 166–7, 223–4
opinion on merit and
  quantum 149–50
performance criteria 224–5
pre-issue applications 152–4
preparation for trial by
  advocate 166–7
presentation 190, 191
  carrying out instructions 218
  gaps in facts 215–16
  intended audience 216–17

CAP (context, analysis and presentation) approach *(cont.)*
   legal framework 215
   preparation of results 217
   selection of theme 214–15
   theory of case and 214
  statements of case drafting 156
  theory of case 207–10
  Wigmore analysis charts 213
case management 143
Case Search **database** 67
cases
  analysis of 3, 4, 97–114
  annotations 49
  application of law to facts 20
  citation *see* **citation of cases**
  finding 45–6
  judicial history 46
  precedent 50, 90–3
  ratio decidendi 50, 90, 93–5
  reported 42
  researching 48
  resources 47
  search strategy 46
  updating 46, 49
  words and phrases used 80
  see also **law reports**
Casetrack 47, 48
CELEX **database** 52, 53, 54, 55, 56, 57, 66
checklists
  conclusions 349–50
  content 348–9
  language 347–8
  practicality 352
  reasoning 350
  structure 350–1
Chronological Index to the Statutes 38
chronology 196
citation of authorities 289–90
  choice of material 299
  Hansard reference, in court 89
  points of law 294–5
  primary sources only 23, 122
  statutes 35
  statutory materials 298–9
citation of cases 289–90, 295–6
  choice of cases 297–8
  facts and judgment 296
  law reports 43–4
    in court 50–1
    neutral 43–4
    online 43–4
  neutral 43–4, 295
  relevance 297
  unreported cases 51
civil advice on evidence
  CAP approach 159–61
  content 314–15
  documentary evidence 321, 322–3, 327
  evidence available on each issue 319–21
  examination of statements of case 317–19, 325

  exchange of statements 321–2
  expert evidence 320, 322
  final considerations 324
  formalities 315
  hearsay evidence 321, 323
  issues
    evidence available on each 319–21
    listing 319
  oral evidence 319–20, 321, 326–7
  purpose of advice 314
  reading the brief 316–17
  sample advice 324–8
  selection of evidence 321–3
  step-by-step approach 316–24
  structure 315
  timing of instructions 316
  writing 324
civil cases
  advice on evidence *see* **civil advice on evidence**
  advising 146
  advocacy 146
  agency relationship 148
  appeals 142, 169
  applications
    CAP approach 158
    to court 157–8
    injunctions 151
    interim payments 157
    orders to assist evidence collection 151
    procedure 151–2
    security for costs 157
    summary judgment 157
  basic legal framework 204
  before action 142
  case management 143
  Civil Procedure Rules 142–3
  costs 142, 144–6, 169–70
    barrister's fee 165
  drafting 146
  enforcement 142, 169
  evidence
    advising on *see* **civil advice on evidence**
    disclosure 158–9
    expert reports 162–3
    preparation 158–63
    witness statements
      drafting 161–2
      exchange 159
  fast track 143
  instituting proceedings 142, 154–8
    claimant's case 154–5
    court documents 154–6
    defendant's case 155
    letter before action 154
    reply by claimant 155
    statement of case 155
  instruction and briefing of counsel 146, 165–7
    acceptance by counsel 165–6
    adequate time 165–6
    CAP analysis 166–7
    delivery of brief 165–6

    endorsing the brief 147–8
    form and content 147
    returning the work 147–8
  interim stage 142
    advising on evidence 159–61
    see also **civil advice on evidence**
    disclosure 158–9
    expert reports 162–3
    further information request 159
    information to/from other parties 158–9
    notice to admit facts 159
    preparation of evidence 158–63
    witness statement
      drafting 161–2
      exchange 159
  legally relevant factors 201–2
  multi-track 143
  opinion on merit or quantum 148–50
  pre-action protocols 142
  pre-action stage 142
    applications
      before issue 151–4
      CAP approach 152–4
      injunctions 151
      orders to assist evidence collection 151
      procedure 151–2
    barrister's involvement 148
    opinion on merit or quantum 148–50
    public funding 145–6
  referral to barrister 143–4
  settlement during process 168–9
  small claims 143
  solicitor's work 144
  stages 141–2
  statement of case 155–6
  trial 142, 167–8
    court date 164
    court documents 164–5
    witness presence 164
  trial bundles 164–5
Civil Procedure Rules 142–3
  case management 142–3
  overriding objective 142
  pre-action protocols 142
  track allocation 143
client
  opinion written for 280–1
Code of Conduct 291–2
Commercial Laws of Europe 56
Common Market Law Reports **(CMLR)** 57
Common Market Law Review 58
communication
  word skills 244
Community Legal Service 145–6, 147, 170
computers
  databases *see* **databases**
  essential skills 236–8
  spreadsheets 237
  word processing 236

see also **electronic research tools;
information technology**
conclusions 300, 349–50
conditional fee agreements 145, 147,
170
content of opinion
citation *see* **citation of authorities;
citation of cases**
civil advice on evidence 314–15
lack of information 290, 352
length 290, 351
questions with no definite
answer 288–9
uncertainties 288–9
contract action
breach 306
causation 308, 309
cause of action 304
losses 307–8
mitigation 308, 309
parties 304
privity of contract 304
proof of breach 306
remoteness 308, 309
structure of analysis 303
terms of contract
express 305
implied 305–6
costs
agreed 169
ascertainment 144–5
assessment 169
civil cases 142, 144–6, 165, 169–70
Community Legal Service 145–6,
147, 170
conditional fee 145, 147, 170
criminal cases 172–3
damages based agreements 145
layout 286
legal expenses insurance 145
numbers/numeracy 228
payment methods 145–6
practitioner books 130
public funding 145–6
security for 157
counsel *see* **barristers; instruction
and briefing of counsel**
Court of Appeal 91
courts
hierarchy 91–2
criminal advice on evidence
admissibility 332
approach 329–30
charge 330
continuity 335
defence 178–9, 341–6
disclosure 334–5
evidence in light of charges 330
expert evidence 333
further statements required 330–1
marking exhibits 335
no admissions by defence 331
photographs 333
plans 333
prosecution 178, 336–41
sample advice

for defence 341–6
for prosecution 336–41
service by defence on
prosecution 335
summarising 335
witnesses
attendance at court 334
further 333–4
police and civilian 331–2
criminal cases
advising
defence 178–9
on evidence *see* **criminal advice
on evidence**
prosecution 178
appeals
case stated 186
from Crown Court 186
from magistrates' court 185–6
judicial review 186
arrest and charge 174
bail
appeal against refusal 174
application 174
Crown Court application 177
duties of counsel 176
magistrates' courts 174
second application 174, 176–7
charge 173
cross-examination 172, 183
Crown Prosecution Service 173
decision to prosecute 173
defence barrister role 171–2
disclosure 180–1
evidence
advising on *see* **criminal advice
on evidence**
disclosure 180–1
proof of 172
instructions to counsel 171–2
legal aid 172–3
legal framework 204
legally relevant factors 201–2
mitigation plea 175, 184–5
mode of trial hearing 177–8
no-case-to-answer submission 182
pre-trial disclosure *see* **disclosure**
pre-trial hearings 181–2
preliminary hearings 181–2
proof of evidence 171
remand hearings 174
sentencing guidelines 185
stages 173–5
trial 182–4
closing speech 182
complex or lengthy 181
counsel role 182–4
'cracked' 181
cross-examination 183
examination in chief 182–3
no-case-to-answer
submission 182
opening speech 182
cross-examination 172, 183
Crown Prosecution Service 173, 174
Curia website 57, 58, 60

Current Law 60
database 60
European materials 55, 56, 60
words and phrases source 81
Current Law Case Citator 48, 49, 58,
62
Current Law Cases 46, 47, 48, 49
Current Law Legislation Citator 36,
38, 39, 48
Current Law Monthly Digest 33, 38,
41, 42, 47, 48, 49, 81
Current Law Service 36, 38
Current Law Statutes 36
Service Files 39
using 39–40
Current Law Statutes Annotated 36,
38, 39, 46, 48
Current Law Statutes Citator 38, 39,
42
Current Law Statutes Service 38
*Current Law Statutory Instruments
Citator* 42
Current Law Year Book 47, 48, 49, 81
Current Legal Information
database 32, 47, 48, 65

D

damages
numeracy and 227
damages-based agreements 145
data protection 239
databases
abstracting and indexing services 65
bibliographic services 66
Case Search 67
CELEX 52, 53, 54, 55, 56, 57, 66
Current Law 60
Current Legal Information 32, 47, 48,
65
full text service 65
HUDOC database 61–2
internet sources 64–5, 70–3
journals 69–70
Justis 48, 66
Lawtel *see* **Lawtel**
Legal Journals Index 65
legislation.gov.uk website 36, 38, 41
Lexis Library *see* **Lexis Library**
types 65–6
updating 17
Westlaw *see* **Westlaw**
debates *see* **Hansard reference**
defence
counsel advising 178–9
see also **criminal advice on
evidence**
pre-trial disclosure 180–1
defence statement 180–1, 334
dictionaries
words and phrases source 33, 80, 81,
82, 126
The Digest 46, 47, 48
Directives
implementation 55–6
Directory of Legislation in Force 54

disclosure 334–5
  alibi evidence 180–1
  by defence 180–1
  by prosecution 180
  civil cases interim stage 158–9
  criminal cases 180–1
  defence statement 180–1
dissenting judgments 300
Document Exchange 235

E

electronic communications
  case preparation 236
  contact with court 236
  data protection 239
  receiving brief 235–6
  security 239
electronic research tools 7, 237–8
  availability 25
  Case Search site 67
  CD-ROM format 65, 69–70, 237–8
  CELEX 52, 53, 54, 55, 56, 57, 66
  databases *see* databases
  encyclopedias 31
  EU legislation 53
  EU sources 60
  EUR-Lex website 52, 53–4, 55, 56, 57, 58
  Euractiv website 60
  internet 64–5
    free sources 70–3
    legal gateways 71, 72
    search engines 70–1
  JustCite 47, 66
  Justis CELEX 52, 53, 54, 55, 56, 57, 66
  Justis UK Statutes 36, 38
  Justis UK Statutory Instruments 36, 41
  law reports 43–4, 69–70
  Lawtel see **Lawtel**
  Lexis Library see **Lexis Library**
  N-Lex website 55, 56
  practical legal research 124–5
  practitioner books 29–30, 69–70
  search strategies 73–9
    analysis of problem 74
    AND 75, 79
    capitals 79
    choice of database 74
    combining Boolean operators 75
    fields 77–8
    hyphenated words 78
    keywords 12–14, 74–5
    NOT 75, 79
    OR 75, 79
    phrases 78
    proximity searching 78
    section numbers 78
    stop words 78
    truncation 75–6, 79
    updating findings 76–7
    wild card characters 75, 79
  taking notes 22
  UK Legislation 35, 36, 38, 48, 67
  websites 238

Westlaw see **Westlaw**
words and phrases 81–2
see also **computers**
emails 237
  case preparation 236
  contact with court 236
  court listings 236
  security 239
Encyclopaedia of Forms and Precedents 33
encyclopedias 30–1, 126
  electronic 31
  noter-ups 31
  supplements 30
  updating 17, 30–1
endorsing the brief 147–8, 223
enforcement 142, 169
English language 247
  see also **plain English**
English Reports 45, 47, 66
essay
  opinion is not 280
Euractiv website 60
Europe Direct website 52, 60
European Convention on Human Rights 61
European Court of Justice 91
European Court Reports (ECR) 57
European Current Law 55, 56, 58, 60
European Documentation Centres 52
European Human Rights Reports 62
European Intellectual Property Review 58
European Law Review 58
European Union materials 51–60
  CELEX database 52, 53, 54, 55, 56, 57, 66
  Commercial Laws of Europe 56
  current awareness 60
  Current Law 55, 56, 60
  EUR-Lex website 52, 53–4, 55, 56, 57, 58
  European Current Law 55, 56, 58, 60
  finding cases 57–8
  Halsbury's EU Legislation Implementator 55, 56
  journals 58
  law reports 57
    finding cases 57–8
  Lawtel 53, 54, 55, 57, 60
  legislation
    directives implementation 55–6
    draft 56
    is it in force 54–5
    primary 52
    secondary 52–4
  Official Journal (OJ) 52, 53, 54, 56
  periodical literature 58
  practitioner books 131–2
  researching 59
  websites 60
Europolitics bulletin 60
Eurovoc Thesaurus 83
evidence
  admissibility 332

advice on 352
  see also **civil advice on; criminal advice on**
alibi evidence 180–1
analysis 307, 312
civil advice on
  CAP approach 159–61
  content 314–15
  documentary evidence 321, 322–3, 327
  evidence, available on each issue 319–21
  examination of statements of case 317–19, 325
  exchange of statements 321–2
  expert evidence 320, 322
  final considerations 324
  formalities 315
  hearsay evidence 321, 323
  issues
    evidence available on each 319–21
    listing 319
  oral evidence 319–20, 321, 326–7
  purpose of advice 314
  reading the brief 316–17
  sample advice 324–8
  selection of evidence 321–3
  step-by-step approach 316–24
  structure 315
  timing of instructions 316
  writing 324
civil cases 158–63
conflicts 278
continuity 335
court documents 164–5
criminal advice on
  admissibility 332
  charge 330
  continuity 335
  defence 178–9, 341–6
  disclosure 334–5
  evidence in light of charges 330
  expert evidence 333
  further statements required 330–1
  marking exhibits 335
  no admissions by defence 331
  photographs 333
  plans 333
  prosecution 178, 336–41
  sample advice
    for defence 341–6
    for prosecution 336–41
  service by defence on prosecution 335
  summarising 335
  witnesses
    attendance at court 334
    further 333–4
    police and civilian 331–2
criminal cases 172, 180–1
disclosure 158–9, 180–1, 334–5
documentary 321, 322–3, 327
exchange of statements 321–2
expert 162–3, 320, 322, 333

facts and 188, 212, 222
  of figures 232–3
  hearsay 321, 323
  marking exhibits 335
  oral 319–20, 321, 326–7
  photographs 333
  plans 333
  practitioner books 132
  pre-trial hearings 181–2
  preparation 158–63
  proof of 172
  refreshment of memory 331
  service by defence on
      prosecution 335
  trial bundles 164–5
  witness statements
    drafting 161–2
    exchange 159
  witnesses
    attendance at court 334
    criminal advice 331–2, 333–4
    police and civilian 331–2
examination-in-chief 182–3

F

fact management process 187–222
  ambiguities 211
  application of legal framework 206,
      207, 220
  CAP *see* **CAP (context, analysis and
      presentation) approach**
  facts *see* **facts**
  strengths and weaknesses
      analysis 184, 211–12, 221
  theory of case *see* **theory of case**
  see also **legal framework**
facts
  admitted 188
  agreed 188, 200–1, 219
  ambiguities 211
  analysis 10–11
  application of law 19–21, 299
  application of legal framework 206,
      207, 220
  checklists 199–200
  collection 195–200
    chronology 196
    dramatis personae 196
    flowcharts 197, 198
    locus in quo 197
    methods 196
    sorting 197
  disputed 189, 200–1, 219, 278
  evidence and 188
    proofs 222
  gaps 211, 215–16
  inferences and 212
  in issue 189
  meaning 188–9
  not in issue 188
  organisation during
      preparation 274–5
  record of 200
  as starting point 272, 348
figures *see* **numbers/numeracy**

**following through between
      sources** 16–17, 120
foreign vocabulary 83
formalities 315, 350
forms and precedents 33–4, 132
funding
  conditional fee agreements 145,
      147, 170
  insurance 145
  legal aid *see* **public funding**
further information requests 159

G

grammar 248–9, 260, 348

H

*Halsbury's EU Legislation
      Implementator* 55, 56
Halsbury's Laws 15, 30, 48, 67
  Cumulative Supplement 31
  index 28
  journal articles 32
  Monthly Reviews 31, 48
  Noter-up 31, 32, 38, 42, 48
  source of keywords 14
  updating 31
  using 31
  words and phrases source 82
Halsbury's Statutes 36, 38, 48
  Cumulative Supplement 37
  Current Statutes Service 37, 38
  Is it in Force? 37, 38, 42
  Noter-up 37, 38, 42
  updating 37
  using 37
Halsbury's Statutes Citator 37, 38
Halsbury's Statutory Instruments 36,
      40, 41
  updating 41
*Halsbury's Statutory Instruments
      Citator* 41, 42
Hansard **reference**
  availability of resources 85
  Bills 87
  citation in court 89
  materials required 84–5
  ministerial statements 89
  no debates found 89
  online 85
  passage of Bill *see* **parliamentary
      procedure**
  Pepper v Hart 83
  running order 87
  Standing Committee debates 87
    none found 89
  starting research 86–7
  time required 86
  when appropriate 83–4
hearings
  mode of trial 174–5, 177–8
  plea before venue 177
  plea and case management 181–2,
      333
  pre-trial 181–2, 332–3

  preliminary hearings 181–2, 332–3
  preparatory hearings 332
  remand 174
High Court 92
HM Courts and Tribunals Service 47
House of Lords
  as court 91
HUDOC database 61–2
human rights
  documentation 60–1
  European Convention 61
  law reports 61–2
  practitioner books 133
  serial publications 62–3
  websites 63
Human Rights Law Reports 62

I

Index to Legal Periodicals 32
inferences 212
**Information Commissioner's
      Office** 239
information technology
  at court 237
  case preparation 236
    research *see* **electronic research
      tools**
  contact with court 236
  data protection 239
  databases *see* **databases**
  Document Exchange 235
  emails 236
  practitioner books 133
  receiving brief 235–6
  research *see* **electronic research
      tools**
  security 239
  see also **computers; internet**
instructing solicitor
  conflicting view of 278
  opinion written for 280–1
**instruction and briefing of
      counsel** 165–7, 171–2
  acceptance by counsel 165–6
  adequate time 165–6
  barrister's involvement 146–7
  brief
    content 302–3
    delivery 165–6
    endorsement 147–8, 223
  CAP analysis 166–7, 223–4
  civil cases 146
  instructions *see* **instructions**
instructions 270
  content 270
  endorsement of backsheet 147, 223
  implied questions 286
  lack of information 290, 352
  questions 270
    on receiving instructions 272
    to be answered 274
  read and digest 273–4
  timing 316
insurance for legal costs 145
interest 227–8

interim stage 142
  advising on evidence 159–61
  disclosure 158–9
  expert reports 162–3
  further information request 159
  information to/from third
      parties 158–9
  notice to admit facts 159
  preparation of evidence 158–63
  witness statements
    drafting 161–2
    exchange 159
internet 64–5
  access at court 237
  directories 71
  evaluation of website content 72
  free sources 70–3
  legal gateways 71, 72
  search engines 70–1
irrelevance 284–5
IT *see* **computers; information
    technology; internet**

J

*Journal of Common Market
    Studies* 58
journals 32–3, 127
  on databases 69–70
  European Union materials 58
  full text 33
  human rights materials 62–3
  Index to Legal Periodicals 32
  law reports 44
  Lawtel 32
  Legal Journals Index 32, 48, 58, 65
judicial precedent
  binding judgment 92
  distinguishing 92–3
  doctrine 90–1
  hierarchy of courts 91–2
  overruling 92
  persuasive precedents 93
  reversing 92
judicial review 186
JustCite 47, 66
Justis 48, 66
  JustCite 47, 66
Justis CELEX 52, 53, 54, 55, 56, 57, 66
Justis UK Statutes 36, 38
Justis UK Statutory Instruments 36, 41

K

keywords
  concealed 13
  electronic searches 74–5
  less obvious 13–14
  starting research with 12–14
  see also **words and phrases meanings;
    words and phrases sources**

L

lack of information 290, 352
language
  legal language

contract terms 256
court order 256–7
lease 255
letter 257
origins 257–8
reasons for use 257–8
recognising and rewriting 254–7
statute 254–5
plain English *see* **plain English**
terminology use 348
see also **writing**
law
  ambiguity 21
  application to facts 19–21, 299
    case law 20
    statutory provisions 20
  citation of authorities *see* **citation of
    authorities**
  citation of cases *see* **citation of cases**
  conclusions 300
  criminal advice on evidence 332
  dissenting judgments 300
  identification 348–9
  important sources 295–6
  lecture not required 293–4
  legal framework construction 275–7
  as means to end 272–3
  minor points 295
  opinion based on 293–301
  statutory materials 298–9
  updating 17
  use in opinion 293–301
  well-known principles 294
Law Gazette 32
law reports 127
  abbreviations 43
  All England Law Reports 44, 48, 51,
    67
  brackets, square and round 43
  CD-ROM 69–70
  citation 43–4
    in court 50–1
    neutral 43–4
    online 43–4
  continuous series 45
  English Reports 45, 47, 66
  European 57
    CMLR 57
    ECR 57
    finding cases 57–8
  human rights 61–2
  journals 44
  The Law Reports
    authority of 44
    indexes 44, 81
    websites 44
    words and phrases source 81
  named reporters 45
  newspaper reports 44–5, 47, 66
  nominate reports 45
  older reports 45
  Weekly Law Reports 44, 48, 51
  Year Books 45
Law Reports (Official Series) 44, 47,
    48, 51, 65, 66, 81
Law Reports Statutes 38
Lawtel 65, 66–7

case law 45, 47, 48
  EU 53, 54, 55, 57, 60
  human rights database 62
  journals 32
  legislation 36, 38
  search strategies 79
  statutory instruments 40, 42
layout of opinion
  backsheet 282
  basic facts and key issues 282
  conclusion 283, 287, 351
  costs 286
  further advice 287
  heading 282
  irrelevance 284–5
  length 290
  liability 285
  opening paragraphs 282
  procedural points 286
  quantum 285
  reasoning 283–4
  rules of structure 285–6
  separate parties 286
  signature of counsel 288
  skeleton plan 281
  subsequent paragraphs 283–5
  subsidiary points 286
  variations in practice 288
legal authorities, citation *see* **citation
    of authorities**
legal costs insurances 145
legal expertise 5
legal framework
  application of facts to 206, 207, 220
  basic frameworks 204
  best-fit approach 205
  choice 205
  construction 275–7
  grouping of legal factors 203
  identification 201–5
  list of relevant factors 201–2
  presentation and 215
  research areas to be identified 205
legal issues
  analysis 11–12, 206, 207
  categorising 12
  meaning 189–90
Legal Journals Index 32, 48, 58, 65
legal language *see* **language**
legislation
  draft 56
  European Union 52–7
  primary 34–40, 52
  secondary 34, 52–4
  updating 17
  see also **Acts; statutory instruments**
legislation.gov.uk website 36, 38, 41
Legislative Observatory 56, 60
length of opinion 290, 351
letter before action 154
Lexis Library 62, 65, 67–8
  All England Law Reports 67
  case law 45, 46, 47, 48
  Case Search 67
  EU materials 52, 53, 54, 55, 57, 60
  EU Tracker 55, 56
  Halsbury's Laws 31, 67

search strategies 79
statutory instruments 40, 41, 42
UK Legislation 35, 36, 38, 48, 67
words and phrases source 82
liability and damages
layout 285
library research 7, 25–7
acts and bills *see* Acts
availability of materials 26
electronic sources *see* **databases;**
electronic research tools
European *see* **European Union**
materials
foreign vocabulary 83
Hansard references *see* **Hansard**
reference
journals *see* **journals**
keywords 12–14
law reports *see* **law reports**
legislation
primary *see* Acts
secondary *see* **statutory**
instruments
new technology *see* **computers;**
databases; electronic research
tools
newspapers 44–5
parliamentary materials *see* **Hansard**
reference
practitioner books *see* **practitioner**
books
primary sources 26
resource format 25
secondary sources 26, 27
starting, keywords 12–14
statutory instruments *see* **statutory**
instruments
textbooks 15, 69–70, 118
words and phrases meanings
authoritative interpretation 80
definitions in other contexts 80
Interpretation Act 80
legal definitions 33
words and phrases sources
Current Law 81
dictionaries 33, 80, 81, 82, 126
foreign vocabulary 83
Halsbury's Laws 81
keywords 12–14
The Law Reports indexes 81
Lexis Library 82
Westlaw 82
locus in quo 197

M

magistrates' courts
appeals from 185–6
bail 174
sentencing guidelines 185
marking exhibits 335
medical law
practitioner books 135
mind mapping 209–10
mitigation plea 175, 184–5
mode of trial hearing 174–5, 177–8
modes of address 291

N

N-Lex **website** 55, 56, 60
neutral citation 43–4
New Law Journal 32
newspapers
law reports 44–5
no-case-to-answer submission 182
notes to pupillage supervisor 21,
121–2
numbers/numeracy 226–34
accountants 229–30
accounts 227
advocacy 232
collecting evidence of figures 233
in conference 231
costs 228
drafting 232
importance of numeracy 226–7
interest 227–8
issues in practice 228–9
negotiation of settlement 232–3
opinion 231
percentages 227
personal relevance 230
preparation of case 231
relevance to practice 227–30
revenue law 227
risk assessment 230
statistics
average 234
mean 234
median 234
mode 234
reliability 234
sources 234
when to use 233–4

O

office management
contact with court 236
Document Exchange 235
emails 236
receiving briefs 235–6
Official Journal (OJ) 52, 53, 54, 56
opinion
checklists *see* **checklists**
content *see* **content of opinion**
law in *see* **law**
not argument, essay, submission or
instruction 280
purpose 279–80
setting out *see* **layout of opinion**
for solicitor or client 280–1
style 291
uncertainty 288–9
opinion on merit or
quantum 148–50
opinion writing
advisory character 270–1
attitude to *see* **practitioner**
approach
citations *see* **citation of authorities;**
citation of cases
instructions *see* **instructions**
meaning 269–71

paperwork 269
planning *see* **preparation**
reason for learning 269
thinking process *see* **preparation**
outdoor clerk 172

P

paperwork 269
paragraphs 350, 351
parliamentary materials
Standing Committee debates 87
none found 89
parliamentary procedure 86
stages of public Bill 86, 87, 88
Pepper v Hart 83
phrases *see* **words and phrases**
meanings; words and phrases
sources
plain English 247
basic rules 260–2
legal language
origins 257–8
reasons for use 257–8
recognising and rewriting 254–7
meaning 253
promotion of 258–9
reasons for use 253–4
writing in 259–60
planning *see* **preparation**
plea before venue hearing 177
plea and case management
hearing 181–2, 333
plea in mitigation 175, 184–5
police
witnesses 331–2
police bail 174
practical research
analysis of problem 10–12
factual analysis 10–11
legal analysis 11–12
application of law 121
assessing performance 123
brainstorming 18
case law 45–6
checklists 18
citation of primary sources 23, 122
electronic sources 119
see also **electronic research tools**
finding relevant material 119–20
flowcharts 18
formal research notes 22–3
'funnel approach' 18
identification of issues 117
interpretation of law 19–21, 120
learning by practice 7
meaning 5–6, 117
methods and techniques 9–24
notes to pupillage supervisor 21,
121–2
nothing found 17
paper sources 124
planning 9–10
primary sources 15–16, 34, 118–19
pupil barrister and 7
recording 21–3
sample exercise 123–4

practical research *(cont.)*
  secondary sources 15, 34
  '7 step method' 19
  sources to use 15–16, 117–18
  stopping 16–17
  systematic 18
  taking notes 21–2
  textbooks 15, 69–70, 118
  updating 120–1
  visual methods 18
Practice Directions
  citation 44
practitioner approach
  academic approach abandoned 271
  answering the question 274
  facts as starting point 272, 348
  law as means to end 272–3
  real situation 271–2
practitioner books 36
  administrative law 127–8
  agency 128
  arbitration 128
  banking 128
  bankruptcy and insolvency 128
  building 128
  CD-ROM 69–70
  charities 128
  children 128–9
  civil litigation 129
  commercial law 129
  company law 129
  competition law 129
  computers 133
  conflict of laws 130
  consumer law 136
  contract law 130
  conveyancing law 130
  coroners 130
  costs 130
  criminal litigation 130
  damages 130–1
  data protection 131
  e-commerce 131
  ecclesiastical law 131
  education 131
  electronic versions 29–30
  employment law 131
  environment law 131
  equity and trusts 131
  European Union law 131–2
  evidence 132
  family law 132
  forms and precedents 33–4, 132
  health and safety 132
  housing law 132
  human rights 133
  immigration 133
  information technology 133
  insolvency 128
  insurance law 133
  intellectual property 133
  landlord and tenant 133–4
  legal profession 134
  legal research 134
  legal skills 134
  libel 134

  licensing 134
  local government 134
  maritime law 135
  medical law 135
  mental health 135
  partnership law 135
  personal injury 135
  planning law 135–6
  probate 137
  rating 136
  real property 136
  road traffic law 136
  sale of goods and consumer
    law 136
  sentencing 136–7
  shipping 137
  social security and welfare law 137
  succession 137
  taxation 137
  torts 137
  updating 17, 28–9
  using 27–8
  wills and probate 137
  see also **textbooks**
practitioner sources 27–30
  see also **practitioner books**
pre-action protocols 142
pre-sentence reports 185
pre-trial disclosure 334–5
  defence 180–1
  prosecution 180
  see also **disclosure**
pre-trial hearing 181–2, 332–3
precedent *see* **judicial precedent**
PreLex 56, 60
preliminary hearings 181–2, 332–3
preparation
  advice consideration 278
  clarification of objectives 352
  consider case as whole 277
  facts
    absorbed and organised 274–5
    as starting point 272, 348
  legal framework construction 275–7
  questions to be answered 273, 274
    all questions 277–8, 349
  reading the brief 273–4, 316–17
  research, *see also* **practical research**
  skeleton opinion 281
  skills 3–4, 225
preparatory hearings 332
presentation 190, 191
  carrying out instructions 218
  intended audience 216–17
  legal framework 215
  preparation of results 217
  selection of theme 214–15
  theory of case and 214
previous convictions 185
professional conduct 291–2
proofs, facts, and evidence 212, 222
proportionality principle 141, 142,
  159
prosecution
  counsel advising 178
  pre-trial disclosure 180

public funding
  civil cases 145–6
  Community Legal Service 145–6,
    147, 170
  criminal cases 172–3
Public General Acts 38
punctuation 249, 260, 348

Q

quantum
  layout 285
questions
  implied 286
  in instructions 274
  with no definite answer 288–9
  preparation 273, 277–8, 349

R

ratio decidendi 50, 90
  altering 94
  discovering 94
  meaning 93
  more than one judgment 94–5
reasoning 350
refreshment of memory 331
remand hearings 174
requests for further information 159
research
  assessing performance 123
  electronic *see* **electronic research
    tools**
  importance 6–7
  IT use 237
  legal expertise 5
  process 8
  selecting sources 15–16
  starting *see* **starting research**
  statutes 34–40
  summary 123
  see also **library research; practical
    research**
research notes 7
  legal answer 23
  preparing 22–3
  research route 22–3
  uses 21
research routes 22–3
revenue law
  numbers/numeracy 227
  practitioner books 137
rights of audience
  solicitors 171
risk assessment 147, 230

S

search engines 70–1
search strategies (electronic) 73–9
  analysis of problem 74
  AND 75, 79
  capitals 79
  choice of database 74
  combining Boolean operators 75
  fields 77–8

hyphenated words 78
keywords 12–14, 74–5
NOT 75, 79
OR 75, 79
phrases 78
proximity searching 78
section numbers 78
stop words 78
truncation 75–6, 79
updating findings 76–7
wild card characters 75, 79
sentences
short as possible 260
sentencing guidelines 185
separate parties 286
skeleton plan 281
solicitors
agency relationship with client 148
civil cases 144, 148–54
pre-claim stage 148–54
rights of audience 171
Solicitors' Journal 32
spelling 248, 348
spreadsheets 237
Standing Committee debates 87
none found 89
starting research 9
Halsbury's Laws 30
keywords 12–14, 74–5
concealed 13
less obvious 13–14
selecting sources 15–16
textbooks 15, 69–70, 118
statements of case 155, 317–19, 325
CAP approach 155–6
statistics
average 234
mean 234
median 234
mode 234
reliability 234
sources 234
when to use 233–4
statutes *see* Acts
Statutes at Large 38
Statutes of the Realm 38
statutory instruments 15–16, 34,
40–2
authority of Parliament 40
citation 40
purpose 40
researching 41–2
updating 41
statutory materials 298–9
see also Acts; **statutory instruments**
Stone's Justices' Manual
index 28
strengths and weaknesses
analysis 211–12, 221
style of opinion
formality 291, 350
modes of address 291
submission
opinion is not 280
Supreme Court 91

T

textbooks 15, 118
on CD-ROM 69–70
see also **practitioner books**
theory of case 184, 190
alternatives 208
identification of potential 207–10
lateral thinking 208–9
logical thinking 208–9
mind mapping 209–10
presentation 214
ways to develop 208
thinking process *see* preparation
Times Law Reports 44–5, 47, 66
tort action
structure of analysis 303–4
trial
civil cases 142, 167–8
complex or lengthy 181
counsel role 182–4
court date 164
court documents 164–5
'cracked' 181
criminal cases 182–4
cross-examination 172, 183
examination in chief 182–3
no-case-to-answer submission 182
opening and closing speeches 182
statement of case 155
witness presence 164
trial bundles 164–5
typographical errors 252

U

UK Legislation (Lexis Library) 35, 36,
38, 48, 67
uncertainties 288–9
unreported cases
citation 51
Upper Tribunal 92

W

Weekly Law Reports 44, 48, 51
Westlaw 62, 68–9
case law 45, 46, 47, 48
EU materials 52, 53, 54, 55, 56, 57,
58, 60
journals 32
legislation 35, 36, 38
search strategies 79
statutory instruments 40, 41, 42
words and phrases source 82
Wigmore analysis charts 213
witness statements
civil cases 159, 161–2
drafting 161–2
exchange 159
witnesses
attendance at court 334
criminal advice 331–2, 333–4
police and civilian 331–2
word processing 236

word skills
barristers and 243–5
communication 244
spoken 244
standards 244–5
written 243, 244
see also **language; plain English;**
writing
words and phrases meanings
authoritative interpretation 80
definitions in other contexts 80
dictionaries 80
Interpretation Act 80
legal definitions 33
words and phrases sources
Current Law 81
dictionaries 33, 81, 82, 126
foreign vocabulary 83
Halsbury's Laws 81
keywords 12–14
The Law Reports indexes 81
Lexis Library 82
online 82
Westlaw 82
writing
appearance 251
bad words and phrases 262–4
choices 246–7
clarity 247, 347–8
completeness 250–1
conciseness 250
elegance 251
English language 247
everyday English 261
plain English 259–60, 348
exercises 264–5
first and second person use 261
grammar 248–9, 260, 348
layout 262
logical structure 248
non-ambiguity 250
order of words 261
paragraphs 350, 351
precision 249–50
punctuation 249, 260, 348
qualities 246
readers 251–2
reading over and correcting 252
sentences, short as possible 260
simple structures 261
spelling 248, 348
structure 311–13, 350–1
style 251
subheadings 351
terminology use 348
typographical errors 252
word order 261
written word skills 243, 244
see also **language**

Y

year books
Current Law Year Book 47, 48,
49, 81